Key to a Cold City

A Personal Odyssey Through Baseball Statistics of the Late Fifties to Understanding Bigotry, Failure, and the Human Soul

John R. Harris, Ph.D.

They are not here. And we, we are the Others
Who walk by ourselves unquestioned in the sun
Which shines for us and only for us.
For They are not here
And are made known to us in this great absence
That lies upon us and is between us
Since They are not here.
Now, in this kingdom of summer idleness
Where slowly we the sun-tranced multitudes dream and wander
In deep oblivion of brightness
And breathe ourselves out, out into the air—
It is absence that receives us;
We do not touch, our souls go out in the absence
That lies between us and is about us.
For we are the Others,
And so we sorrow for These that are not with us,
Not knowing we sorrow or that this is our sorrow,
Since it is long past thought or memory or device of mourning,
Sorrow for loss of that which we never possessed,
The unknown, the nameless,
The ever-present that in their absence are with us
(With us the inheritors, the usurpers claiming
The sun and the kingdom of the sun) that sorrow
And loneliness might bring a blessing upon us.

                    Edwin Muir, "The Absent"

To Dr, Cliff Henry, Wherever You May Be:
eternal thanks for your brief but true friendship in a hard town
during hard times…

and to George Altman.

CONTENTS

Preface: How a Statistical Inquiry Became a Personal Odyssey

I began writing this book in 2005, or perhaps even a year earlier. My purpose then was just as the first chapters continue to portray it now: i.e., to inquire into the curious cases of several promising young black ballplayers of the late 1950's and early 1960's who "dropped off the radar" in ensuing years for no very clear reason. I anticipated finding residual racial animosity; I expected that the arrival of Jackie Robinson in the big leagues a decade and a half earlier had not magically dispelled all of the hostility that had once banned his brethren from admission. I thought that a closer examining of the statistics, a researching of specific incidents, and maybe even an exchanging of friendly correspondence with a few surviving players might easily result in a powerful exposé.

I was naive in those assumptions. Statistics are always, in any walk of life, subject to varying interpretations. If I flip a coin to land "heads" five times straight, does it make a sixth "heads" highly likely (attributable, perhaps, to how I'm flipping and catching the coin)... or does it, rather, make "tails" the preemptive favorite, so far denied only by gross improbability? Does a .325 batting average in very occasional play mean that a ballplayer deserves to start regularly... or does it mean that he would make the ideal pinch-hitter and should continue to be held in reserve?

That argument is a bit of a strain, I grant you—but it's not without logic. More compelling—and less susceptible to exposure by a study like mine—is the influence of off-the-field factors, ranging from attitude in dugout and clubhouse to problems with alcohol to marriage difficulties or "girl-craziness" to poor handling of money and indebtedness. Such areas can intrude so deeply into the personal that no amount of poking around, even by a seasoned sportswriter who has the ear of several insiders, is likely to reach the truth. Indeed, precisely because no writer of publicly displayed copy wanted to stray too far into territory that was distinctly forbidden in 1960, the merest hint of a dark impropriety could shut down all discussion—and the hint might have been slanderous, something cooked up by a bigoted front office to cover its sordid tail; but because it led to a "no go" zone, nobody went. What, then, is someone like me to do half a century later—a professional classicist and grammarian whose closest approaches to players have come from buying a ticket?

Oh, yes: I could write letters. I wrote dozens. God bless George Altman. He responded instantly, often, and with candor and thoroughness. But I can't blame the remaining dozens who shrugged me off. Even if I were a known quantity to them—an established sportswriter with a track record of *bona fides*—why would they want to relive times whose memory must be painful, particularly if my suspicions were true? Those men who were yet alive had moved on to explore new trails in this earthly valley of joys and tears. Why should they submit to being dragged back to roads long abandoned? I myself didn't enjoy rereading the account of my son's struggles in high school with a coach who was prosecuting some kind of vendetta against me personally for years. (I'll explain later how such a chapter could have crept into this work.) If I would as soon forget about those days and pass on, why would my subjects feel any differently about their soul-wrenching ordeals?

The book's first draft, in short, didn't build neatly to a crescendo like a well-orchestrated symphony. It seemed to curl back upon itself, instead, and to end in the same uneasy rustles of questions where it began. I worked it over to give the whole a somewhat more philosophical spin; for in the final analysis, a problem like racial prejudice—and I'm not talking here about civil rights or legal standing—owes much of its reality to the mind of the beholder. You can choose to ignore the doors that don't open (the option of Willie Mays when asked to contribute to Jackie's anthology) or to bull your way down each passage with a robust, aggressive kind of humor (I think of Leon Wagner), or you can take it all deeply to heart and let it gnaw away at you in silence (as I believe the young Henry Aaron must have done). Bigotry can be just another circumstantial nuisance, like your hometown's rainy weather, or it can be a poison that saps the energy from everything you undertake.

Such a general insight as this, however, wouldn't have been a very satisfactory endpoint, either. Heaven forbid that I should appear to finish the project in a bland exhortation that those impeded by bigotry have a better attitude! Again, I'm a very poor example of "positive thinking" myself, so I'm not likely to recommend it as a remedy to anyone else.

I put the book on a back burner for several years, therefore. I should say, more specifically, that a major publisher was indeed interested in it for a while... but I didn't like the equivocal signals I was receiving. The numerous photographs of my old baseball card collection—the nucleus of my study group—became a major issue. We couldn't reproduce the cards in full color and keep the price down: I understood that. The deeper concern, however, was a kind of paranoia that someone somewhere might sue because we had generated a facsimile of Uncle Jethro's face. Lawyers would not say "yea" or "nay" on the issue, though I've seen photos of baseball cards in books several times and am unquestionably the purchaser and sole owner of my private card collections. The paralyzing indecision of the industry today about such issues is perhaps not a problem of its own making... but being as insecure about the manuscript as I already was, my would-be publisher's wishy-washy response about relatively minor issues was all I needed to grow sick of the whole thing.

At least for the time being. Years passed. Racial tensions in our nation and throughout the world appeared to go into overdrive rather than subside into a crawl. As I sit here writing in early November of 2018, everything is potentially "racist". A Halloween costume, a reference to a chimp or gorilla, mention of fried chicken or watermelon... O Leon Wagner, where is thy noble, jocund, manly spirit today? A distaste for rap or hip-hop is racist—but listening enthusiastically to one or the other is "cultural appropriation" if your skin tone is light. Sending jobs overseas and out of blue-collar urban neighborhoods is racist... but bolstering the economy so that Americans can liberate themselves from welfare dependency is also racist. Exploiting "sex workers" is racist, but not having a few girls of color among your brief flings is racist, too. What could be more genuinely racist than murdering babies of a certain demographic by the million? Yet the word is reserved, rather, for those who would inhibit the slaughter.

The situation has passed beyond the laughable and entered the precincts of the disgusting. Naturally, those who attempt to play these mind games with us are seldom of the race in question—and never, it seems, part of the world of sensible working people. They are academics and intellectuals, rather; and, yes, most of them are white. They seem driven to torment the rest of the Caucasian populace in order to prove to us (or to themselves?) that they do not share our filthy vices. They create sins from their fevered imaginations that could never prosper in daylight and clean air... and then they project these onto everyone around them and congratulate themselves theatrically for being uniquely unaffected. They truly disgust me. I pity whatever pathology makes them so miserably dysfunctional... but it also angers me that they dare make a silly word as lethal as a bottle or a battery flying at a left-fielder's head.

At about this point (with the chronological "point" beginning, say, around 2012, when we had scaled to our present plateau of cultural insanity), I admit that my inclination to publish the manuscript was weaker than ever, despite all the work I had put into it and despite an implicit kind of promise I had made to George Altman to share my research with the world. If anything shifted my critical mass of determination to the other side, it was the experience of my own son. He graduated from high school in 2013, amid a lot of pain that isn't usually associated with such a milestone. Baseball had been an important part of his life (probably too important); and, because I loved him, it had grown to be an important part of mine. Much of his final season in high school, though, was spent riding the bench—this as his coach's means of venting rage over the boy's excelling and receiving a college athletic scholarship. The rage was aimed at me: I was viewed as having aspired to prove that I could make the kid a good ballplayer without the coach's help, and as now having produced hard proof. No such aspiration had ever occupied even the most secret space in my mind... but the coach had some vaguely paranoid notions about parents who showed an interest in their sons' baseball growth, and I was an "idiot intellectual", to boot. Those were two good reasons, in his mind, to detest me.

I tell the whole tawdry tale at the end of this book. I added it after 2013. I did so because my personal experience suddenly made the issue of bigotry very real to me. So many of the underhanded dealings I had read about or surmised in the case of young black ballplayers had surfaced while my son was in the hands of this man that I couldn't help but dust the manuscript off again and give it a new look. A really thorough proofread followed, and then the second section of Part Four was added. The study once more finished up in a mist of questions, with only fleeting rays of optimism slipping through here and there. I decided that I couldn't do any better, if I were to be faithful to the truth as I saw it.

For the ultimate problem here is people: not white folks, or a poor upbringing, or Western "patriarchal" culture, or any of the other villains generated by hifalutin Ivory Tower rigamarole—but human beings. We oppress each other. We do it all the time. A microscopic few of us are despicable megalomaniacs who just like to feel others squirm under our thumb. Far more of us, though, are poor buggers who are scared of being bumped to a lower rung of the ladder and doubt our own ability to hold on or climb higher. We therefore make others look worse to make ourselves look better; and if we can designate an entire group of potential rivals as tainted by some undesirable or disqualifying characteristic, then… well, that's killing a bunch of birds with one stone, isn't it? For instance, if we're trying to scale the academic ladder and we convince college administrations that no more white males need to be hired—that they've exercised their unfair advantage to the hilt long enough—then our own chances for hire and promotion are much enhanced.

I can hear the screams and screeches now. "Wait a minute! First you were drawing an analogy between your son's being bullied by a prickly coach with the black experience of the Fifties; now you're suggesting that white males go through something similar in pursuing their cushy careers. You've got to be kidding!" In the first place, the parallel with the academic world is just what the objection calls it: a mere analogy. I'm not equating loss of employment with being chased off buses and out of restaurants, only proposing similarities in the thinking behind these widely different kinds of harassment. In the second place, I would indeed say that my son's experience was about as bad for him as a kid's who was denied a uniform because of his skin color. Both were no doubt disparaged to their faces and before teammates (or would-be teammates); both had their self-confidence undermined; both had the most important thing in their young lives taken from them. No, they weren't both told that they couldn't drink from a public water fountain—but they were kids. They didn't care about water fountains: they cared about baseball, and pretty much nothing else.

If you can't see that cheating a child of his confidence and his opportunity to test his talent while building his skill is at the very core of what makes racial bigotry wrong—spiritually wrong, wrong in God's eyes—then you won't like where my long research ends its exploration. If you're going to insist that one group needs a kind of "lifetime headstart card" to flash in the company of other groups, then I'll tell you, in turn, that you are discrediting the worthy cause of those who just want an equal chance. If you and I must compare different kinds of prejudice and compete with each other for the "prize" of having suffered the worst prejudice, like a pitiful crew of old soldiers showing off their wounds ("You just got yours from shrapnel, but I was charging a machine gun!"), then we're bound to miss the real tragedy of racial discrimination.

All of the men whose cases I review below were *young* men at the time the Post Cereals camera snapped their portrait. They were immensely closer to a high school student's age than to mine today, or probably to yours right now. What I grieve over most is the blows absorbed by their young spirits. We oldtimers either repel hard knocks with our thickened hides or apply the salve of long experience and mature philosophy; but a person still measuring his adequacy to run the pitiless gamut of adulthood should not have to handle traitorously whispered criticisms of his powers on top of warding off direct frontal attacks. There's something wicked—I venture to say even diabolical, as in "devilish"—about distilling doubts into an innocent, naïve mind that cannot spot a scheming saboteur behind a teacher's mask or an envious rival behind a friend's. A big difference exists between telling a boy that he'll never be an astronomer because the math is just too hard for him and saying that he will have to get to work really, really hard on math if he wants to study astronomy. On the other hand, virtually no difference exists between telling him that he'll never understand math because the DNA of his race has no "calculus gene" and because the backwoodsy dialect of his childhood has slowed his brain.

A few young men in my study group excelled despite the constant discouragement thrown up in their path—or, some would say, because of it. We celebrate them as heroes, and justly so. Many, many more young men, however, were beaten down by the obstacles in this particular case (as they are in so many similar cases), and their failure was certainly not un-heroic. In my opinion—and here is my last word on the subject—we do them a disservice merely to label them victims of racial discrimination. Yes, they were that— but they were more than that. They were human beings whom other human beings treated with duplicity and manipulated into despair. Forgive me, then, if I do not turn my work utterly into an echo chamber for the present day's "racism, racism" cries. I am not a white scholar trying to advertise a moral enlightenment far brighter than the haze engulfing his dull bourgeois brethren. I am a father who once felt the anguish of looking on helplessly as his son's confidence was sabotaged—and who has re-aggravated that anguish in pondering the young lives of a few talented men now gone from this world.

Let me briefly issue a warning, and an apology. A few of the graphs and charts in Part Two made a very rough transition to the present format. At the same time as their margins were being pinched, the letters designating individual players were throwing out their elbows in a bid for more space. Obviously, pinpointing exact values isn't possible in such circumstances. Saving the graphs as picture files, on the other hand, was a non-starter. Not only would the lettering be shrunk to microscopic sizes, but the technology producing the book's hard-copy version apparently cannot handle JPEG's of print documents. Pardon the many inaccuracies in my graphs, therefore—and stay generous for the moment, please. I must also warn that the red color-coding of black players' initials in these graphics will only appear as a lighter gray in all e-book formats (and perhaps even in the print version; at this instant, I'm uncertain of exactly what Amazon's hard-copy options will allow me to do).

I'm a perfectionist, and such flaws bother me. Yet I take comfort in knowing that the discussion after each graphic is based on solid evidence, even though the reader may not have been supplied, in specific cases, with a useful condensation of that evidence into a picture. Please concentrate on the discussions, then, and forgive the visuals. You can construct your own magnificent graphs with information from baseballreference.com if you feel the need and have the time.

I will *not* apologize, finally, for having scuffed up several generic boundaries in writing a book about sports history that seeks to fathom a cultural problem and, in doing so, uncorks a little psychology mixed with philosophy while spilling in a long personal anecdote. I don't quite know how I managed to stir these ingredients together so indiscriminately, in retrospect, but... well, they say that the melting pot is the American ideal, and I've certainly added almost everything to my stew. I hope you find the result not entirely inedible. For me, the experience has been a little exhausting, but deeply rewarding. I feel myself a better person because of it.

J.R.H.
Rome, Georgia
2018

Part One

Ground Rules: Pointing a Microscope Half a Century into the Past

I

Baseball for Breakfast: Growing Up White, Upwardly Mobile, and Clueless in the Early Sixties

The Italian poet Giovanni Pascoli once wrote that everything painful is strangely pleasant in being recollected, and everything pleasant strangely painful. I don't know which of those two categories explains the gilding of childhood memories. I was not a particularly happy child. There were few kids my own age on the block, we lived at very close quarters in the sort of house which was mass-produced for demobilized GIs, my father often had a short fuse after a day of being a cog in General Dynamics' vast machine, the Texas summers beat hot on a brown plain as flat as an anvil, and—worst of all—the early rumblings of "upward mobility" were throwing me among kids at school who could buy my entire Christmas list with their pocket change. Maybe all this misery explains the golden haze through which I see the Fifties now: maybe Pascoli was right.

But then, you don't really know that you're miserable when you're a kid. You have nothing to which your day's misery may be compared. Maybe I perceive those times as predominantly gloomy, despite their present gilding, because I now know that they must have been so. Only the adjustment to private school struck me as a hellish torment while it was happening. The rest... I may even have enjoyed it. We would soon move into a more accommodating house—and I would quickly lose my brother and sister as close friends (though puberty may have been the primary villain in that loss). I don't really recall the heat with any anguish: I recall, rather, Kool-Aid in the shadows of a chinaberry tree and afternoons splashing in a plastic pool which must have held all of two feet of water. As for that flat vista rumpled by oak and cottonwood outcrops here and there, I miss it to this day: I feel that my adult surroundings have cheated me of the sky. And my father's short temper, as far as I knew, was standard issue for fathering. I wouldn't find out otherwise for a long, long time.

I begin my book about baseball and life with these whimsical musings because, it seems to me, baseball holds the key to life (or to a few of its doors). When you think about baseball (if you are a typical American male of a certain age), you think about the first back yard or park you can recall, and about summer, and about Dad. The playgrounds, the summers, and (God knows) the dads are different in every individual case... yet together they yield something like an objective response. Pascoli might well have become baseball's premier philosopher if his parents had thought to emigrate from San Mauro. With all of its frustrations (baseball is full of failure: the pitcher who wins half his starts and the hitter who beats the throw to first one in three times both end up in the Hall of Fame), the game charms those who play it and those who watch it for a lifetime after the Fat Lady sings. Yet it also produces fallen eagles and zeniths with steep descent on the other side—an inexhaustible supply of matter for proving that heroes die tragically and that no fingers can hold the sands of time.

Baseball is poetry. In a dog-eat-dog, utilitarian culture of loud motors and louder billboards, it is sometimes the only poetry we males ever see. When I try to recollect that tiny house where five of us competed for one bathroom and one crackling black-and-white TV (Marshall McLuhan, insisting that television forces the imagination to complete its images, must have had our set in mind), I think of baseball cards at once. I can see myself seated at the one table where we ate all our meals, staring at the back of a Post Cereal box as I munch away. I can once more see the summer sunlight filtering through a curtain, so that I have to turn the box away in order to read it. I half-believe that I learned the love of reading from those boxes. I certainly learned to appreciate mathematics more than I had before. There were six cards to a box, if memory serves—maybe eight on a large box—and all were actually part of the back panel. You clipped them out with scissors when you had emptied the box's contents (not a bad motivation for making little lads eat their Oat Flakes). I'm sure the stock boys at Safeway must have grown mildly irritated on occasion as I displaced their hard work toward summer's end, looking for a box that displayed just one new card. Heaven help me—how many duplicates must I have thrown away! Imagine tossing out an extra Al Kaline in the joy of snipping around Don Buddin!

Much my clearest memories, however, are of the faces. Since the cards were one-sided, the players' faces appeared above their stats and beside a brief description of their accomplishments or expectations. To this day, I like not having to flip a card over in search of season or career numbers. I've also noticed (and I don't think this is just another of my grumpy-old-man prejudices) that more recent cards disdain to show the player's face in a humane, hand-shaking sort of close-up. Instead, you get bodies in action, frozen by high-tech photography as they execute a swing or a throw in an actual game. The players are finely tuned robots, not thinking, feeling men with a stern or mild or faraway look in their eyes as they await the next burst of action. Frankly, that look, for my money, is closer to the truth; for as baseball is full of failures, so it is full of waiting—and the way a man waits tells a lot about how he plays.

I didn't know all that as I sat chewing my cereal, though—or perhaps only intuitively. What I saw were men whose eyes I was not afraid to search—who would not suddenly grow angry, like my father, or suddenly denounce me for staring, like the rich kids at my new school. In some ways, they may have been my best friends. I connected a few of them to people in my small circle of acquaintance whom they may remotely have resembled, but whose twins I took them to be. Harmon Killebrew, I decided, must be related to our minister, both because they looked alike to me and because the Reverend's last name was Harmon. (I didn't see any inconsistency in the reasoning.) Henry Aaron (the cards all called him Hank) had a sister or close cousin, I was convinced, who lived in our city and came over to do our ironing after my mother took a job to help pay for the new school. The "cousin's" name was Bonita, and I loved her faint, modest smile—just like Hank's. I do not recall being impressed in any way whatever by the darker skins of some players. They simply had darker skins. In fact, the cards didn't always betray a difference between black and white, both because some of the black players were fair-complected (e.g., Billy Bruton and "Sad Sam" Jones) and because some of the photos were shot in ambiguous lighting (e.g., Vada Pinson's). I didn't learn that the men named parenthetically above were of African extraction until years later.

I repeat, however, that it wouldn't have mattered to me one way or the other back then to have possessed such knowledge. Only after attending my new school for a year or two did I come to realize that there was something "dangerous" about being dark-skinned—or come to realize, I should say, that people around me perceived a danger. The blonde-haired, blue-eyed girl that I was head-over-heels in love with for years (and to whom I addressed perhaps a dozen words in all those years) once said something to someone about "colored town": something about having to drive through there quickly, about having to be careful. To be honest, "colored" wasn't quite the word she used. I remember feeling as though I had been dealt a swift blow in the diaphragm. I couldn't imagine how such a sentiment could have taken wing from my goddess's glorious lips, and I soon decided that others had primed her—that she really didn't know what she had said. Not that I was coached at home in civil rights like Scout in *To Kill a Mockingbird*; but if my father was no Atticus, neither was he a beer-guzzling red-neck. Our next-door neighbor had conferred upon the "n" word a privileged place in his mostly monosyllabic vocabulary, and his son (my brother's playmate) wielded it against his sister whenever she vexed him... but no one in our house ever repeated it. I don't recall ever being threatened about the matter. We just didn't use it: we didn't even want to use it.

Perhaps, too, I had learned first-hand what it means to be "dark" and to be despised for it. I sported very broad, very black eyebrows over my deep brown eyes when I was young. (Age has since decimated my supercilliar shrubbery.) I would discover years later, through travel, that people of Welsh lineage often have such features, and that indeed I could easily blend into a crowd in Aberystwyth (on those rare occasions when its streets collect a crowd). But at my new school, I was constantly scolded for frowning when I was not, or for staring when I was not. A photo in the yearbook taken shortly before I graduated caught me unawares in a classroom as I glanced over the shoulder of the girl seated in front of me. The photo carried the caption, "John Harris contemplates violence," as if I were about to assault the girl. All because of my dark eyes. The photo and its caption bothered me for years, in a way that I'm sure none of my classmates could begin to understand.

Maybe that's why I was so smitten with a golden-haired girl—because she represented the photographic-negative opposite to my own suspicious appearance. And maybe that's why, having become her thrall, I could seldom muster the courage to peep out a word in her presence. I was not worthy: I was dirt under her divine step.

It is not altogether impossible, you see, for a white man to understand something of what a black man goes through in American society. There's more than one way to skin a cat—and there's more than one way to make a person feel embarrassed about or ashamed of his appearance. And invariably, these ways are after the fact: those who would embarrass you have already taken a disliking to you for other reasons, your physical appearance supplying a mere pretext for the deeper hostility. I would re-discover this truth years later as a teacher, when I was frequently criticized at my more chintzy places of employ for having a gentle voice incapable of those thrilling modulations much affected by charismatic preachers. My audibility was never in question during these "cut-down" sessions before contracts were issued. I was simply being intimidated for having the voice God gave me so that I would not protest my nugatory raise. Other teachers were bled for other reasons: all of us got eviscerated.

On such fully adult occasions, I would sometimes ask myself why I hadn't pursued baseball as a profession. After all, they *can't* hold you back if you hit a steady .333 or zip the ball past the opposition's line-up. In baseball, accomplishment speaks for itself. You might have horns and a tail, but somebody will still give you a contract for your hot bat. Owners want to win, they want players who will help them win, and they don't really give a damn about how many shades of the rainbow are represented in the dugout.

I suppose I carried forward this naïve vision of baseball's equality, fostered by the Jackie Robinson story, because I did not in fact have the chance to play much formal baseball. My new school dissolved our team rather early on (just my luck: with the quick wrists I had inherited, I was our heavy hitter). A command decision was made to throw all resources into football—for football is the *de facto* religion of Texas, informing even the kind preached in churches. When we do play baseball down here, we play it as though it were football, refusing to keep calm, swinging viciously from the heels so as to "impose our will" upon the pitch. After a brief and forced exposure to football on our campus (*everyone* was expected to try out), I decided that I bitterly detested the Dionysiac orgy—the berserk mania—which fuels the game, and I retreated further than ever into my books. Baseball virtually disappeared from my life: life proceeded to lose its poetry.

I have since recovered my devotion to the game (I won't say "passion", for emotional debauch belongs to football). After my own son was born, I spent years learning how to pitch from both sides and at all angles so that I could expose him to The Lefty and The Submariner. (My efforts eventually led my boy down a baseball path that I hadn't anticipated: I shall get to that much later, for it becomes the last leg of this book's journey.) I also wore myself out on tee and hitting machine in search of The Swing With No Holes. Inevitably, I unearthed my baseball cards once again. If I were to take a stroll through my house right now, a few of those Post Cereal cards in a glassed frame would be the *single* relic of my early childhood which has not been confined to a dark closet. (The dozen moves around the country which I endured for my career as a professor pretty much scattered or destroyed all my other keepsakes: ballplayers and soldiers aren't the only ones who get shuffled from state to state.) Very lately, I have learned that the Post cards, in particular, fetch a great deal of money on e-Bay. I don't know why they wouldn't: most of them must have been thrown away with the cereal's empty wrapper, or else jettisoned later as too "cheap" to preserve. The boys at school all scoffed at me for collecting them (as opposed to bubblegum cards). Now I have about four hundred in excellent condition, mostly from the 1961 and 1962 seasons. After our move to the "upwardly mobile" house when I was about ten, I apparently never clipped another card again... but then, I couldn't have, as I realized only recently. Post discontinued the cards after 1963 (i.e., the 1962 season was the last run).

Impressed with my new-found treasure, I undertook the insertion of all the cards into plastic sleeves which would keep them clean and uncreased. As I did so—as I looked at these hundreds of faces for the first time in decades—I was struck by how many had vanished without a trace from baseball's corridors of glory. Several are still iconic, to be sure. Any fan of more than adolescent years must surely recognize Mays's mug, or Aaron's, or Mantle's or Yogi's or Sandy's. But back in 1962, who would have dared to assert that Tommy Davis or Norm Cash or Rocky Colavito would be a mere footnote in baseball history? My exercise of *triage* grew rather sad, as Pascoli promises us such exercises must always be. In the words of another poet, where are the snows of yesteryear?

I might have left my reflections there: *vanitas vanitatum*, sayeth the Preacher. I don't know why I didn't... but for some reason, I started looking more closely at the "footnotes". Norm Cash had a good career, in fact—just not up to sustaining his 1961 batting average, which exceeded his lifetime average by about one hundred points. Tommy Davis was more troubling: he seemed to fall off slightly after winning two consecutive batting titles, and then to be traded around with the dizzying speed of a clown caught in a revolving door. My research indicated that he had declined irrecoverably after a badly broken leg, and I accepted that verdict at face value—for the time being. But what about Vada Pinson? His numbers compared favorably with those of Ernie Banks or Eddie Mathews, yet he came to be passed around almost as feverishly as Davis.

And what about Leon Wagner? I could vaguely recall seeing Leon hit on our dim black-and-white TV during the 1962 All-Star Game, a contest which he won with a homer. Leon's highly distinct three-inch space between the hands (which I could plainly make out on the 1962 Post Cereal card) had always fascinated me. Every coach I have ever known has rejected hand-spacing contemptuously: most call it childish, or even "girlish". Yet Leon hit long home runs, and lots of them. He had logged 211 of them when he hung it up after only about 4400 at-bats. He had been on a Hall of Fame pace, and he had simply quit. Once again, Internet sources volunteered the answer confidently. Leon was a lousy fielder—he butchered too many plays on defense for his offense to earn him a perpetual free pass. Yet I found no evidence of exceptional incompetence in his fielding record; and since when was a man coordinated enough to hit .300 not coordinated enough to shag flies or play first base?

The deeper I dug, the more journeys to glory I found inexplicably waylaid. Charlie Neal, Gold Glover and owner of a new Dodger record for homers by a second baseman... Bill White, a steady 100-RBI-per-year powerhouse who suddenly disappeared from the Cardinal line-up... Jake Wood, a rookie who led his league in triples and then vanished... Wes Covington, a slashing speedster who was also zapped off the screen as if by a laser.... *Most of these unaccountable casualties were black.* Were they casualties of *being black*? I had always been led to believe by popular lore and documentary truism that Jackie Robinson broke the color barrier, and that talent thereupon came trickling in, slowly but with irresistible acceleration, from the Negro Leagues—so much so that these leagues had soon perished. Could it be that the problem for young black players in the generation immediately following Jackie was no longer getting to the Majors, but staying there? Was effort now being expended not to keep them out, but to keep them from settling in?

I should quickly add that white players were sometimes "victimized", as well (if I could call these men victims whose stories, at the time, I could only guess at). Dick Stuart and Don Demeter, for instance, seemed headed for great things when Post pasted their photos and stats on the backs of cereal boxes. Stuart had some awe-inspiring power years with Pittsburgh, while Demeter showed that magical combination of power, speed (reflected in extra-base hits), and average which I had noticed in Vada Pinson. Yet the careers of both men were short-circuited, it appeared, by their having been forcibly packed off where they probably didn't want to go. Some of us are more sensitive to our surroundings than others. The notion of having to pull up stakes and move across country may be exciting to certain young men—but to others it can be completely demoralizing; and to older young men with families, it can mean domestic chaos—wives torn from their blood relatives and children from their schools and friends. Maybe I was just observing in retrospect the "winnowing out" of homebodies and conscientious fathers from the pool of Major League ballplayers.

Something in me wanted a firmer answer, though. As I looked further into the matter, I grew more suspicious, and I eventually started taking formal notes. I began to convince myself that the generation of players following Jackie Robinson into the big leagues faced a fairly widespread kind of hazing—destructive hazing, not benign initiation. A black recruit, for instance, might be given a few pinch-hit or late-inning at-bats to test whether or not he was in fact equal to the pressures of an elite existence. Naturally, a kid who sees batting-practice fastballs six days a week and then Major League heat and junk on the seventh is unlikely to perform well, particularly if he understands (and how could he not?) that his future rests on those few spot-starts. Another pattern seemed to suggest that players like Pinson and White who met the challenge and won themselves regular starts throughout the year were prime targets for ambitious trades if they proceeded to turn in All-Star performances. What a life it must have been! The skipper gives you 50 at-bats all year, you screw up because you're nervous and out of sync through lack of playing time, and then he mutters to a nodding coach, "Good thing we didn't make the mistake of starting him—he just can't do the job up here." Or if you do the job, then you spend December waiting for the phone to ring behind the Christmas tree and announce that your family will be taking up residence in the Windy City.

I grasp that these are pretty stiff charges. To this day, I don't know if they're substantially true. In this book's first couple of sections, I propose to do no more than share my statistical evidence (whose cloudy witness always begs interpretation) and whatever testimony I have managed to glean from the scant writings of players belonging to that era. Pinson, Neal, Bill Bruton, "Daddy Wags", and many others are gone. Still others, I discovered rather guiltily, have moved on in life and don't wish to reminisce about "the great ballplayer" they might have been. Finding such bitterness in the latter, I only hope the former—the lately deceased, most of them within the last dozen or so years—did not make a hastier exit because of the same bitterness, the same sense of having been denied a proper chance. Life can do that to people—deprive them of chances, and then eat away at them in reduced circumstances which remind them every day that they missed fortune's high tide.

Such misery is part of the human condition, and we will not resolve it, in the words a Shakespeare's wag Lucio, "till eating and drinking be put down." Yet we should not therefore complacently ignore inequity when we find specific cases of it. On the contrary, we should put such cases under the magnifying glass that we may learn from them whatever there is to learn. More than one important lesson, I think, circles the sad heap of crumpled possibilities I found among my baseball cards—and the most important of these lessons has nothing directly to do with baseball.

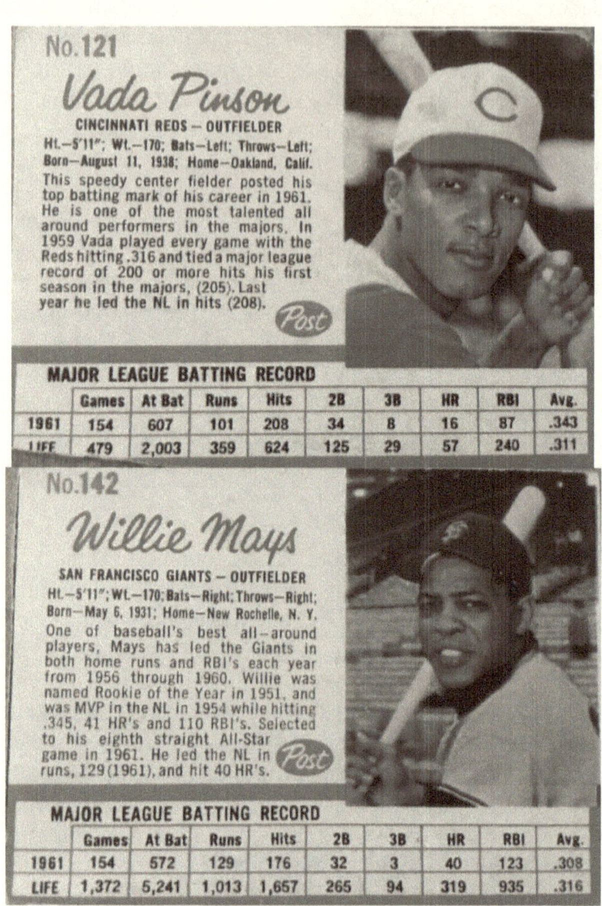

No. 121

Vada Pinson

CINCINNATI REDS — OUTFIELDER

Ht.—5'11"; Wt.—170; Bats—Left; Throws—Left; Born—August 11, 1938; Home—Oakland, Calif.

This speedy center fielder posted his top batting mark of his career in 1961. He is one of the most talented all around performers in the majors. In 1959 Vada played every game with the Reds hitting .316 and tied a major league record of 200 or more hits his first season in the majors, (205). Last year he led the NL in hits (208).

Post

MAJOR LEAGUE BATTING RECORD

	Games	At Bat	Runs	Hits	2B	3B	HR	RBI	Avg.
1961	154	607	101	208	34	8	16	87	.343
LIFE	479	2,003	359	624	125	29	57	240	.311

No. 142

Willie Mays

SAN FRANCISCO GIANTS — OUTFIELDER

Ht.—5'11"; Wt.—170; Bats—Right; Throws—Right; Born—May 6, 1931; Home—New Rochelle, N. Y.

One of baseball's best all-around players, Mays has led the Giants in both home runs and RBI's each year from 1956 through 1960. Willie was named Rookie of the Year in 1951, and was MVP in the NL in 1954 while hitting .345, 41 HR's and 110 RBI's. Selected to his eighth straight All-Star game in 1961. He led the NL in runs, 129 (1961), and hit 40 HR's.

Post

MAJOR LEAGUE BATTING RECORD

	Games	At Bat	Runs	Hits	2B	3B	HR	RBI	Avg.
1961	154	572	129	176	32	3	40	123	.308
LIFE	1,372	5,241	1,013	1,657	265	94	319	935	.316

Except for Mickey Mantle, Willie Mays may have been the most recognizable ballplayer—black or white—across Middle America in the early Sixties. But who was Vada Pinson? Only a kid who snatched the Gold Glove for center field away from Willie in 1961, and whose .343 average that year was surpassed just twice—barely—by Mays. Unfortunately, Vada himself scarcely managed to top .300 twice again in his long career. What happened to him?

II

Criteria of Selection: A Box of Old Baseball Cards and the Calculus of High Hopes

In the previous chapter, I describe my rediscovery of a box of old baseball cards. For reasons which I shall detail in the present chapter, I consider that collection an excellent point of departure. Most of the players whose careers I shall analyze belong to the "elite four hundred" who were represented on my Post Cereal cards from the 1961 and 1962 seasons. (Of course, there aren't really four hundred different players in this group: the overlap from year to year was considerable—probably 75%.) Naturally, the selections from each team were essentially the starting line-up. Most of my subjects, therefore, were thought to be very good at what they did when the cards were printed. I am thus able to say right off the bat that, in comparing black players with white players, I'm not juxtaposing apples and oranges with regard to playing time. These men were considered the cream of the crop at a magical moment in the early Sixties, whether or not their own talent, Lady Luck, and social circumstances would allow them to advance as predicted.

A few of the subjects I eventually decided upon, however, did not pass muster before Post's judges in '61 or '62. There are two reasons why I included in my study groups players whose affable, shy, or competitive faces never made it to my cereal boxes. One is that I had to expand my search for black players, not because there were so few good ones in those days, but because so few good ones had found their way to public recognition. Precisely because the Major Leagues had not flung the doors of integration wide open after Jackie Robinson, players like Bob Boyd, Jim Grant, Mack Jones, and Ted Savage passed beneath Post's notice. Grant actually appeared in Post's 1960 collection, of which I had rounded up only a smattering as a boy. It turns out that my lacking the first set of cards (they were produced only for the seasons running from '60 to '62) did not alter my sample except for Grant and a Bahamian named Tony Curry: all the other black players in that year's run appeared somewhere in the next two.   Left out entirely, then, were stars whose careers, like Boyd's, were winding down by 1960—or else whose big-league life had barely begun by 1962, as with Jones and Savage.

I had to go looking for such players in other sources. I wanted to include every American of African descent playing competent baseball during the late Fifties and early Sixties. I know now that I missed more than a few; but I did succeed in coming up with names like Pumpsie Green, Larry Raines, and Joe Gaines—players who never made anyone's list of "greats" at the end of any Major League season. Significantly, what meager statistics these "ne'er-do-wells" had been allowed to rack up didn't look at all bad when compared to some of Post Cereal's white players: Gene Stephens and Haywood Sullivan hardly put them to shame. When I sought to expand the envelope in the other direction, however—that is, when I lowered the bar to let in a few whites who had not been honored with a Post card—I did not always find the same level of competence. Wally Moon and Johnny Logan were fine ballplayers who might have been selected. Logan's career had essentially ended by '61, and Moon's Dodgers were so crammed with talent that Post must have run out of room. But the career of Doug Clemens, representing nine years of flirtation with the Mendoza Line (a batting average of .200), must be seen on paper to be believed. I included Clemens in my study because Wes Covington was once traded for him, and because Doug's relative longevity begs the question, Why couldn't Ted Savage achieve even a half-season's worth of at-bats over his six big-league years collectively after 1962?

Among the white players of my card collection, I selected subjects more or less randomly. I did tend to avoid choosing Hall-of-Famers like Al Kaline and Carl Yastrzemski, for I was more interested in seeing how black players compared with routine starters whose experience of being traded around and benched once in a while was similar to the black experience. Nevertheless, I threw in Mantle and Santo and Ken Boyer to leaven the effects of Aaron and Mays and Robinson—a very partial leavening, I know. But then, there really *were* no Caucasian stars hitting their stride at about 1960 who could compare to Henry and Willie and Robby. Most of Mickey's best years were behind him, Yaz was just about to appear on the scene, and Kaline, Eddie Mathews, and Harmon Killebrew never quite reached this amazing combination of high average and raw power.

If anything, then, I may have undershot the standard of the typical black Major Leaguer with the caliber of white Major Leaguers I chose. This was somewhat calculated, inasmuch as the statistical part of my study deals heavily with issues involving frequency of trades and length of career. If such figures were rather more accommodating for whites even when many of them had been out-performed over the short haul by their black counterparts' brief audition, then I had to be on to something. I wanted to be sure that I wasn't verifying my own suspicions, at any rate, by compiling a list of Caucasian superstars whom only a front-office lunatic or a compulsive gambler (Frank Lane falls in there somewhere) would have traded. One must always bear in mind, too, that many of these players, both black and white, looked as though they might *become* superstars in 1962. In other words, I am not comparing the results of actual careers, but the expectations of those careers as they were unfolding. Even more than that, I am comparing the *opportunity* of young men similarly gifted by nature to have a successful career.

I hasten to add, as well, that I tried for a reasonably balanced pairing of black and white players even in the matter of short careers and frequent trades. Chuck Essegian and Joe Koppe, despite their honorary appearance on boxes of Post Cereal, lasted only a few years. Tito Francona and Frank Thomas, though outstanding players in many ways, were passed around like a bad penny. The proportion of the short-lived and the oft-traded may well be uneven, with both groups represented much more abundantly among blacks than whites; but this is primarily because of the times, not because I refused to allow Caucasian players into the study who failed to "catch on". I admit that a few black players like Curt Roberts and Pumpsie Green gave very few signs of greatness in their very brief stints of Major League ball. Let's just say that they somewhat balance out the effect of Aaron, Mays, and Robinson.

Jackie Robinson put on a Brooklyn uniform in 1947. The earliest rookie year of any of my subjects is 1951: Bob Boyd and Harry Simpson. This is really a bit early as a cut-off point for the "next generation" of black players. Both Bobby and Harry were extraordinary talents and managed to hang around for the rest of the decade, so I feel justified in throwing them into the mix. There were many other players, though, who came up for "a cup of coffee" in the early Fifties, were never given a chance to show their stuff, and were gone in a couple of years. These I suppressed for the most part, with regret. I do not in the least consider their story unworthy of telling: on the contrary, I consider that I am already telling it as I talk about their slightly later brethren. (R. C. Stevens and Ted Savage are excellent examples of black players who *did* show their stuff through a tiny window of opportunity— which was promptly shut on them: they are included in my group.) The danger of roping into my analysis every single black player from the Fifties I can find would be that, having taken the stars featured on Post Cereal cards from the 1961 and 1962 seasons as my original pool, I might have ended up undermining any meaningful comparison by departing too far from the cards. I didn't want this to happen. I wanted all of those who might read my study to be convinced that I was not tossing in a bunch of "second-rate" black players with a bunch of "first-rate" white players and then arguing that the former were mistreated because they didn't play as much as the latter. I have already erred, perhaps, in admitting as many black players from outside the original pool as I have—a total of twenty: but I defend my decision on the basis of necessity. There were too few black position-players (thirty) on the backs of my cereal boxes to fuel a really thorough study. Many very good ballplayers from outside the group just didn't fare well in '61 or '62, or else simply were no longer around by then.

Judge for yourself. The players I added from outside the card collection were these: Tommie Aaron, Tommie Agee, Gene Baker, Bob Boyd, Lou Brock, Joe Caffie, Donn Clendenon, George Crowe, Joe Gaines, Pumpsie Green, Mack Jones, Bubba Morton, Jim Pendleton, Larry Raines, Curt Roberts, Ted Savage, Harry Simpson, R. C. Stevens, and Bob Thurman.

Boyd, Caffie, and Crowe could have played on anybody's team: their heyday had passed before my cards were printed (including the 1960 run), pure and simple. Agee and Clendenon were just breaking in by 1962, and none-too-spectacularly: they would go on to have fine careers. Young Lou Brock didn't make much of a splash in '62, either. He would end up in Cooperstown. I mentioned parenthetically above the players like Savage and Stevens who showed great promise when allowed off the bench more than once a week—but who were nevertheless confined to the bench after an impressive showing. There are a good many of these—too many. Even Tommie Aaron, typically treated as a comical attachment to big brother Hank's coattails, might well have scored 100 runs in his first and only significant season if he had been allowed to play it out. In my opinion, Pumpsie Green's record also indicates that he could have blossomed with more playing time: with 21 extra-base hits in 219 at-bats for the 1961 Red Sox, he was putting himself in scoring position every tenth trip to the plate—much more often than one would expect of a second baseman. Curt Roberts is perhaps the one player for whom not much of a case may be made on paper. (He turned out to need glasses: the problem once corrected, he launched into a hitting spree—but not in time to impress the front-office gods.).

Sometimes I wonder if the very few of my group who shed only a scintilla of promise might have been victims of attention rather than negligence. What I mean is this: perhaps an effort was made in certain quarters to bring up "first" black players (Curt and Pumpsie were both franchise "firsts") whose failure was all but a foregone conclusion, given their retiring nature. Perhaps certain owners had a longing to discredit integration. Howard Bryant strongly implies in his book *Shut Out* that such may have been the motive behind calling up Pumpsie. I shall deal with this possibility later. I certainly don't think that including a few players in the study who raise it was a mistake.

To return to the "cut-off date": most of my subjects were rookies in the mid- or late-Fifties, but not all. My chronological breadth of admission raises a question: had things gotten any better for black rookies by 1961, when Jake Wood came up? To this matter, too, I shall devote a few paragraphs later (in Part 3, Chapter 5), based less on statistics than on contrastive experiences. If I may anticipate my answer, things *had* and *had not* gotten better. The methods of keeping black players off the field, or ensuring that they failed when on the field, had grown refined after a decade of simply displaying them in the dugout. It also seems to me that the pressure had really been turned up by the early Sixties, in the luminous wake of Aaron and Mays, for young black players to swing for the fences. This is not racism *per se*, though it is a rather hostile approach to the exciting baseball of the Negro Leagues. On the subject of the home run, I shall have very much more to say throughout the book.

I did not admit any Caucasian players into the study who did not come from the Post Cereal cards, with the single exception already mentioned: Doug Clemens, whom I included because his name came up in a trade for Wes Covington. Someone of influence must have thought these two players equal in ability after the 1966 season. The apparent absurdity of such trades seems a red flag; and, while I'm sure Mr. Clemens was a delightful human being (the only picture I found of him showed a big-eyed kid who might have been an angel), none of my black subjects could match his special talent for hanging around year after year without manifesting any proclivity for getting on base. I'm afraid I really should apologize to Doug, wherever he is: he is likely to become something of a whipping boy whenever I have to pose the question, "If a white player were even less productive than Curt Roberts, would he still catch a break?" Doug wasn't the only offensive dud whose guardian angel (or fellow angels) worked overtime. I might have included Coot Veal—and probably should have, because his card is actually among Post's selection for the 1961 season. Even Coot, however, failed to match Doug's longevity. You've got to love that kind of knack for survival!

I hesitated to admit catchers into my study, and I did *not* include pitchers in the study's major part. These two positions seem to me to have different standards in matters of career length and active playing time, if not frequency of trades. Only the most confirmed racist, assigned the task of winning ball games, would bench a catcher or exile his best starting pitcher to the bullpen for being of the "wrong" complexion. I know there are those who would assail this proposition. Bob Gibson would disagree with me, as would, probably, Sandy Koufax (who has always believed that his being Jewish limited his early opportunities).[1] In fact, I do not agree with it categorically myself, and I do not intend it to be understood in that fashion. In my special chapter on pitchers (and in the questions of the very next chapter), I shall suggest that Al McBean's senseless consignment to the bullpen after a brilliant sophomore season has every appearance of a demotion whose greatest cost was to the teams Al played for. The same is true of catchers: Valmy Thomas seems to have been a good one; yet not only was he never allowed to play even half a season in a starting role—he was traded three times in his brief five-year career!

All of that having been said, I still believe that good catchers and pitchers tended to get more playing time and a few more years on their career than the typical black position player of the era. Gibson himself fared far better than Bill White, who should have ended up in the Hall of Fame rather than on the trading block. And Thomas notwithstanding, I noticed repeatedly that Earl Battey, Elston Howard, and John Roseboro tended to resemble white players more than black players in their amount of playing time and their career length. Battey rode the bench for a long while in the beginning—but so did the highly accomplished Caucasian catchers Ed Bailey and Sherman Lollar. Along with Bailey and Lollar, I added John Romano and Clay Dalrymple to balance out the "catcher effect"—whatever it might be—in my graphic comparisons; for I did, at last, decide to put the catchers on all the graphs (except for Valmy Thomas: I explain his exclusion in the following chapter).

Anyway, here you have it—the complete study group of one hundred:

black players	_white players_
Hank Aaron	Bob Allison
Tommie Aaron	Ed Bailey
TommieAgee	Steve Bilko
George Altman	Frank Bolling
Gene Baker	Ken Boyer
Ernie Banks	Don Buddin
Earl Battey	John Callison
Bob Boyd	Andy Carey
Lou Brock	Norm Cash
Bill Bruton	Gino Cimoli
Joe Caffie	Doug Clemens
Ed Charles	Joe Cunningham
Donn Clendenon	Clay Dalrymple
Wes Covington	Jim Davenport
George Crowe	Don Demeter
Tommy Davis	Chuck Essegian
Willie Davis	Ron Fairly
Curt Flood	Tito Francona
Joe Gaines	Gary Geiger
Jim Gilliam	Jim Gentile
Lenny Green	Woodie Held
Pumpsie Green	Ken Hunt
Chuck Hinton	Marty Keough
Elston Howard	Ted Kluszewski
Mack Jones	Joe Koppe
Willie Kirkland	Harvey Kuenn
Lee Maye	Jim Landis
Willie Mays	John Logan
Willie McCovey	Sherman Lollar
Bubba Morton	Al Luplow
Charlie Neal	Jerry Lynch
Jim Pendleton	Frank Malzone
Vada Pinson	Mickey Mantle
Larry Raines	Roger Maris
Curt Roberts	Dick McAuliffe
Andre Rodgers	Wally Moon
Floyd Robinson	Wally Post
Frank Robinson	Boog Powell
John Roseboro	Bobby Richardson
Ted Savage	John Romano
Harry Simpson	Pete Runnels
Al Smith	Ron Santo
R. C. Stevens	Norm Siebern
Willie Tasby	Roy Sievers

Bob Thurman
Leon Wagner
Bill White
Billy Williams
Maury Wills
Jake Wood

Bob Skinner
Bill Skowron
Russ Snyder
Dick Stuart
Frank Thomas
Lee Walls

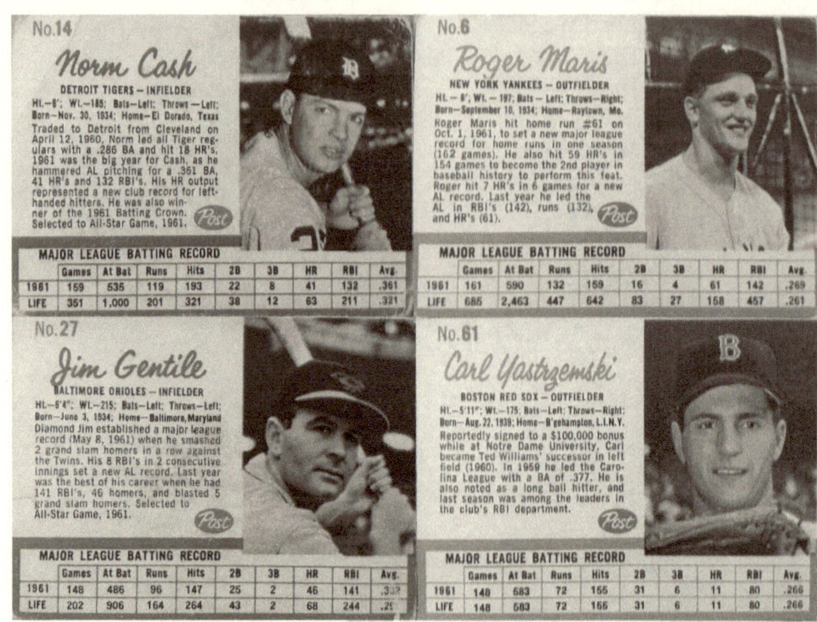

No. 14

Norm Cash

DETROIT TIGERS — INFIELDER

Ht.—6'; Wt.—185; Bats—Left; Throws—Left; Born—Nov. 30, 1934; Home—El Dorado, Texas Traded to Detroit from Cleveland on April 12, 1960, Norm led all Tiger regulars with a .286 BA and hit 18 HR's. 1961 was the big year for Cash, as he hammered AL pitching for a .361 BA, 41 HR's and 132 RBI's. His HR output represented a new club record for left-handed hitters. He was also winner of the 1961 Batting Crown. Selected to All-Star Game, 1961.

MAJOR LEAGUE BATTING RECORD

	Games	At Bat	Runs	Hits	2B	3B	HR	RBI	Avg.
1961	159	535	119	193	22	8	41	132	.361
LIFE	351	1,000	201	321	38	12	63	211	.321

No. 6

Roger Maris

NEW YORK YANKEES — OUTFIELDER

Ht.—6'; Wt.—197; Bats—Left; Throws—Right; Born—September 10, 1934; Home—Raytown, Mo. Roger Maris hit home run #61 on Oct. 1, 1961, to set a new major league record for home runs in one season (162 games). He also hit 59 HR's in 154 games to become the 2nd player in baseball history to perform this feat. Roger hit 7 HR's in 6 games for a new AL record. Last year he led the AL in RBI's (142), runs (132), and HR's (61).

MAJOR LEAGUE BATTING RECORD

	Games	At Bat	Runs	Hits	2B	3B	HR	RBI	Avg.
1961	161	590	132	159	16	4	61	142	.269
LIFE	685	2,463	447	642	83	27	158	457	.261

No. 27

Jim Gentile

BALTIMORE ORIOLES — INFIELDER

Ht.—6'4"; Wt.—215; Bats—Left; Throws—Left; Born—June 3, 1934; Home—Baltimore, Maryland Diamond Jim established a major league record (May 8, 1961) when he smashed 2 grand slam homers in a row against the Twins. His 8 RBI's in 2 consecutive innings set a new AL record. Last year was the best of his career when he had 141 RBI's, 46 homers, and blasted 5 grand slam homers. Selected to All-Star Game, 1961.

MAJOR LEAGUE BATTING RECORD

	Games	At Bat	Runs	Hits	2B	3B	HR	RBI	Avg.
1961	148	486	96	147	25	2	46	141	.302
LIFE	202	906	164	264	43	2	68	244	.29

No. 61

Carl Yastrzemski

BOSTON RED SOX — OUTFIELDER

Ht.—5'11"; Wt.—175; Bats—Left; Throws—Right; Born—Aug. 22, 1939; Home—B'gehampton, L.I. N.Y. Reportedly signed to a $100,000 bonus while at Notre Dame University, Carl became Ted Williams' successor in left field (1960). In 1959 he led the Carolina League with a BA of .377. He is also noted as a long ball hitter, and last season was among the leaders in the club's RBI department.

MAJOR LEAGUE BATTING RECORD

	Games	At Bat	Runs	Hits	2B	3B	HR	RBI	Avg.
1961	148	583	72	155	31	6	11	80	.266
LIFE	148	583	72	155	31	6	11	80	.266

1961 was a career year for more players than Roger Maris. Norm Cash hit 90 points above his career batting average and topped the .300 mark for the only time in a 17-season career—this while slamming 41 homers! Jim Gentile would never again visit the .300 mark, either (a .302 hides within the corner crease), and his second-best home run total after this season's 46 would be 33. Who would have suspected when these cards were clipped off a cereal box that only the humble rookie with the unspellable name would reach the Hall of Fame?

1 Gibson protests, for instance, that under Cardinal manager Solly Hemus, "I never knew where I stood.... I pitched and sat and pitched and sat" (*Stranger to the Game*, with Lonnie Wheeler [New York: Viking, 1994], 55). Jane Leavy repeats throughout her biography, *Sandy Koufax: A Lefty's Legacy* (New York: HarperCollins, 2002), that Koufax felt his ethnicity had postponed his entry into the Dodgers' starting rotation.

III

Unas Palabras Más: The Special Case of the Latino Ballplayer

I must say a few final words—or rather, a great many—about Latino players before I move on. Vic Power and Minnie Minoso were clearly made to feel uncomfortable because of their dark skin, even though the former was Puerto Rican and the latter Cuban. They have written forthrightly of their experiences. Power was actually harassed by Kansas City police so often for driving about with his fair-skinned Puerto Rican wife that he went down to City Hall at last and "had it out" with them.[1] In other words, skin would seem to trump nationality: a black was apparently submitted to certain ordeals when playing ball in the Fifties, not because some tendentious logic connected him to earlier centuries of slavery, but simply because his skin was dark.

Well… yes and no. Far be it from me to minimize the miseries which players from Mexico or the Caribbean were made to endure because of an African contribution to their bloodline. And a certain amount of anecdotal evidence suggests that even native sons of Alabama or California might meet with somewhat better treatment if their skin were a pale brown. Players like Bill Bruton and Maury Wills, whose skin was relatively fair, were received rather warmly by their franchise's surrounding community (or perhaps I should say "less coolly"). Tint of skin color most certainly played a part in how Latino players were regarded. Some were no more snubbed than a dark-haired Italian or a swart Central European would have been: that is, their routine was not uncomplicated by any prejudice at all, but they enjoyed the mainstream's comparative tolerance. Observes Bill James, "The unwritten rule was that you could play Cubans or other Latin American players, but only if they were light enough to pass for white guys."[2]

The focus of this distinction was not lost on any African-American player. Curley Williams remarks the bitter irony of watching foreign nationals be greeted with open arms by cities and towns around the country while a slightly darker shade of skin instantly shut the doors of restaurants and boarding houses:

I'll tell you another thing that really… [made me angry]. They'd have players—sort of light-colored players—from the Dominican Republic and Puerto Rico and all and they could stay *any*place [during spring training or road trips]. They always put us someplace—in a black neighborhood. That kind of got to me, too.[3]

But was it all *just* a matter of skin tone? Could having an "o" or a "z" at the end of your surname drive the tolerance threshold a notch lower, even if your sun tan was "excessive"? Granted, an amiable chap called Pancho from south of the border, if he were a shade too dark, could not appear at all in a Major League game before Jackie Robinson broke the taboo: I am not suggesting otherwise. Yet fair Latinos like Lefty Gomez (a California native of Mexican lineage) had been allowed in the big leagues throughout the century. Jackie's trail-blazing was not needed to clear a path for Luis Aparicio (a Venezuelan), Leo Posada (a Cuban whose career was doomed to brevity by his weak hitting), and Camilo Pascual (another Cuban—whose last name, I suspect, was sometimes misspelled with a "q" to sustain the illusion of Italian origins). I'm not so sure about Lefty, but the other three plainly had dark hair and dark eyes. Yet they had cleared a significant hurdle.

Jim "Mudcat" Grant once stated the relationship between darkness of color and degree of intolerance suffered by Latinos quite succinctly: "There was always a bond between blacks and Latin players of color. However, a white-skinned Latin player may have wanted all the advantages he could get, so he may have gone by the rules set down for white players and become part of the white-player clique. That's why there was often trouble between blacks and light-skinned Latin players."[4] The "bond", at any rate, had a certain instability when extended to Latinos as a group—and it doesn't take much imagination to suppose that Latins neither very fair nor very dark might have turned up the pressure by accepting the patronage of a light-skinned countryman. I have no way of knowing, by the way, how Grant would have classified Aparicio and the others just named. Pascual and Vic Power certainly seemed to be good buddies.

That the dividing line could indeed be nudged over sometimes for Latin ballplayers is strongly suggested by a story I once heard repeated in a documentary entitled *There Was Always Sun Shining Someplace*. The film featured live interviews with immortals like Cool Papa Bell, Satchel Paige, and Buck Leonard. The story I have in mind, though, was recounted to an appreciative gathering by former Negro Leaguer Chet Brewer. A black kid (said Chet) was watching a ball game from beside one of the dugouts during the days of segregation. He kept insisting to the white manager that he could play as well as any member of the team on the field. For a few innings, the manager tried every form of verbal abuse at his command to drive the kid away—but the youngster was persistent. At last the manager decided upon a change of tactics: he would let the kid suit up and go to the plate so that, after an inevitable humiliation, he would never return to the park again. But the young man thwarted the manager's expectations. He walloped the first good pitch deep to center field, where it bounced off the wall and rolled while he circled the bases. As his new star rounded second and streaked toward third, the manager could be heard to bellow for public consumption, "Look at that Cuban go!"[5]

The humor, of course, is wry. The story itself may or may not have been true as told. Its central point, however, was a stark reality, and one very well known to every black man of that era who ever wore cleats: dark skin is a handicap, but it can be eased if you happen to be a Cuban, a Cherokee, or some other dusky being whose ancestors didn't pick cotton in the Carolinas. (John McGraw had literally tried to sneak Charlie Grant into big-league ball as a Cherokee Indian rather than an African-American in 1901: it didn't work.)

The truth is that certain factors, even in the dark-skinned Latin ballplayer's situation, were distinctive—were more favorable to his survival and prosperity—when viewed beside the realities facing his American-born black counterpart. (This is the main reason I never went back and introduced Tony Curry—whose home was Nassau—into my sample.) For one thing, black players from outside the States had their *indignation* working for them. They did not accept the abuses of segregation with resigned patience: one way or another, they often made noise. Vic Power is said to have been arrested for crossing against a traffic light during spring training in heavily segregated Florida. When hauled before a judge, he explained with impeccable logic (if in broken English) that, since America had everything else separated for black use and white use, he assumed that traffic lights were the same way and that only white people were meant to cross on green. The judge let him off without a fine.[6] In an interview already cited, Jim Grant recalls, "We American blacks loved when the black Latin players did things that weren't expected of black ballplayers. For instance, it cheered all of us when they wouldn't allow 'Colored' to be written on their passport. Vic [Power] would argue, 'I'm Puerto Rican, not colored.' Minnie Minoso would say, 'I'm Cuban. Don't put no colored stuff on my passport!'"[7]

Latin players trapped in the segregated South during their Minor League experience might also sometimes be boarded in the homes of Spanish-speaking Americans who adopted them into the local "Little Mexico" or "Little Cuba". American blacks, of course, didn't need to have mentors fluent in a second language (despite the widely circulated myth, discussed later in this book, that they had their own secret lingo). That's exactly the point, really. Admittance into an intimate community of immigrants meant for Latinos that they spoke their native tongue, ate their native food, listened to their native music, and enjoyed their native amusements during their free time. For blacks, native food and music and amusement were to be had throughout the town—but often a much better quality was served up in the white part of town, to which they were strictly denied access. Black catcher John Roseboro once had the unique experience of bedding down in a hotel right along Miami's racial seam. "Standing on the balcony of my room, overlooking the front of the hotel, I watched well-dressed people pour in to see his [singer Roy Hamilton's] show. I wanted to see the show in the worst way, but I didn't have the guts to go."[8] Room and board in the black part of town also meant lousy bedding (literally) and greasy food, more often than not; for, in the

South, that part of town was the *poor* part, by definition—much more so than up North or out West.

For another thing, mainstream white America nursed subtly but significantly different stereotypes about native-born blacks and Latinos. The average Eisenhower American, sitting at home before his miraculous new television, was quite comfortable with the dark eyes and hair of Desi Arnaz on the *I Love Lucy* show. Rickey Ricardo (Desi's character) was lyrical, graceful, passionate, creative, and... well, no one would have said "sexy" back then except for Alfred Kinsey, but that was the idea. Even the more buffoonish Bill Dana, who played bellhop José Jiménez on another TV comedy, was not laughed at by the mainstream white audience as were the characters of *The Amos and Andy Show*. Dana presented a puppet-like figure with his small, stocky build and huge dark eyes. He was able to bring in his shoulders, hang his head, and speak in mincing, thickly accented tones—all of which implied a child-like naiveté. You wanted to throw an arm around José sometimes, smile, and say, "Don't you understand what's going on?" Andy and the Kingfish, in contrast, were studies (respectively) in lazy gullibility and devious trickery: they drew an altogether different kind of laughter.

In serial dramas or on the big screen, to be sure, unsavory racial stereotypes differed from their sit-com versions—but the gap between Latino and American black remained wide. The "bandido" type played by actors like Eli Wallach, Charles Bronson, John Saxon, and Rick Jason (i.e., by men with little or no actual Spanish blood) was a ruthless cutthroat, but also possessed his own variety of manly honor. What few black male parts existed placed bit-actors in a "man Friday" posture behind some rugged-individualist white hero. Black women made no appearances at all, except perhaps to cluck comically after Scarlett O'Hara's skirts. Hispanic women, on the other hand, were sometimes permitted to steal the Caucasian hero's heart. Ruth Roman was Gary Cooper's lady in an energetic western titled *Dallas*, while a much more dark-skinned—and perhaps more ravishing—Linda Crystal turned Jock Mahoney from his lawless ways in a B-film called *The Last of the Fast Guns*.

In the part of the southwest where I grew up, Caucasians like us sometimes married people with Hispanic surnames. Betty Andujar was our county's state senator for years and years. Yet nobody of my acquaintance had ever heard of a black person and a white person marrying, and no person of African descent would win a general election among us for quite some time. The Latin population was different from us, but not in the same way as the black population. It may seem paradoxical to some... but if one had to make his way in our majority culture back then, he would have had a much easier time as Pete Ayala, car dealer, than as Joe Davis, great grandson of a freed slave.

Still not convinced? Reflect upon how many hundreds of thousands of black kids played baseball back then—and played it extremely well. Then explain why Andre Rodgers, a star cricket-player from the Bahamas who scarcely knew the rules of baseball before he was given a Minor League contract, soon found himself patrolling the infield for the Giants. Similarly, future Pirate hurler Al McBean was photographing baseball try-outs one spring when, on a lark, an official invited him to throw a few fastballs. There's no doubt that Al had an exceptional arm—but so did a lot of young men whose talent remained buried in the obscurity of the Negro Leagues. Like big-leaguers Joe Christopher and Valmy Thomas, McBean hailed from the Virgin Islands. These four lucky "finds" were about as far from any tie to the conquistadors, and about as pure-blooded African, as anyone who ever wore a Major League uniform: *but they were not from the mainland United States*. Their association with a Latin part of the hemisphere—or, in the case of Bahamians and Virgin Islanders, with British manners and speech habits—sufficed to draw an interest to them, apparently, out of all proportion to the fragment of the baseball-playing population which they represented.[9] I don't say that any of the Caribbean talents named above was not an extraordinary ballplayer. I say that other fine ballplayers in rural Georgia or the Carolinas had far less of a chance to show their stuff, not because they were black, but because they were *mainland North American blacks* with no tie to European culture whatever.

My conclusion, then, is that it wouldn't have been accurate to suppose all the Latin players in my set of Post cereal baseball cards to have been automatically exposed to the same pressures and double-standards known so well to black American players. My suspicion, frankly, is that the struggle was equally arduous in very few cases—though Henry Aaron, reflecting on the experiences of his friend Felix Mantilla, insists that Latin players had it worse precisely because they had grown up in better conditions.[10] It is certainly true that Mantilla played on many of the same Minor League teams as Aaron and Wes Covington (in fact, he became the godfather of Henry's oldest daughter Gaile). Cuban Pancho Herrera had played in the Negro Leagues, and outfielder Tony Gonzáles was considered to be one of the young men integrating the game when the Reds called him up in 1960. A magnificent rookie star from 1962 named Manny Jiménez showed in his subsequent career all the sad signs of having been fiercely discriminated against for no sane reason, just as Mantilla's many talents were inexplicably ignored in the big leagues. Manny and Felix both appear in the Post cereal trading cards for 1962—and both have decidedly dark complexions in their photos. The way Major League baseball treated them seems suspect, to say the least.

On the other hand, dark-skinned Latin players such as Gonzáles and Tony Taylor had good, long Major League careers over these years. (Pancho Herrera piled up record-breaking numbers of strikeouts: nobody could be too puzzled at his quick exit.) These players, too, were among my cards, as were the not particularly fair-skinned—but Hall of Fame-bound—Orlando Cepeda and Roberto Clemente. If being a copper-toned Latino did not assure you of faring better than a mainstream African-American during these times, it clearly wasn't an insurmountable obstacle, either. And we shall see, finally (in my concluding section), that baseball jettisons its best young talent for many, many reasons. Race was no doubt one of these until the Seventies—but it also worked in tandem with others, or occasionally was a complete red herring.

40

Be that as it may, most of the Latin players just named are listed in Moffi and Kronstadt's encyclopedic work, *Crossing the Line: Black Major Leaguers, 1947-1959.* (Gonzáles and Jiménez appeared on the big-league scene too late to fit the study's parameters). I assume that these authors selected which Latin players to categorize as black by having recourse to a Negro League pedigree. (Light-skinned Latinos like Aparicio and Pascual are not included in their book.) Now, if a ballplayer appears in the set of trading cards upon which I have based my own study, and if he also played in the Negro Leagues, why should my survey not admit him just because his last name is Herrera or Pagán?

In the first place, there are points in the book where I do mention Latino players. Jiménez and Mantilla are named in the next chapter as two of the players in my ancient card collection whose curious disappearance from baseball's annals, despite so much promise, got me to thinking about this subject. I shall be reviewing the cases of these two and others mentioned in Chapter Three when I begin the book's third part. (I may anticipate that moment by saying that, upon closer inspection, I continued to find the careers of Jiménez and Mantilla to show signs of grossly unfair treatment, but partaking more of managerial stupidity than racial bigotry.) Andre Rodgers is actually included in the sample analyzed throughout the book—though, for reasons given above, I should perhaps have disqualified him. That is, despite something very close to a pure African bloodline without any Hispanic component at all, Andre hailed from the Caribbean rather than the North American mainland and hence was apt to be viewed a little differently. Al McBean appears among my small sampling of pitchers for the same reason: that is, his Caribbean pedigree notwithstanding, he was one of the few dark fasces in my baseball card collection. In the last analysis, I did not exclude these two from the study sample because there were so few non-Latin black players in my cards, to begin with.

But I am arguing in circles now. I might simply say that the "Latin variable", while perhaps negligible, was one that I didn't want to admit into my final calculations, *just in case* it might prove influential in certain circumstances. By excluding the Latin players from my group, I had something like a more homogeneous bunch to test for the career effects of prejudice... but I can go that argument one better. For the truth is that, while dark Latinos most certainly had a tough time in the Majors just after Jackie broke the color barrier, I very soon stumbled upon an example of their enjoying preferential treatment in a significant way. I don't remember precisely when it dawned upon me—but at some point, as I sat among my aging cards and emerging graphs and evolving lists, I noticed that *Latino ballplayers enjoyed a very liberal representation in the middle infield, whereas American blacks almost always tended to end up in the outfield.*

Why was this such an important discovery? Because middle infielders—shortstops and second basemen—are skilled labor, while outfielders are relatively unskilled labor. Playing the middle infield is considered such a delicate, intricate craft in baseball that those who do it well can survive for years with puny batting averages and risible power numbers: they're on the team because of their glove. Outfielders, on the other hand, are expected to supply both high averages and big power numbers. The center fielder may need a little more skill than those who play at his sides (or a lot more, if he must minimize the errors of a couple of heavy-hitting clods): the right fielder only has to be able to throw, and the left fielder doesn't even need that much defensive mastery. When outfielders go into a prolonged hitting slump, therefore, it tends to be terminal. Even when they do well, they constitute what is viewed as the most easily replaceable piece of the puzzle, so they are frequently uprooted and packed off in trades. Unless they develop into superstars, they're lucky to eke out a decade in the big leagues.

This contrast is perhaps somewhat exaggerated. Guys like Joe Cunningham and Russ Snyder managed to get past the decade mark without demonstrating great power because they played a very solid outfield (where Joe was moved when the Cardinals eased Stan Musial over to first base). But both Cunningham and Snyder were white; and my point is that if a player's career did indeed risk sabotage by bigotry, he would be far more exposed to such undermining in the outfield than the infield. So Latino players, in this regard, held a substantial advantage even if their skin were as dark as an American black's: the thinking of the day had "typed" them as endowed by Mother Nature to play second or short, where a very nice living could be made.

<u>Players by Most Commonly Assigned Defensive Position</u>
Bold=African-Americans　　　　*Italics*=Latinos

<u>catcher</u>	<u>1st base</u>	<u>2nd base</u>	<u>shortstop</u>	<u>3rd base</u>	<u>outfield</u>
					Aaron
					Alou
					Altman
					Bruton
					Clemente
					Covington
					T. Davis
					W. Davis
					Flood
					González
					Green
					Herrera
					Hinton
					Jiménez
					Jones
					Kirkland
			Amaro		**Maye**
			Aparicio		**Mays**
			Cárdenas		*Mejías*
			Banks		*Minoso*
		Fernández	*Gotay*		*Posada*
		Gilliam	*Mantilla*		**Fl. Robinson**

	Cepeda	*Javier*	*Pagán*		**Fr. Robinson**
Battey	**McCovey**	**Neal**	**Rodgers**	**Charles**	**Tasby**
Howard	*Power*	*Taylor*	*Versalles*	**Smith**	**Wagner**
Roseboro	**White**	**Wood**	**Wills**	*Torres*	**Williams**
<u>catcher</u>	1st base	2nd base	<u>shortstop</u>	3rd base	<u>outfield</u>

Just above, I introduce my first table, whose facts speak for themselves. Both the African-Americans and the Latinos named here were selected strictly from my card collection for the 1961 and 1962 seasons. The resulting samples are not balanced (the Latinos are outnumbered two to one), nor do they represent in either case an exhaustive inventory of the numbers actually to be found in the big leagues during these years. Yet the very fact that the arbiters at Post Cereals chose these names and not others for their elite collection declares that the given player had found unusual success at the given position. In other words, by working only with the groups that Post has provided, we are able to see with particular clarity where African-Americans tended to do well in professional ball, and at what positions Latinos often scored their greatest triumphs.

Even taking into account that the black sample is 50% larger than the Latino sample, the former clearly dominates the outfield by an enormous margin. Roberto Clemente was arguably the best right fielder ever to play the game. Tony González was also a superior fly-hawk. Felipe Alou and Minnie Minoso were above average defensively, but their bats were responsible for keeping them in the game. Otherwise, the Latinos named in the table who failed to break into the infield were doomed to brief, undistinguished careers. This, of course, is my primary point: playing the outfield was the fast track to sudden trade and early retirement.

Now ponder the middle-infield positions: second base and shortstop. Of the 16 players at both positions, 10 are Latino. Most of these middle infielders had much longer careers than their bats would have earned for them if they had roamed the outfield: e.g., Fernández, Javier, Pagán, and Rodgers. Three of my just-cited examples were racially Latin—and the fourth, Andre Rodgers, was strongly associated with the Caribbean and things Latin. Andre had the finely clipped accent and the confidence which growing up in the Bahamas had bestowed upon him, not the heavy drawl and the head-hanging manner which mainstream white America projected upon its native blacks. Even Felix Mantilla, about whom I have already said that I see distinct signs of cheated talent and a thwarted career, enjoyed a much longer day in baseball's sun than the promising American-born Jake Wood. (Jake was given all of one year to succeed—his rookie season—during which he only led the league in triples: not good enough.) Ernie Banks, of course, built a Hall-of-Fame career out of fielding shortstop and (after his legs gave out) first base; but Jim Gilliam, whose play was always sure if not dazzling, was elbowed over to second base, then to third, and finally to the outfield.[11] (Another superior shortstop in the Dodger organization—Jim Pendleton—would reach the Majors only as an outfielder.) Similarly, Al Smith had scintillated in the

Minors as a shortstop and Ed Charles as a second baseman. By the time they made it to the top, however, both had been shouldered to third, where they were somewhat more expendable. Smith was eventually relegated to outfield duties: Charles's exit was a less ceremonious trap door after his batting average fell off.

The message here seems to be that, as important as second base and shortstop are to winning ball games, we don't want them fouled up by people who can't really do the job. A black player at these positions always (unless he was Ernie Banks) seemed to be suspect. As a matter of fact, a great many legendary middle infielders in the Negro Leagues—not Latinos, but American-born blacks—never attracted the slightest interest in the white Major Leagues. Clifford Brown, Pee Wee Butts, Bus Clarkson, Willie Wells, and Art Wilson could have left their teams any day of the week, played shortstop on a Major League field the next afternoon, and struck the crowd dumb. Eddie Brooks and Marvin Williams at second base were just as good. The big leagues, however, were not interested in blacks at these positions. Larry Doby was converted from second base to the outfield before he was brought up, and Monte Irvin was persuaded to make the same shift from shortstop. Henry Aaron, Curt Flood, and Willie Mays were all middle infielders before a paternal hand put them farther out in the pasture. To be fair, Negro League legend Piper Davis moved Willie after assessing his extraordinary ability, and Aaron and Flood both insisted later that their infield play was malodorous. Mickey Mantle said the same thing of his own shortstop days in Single A: high achievers can be devastating critics of their best efforts when these manage only to humiliate them. A position like shortstop isn't learned in a day, a week, or even a year. One has to stick with it, to receive encouragement—but young black players, it appears, were encouraged only to give it up.

Now, a position like first base might just about lie within the capacities of a big, lanky, bucket-footed black kid. The Major Leagues of the Fifties and early Sixties didn't seem to mind letting Bill White and Willie McCovey have a shot at the first sack (though both men started with the Giants' organization, an exceptionally tolerant one). First basemen in my book's sample who did not appear on Post trading cards over the two specified years are Bob Boyd, Donn Clendenon, George Crowe, and Hank's brother Tommie Aaron (who also played outfield, third, and a very little second base). Ironically, at the same time as the assumption reigned that black players were not quick-witted enough to play up the middle, three of the greatest catchers of the era—Earl Battey, Elston Howard, and John Roseboro—were following in the footsteps of Roy Campanella. The obvious fact of having success at blocking bad pitches and at throwing out runners was hard to argue with. Perhaps because catching was such very physical labor, the American black possessed of exceptional intelligence (there had to be a few, right?) could make a go of it. On the other hand, those clever, quick-footed Latin types, with their flamenco-dancer build and their machine-gun jabber, were ideal for turning double plays but would have been ground to pieces under catcher's gear in one afternoon. It is truly amazing to reflect, in this day when almost every Major League catcher seems to be Latino, that about the only Latin behind a big-league plate in the early Sixties was Camilo Carreón. The perfect person for the job would have been an Italian.[12]

In summary, since the one thing that *every* black kid could do was run (I have occasion later to cite Casey Stengel's painful remark about Elston Howard, "We finally get one, and he can't run!"), then young black men were waved into the outfield. There they could be stroked or cut loose, depending upon how they fared at the plate. One must wonder how much coaching was invested in showing them how to match their fleet feet to sound outfield technique, for the front office frequently played the "butcher fielder" card in explaining a trade or release and must surely have liked to hold it ready. A cruel world… cruel for black ballplayers and Latin ballplayers—and for white ballplayers, too. But the American-born blacks were given the dregs to drink in the Fifties, and it is upon them, therefore, that I primarily focus this book's statistics.

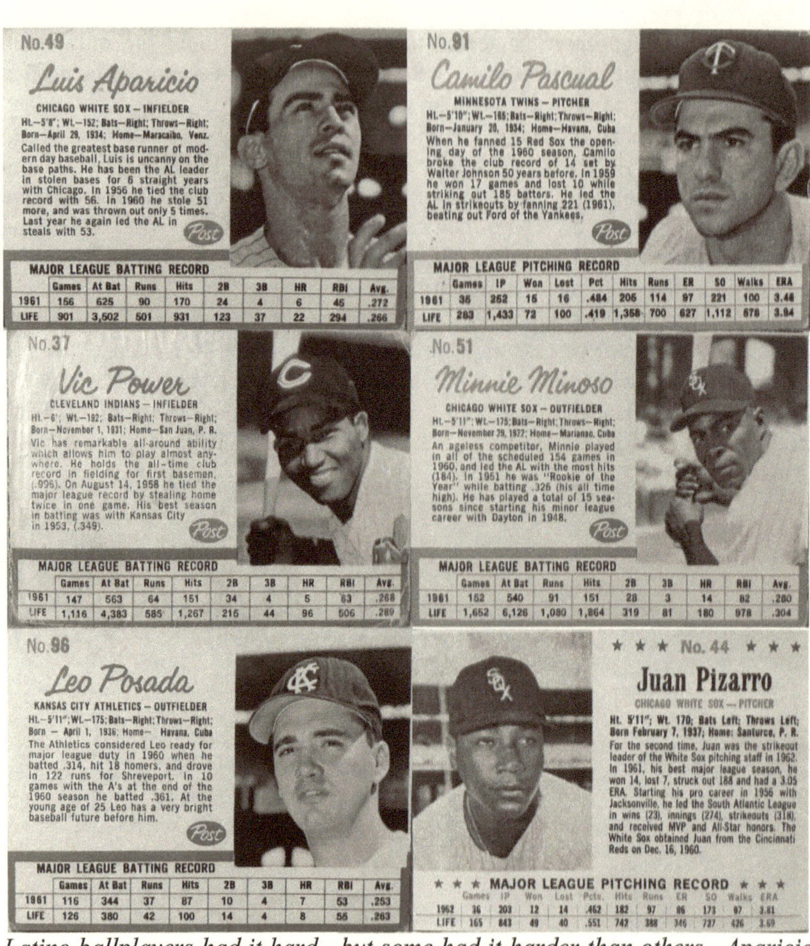

No. 49

Luis Aparicio

CHICAGO WHITE SOX — INFIELDER

Ht.—5'8"; Wt.—152; Bats—Right; Throws—Right; Born—April 29, 1934; Home—Maracaibo, Venz.

Called the greatest base runner of modern day baseball, Luis is uncanny on the base paths. He has been the AL leader in stolen bases for 6 straight years with Chicago. In 1956 he tied the club record with 56. In 1960 he stole 51 more, and was thrown out only 5 times. Last year he again led the AL in steals with 53.

MAJOR LEAGUE BATTING RECORD

	Games	At Bat	Runs	Hits	2B	3B	HR	RBI	Avg.
1961	156	625	90	170	24	4	6	45	.272
LIFE	901	3,502	501	931	123	37	22	294	.266

No. 81

Camilo Pascual

MINNESOTA TWINS — PITCHER

Ht.—5'10"; Wt.—165; Bats—Right; Throws—Right; Born—January 20, 1934; Home—Havana, Cuba

When he fanned 15 Red Sox the opening day of the 1960 season, Camilo broke the club record of 14 set by Walter Johnson 50 years before. In 1959 he won 17 games and lost 10 while striking out 185 batters. He led the AL in strikeouts by fanning 221 (1961), beating out Ford of the Yankees.

MAJOR LEAGUE PITCHING RECORD

	Games	IP	Won	Lost	Pct	Hits	Runs	ER	SO	Walks	ERA
1961	36	262	15	16	.484	205	114	97	221	100	3.46
LIFE	263	1,433	72	100	.419	1,358	700	627	1,112	676	3.94

No. 37

Vic Power

CLEVELAND INDIANS — INFIELDER

Ht.—6'; Wt.—192; Bats—Right; Throws—Right; Born—November 1, 1931; Home—San Juan, P. R.

Vic has remarkable all-around ability which allows him to play almost anywhere. He holds the all-time club record in fielding for first basemen, (.996). On August 14, 1958 he tied the major league record by stealing home twice in one game. His best season in batting was with Kansas City in 1953, (.349).

MAJOR LEAGUE BATTING RECORD

	Games	At Bat	Runs	Hits	2B	3B	HR	RBI	Avg.
1961	147	563	64	151	34	4	5	63	.268
LIFE	1,116	4,383	585	1,267	215	44	96	506	.289

No. 51

Minnie Minoso

CHICAGO WHITE SOX — OUTFIELDER

Ht.—5'11"; Wt.—175; Bats—Right; Throws—Right; Born—November 29, 1922; Home—Marianao, Cuba

An ageless competitor, Minnie played in all of the scheduled 154 games in 1960, and led the AL with the most hits (184). In 1951 he was "Rookie of the Year" while batting .326 (his all time high). He has played a total of 15 seasons since starting his minor league career with Dayton in 1948.

MAJOR LEAGUE BATTING RECORD

	Games	At Bat	Runs	Hits	2B	3B	HR	RBI	Avg.
1961	152	540	91	151	28	3	14	82	.280
LIFE	1,652	6,126	1,080	1,864	319	81	180	978	.304

No. 96

Leo Posada

KANSAS CITY ATHLETICS — OUTFIELDER

Ht.—5'11"; Wt.—175; Bats—Right; Throws—Right; Born — April 1, 1936; Home— Havana, Cuba

The Athletics considered Leo ready for major league duty in 1960 when he batted .314, hit 18 homers, and drove in 122 runs for Shreveport. In 10 games with the A's at the end of the 1960 season he batted .361. At the young age of 25 Leo has a very bright baseball future before him.

MAJOR LEAGUE BATTING RECORD

	Games	At Bat	Runs	Hits	2B	3B	HR	RBI	Avg.
1961	116	344	37	87	10	4	7	53	.253
LIFE	126	380	42	100	14	4	8	55	.263

★ ★ ★ **No. 44** ★ ★ ★

Juan Pizarro

CHICAGO WHITE SOX — PITCHER

Ht. 5'11"; Wt. 170; Bats Left; Throws Left; Born February 7, 1937; Home: Santurce, P. R.

For the second time, Juan was the strikeout leader of the White Sox pitching staff in 1962. In 1961, his best major league season, he won 14, lost 7, struck out 188 and had a 3.05 ERA. Starting his pro career in 1956 with Jacksonville, he led the South Atlantic League in wins (23), innings (274), strikeouts (318), and received MVP and All-Star honors. The White Sox obtained Juan from the Cincinnati Reds on Dec. 16, 1960.

★ ★ ★ MAJOR LEAGUE PITCHING RECORD ★ ★ ★

	Games	IP	Won	Lost	Pct.	Hits	Runs	ER	SO	Walks	ERA
1962	36	203	12	14	.462	182	97	86	173	97	3.61
LIFE	165	843	49	40	.551	742	388	346	737	426	3.69

Latino ballplayers had it hard—but some had it harder than others. Aparicio and Pascual didn't come up through the Negro Leagues, nor were they shuttled to the black part of town during Florida spring training. Not that Power and Minoso took indignity lying down: both were outspoken about the stupidity of segregation, and their African American teammates enjoyed watching them take up the gauntlet. Camilo and Minnie were good friends, by the way—but there was often friction when a fair-skinned Latino chose to blend in quietly with the whites. As for Posada and Pizarro, when Juan pitched for the Milwaukee Braves in the late Fifties, a "gentlemen's agreement" determined that only three other blacks (usually Aaron, Covington, and Bruton) could take the field. Leo, a fair Cuban, would not have created the same problem.

Notes

1 Vic Power's narrative account of the incident appears in Jackie Robinson, *Baseball Has Done It*, ed. Charles Dexter (Philadelphia and New Rork: Lippincott, 1964), 168-169.

2 See Bill James, *The New Bill James Historical Baseball Abstract* (New York: Free Press, 2001), 196. This remark appears in James's discussion of Cuban player Bobby Estalella, who performed brilliantly in the Negro Leagues but also slipped under the race-radar to serve a brief stint with the Senators— this *before* Jackie Robinson's emergence on the scene. The incident demonstrates the absurdity of the whole situation, and may suggest why I find frustrating the selection of just which Latinos to earmark as special victims of racial prejudice. Estelella was apparently *rather* dark without being downright black (or something like that). Honestly, I looked at several cards of Jackie Brandt and Bob Johnson before concluding that they were *Caucasian*! The shadows cast by baseball caps and the presence (I would wager) of some of that swart Central European blood made for several minutes of inane—and at last degrading—calculation.

3 Brent Kelley, *Voices From the Negro Leagues* (Jefferson, NC: McFarland, 1998), 179-180.

4 From an interview in Danny Peary (ed.), *We Played the Game* (New York: Black Dog and Leventhal, 1994), 440-441.

5 Directed by Craig Davidson (1989). The documentary was narrated by James Earl Jones.

6 Henry Aaron relates a slightly more plausible version of this now legendary adventure in *I Had a Hammer* (New York: HarperCollins, 1992), 136. In Henry's version, the cop is persuaded by Vic on the spot.

7 Peary (ed.), *op. cit.*, 441.

8 From John Roseboro (with Bill Libby), *Glory Days with the Dodgers and Other Days with Others* (New York: Atheneum, 1978), 84. It sounds as though Roy Hamilton was actually performing in John's hotel at the time and that he simply didn't have suitable clothes to attend; but celebrated black singers and musicians would also be invited to perform in parts of town where no amount of fancy dress would have made a black customer permissible.

9 Of the few black players who penetrated the Major Leagues in the Fifties, Charley Peete, Pat Scantlebury, and Ozzie Virigl were also not from the North

American mainland (Venezuela, Panama, and the Dominican Republic, respectively), despite their anglicized names.

10 *I Had a Hammer* (*op. cit.*), 81. Aaron writes, "All of that [the racist heckling in the Minors] was harder for Felix than it was for Horace [Garner] and me. We were both accustomed to it, being from the South, but Felix never heard that sort of thing growing up in Puerto Rico It wasn't as easy for him to turn the other cheek."

11 I have seen varying assessments of Gilliam's fielding ability. Bill James always lauds him to the skies, no doubt consulting the statistics. Teammate John Roseboro would reminisce that Jim "was slow-footed and slow-armed and had to cheat like hell to get by in the infield" (*Glory Days with the Dodgers and Other Days* [*op. cit.*], 101). There's something to be said, of course, for being able to get away with cheating like hell.

12 For those who are curious about the breakdown of pitchers in my card collection, I found very few in either group: three American-born blacks (Bob Gibson, Al McBean, and Earl Wilson) and five Latinos (Hank Aguirre, Luís Arroyo, Juan Marichal, Camilo Pascual, and Juan Pizarro). There are few generalities worth advancing here. Pitching, as I argue later, is a unique position in many ways, and bigotry did not necessarily make itself felt in a pitcher's career as it would have in, say, an outfielder's career. At most, one might look at the number of career starts given to these eight men and conclude that McBean, Wilson, and the darkest of the Latinos—Pizarro—were used much more sparingly than they deserved.

IV

Questions in the Cards: A Few Tentative Posers for Those Who Think Jackie Vanquished Racism

An Argentine proverb goes, *conocer su ignorancia es principio de saber*: "To recognize one's ignorance is the beginning of wisdom." The sentiment could be traced much farther back to Socrates' quip that he was the wisest of men because at least he knew that he knew nothing. Either way, there's a long tradition of fools like me wincing at their own folly. An endeavor like this book's, whose answers hide in bygone years and require missing testimony, can only grope after the truth—and must grope, even, to frame the right questions. I did not quite know what I should ask. Yet ask I did—and rather feverishly, scrawling two pages of indignant or bewildered questions addressed to no one in particular. This book grew out of my list. The questions emerged one by one as I shuffled through my old cards and began to wonder why such-and-such an outstanding player of 1961 or 1962 had simply disappeared from baseball's radar. I sometimes found that I was writing down accusations which just happened to be framed interrogatively. My list sadly reminded me of the surveys one receives routinely in the mail nowadays, their disingenuous queries usually intended to market some political cause or candidate. Respondents are asked if they hate crime, value a good education, and think gas prices are too high; then they're invited to enclose a contribution along with the useless answer sheet in the pre-stamped envelope addressed to The Society for a Sunnier America.

I confess that my own questionnaire has the same tendencies. I realize that when I write, "Why was so-and-so traded at the peak of his career for twenty-five boxes of Cracker-Jack?" I am really remarking, "Wasn't this a stupid trade?" I am probably even soliciting the answer, "Because he was black." I don't mean to be tendentious, and I did strive after new phrases later on that might come across as something more than a bald protest. Yet the truth is that several incidents in the careers of these players do seem outrageous at first glance. In fact, the almost insane imbalance and the almost red-letter unfairness of certain trades and certain refusals of playing time are my best evidence that something was amiss in these days.

Still... you never know. Players may have requested to be traded in some instances, or they may have been nursing hidden injuries or grievances known only to the game's insiders. The "nobody" for whom they were traded may strongly have impressed the right people as a "somebody" in the very tricky business of predicting performance on the field. The player who appears to have been deserted by the game may instead have deserted the game. Did Leon Wagner undertake a career in acting because his new Hollywood contacts truly enamored him of the industry, or because he discovered a latent love of posing for the camera? Would he have departed baseball, anyway, even if the Los Angeles Angels had not sent him packing during his best years?

Questions like these may perhaps not be answerable even for the person they directly concern—and who, as in Leon's case, is often no longer with us. They require mind-reading or soul-searching responses, and only the rare person is given to intense self-dissection. His friends and teammates may be expected to have blind spots and gaps of awareness about his life, as well. At the other end of the victim/villain spectrum, we find that the nuts and bolts of arranged trades often remain hidden in the motives of general managers and owners: such things don't get typed out in agreements.

The probability, then, that a brother, a teammate, or a manager commenting upon these matters over half a century later would be able to convey anything but suspicions is slim... and the suspicions, I repeat, are already justified to the casual outsider's eye by the frequent inequity of such arrangements. I nevertheless sought the commentary of whatever teammates and contemporaries I could locate, and I shall discuss the results later. For now, I suggest that the sheer volume of odd incidents involving the trade, benching, or release of black players appears to conceal a story, even if a few such incidents were wholly free of uncharitable motives.

I offer my "questionnaire" below, therefore, in all its weaknesses and limitations. Make of it what you will. The questions, at least, are forthright in that they flowed from the information I possessed. Their disbelief is frank disbelief. They come in no particular order: they are literally lined up as I recorded them while browsing through baseball cards and statistics.

1) Why did Jake Wood never approach 400 at-bats after his rookie year, in which he led the American League in triples, stole thirty bases, and scored almost 100 times?

2) Why did the Cubs so glibly part with George Altman after he had collected 67 extra-base hits in 1961 and nearly won a batting title in 1962?

3) Why was Bill White traded by the Cardinals after the 1965 season— was it because he "slipped" to a .289 average and 73 RBI after three consecutive seasons of batting over .300 and driving in over 100 runs? Inasmuch as the Cardinals had already traded Ken Boyer, who was clearly near the end of his career, why did Mr. Busch allow his

only other big run-producer to be sent packing in the same off-season?

4) Charlie Neal earned a Gold Glove for the Dodgers in 1959, was one of the heroes in the Dodger-dominated World Series of that same year, and had set the team record for homers by a second baseman one season earlier. Although the franchise had already built up a tradition of doing right by its black players, Neal was traded to (not drafted by) the expansion Mets at the end of 1961. In return, the Dodgers received a raw pitcher without a Major League record and offensive featherweight Lee Walls. Why was this considered to be a good deal?

5) Floyd Robinson had logged several fine seasons with the White Sox when, at the end of 1966, he was sent to the Reds for aging pitcher Jim O'Toole (who would go 4-3 for Chicago the next season—his last). In five years of full-time starts with the Sox, Robinson had batted over .300 three times. In 1966, his at-bats were almost halved (due to injury?) and his average dipped; yet he still walked more often than he struck out and still scored almost 50 times. Was this sufficient reason to consider him washed up? Cincinnati gave him no playing time and promptly traded him off: he retired soon thereafter. What justified the interruption of a brilliant career in this manner?

6) Bill Bruton was traded to the Tigers by the Braves in late 1960 for an aging Frank Bolling and ne'er-do-well Neil Chrisley. (Actually, three other Braves were included in the deal!) Bruton had broken a leg a few years earlier, but it had healed completely, and he would have some of his best power-years in Detroit. What was *really* behind this nonsensical trade?

7) Why did Wes Covington *never* receive 400 at-bats with either the Braves or the Phillies, even though he consistently batted around (or above) .300 for both teams, cranked out home runs in double-digits, and proved his worth under pressure in the 1957 World Series? His walks-to-strikeouts ratio was almost even: most teams would not let a player of this caliber sit a game out.

8) Why was Leon Wagner with five teams over eleven years when his "power stats" rivaled those of the day's best hitters? For eight of those years, Leon's slugging percentage was over .400—and for three, it exceeded .500.

9) Did Cincinnati consider that Vada Pinson was washed up when he hit only five homers and batted a "mere" .271 in 1968, the so-called Year of the Pitcher? Did the management believe that eleven years was his limit? Why did teams in the American League continue to shuttle him around thereafter, giving him ever fewer at-bats even though his average remained fairly steady?

10) How could Tommy Davis's broken leg be said to have ruined his career when he came back to hit .313 in 1966, and followed with .302 the next year after being traded to the Mets? Not until he arrived in

Baltimore six years later did Tommy ever again spend more than a year with the same team. Is this not suspicious treatment of a man who won two consecutive batting titles in 1962 and 1963, when Aaron, Mays, and Robinson were in their prime?

11) Why did the Reds trade Frank Robinson in 1965—did they simply decide that Milt Pappas's respectable 60% win-to-loss percentage was adequate compensation for a man who had only once batted in fewer than 80 runs in 10 seasons?

12) Why did highly rated rookie Ted Savage never again receive 300 at-bats after 1962, although—in only 335 at-bats—he had scored 54 runs during his initial campaign and slugged at a .373 percentage?

13) How could Kansas City have sold Ed Charles to the Mets in 1967 (even though Larry Elliot was thrown in)? Charles's slugging percentage had been at or near .400 with the Athletics for five years. He carried right on with the Mets, hitting .276 during the Year of the Pitcher (with 15 home runs)—yet New York gave him few at-bats in 1969 before releasing him.

14) Al Smith collected 142 home runs and almost 1400 hits in ten years of being a starter. He batted .292 the season before the White Sox traded him to Baltimore—where he batted a solid .272 before relegation to permanent part-time duty. Why did baseball pull the plug on him when there was no strong evidence of a down-turn in his abilities??

15) A young man named R. C Stevens hit seven homers in 90 at-bats for the Pirates in 1958 (i.e., he was on track to collect close to 40 in a full season). Over the next two years, he was rewarded with 10—as in *ten*—at-bats! Is there a reasonable explanation for this show of lunacy?

16) Harry "Suitcase" Simpson batted in 105 runs for Kansas City in 1956. This apparently got him traded: he proceeded to win his sobriquet by doing stints with five teams over the next three years. Is there another 100-RBI man in baseball history who has been thus rewarded?

17) How did the White Sox manage to allow eventual All-Star catcher Earl Battey only 356 at-bats in five years?

18) In 1962, Al McBean started 29 games as a sophomore pitcher for the Pirates. He went 15-10 with a 3.71 ERA. In return for this stellar performance, he spent most of the rest of his 10-year career in the bullpen (from which—and with seven spot-starts—he compiled a 13-3 record the following season). Why were McBean's obvious talents not properly exploited?

19) Bob Thurman played five seasons in the big leagues—all with Cincinnati—and not a one consisted of 200 at-bats. Yet he managed to club 16 homers, bat in 40 runs, and score 38 in only 190 at-bats during 1957, a performance which might have put him in contention

for the MVP award if extended over 500+ at-bats. Thurman earned a shot at a starting role, but he was never given one. Why not?

20) Speedster Joe Caffie, who played with Henry Aaron in the minor leagues, had all of two years with the Cleveland Indians. His first season consisted of 38 at-bats, over which he batted .342; his second of 89 at-bats, which produced 10 RBIs and 14 runs scored. Caffie's big league career ended at this point. Exactly what kind of audition would have won him another year with the Indians, or with someone else?

21) Manny Jimenez batted .301 for the Kansas City Athletics and knocked in 69 runs during 1962, his rookie season. Manny hailed from the Dominican Republic—but, like Vic Power and Minnie Minoso, he was visibly more African than Hispanic. His 479 rookie at-bats were to be almost *half* the total he would ever receive in *seven seasons* of Major League play. Is there a rational explanation for why 1962's runner-up Rookie of the Year was shelved forever after that season?

22) Felix Mantilla was another dark Puerto Rican, like Vic Power. There is no question that he was considered "black" in the same way: the Braves organization brought him through the system to be integrated into the white Major Leagues along with Henry Aaron and Horace Garner. Mantilla exceeded 200 at-bats only five times in an eleven-year career. His biggest chance came with the Red Sox in 1964-1965. In the former year he hit 30 homers, and in the latter he batted in 92 runs. His reward for this impressive two-year stretch was to be traded to Houston—where he had 151 at-bats the next year and was then released. Has another hitter of such demonstrated potential—but with fairer skin—ever been nudged from the game so quickly?

I recall that when I first looked over this laundry list of gripes and scowls, I was amazed that certain organizations kept cropping up. The Milwaukee Braves authored the dubious trades of Bruton and Covington (and a rather shaky one of Lee Maye). The Chicago White Sox confined Earl Battey to the bench for years while Sherman Lollar was leading a very full life behind the plate. Meanwhile, Larry Doby (whom "Frantic Frank" Lane had jettisoned from the Indians just two years earlier) and Minnie Minoso were traded away, even though the strategy opened the Sox up to public criticism that they had unloaded what little power they possessed. Manager Al Lopez was delighted to have black slugger Al Smith, in return... but Smith's days with the franchise were strangely interrupted while he was in his prime, as were the talented Floyd Robinson's. Cincinnati disposed of Vada Pinson just three years after swapping Frank Robinson for Pappas. The Phillies benched Ted Savage after his very promising rookie season, and they never made Wes Covington into the full-time player he so transparently deserved to be. The Kansas City Athletics similarly benched Jiménez after his spectacular debut and traded away Ed Charles when he had given every indication of having hit a long, confident stride. The Athletics had earlier tossed away Simpson right after he showed them his stuff with a 105-RBI season.

Was I seeing behind the recurrent names of a few cities that Middle America didn't want black men as heroes? In most cases, I was eventually led to answer "no"—but I will admit here, in the early going, that the question occurred to me. It was no doubt impossible to contain Henry Aaron's light under a bushel, and catchers like Battey (once he was given a chance in Minnesota) seemed to receive exceptionally generous playing time if they demonstrated a mastery of their position. In the case of position-players within fair territory, however, and of men whose abilities were slightly short of phenomenal, I was beginning to wonder if starting for a team somewhere east of Los Angeles just didn't mix with African blood. The Cubs franchise was admirably loyal to Ernie Banks and Billy Williams, at least on the surface.[1] Yet it would be the St. Louis Cardinals, more than any other mid-American team, which was to lead the way in a few years, assigning Gibson, Flood, Brock, and White all primary roles on the squad. Yet Bill White is prominent among my case files above: August Busch's Cardinals bundled him off quite unceremoniously.

The seasoned baseball historian will already have glimpsed two naïve oversights in my objections: 1) that most of the teams I am indicting sent off more black players in trades because they *employed* more blacks, to begin with; and 2) that my assumptions often underestimate the giddy childishness which moves wealthy owners of sports teams to make deals, and which did so especially in the days of baseball's Reserve Clause. As I say, these deficiencies would strike me later—but my research, if I may again anticipate my own defense, did not always wipe away every trace of a racially tinged double standard. Far from it.

Then we have the East Coast, where the nation's most liberal minds have long been thought to nestle. Elston Howard, a brilliant young catcher who (with John Blanchard) was employed to take some of the strain off of the aging Yogi Berra, was for many years not only the first African-American on the Yankees, but the *only* one who received serious playing time until pitcher Al Downing arrived about a decade later. (Harry "Suitcase" Simpson had meanwhile paid a brief visit.) Even in my pristine naiveté, I was aware that imbalanced, unjustifiable trades involving black players do not besmirch the Yankee record of this era because there was only one black man worth trading for on the Bronx Bombers. The Boston situation was similar, only worse. Howard Bryant's *Shut Out: A Story of Race and Baseball in Boston* details such incidents as the Red Sox' declining to scout a minor leaguer named Willie Mays because it was raining too hard in Alabama! The Sox front office tossed a bone to the nation's hunger for change by signing Pumpsie Green, Willie Tasby, and a few other talented blacks over the decade to occupy the dugout. Bryant observes, however, that though Boston had officially integrated, "the club's racial attitudes of the 1950s were perfectly intact. [Manager Pinky] Higgins was known throughout the league as an alcoholic and a racist, the classic old-boy drinking buddy of [owner] Tom Yawkey's who always found himself with a job in the Red Sox organization."[2] Boston was in fact the last team in the Majors to integrate: no need to worry about outrageous trades emanating from *this* franchise until the '60s!

You will perhaps now see, as I soon saw, the difficulty of conducting a study of *sub rosa* bargains and unpublicized attitudes. The best evidence is often no evidence at all: or rather, the absence of doubtful judgments in dealing with black players may hint at the presence of a persistent refusal to have *any* dealings with them. Such frustrating elusiveness characterizes a host of related issues. How do you demonstrate that a trade or a release was racially motivated when another black player is acquired right away? How can you maintain that the trade was unjustified if the player's productivity had fallen off—but how could his numbers *not* have declined when he had spent three-quarters of the season watching games from the water cooler? But again, how do you prove that the manager was disingenuous in claiming to have benched said player because of the decline—i.e., that the decline did not cause the demotion rather than the demotion the decline?

Capturing statistical evidence to support allegations of unfairness in these matters is like trying to get a snapshot of a ghost. We have all seen photographs of blurry objects whose author claims that they prove the existence of the supernatural, leaving us to decide whether the whole thing is a hoax. I have no training as a statistician, and I am incapable of the subtlety needed to pull off a hoax in numbers. The figures and graphs I offer in the succeeding chapters will be readily dismantled by people brighter than I if they are the result of cooked books. I repeat: make up your own mind.

After I have taken my shot at making the statistical case, I shall return to this chapter's questions at the beginning of Part 3. I shall also be introducing a great deal of anecdotal evidence in that part of the book. With numbers on one side and eye-witnesses on the other, we can perhaps get to the bottom of some of the charges. And then again, there are some issues about which we shall never know the full truth.

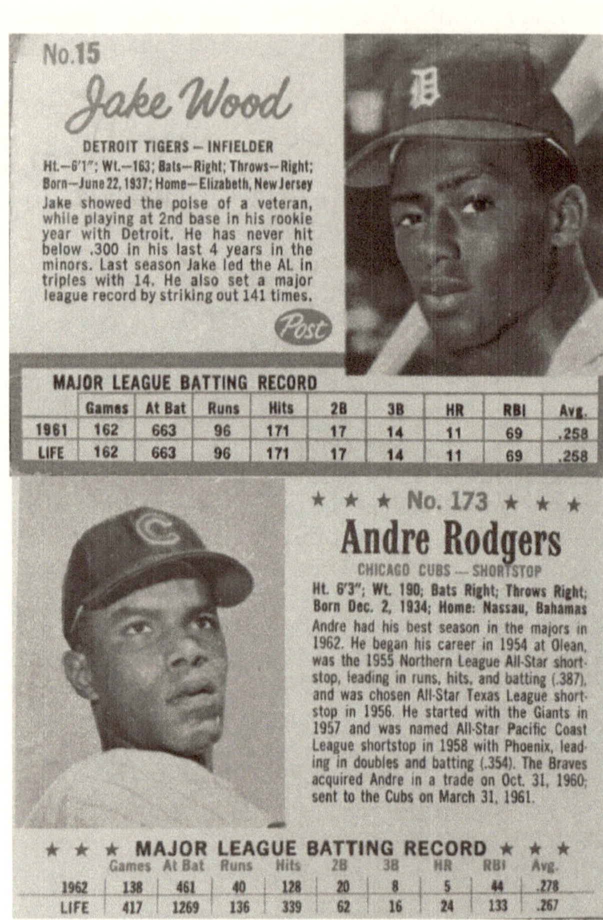

| MAJOR LEAGUE BATTING RECORD | | | | | | | | |
	Games	At Bat	Runs	Hits	2B	3B	HR	RBI	Avg.
1961	162	663	96	171	17	14	11	69	.258
LIFE	162	663	96	171	17	14	11	69	.258

| ★ ★ ★ MAJOR LEAGUE BATTING RECORD ★ ★ ★ | | | | | | | | |
	Games	At Bat	Runs	Hits	2B	3B	HR	RBI	Avg.
1962	138	461	40	128	20	8	5	44	.278
LIFE	417	1269	136	339	62	16	24	133	.267

Andre's 1962 card credits him with a career year—but his stats look puny compared to Jake's rookie season, especially the "power" categories and the runs scored. Yet Wood was washed up as a starter after 1961. Few black players were allowed to get a firm hold on key middle-infield positions. It may not be irrelevant that Rodgers, who was one of those few, hailed from the Bahamas, where he had starred in cricket but played little baseball.

1 [1] In *The New Bill James Historical Baseball Abstract* (*op. cit.*), Mr. James notes that Baltimore approached the Cubs about trading Williams after a "bad" year in 1966—when he logged a .276 average, hit 29 homers, and drove in 91! "The Cubs demanded Mike Epstein, who at the time was the minor league player of the year. The Orioles turned them down..." (658). If Norm Cash and Ron Fairly had been the beneficiaries of such loyalty, their career would have been done in five years.

2 From Howard Bryant, *Shut Out* (New York and London: Routledge, 2002), 62.

V

O Tempora, O Mores: Some of Baseball's Peculiar Years and Obscure Necessities

There are several observations which should be made right away before I begin to toss statistics around. I apologize if the matter of this chapter seems condescending to some readers—but my perception is that many fans, and far too many professional commentators, know a lot less about the physical exigencies of playing baseball than they should if they are to appreciate genuine accomplishment. How many "great catches", for instance, are featured over and over again on highlight reels which show a fielder diving or leaping to make a last-second grab? Most of these catches reflect nothing so much as bad judgment: a better fielder would have gotten and better jump and cruised under the ball like Joe DiMaggio or Andrew Jones. Or take the notorious space-between-the-hands which Leon Wagner employed when gripping the bat. This technique is universally derided.[1] Yet it was routinely used by earlier ballplayers like Gavy Cravath (the pre-Ruthian home run king), Ty Cobb, and the *other* Wagner—Honus—and used modestly under high-pressure circumstances by such recent superstars as Ted Williams, Billy Williams, and Jim Rice. I shall have more to say about such colorful subjects as now-extinct batting styles in the book's concluding section, for many of these curiosities are relics of the "dead ball" and Negro League days. They patiently await rediscovery by anyone interested in acquiring three thousand hits—a surprisingly small club at present (I mean, that of those even *interested*).

My comments for now will be of a rather more general nature. The first is this: that higher batting averages accrue to higher numbers of plate appearances. The novice may scratch his head and wonder why the average-to-at-bats ratio isn't simply a crap shoot. What if you're just lucky for your first twenty or thirty at-bats of the year—or what if the pitchers need that long to figure out your rookie fallibilities? It might be that being rewarded with another 100 at-bats would simply plunge you into a 3-for-51 slump.

To make such an argument, a person must be either naïve or disingenuous—either a novice indeed or else a trouble-maker. *Anything* can happen in baseball, yes… but only a few things *tend* to happen. At the Major League level, a hitter needs to see lots of pitches if he is to handle them with success. You can take all the batting practice you like: the guys who throw batting practice rarely pump in a ninety-mile-an-hour fastball, let alone a first-rate change-up or a sharp breaking ball. Furthermore, batting practice too seldom replicates a "game" situation with a count to be worked. The hitter simply walks into the cage and proceeds to hack away at anything he can reach. Even at the highest levels, hitters rarely practice taking close pitches or altering their approach with two strikes. Rookies, in fact, are particularly vulnerable to being worked over in a real live confrontation—for a hitter seldom appears out of the blue who has a completely off-beat or "reverse" batting style, while virtually every Major League pitcher has an array of kinks, quirks, and tricks which has helped him to reach the top.

The directly proportional relation of at-bats to average is vitally important in understanding how young black players were short-changed a few decades ago. (I focus on official at-bats rather than plate appearances in this and subsequent chapters because few Major League managers prized the ability to draw walks in the Fifties, and few young hitters bothered to angle for them.) To bring a kid to the "big team" and then sit him on the bench five days out of seven is to set him up for failure. Even if the youngster were not overwhelmed by the pitching he faced, he would quickly grasp that increased playing time—if not his entire professional future—depended upon how he fared in his three or four plate appearances per week. He would press. He would swing at marginal pitches, and he would try to pull everything. Every big-league pitcher has a nose for rookies' sweat and understands how to exploit their over-eagerness. It is amazing, indeed, that as many young black players, saddled with an awareness of hostility to their race as well as with normal rookie pressures, performed as well as they did. Larry Doby tells a story of how race-baiting once induced him to attempt a steal of home with the bases loaded and his team down 7-4: in circumstances, that is, which any ballplayer knows preclude such an attempt.[2] He failed, and looked like a fool. The pressure had affected his judgment. How much more often must the same kind of pressure have lured young black players to swing at bad pitches! The career stats of Larry's immediate successors are beset with seasons of around 200 at-bats (equivalent to playing every third game), and even of fewer than 100 at-bats. One can only wonder how many such seasons actually involved one start per every three games, when the player would at least see the same pitcher three or four times, and how many consisted mostly of pinch-hit appearances, a much tougher assignment for a freshman.

Besides at-bats, my graphs will consider the number of times a player was traded. All of us who have worked at a job where we were frequently moved by a single employer—or, worse, had to move continually in search of new employment—know what pure misery it is to be forever relocating. The early hope that things will work out better this time is soon throttled by the self-preservative refusal to become attached to anything in one's new surroundings. If one has a family, then one must either forego seeing one's wife and children for months at a time or else uproot them every year or two and thrust them into friendless, alien circumstances. Even if one is young and single, the experience of having to enter an entirely new environment where one is expected to excel instantly does not inspire maximum performance. No less a talent than Mickey Mantle was reduced to tears when he first encountered the "success" of being called away from everything and everyone he had ever known:

> I knew I looked pale and frightened as I turned at the steps to the train, took my suitcase in my hand, and tried to say good-byes to my mother and father. I was just about able to speak. I got on the train, looked for a seat by the window where I could see my parents, and tried forlornly to smile as they waved up at me. The train began to roll at last and then the sobs rose up and choked me. For a whole hour I sat with my fist pressed tight to my mouth and my swimming eyes fastened unseeing on the blurred country outside as I tried to keep from weeping aloud. Tears kept welling up, in spite of me, and ran hot on my nose and cheeks. What a jerk I felt like! And how hard I tried to breathe deep and square up like a professional ballplayer. And how completely lost and woebegone I was![3]

Black players were not only being moved around in the Fifties and Sixties at a rate exceeding what their white counterparts usually endured: they were also commonly unwelcome *as blacks* wherever they went, and they could seldom count on finding more than one or two other black faces in the new locker room.

I also track at one point the number of times black players were traded across league boundaries, which turns out to have been slightly higher than for white players. The change of leagues was far more challenging half a century ago than it is today. The National League was known as a low-strike league, the American League as a high-strike league. The calling of various breaking pitches was also "league-specific", it was claimed. The explanation of this phenomenon pertains to the different gear worn by the umpires. National League umpires carried a chest protector inside their coat, whereas American League umpires held a vast shield-like protector on the outside of their clothing. The American League protector prevented its wearers from crouching as low as National League referees. Naturally, this caused the AL blues to see the strike zone from a higher angle. Pitchers in both leagues threw the same kinds of pitch, to be sure; but the difference in how those pitches were arbitrated was significant enough to draw frequent comment, and switching from one league to the other must certainly have required an adjustment of any hitter (and, to a lesser degree, of any pitcher).

Today the difference has been largely erased, not only because all umpires wear the same gear and because a new routine has each league frequently playing the other, but also because so many pitchers, in pursuit of the best deal, choose to cross league boundaries so often. Several decades ago, however, the cross-over might possibly have been a death sentence to a hitter's career, particularly if he were not allowed more than one sub-par season before being released or traded yet again. Such a "quick hook" was precisely the kind of handling portioned out to most black players.

I do not feel entirely comfortable, on the basis of my research, asserting that blacks were deliberately and consistently shuttled across league boundaries more than whites. The figures are about even, and I am not sufficiently enamored of conspiracy theories to find attractive the proposition that the whole "old boy" network somehow got together and agreed to disadvantage its young black players in this very subtle manner. Yet when the roughly even figures are realigned to take into account the much shorter careers of most black players (the incredible longevity of Aaron, Mays, and McCovey tends to create the illusion of balance), black players of the late Fifties and early Sixties did indeed seem to be getting more than their fair share of exposure to the other league... and after that, often, to the former league no longer so familiar. For I must also emphasize this point: that a National Leaguer returning "home" after a year or two in the American League would not find his surroundings as he left them. New pitchers are constantly being brought up. A hitter can't get the better of the good ones simply by hearing about their lively fastball or watching their sharp curve during warm-ups. Nothing can substitute for actual time in the batter's box against the league's best arms. A player who has taken a year or two's "vacation" from this study must start his apprenticeship all over again.

After receiving adequate at-bats and being allowed to play without fear of a life-altering trade from month to month, the young black player must have wanted most of all just to be evaluated by a sensible standard. My research suggests that the kind of baseball played in the Negro Leagues— bunting, stealing bases, advancing runners with productive outs—was either not fully understood or not fully appreciated throughout the Major Leagues. I believe, indeed, that black players were expected to hit home runs, or at least were most prized when they did so. The "immortals" from this era whose names are household knowledge—Aaron, Banks, Mays, McCovey, Robinson—all ground out four-baggers at energetic yet steady rates. They did other things, too. They were exceptional fielders, they ran the bases extremely well, and they were contact-hitters by any standard that might fairly be applied to a slugger. Yet they were most widely heralded in white society for hitting home runs. The one black ballplayer in my group who seemed to have gotten more than a fair shake (or a fairer shake, anyway, than his peers) was Willie Kirkland—and Willie's mediocre-to-abysmal average does not appear to have hampered his homering abilities. Would Tommy Davis have been traded at a pace that eventually set a Major League record if he had not clobbered 27 home runs in 1962? Though never so prone to clear the fences either before or after that red-letter year, Davis became a one-season experiment for several teams. The experiment didn't seem to yield positive results if he merely hit over .300. Vada Pinson better justified such expectations, no doubt; yet Vada was also fleet afoot, and could be relied upon to generate doubles and triples even when his home run numbers declined. This did not prevent his being passed around almost as frequently as Davis in the latter half of his career.

In fairness, I should say that Caucasian players got swapped in much the same manner for much the same reasons during their twilight years. If predicting a player's inevitable decline based upon minute statistical down-turns was a fine art, then most general managers don't seem to have mastered it at the time (and don't do much better today). After seven or eight years of steady service, you get little slack from the front office when your home run or RBI curve noses downward. The assumption is made that you have passed your prime, and that you'd better be traded now while you can still fetch something on the open market. The statistics bear out the assertion that most white sluggers got a little more leeway in these calculations—yet the prospect of ending your professional days by wearing several uniforms about half-a-year apiece loomed over both black and white stars. (Such prophecies, I might add, are often self-fulfilling: the player expected to decline *does* decline when traded into an unfamiliar environment... and who knows how much of the cause is age?)

All the same, it appears that the criteria for determining when a black player was "past it" were pretty crude—that, once again, they had little bearing on anything but power. Davis hit .313 in his last year with the Dodgers, then .302 in a full season of at-bats with the Mets—which won him a trade into the American League. The rap about Tommy was that he would never recover his peak form after a severely broken leg. Yet he would end up stealing a career-high 20 bases (with Seattle and Houston) in 1969—and swatting a career-high 32 doubles, as well, in parks which were not friendly to homers. Exactly how was the unwholesome leg supposed to be inhibiting his performance? Pinson's average did indeed descend from .288 (where it had been two years running) to .271 in 1968, just before he was traded; but his usual 600 at-bats were also reduced to just under 500, and he still managed to pound out 29 doubles and 6 triples. To be sure, a trade could easily be justified in such circumstances... but we shall see that white players of established reputation suffered far worse fall-offs for a season without having their plug pulled.

1968: the so-called Year of the Pitcher. If the front office had inspected something beyond the power stats of its black players, it might well have found averages also declining throughout the mid-Sixties. *Everybody's* stats declined. For several years, life had been getting better and better for pitchers. After the 1963 season, the strike zone was altered to include the entire height of the knee-cap rather than stopping where thigh becomes knee. Though the adjustment may seem no more than three or four inches, one cannot actually see a uniformed ballplayer's knee-cap very well. The effect was that men who had spent all of their adult (and much of their juvenile) life learning precisely where to lay off a pitch now had to go back to school, while umpires entered their crouch with really no more a sense of their new duty than that they should be calling low pitches strikes. In the American League, three hitters reached the .300 mark in 1968: Carl Yastrzemski won the batting title with a .301 performance (the lowest ever to be so crowned). More night games were being played, as well (with lighting which was not always up to the task), and newer stadiums, as Bill James observes, were springing up which turned one-time fouls over the stands into easy catches for first and third basemen.[4] James also astutely notes that pitching mounds were not systematically checked for violation of the rules. He plausibly attributes some of Koufax's and Drysdale's spectacular success during these years to a mound at Chavez Ravine that was both too high and too sharply sloped. I might add that the slider was also becoming a very popular pitch at this time. Different eras favor different pitches, and whenever anything is first introduced, it leaves hitters nonplussed for a while. A good slider from a righty to a righty is still unhittable unless the batter manages to poke it to the opposite field—and pokes would only result in home runs during the steroid days of the Nineties, *not* during the Sixties.

The home run again: one cannot escape its influence. James believes that ballplayers—or at least their managers—became home-run crazy when they found that they could no longer expect to grind out three hits in an inning. So dominant had pitching grown that the best recipe for scoring was simply to hope that a couple of hard-swinging batters, in the course of the allotted twenty-seven outs, would drive a pitch to the seats. I confess that I find this reasoning backward. It is precisely when a pitcher is dominating your line-up that you try to draw walks, drop bunts, advance runners, and make productive outs. A savvy pitcher longs for nothing so much as for the opposition to start swinging from the heels at whatever he offers. Yet James may be quite right that a good many managers of the day thought otherwise.

So here we have a chicken-or-egg conundrum—and it is the key, I believe, to understanding the mid-Sixties in general and the dilemma of the black player in particular. Did the dominant pitching of Koufax, Gibson, Juan Marichal, Jim Bunning, and others reduce batting averages and elevate the stock of the home run... or, instead, did an infatuation with the home run contribute to making a generation of great pitchers and sub-.300 hitters? I tend to argue for the latter: I think a primary cause of those years leading up to the Year of the Pitcher (which induced baseball's wise men, in a predictably obtuse response, to lower the mound in '69) was a silly infatuation with the home run.

If you believe as I do, then the next question must be this: did franchises exhort their players to swing for the fences because the results electrified the public and made the turnstiles spin... or did they, rather, *encourage a predominantly white style of baseball so as to minimize the black contribution?* To the extent that black players succumbed to the allure of the "long fly", they were playing someone else's game and working against their area of greatest strength. Might Davis have led the league yet again in hitting if he had not been made a little "power conscious" in his final Dodger years? Would Pinson have done so if he had retained his poise of a few years earlier? Dixie Walker, with apparently the best of intentions, is on record as declaring of Mack Jones, "I'm going to try to make him into another Henry Aaron"—by which he plainly meant "a prolific long-ball hitter", since the remark follows another about Mack's losing a little power by not keeping his weight back.[5] (What an irony: Aaron himself was a front-foot hitter!) Would Jones have managed to log a respectable Major League career if well-meaning white coaches had not forced him out of his style to worship at the home run's altar?

These, of course, are unanswerable questions—but they are *not* frivolous ones. It does no good to scoff at my suggestion by observing that, in fact, Davis hit only 3 homers in his last Dodger year and Pinson only 5 in his last Reds year.[6] You hit fewer home runs when you press to hit more: you hit more when you simply try to drive the ball. Henry Aaron has often described himself as a doubles-hitter whose low liners sometimes happened to clear the fence. In other words, Aaron became the all-time drug-free home run king by making solid contact and not worrying about the ball's elevation. The World Series of those pitcher-dominated years just mentioned were most often visited by two teams with scrappy, contact-hitting offenses: the Dodgers and the Cardinals. Why, then, were Major League franchises clamoring for more homers as loud as any bellicose bleacher-mom exhorting her Little Leaguer? Why did Tommy Davis in fact hit 16 homers in 1967 (tied for his second-highest total) and Pinson 24 homers in 1970 (his highest total ever) if they, and their peers, were not trying harder than ever to go for distance? Yes, I just wrote that homer totals usually descend when you try to elevate them... but not so much if your commitment is utter and you don't mind ruining your average. Davis's average for the same year was thirty points below his career mark, and Pinson's right at his career median when he should have been in his prime; so their "success" appears to have come at a cost.

Eventually, black baseball won out—for a while. The Seventies and Eighties saw the successors of Maury Wills and Lou Brock—Vince Coleman, Rickey Henderson, Tim Raines—transforming the game into a complex ballet of hitting pitches into gaps and taking an extra base right under the defense's nose. Then the Nineties put a stop to the thinking man's game and fed an undiscriminating public a constant home run derby. Black players began to disappear. The causes of baseball's current crisis—its tiresome absence of subtlety, I mean (since its lack of black players is perhaps a social problem, but not *per se* a strategic one)—is due to many causes. I have a suspicion that television has made baseball audiences worship the home run to the severe detriment of the game. Televised contests were not a fixture of the Sixties world. While homers and their authors were highly popular, sales of tickets and "collectibles" did not depend upon sluggers to the degree that they do now. For instance, there is no indication that Mickey's mighty wallops and Roger Maris's shattering of Ruth's record (without benefit of steroids and juiced balls, I say in asterisk) had much effect on the game's popularity, one way or the other. Mantle, describing later the "capacity crowds" of mid-August as his duel with Roger for the Ruth record came down to the wire, would stress the "Home Run Derby" quality of the drama, involving two great sluggers on the same team.[7] In his view, the public was captivated as much by a neck-and-neck race as by the rapid, towering ascent of a small white globe.

As we look at these years, then, with their very peculiar inversion of typical numbers, we must again ask just what was going on. And we can hardly rule out immediately the notion that the whole thing was some sort of nervous "gut" recoil from the talents which young black players, especially, were introducing into the Major Leagues.

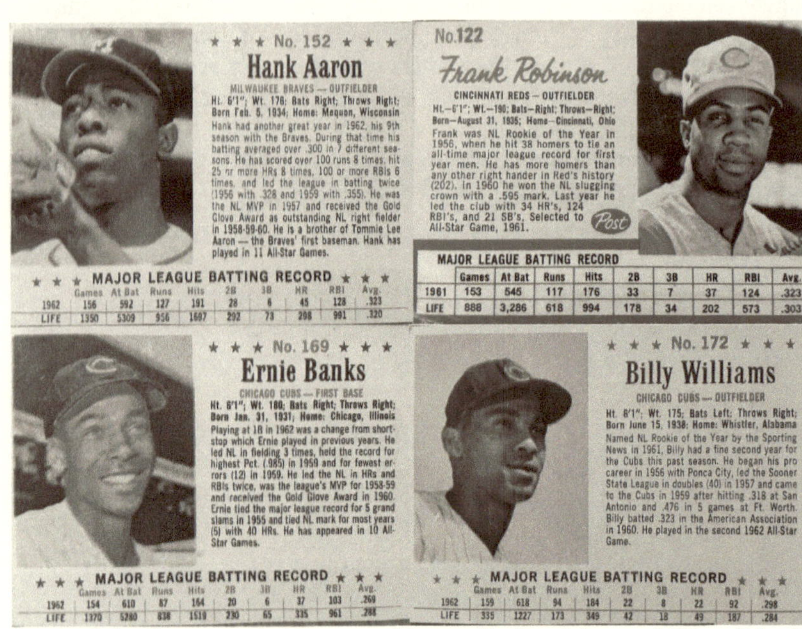

★ ★ ★ No. 152 ★ ★ ★

Hank Aaron

MILWAUKEE BRAVES — OUTFIELDER

Ht. 6'1"; Wt. 176; Bats Right; Throws Right; Born Feb. 5, 1934; Home: Mequon, Wisconsin

Hank had another great year in 1962, his 9th season with the Braves. During that time his batting averaged over .300 in 7 different seasons. He has scored over 100 runs 8 times, hit 25 or more HRs 8 times, 100 or more RBIs 6 times, and led the league in batting twice (1956 with .328 and 1959 with .355). He was the NL MVP in 1957 and received the Gold Glove Award as outstanding NL right fielder in 1958-59-60. He is a brother of Tommie Lee Aaron — the Braves' first baseman. Hank has played in 11 All-Star Games.

★ ★ ★ MAJOR LEAGUE BATTING RECORD ★ ★ ★

	Games	At Bat	Runs	Hits	2B	3B	HR	RBI	Avg.
1962	156	592	127	191	28	6	45	128	.323
LIFE	1350	5309	956	1697	292	73	298	991	.320

No. 122

Frank Robinson

CINCINNATI REDS — OUTFIELDER

Ht.—6'1"; Wt.—190; Bats—Right; Throws—Right; Born—August 31, 1935; Home—Cincinnati, Ohio

Frank was NL Rookie of the Year in 1956, when he hit 38 homers to tie an all-time major league record for first year men. He has more homers than any other right hander in Red's history (202). In 1960 he won the NL slugging crown with a .595 mark. Last year he led the club with 34 HR's, 124 RBI's, and 21 SB's. Selected to All-Star Game, 1961. *Post*

MAJOR LEAGUE BATTING RECORD

	Games	At Bat	Runs	Hits	2B	3B	HR	RBI	Avg.
1961	153	545	117	176	33	7	37	124	.323
LIFE	888	3,286	618	994	178	34	202	573	.303

★ ★ ★ No. 169 ★ ★ ★

Ernie Banks

CHICAGO CUBS — FIRST BASE

Ht. 6'1"; Wt. 180; Bats Right; Throws Right; Born Jan. 31, 1931; Home: Chicago, Illinois

Playing at 1B in 1962 was a change from shortstop which Ernie played in previous years. He led NL in fielding 3 times, held the record for highest Pct. (.985) in 1959 and for fewest errors (12) in 1959. He led the NL in HRs and RBIs twice, was the league's MVP for 1958-59 and received the Gold Glove Award in 1960. Ernie tied the major league record for 5 grand slams in 1955 and tied NL mark for most years (5) with 40 HRs. He has appeared in 10 All-Star Games.

★ ★ ★ MAJOR LEAGUE BATTING RECORD ★ ★ ★

	Games	At Bat	Runs	Hits	2B	3B	HR	RBI	Avg.
1962	154	610	87	164	20	6	37	103	.269
LIFE	1370	5280	838	1519	230	65	335	961	.288

★ ★ ★ No. 172 ★ ★ ★

Billy Williams

CHICAGO CUBS — OUTFIELDER

Ht. 6'1"; Wt. 175; Bats Left; Throws Right; Born June 15, 1938; Home: Whistler, Alabama

Named NL Rookie of the Year by the Sporting News in 1961, Billy had a fine second year for the Cubs this past season. He began his pro career in 1956 with Ponca City, led the Sooner State League in doubles (40) in 1957 and came to the Cubs in 1959 after hitting .318 at San Antonio and .476 in 5 games at Ft. Worth. Billy batted .323 in the American Association in 1960. He played in the second 1962 All-Star Game.

★ ★ ★ MAJOR LEAGUE BATTING RECORD ★ ★ ★

	Games	At Bat	Runs	Hits	2B	3B	HR	RBI	Avg.
1962	159	618	94	184	22	8	22	92	.298
LIFE	335	1227	173	349	42	18	49	187	.284

Some of the Superstars: Aaron would actually be nicknamed "Supe" by his teammates. Billy Williams—called "Sweet William" for his level, effortless swing—was in fact still little known in 1962, and would remain a very quiet performer throughout his career.

1 Bill James (*op. cit.*, 702-703) recalls that "Wagner had an odd batting stance, actually a series of odd batting stances..."; and he proceeds to reproduce Jack Zanger's exclamation from *Baseball Stars of 1963*: "...his hands—look at his hands, will you?—spread apart on the handle." It is true that Leon's hands were spaced dramatically far apart when compared, say, to Bill Madlock's or (with two strikes on him) Billy Williams's; but the top fist slid down on the bottom fist upon its initial thrust—there was none of that awkward bump in the swing which causes some hitting coaches to decry the practice. James, of course, is a very entertaining writer. Too many people, however, earnestly caricature Wagner as a freak or a clown without understanding the advantages of his technique or, indeed, knowing squat about hitting.

2 Doby recounts the incident in Jackie Robinson's *Baseball Has Done It* (Philadelphia and New York: Lippincott, 1964), 62.

3 From Mickey Mantle, *The Education of a Baseball Player* ((New York: Simon and Schuster, 1967), 54-55.

4 *Op. cit.* This and subsequent references to Bill James here and in the next paragraph are drawn from his section, "How the Game Was Played," for the 1960s, 249-250.

5 See pp. 46-47 of Jackie Robinson's *Baseball Has Done It* (*op. cit.*).

6 My suggestion that Pinson may have been preoccupied with homering is not entirely whimsical. Bill James (*op. cit.*, 736) cites sports reporter Earl Lawson on the subject of Vada's losing the 1961 MVP award to Frank Robinson: "I have to think that during the winter of 1961 Pinson came to the conclusion that the top awards and big bucks came with home runs." He would naturally have figured this out: anyone could have, with far less cause to brood over the fact than Vada. It is a small step from here to the supposition that Pinson began to press for the long ball.

7 See especially 203-206 of Mickey Mantle, *The Mick* with Herb Gluck (New York: Doubleday, 1986).

Part Two

In Search of Facts: Inferences to be Drawn from Graphs, Tables, and Statistics

I

Slow Death by Benching:
The Hit/Sit Differential

It is surely self-evident that the more good pitching you see, the better hitter you become. Batting practice itself is only of limited value—for you play the way you practice, and too many BP pitchers simply lob tired fastballs up to the plate. Ted Williams insisted that pitchers in such warm-up exercises should simulate the conditions of a game-quality performance as much as possible, but Ted knew better than anyone that nothing could substitute for game-time experience. Even pinch-hitting, in and of itself, cannot tap a young hitter's potential:

> One pinch hit every other day isn't enough to keep you sharp, 100 pinch hits a year aren't enough, but if you play twice a week, or once a week, and pinch-hit a couple of times in between, then it's not completely foreign to you when you're sent in there. You're playing, you feel good, you win a game once in a while with an important hit—it gives you a little incentive, makes you want to practice more. But if you just sit a guy on the bench and leave him there, sooner or later he says, "Well, nuts with this outfit," and you can't blame him.[1]

Particularly for a young player just getting to know the league's legendary hurlers, nothing can substitute for a few humbling encounters. After he has seen the break in Jones's curve ball or realizes that Smith will mercilessly work him over inside, he begins to make adjustments and to meet with a certain amount of success. This happy day may require a full tour of the league before it arrives: in a league of eight teams and playing every second or third day, maybe 50 at-bats. A hundred for good measure—100 at-bats, just to get started. The grizzled veteran who has long ago seen every trick in the book and merely wants to add a couple of years to his career by contributing clutch pinch-hits is in an altogether different category, and may be able to log a .333 average with the paltry 50 AB's which he receives all year. For most rookies, such severely limited exposure gives little indication of their ability.

Yet for many black rookies of this era, a few dozen at-bats were precisely the predestined allotment. They never really had much of a chance. As I have written already, they must have been keenly aware that the door was only slightly ajar for them, and they must have pressed at the plate even more than their young white counterparts. They must have known that a .250 average in 50 or 60 plate appearances would win them—if they were lucky—another season of the same very limited playing time. The worst-case scenario (which was none too rare) was that so brief a trial would be used to evaluate their potential, and perhaps become the justification for sending them home. Even players who did extraordinarily well in a rookie season of 100 at-bats or so sometimes found themselves inexplicably relegated to the same restricted role ever after. Perhaps they had so well pleased their managers that they were perceived as doing their best work at 100-AB's-per-season!

In this chapter, I have devised a rather crude means of correlating the amount of playing time allotted to a player and the success of his performance during that time of play. I call it the *hit/sit differential*. I calculate it by finding the difference between the player's lifetime batting average and the percentage of seasons in his career when he received fewer than 200 at-bats. For instance, a player with a career average of .250 who played eight years and had 86 and 155 at-bats in two of those years has a differential of 0. Where the percentage of sub-200 AB seasons exceeds the lifetime average, the differential is a negative value. The player I just mentioned hypothetically, if he had passed four rather than two seasons getting to the plate fewer than 200 times, would have a -.25 differential, since we should be subtracting .5 from .25.

I staged this dramatic descent into sub-zero territory because it seems to me that such numbers usually point to a below average performance. After all, in the case of the -.25 player, why would you want to have him on your team? Good pinch-hitters go better than one-for-four, and excellent fielders at key positions tend to start more than half of the season's games even with a mediocre batting average. Our -.25 player is lucky that he managed to stick around for eight years. He must have been somebody's nephew!

As far as proving anything, I admit that this correlation runs the risk of being self-defeating. That is, since I make the claim (and I hope it is transparently obvious) that performance improves with playing time, a possible revelation that lower batting averages tend to go along with fewer at-bats would tell us what we already knew *without* demonstrating how much a given player would have improved with more exposure. What the table of differentials *might* show, then, is that managers were right in not putting the "sub-zero" players in the starting line-up. Since they didn't hit very well, they would have cost the team several games in the standings. Should a mediocre hitter be played more on the gamble that he will become an exceptional hitter—or should he not, rather, be made to prove first that he's an exceptional hitter before he is played more?

In reality, however, the table shows us that several names are not at all where they should be in the preceding paragraph's reasonable scenario.

Players with deeply negative differentials often turn out *not* to have mediocre batting averages at all—or to have demonstrated, in some cases, that they *would* perform exceptionally if given 200 at-bats. Let me put it this way. A reasonable hit/sit ratio for a player would probably range between -.05 and .2. Some players are not starters when they are first called up, and some linger in the game to pinch-hit or start every third game after age has sapped their energy but not robbed them of all ability. In other words, the average player in this study might reasonably be predicted to have fewer than 200 at-bats about 10% or 20% of the time. If his career average is around .270, he would end up with a slightly positive ratio. Catchers are a special case, here as in so many other statistical profiles. They incur more injuries than other position-players, and a good catcher may be kept on for years after his prime just to catch a particular pitcher in every fourth game and to work in practice with upcoming talent. For a catcher, a -.1 ratio is not unusual.

When we see the ratio falling around -.4 or -.5, however, we must assume that we're dealing with a player who has seldom been a starter *and* who has never been much of a hitter. And this, as I have said, cries out for further explanation, because a position-player who can't hit had better be a stellar performer at shortstop or second base—but a player who stands out at these positions is typically allowed to start in spite of a weak average (or was allowed to do so half a century ago). What are we going to find, then, at the bottom of the table? What kind of player gets to ride the bench and draw a check for years without hitting .200—or what kind of player hits .285 and has to ride the bench for years?

The Hit/Sit Differential
black players italicized (Latinos in parentheses)

.31	*H. Aaron*
.3	
.29	
.28	Santo
.27	*Bruton, Gilliam, Howard*
.26	*Mays*
.25	Bolling
.24	*Brock*, Mantle
.23	*Pinson*
22	Boyer, Runnels
.21	
.2	*Frank Robinson* (Power)
.19	Skowron, Snyder
.18	Davenport, Maris, *McCovey, Williams*
.17	*Banks, W. Davis*
.16	
.15	Powell
.14	*Charles, Simpson*
.13	*T. Davis, Kirkland, Neal, White*
.12	Cunningham, Fairly, McAuliffe, Moon
.11	*Clendenon, Roseboro, Smith, Wagner*
.1	Cash, *Covington*, Kluszewski, Kuenn, Richardson

.09   *Flood*
.08   *Tasby*
.07   Buddin, Callison, Landis
.06   Stuart
.05   *Jones*
.04   *Mays*, Lollar
.03   Sievers, Skinner
.02   Malzone, Siebern, F. Thomas
.01
.0   *Hinton*
-.01
-.02.
-.03
-.04   Logan
-.05   Allison, *Floyd Robinson*, Romano
-.06   *Altman*, Francona
-.07   Gentile
-.08   *Agee*
-.09
-.1   Bailey, Carey, Dalrymple, Demeter
-.11   *Rodgers*
-.12
-.13   Post
-.14   Cimoli, Walls
-.15
-.16
-.17
-.18   *Wood*, Held, Lynch
-.19   *Battey*, Luplow
-.2
-.21
-.22
-.23   *L. Green*
-.24   *Baker*
-.25   *Raines*
-.26   *Boyd*
-.27
-.28
-.29   *Crowe*, (Mantilla)
-.3   Keough
-.31
-.32
-.33
-.34   Geiger
-.35   *P. Green*
-.36
-.37
-.38
-.39   Koppe
-.4
-.41   Essegian
-.42
-.43   *Savage*
-.44   *Roberts*, (Jiménez)
-.45   Bilko
-.46
-.47   *Gaines*

-.48
-.49   *T. Aaron*
-.5   *Pendleton*
-.51
-.52
-.53
-.54
-.55
-.56
-.57   (V. Thomas)
-.58
-.59   *Morton*
-.6   Hunt
-.61
-.61
-.63
-.64
-.65
-.66   Clemens
-.67
-.68
-.69
-.7
-.71   *Caffie*
-.72
-.73
-.74
-.75   *Thurman*
-.76
-.77
-.78
-.79   *Stevens*

Several observations at once recommend themselves. For one thing, the range between "plus" and "minus" .05, where I predicted we might find many players, is populated much more densely by Caucasians than by blacks. We can extend the boundaries about five percentage points into positive territory and ten into negative territory to dramatize the fact further. Once again, what this range generally tells us is that a player within it probably batted from .240 to .270 for his career and received fewer than 200 at-bats in somewhere between 10% and 25% of his big-league seasons. Most fairly successful players surely ought to be here. Unless they were rookie "phenoms", they could expect to see limited playing time to start with; and unless they achieved a superstar's level of productivity later on, they would likely cling to baseball for a year or two in a largely pinch-hitting or "platoon" capacity as their joints began to age and their quickness to wane. This profile fits Joe Cunningham, Wally Moon, Ted Kluszewski, and most of the other Caucasian players down to Andy Carey and Don Demeter pretty well. The white catchers—Bailey, Dalrymple, Lollar, and Romano—are all within this span, too. We have already discussed why a catcher's playing time might be reduced, and why a veteran catcher might be kept around for a season or two even though making few appearances in games.

The black players, on the other hand, tend to fall either above or below the boundaries of the predicted norm. The catchers themselves emphasize what applies to the broader group. Earl Battey had too few seasons of 200+ at-bats, even allowing for his position's wear and tear: the White Sox kept him busy doing almost nothing for five years. Caribbean player Valmy Thomas, at -.57, did less than nothing for four teams within five years. One must wonder if his appearance on various benches was supposed to add a pleasant window-dressing to be seen by a public restless for integration. At the other extreme, the Yankees would scarcely let Elston Howard out of the line-up (once they finally called him up—which is another story). They needed his right-handed power, and they often had him playing somewhere other than behind the plate. John Roseboro was used steadily by the Dodgers from the very start of his tenure with them (thanks to Roy Campanella's tragic car wreck). Like so many players who were talented on defense, he found that the franchise was willing to give him work whether or not he was suffering through an off-year at the plate.

It helps, of course, to be talented at a particularly tough defensive position, such as catcher or middle infielder. Gilliam, Wills, and Neal rank high on the table because they had such talents—or (should I say) because the Dodgers permitted them to exercise these talents. Significantly, Neal sits lowest on the chart. Once Charlie departed LA (to make room for Maury Wills after an off-year of reduced at-bats), he was essentially finished, despite hitting a hard .260 for the new-and-struggling Mets in '62. It's amazing that other teams took so long to learn from Los Angeles. The club's history over these years was scarcely one of cellar-dwelling: the Sixties, on the contrary, would stand out as among the Dodgers' most splendid decades.

Before the mid-Sixties, however, the teams that learned to play rather than display their black stars were few, even if these few enjoyed Dodger-like prosperity. The Braves went to the Series twice in the late Fifties with the help of Aaron, Bruton, and Covington. The Giants worked Mays and McCovey hard to good effect, and the Reds succeeded as long as Robinson and Pinson were plugging away in the same line-up. The Cubs *ought* to have done well, by this same formula—and they did, offensively: their perennial problem was pitching. On the other side of town, the White Sox, who boasted of having Larry Doby, Harry Simpson, Minnie Minoso, Al Smith, Chico Carrasquel, and Luis Aparicio at various times (some of these passed each other like ships in the night during the era's frenzied trades), were the Yankees' only serious intra-league rival throughout the decade—except Cleveland, which also played black stars (some of the same just listed) liberally.

Perhaps the other most notable feature of the table's upper reaches (I mean, besides the World Series visits of the teams whose black players are listed near the top) is the implied importance of the *home run* in securing a starting role. When the Dodgers' infield wizards are filtered out, we are left with one black super-slugger after another. The African-American players who were thrust out on the field with greater regularity than the most frequently played whites were the home run hitters deluxe whose names are household words to this day: Aaron, Banks, Mays, McCovey, Robinson. Al Smith and Vic Power, too, were considered to be wall-bangers, though of a reduced class. (Power, a black Puerto Rican, would rank at .20 on the chart.) Willie Kirkland and Willie Tasby, to be honest, were less skillful with the bat than Floyd Robinson, Bob Boyd, and several other black players with a much lower percentage of 200+ AB seasons. They were played in the hope that their power would blossom to Mays-like proportions (which, of course, never happened). Billy Bruton, Wes Covington, and Minnie Minoso (a black Cuban whose value would be .1 without his "ageless wonder returns" gimmick seasons) legged out many a double and triple to go with their moderate home run output. Vada Pinson may well have swung himself into a mid-Sixties slump trying to replicate the 20+ home run years of 1962-1965. He might have been better advised to take a page from Lou Brock's book, who ended up being an everyday player when the black-dominated Cardinals of the mid-Sixties once again made speed respectable. In the years before Brock's heyday, however, power was clearly the young black player's ticket to a steady job.

The white players of this same group were scarcely less formidable—or some of them, anyway. Mantle, Maris, Ken Boyer, and Boog Powell all appear in this range. Dick McAuliffe, too, was a powerhouse for a second baseman; and Ron Fairly (like black player Willie Davis), while his stats argue for only a modest slugging ability, was a veritable dynamo by the distorted standards of the new Dodger Stadium in Los Angeles. Jim Davenport showed early signs of power, although the Giants very generously allowed him to spend almost two-thirds of a 13-year career disproving their high expectations. Jim did play an exceptional third base. What is Russ Snyder doing in such elite company, however? Snyder was particularly speedy, and a fine outfielder—but of how many black players, deep in the chart's negative territory, could the same thing be said?

Bobby Richardson and Harvey Kuenn were lead-off men with little power, no great speed, and no particular knack for drawing walks, though both hit for average and Kuenn, indeed, was a one-time batting champ. What about Buddin, Callison, and Landis at the .07 level? Well, Johnny Callison had considerable pop in his bat, and—like Joe Cunningham (a few notches above)—logged several seasons when he batted over .300. Comiskey Park flattened out Landis's power numbers, and Jim was a Gold Glove center fielder. But Buddin? Why did Boston award Don a starting role when the likes of Lenny Green, Manny Jiménez, and Jake Wood hit better and ran better? The very skills at which veterans of the Negro Leagues had excelled were apparently not prized in the Major Leagues—or not, at any rate, in black players, only in a Snyder or a Landis. A moderately fast white player like Bobby Richardson who put the ball in play but hit one homer every other season went year after year starting virtually every game; but a black player with far greater speed who drove the ball far better would have to be considered the next Henry Aaron to receive the same opportunity.

(Bobby, I should note, received rave reviews as a second baseman. Finding testimony about the defensive skills of obscure black players is hard-to-impossible... and then one would have to rate the value of such testimony by estimating the motives of its source!)

The most revealing part of the table is clearly its bottom. These depths we find inhabited exclusively by black players and white ne'er-do-wells—yet all of the latter except Doug Clemens did well enough to earn a spot on Post's baseball cards. Of the black players below the -.02 level, only Lenny Green and Latin player Manny Jiménez (whose value would be an incredible -.44) appeared on the backs of cereal boxes in '61 and '62, when both were having career years. Yet other black players whose best years were past them might not have made the cut even if their glory days had fallen in the early Sixties. They were not starters: they were not played regularly. How could you justify printing thousands of images of Bubba Morton or Tommie Aaron when the two passed brief careers coming off the bench?

One might charge, then, that I am cooking the books by slipping in bench-warmers with regulars. Why include Doug Clemens as the only white player not to make the card selection? There must surely be hordes of Caucasian cannon fodder like Clemens in baseball's footnotes.

The point to be stressed, however, is that most of these little-known black players are *not* Doug Clemens. Only Curt Roberts (who had little more than one season in the big leagues) failed to post a higher career batting average than Doug. And yet, among the "cellar-dwellers", only Ted Savage and George Crowe managed to eke out a career as long as Doug's. That Clemens's talents were not commensurate with most of this company is painfully evident. Savage was either riding the bench or being shuttled to the Minors for eight years after a fine rookie season (or half-season) in which 335 at-bats led to 54 runs scored and 39 RBIs. Crowe smacked 31 home runs in his only season of more than 400 at-bats, and Tommie Aaron scored 54 runs (like Savage) following 334 at-bats in his first season. *In his whole career*, Clemens hit 12 home runs, batted in 88 runs, and scored 99. Doug, by the way, played the outfield—just in case you conceive the notion that he had hidden merits as a utility infielder.

But what, then, about the white "stars" chosen by Post who appear at the table's bottom? Lynch and Bilko were journeyman "platoon-players" who could bring a good left-handed bat to the line-up; Keough and Geiger were infielders who probably handled ground balls better than sliders. Luplow was an outfielder who showed promise as a rookie in 1962 (though not nearly as much promise as Manny Jiménez) and then proceeded to fizzle out. Woodie Held was a miscast shortstop whose home runs kept him hanging around the game, but whose strikeouts kept him—eventually—out of the starting line-up. Held played for fourteen seasons: Bilko, with a mere ten tours of duty, played fewest of this group except for the hapless Luplow, who managed seven. Among the black players below the -.25 level (a number more than twice that of white players), not a single one reached double digits in Major League seasons other than Felix Mantilla.

If we dip a little nearer to the Caucasian bottom, we find Joe Koppe, who probably garnered the glories of the cereal box only because the expansion Los Angeles Angels had picked him up in an initial motley assortment. His '62 batting average of .227 (misreported by Post as .277) was indicative of where he would remain for most of his career. Joe's LA teammate that year, big Ken Hunt, clubbed 25 home runs and seemed at the beginning rather than the near-end of a fine career. The truth is that Hunt never really had another year: but for 1962, all of his six seasons were quite fragmentary. Ken (who should not be confused either with the pitcher of that name or rookie Ron Hunt of '63, destined to set records for being hit by pitches) possessed a frightening, perhaps sociopathic side. He was constantly surly with his peers and resistant to coaching. I have little doubt that his attitude—which no one around him failed to comment on—is the complete story behind his appalling -.60 hit/sit ratio. Even his photo on Post's baseball card would make any little tyke tremble! Such gloomy stories, of course, are routinely kept under wraps by Major League publicists—but they are real, and not infrequent. I can't do better than quote John Roseboro on the subject:

> There are a lot of fellows with ability who get kicked around [i.e., traded and demoted], and you wonder why. Then you find out, you learn there's a reason. Maybe they chase women and booze it up or pop pills or take dope and get in fights and get into trouble. The time comes when no one wants to bother with them anymore.[2]

Chuck Essegian, as far as I can tell, was *not* this kind of player. Frankly, Chuck deserved a better fate. In 1962, he received over 300 at-bats—just barely—for the first and last time, and responded by hitting 21 home runs and batting .274. He was rewarded by being traded to Kansas City for a year, where he warmed a bench throughout 1963 for ultra-hands-on owner Charlie Finley and was then released. His pitiable six-year career, with its distinct promise of unused talent, could easily be that of a black man. Did the Major Leagues have something against swarthy Armenians, as well?[3]

As we plumb the table's murky bottom, we might want to ask, not unfairly, if some of the black ballplayers—perhaps most of them—who swim in this gulf were surly Ken Hunts, or were otherwise trouble-makers. Bitter about racism—or maybe about a broken marriage—perhaps they drank too much or got into fights. I have not exhaustively researched the personal histories of the group, but I can honestly declare that I have never run across a single such charge leveled at any of its members. The nearest thing would be the strange case of Alex Johnson. Alex didn't like people of any race or walk of life, it seems, though he preferred simply ignoring their presence to smacking them in the face. Johnson was not included in this study—his arrival was slightly too late; but if I were to list him on the table above, his hit/sit ratio for a 13-season career would stand at +.057. General managers never tired of giving him second chances.

Certainly Bob Boyd was one of the most docile, pleasant, unassuming men ever to play the game. Yet Bob nestles in the sad company of the trench-dwellers, even though he had batted over .300 *for three straight years* during the late Fifties in Baltimore. The kind-hearted George Crowe, too (who took a young Curt Flood under his wing), is in the group, a slugger who hit 31 homers (as I have said) and batted in 92 runs in 1957, his only approach to a full season. Farther down still, we find the hapless Pumpsie Green and Jim Pendleton. Pumpsie was a quiet family man, while Jim was a lady-killer whom Henry Aaron called "the only guy I ever saw who would take his paycheck right to the tavern";[4] but it was Pendleton, in fact, who would hang around the big leagues longer. Green felt keenly in Boston that his last day on the squad was always imminent. The high-rolling Pendleton had the kind of confidence (or swagger, if you prefer) that it took to stay afloat year after year of half- and quarter-seasons. He perhaps represents the flip-side of Roseboro's disappearing mystery-men: that is, the reason so many ballplayers drank and caroused was precisely because it relieved the pressure of a gladiatorial existence.

Yet closer to the ocean floor, Bubba Morton batted .313 one season when given a career-high 201 at-bats. Years before Bubba's debut, Joe Caffie and Bob Thurman had logged their brief Major League stints: you can find them where the chart has almost run out. They, too, had shown special promise during their pitiable opportunities—Caffie for collecting hits and Thurman for banging home runs. Yet we find both of them beneath the -.7 range.[5]

One could argue that a few of the players toward the bottom should probably never have been admitted to the Major Leagues. Flashy second baseman Curt Roberts did not post stellar offensive numbers, though neither was he given a chance to get his feet wet above the cleats. (Doug Clemens, with an almost identical career batting average, was allowed to hang around for nine seasons compared to Curt's one and parts of two more.) Yet ineptitude simply cannot explain many of the names on the lowest rungs—that is, not the players' ineptitude. At the uttermost edge of outer darkness, we discover the invisible R. C. Stevens. Who was R. C. Stevens? Why, nobody: a kid who hit 7 home runs and batted in 18 during 90 at-bats for the Pirates in 1958, and received a total of 72 at-bats *over the next three years* prior to being released. If R. C. had played two-thirds of a season in 1958—say, 400 at-bats—and had failed to improve upon his initial rate of success, he would still have posted over 30 home runs and knocked in about 80. Stevens had also won multiple Gold Gloves as a Minor League first baseman. Whose ineptitude do *these* figures indict?

Recall what the hit/sit differential represents: the percentage of under-200-at-bat seasons in a player's career subtracted from his career batting average. If a player's career average were an outrageous .200 (exceeded by some pitchers) and he somehow managed to play five years in these circumstances, receiving—understandably—a single season of over 200 at-bats, his hit/sit ratio would be -.6. Imagine a player that bad, if you can, and then ponder how many black players hover around—or even below—this abysmal mark on the table. Now consider the quality of the dark-skinned players… and tell yourself that nothing at all is amiss here!

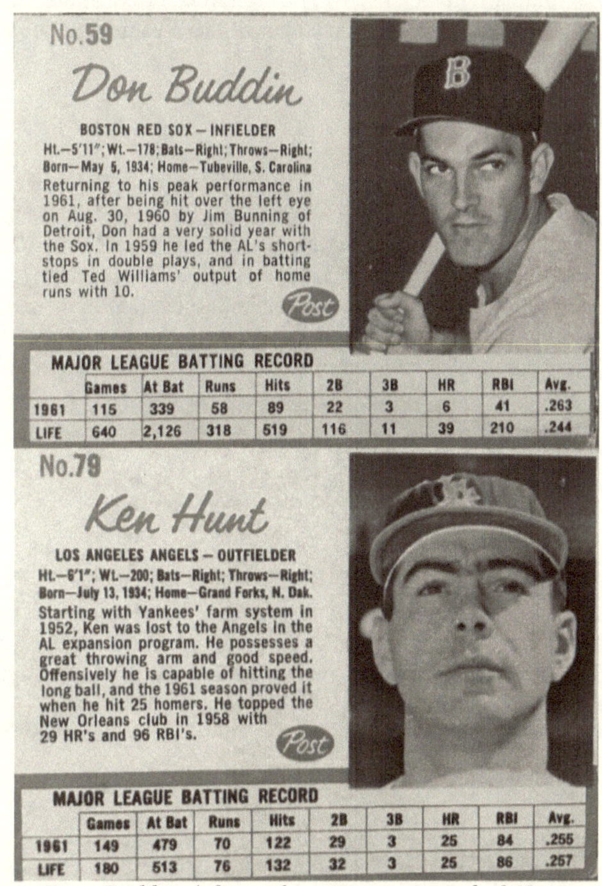

Light-hitting Don Buddin (who only once surpassed .245 in six seasons) logged almost 2300 at-bats with the Red Sox. Switch-hitting black infielder Pumpsie Green, who batted .246 for his career, received 742 at-bats over four seasons in Bean Town. Sometimes reasons for short-circuited careers were less visible. Ken Hunt, a rookie in 1961, looked like the answer to an expansion team's prayers… but Hunt had a very complex personality.

1 See Ted Williams, *The Science of Hitting* (New York: Simon and Shuster, 1986), 82. Ted, of course, was the manager of the Washington Senators/Texas Rangers after his Hall-of-Fame career.

2 From *Glory Days with the Dodgers and Other Days* (*op. cit.*), 93-94.

3 Actually, this query is not intended to be frivolous. Prejudice of several kinds, including anti-Semitism, was widespread in the upper echelons of the Major Leagues as well as throughout mainstream America. Bill Veeck, in his delightful autobiography (with Ed Linn), *Veeck—As in Wreck* (New York: Bantam, 1963), observes that there was a stunning overlap in the authorship of his hate-mail after Larry Doby's signing and that of other letters denouncing his philanthropy for Jewish and Catholic causes (173-176). He reminds us, as well, that Jews were not permitted on most "dude" ranches in the Southwest during the late Forties.

4 In *I Had a Hammer* (*op. cit.*), 124.

5 Though I have explained my reasons for not including Latinos in this part of the study, I might add—having mentioned him here already—that Manny Jiménez narrowly resembles Chuck Essegian in how badly his talent was squandered and Ted Savage in how bluntly his brilliant rookie season was ignored. But for Tom Tresh, who played in the New York spotlight, Manny might have been Rookie of the Year.

II

Not "One of Us": The Suspicious Ratio Between Playing Time and Length of Career

At the very least, the previous chapter shows that players of the late Fifties and early Sixties were not necessarily awarded with playing time when they performed well at the plate—and that black players, in particular, found such awards difficult to harvest. Of course, there is more to baseball than offense. An exceptional "glove man" will usually be indulged somewhat if he embarrasses himself at the plate: his defensive contributions may be felt to save more than as many runs as he fails to drive home with his bat. Yet one would be hard pressed to argue that the black players consistently denied a starting role were worse defensive players than the white players who were consistently put out on the field despite their modest hitting. Jerry Lynch was a fine outfielder—but were he, Gus Bell, and Wally Post really so dazzling that Bob Thurman could never pry his way into more than twenty or thirty games a season, as Hershell Freeman claims?[1] R. C. Stevens was the top-fielding first baseman at three consecutive levels of Minor League play: was Steve Bilko his superior by Major League standards?

The bitter truth is that ballplayers who receive rather few at-bats per season tend not to be employed for many seasons, even if they drive the ball hard when given a chance and suck it up in the field like a human vacuum-cleaner. Being given few at-bats is a recipe for having a short career. This, after all, makes perfect sense. A player who isn't sent to the plate very often must not be very good; or, if he's a good hitter but lost in a squad of established stars, then the team may be forced to trade or release him as it pursues another pitcher or performer whose special skills are in short supply at the moment. Sustaining a career in professional baseball requires a certain amount of luck, even for the talented. If we were to graph the number of 200-and-over-at-bat seasons, therefore, against length of career, we should expect to see a steadily rising cluster of coordinates: the more 200+ seasons, the more years in the big leagues.

I have created just such a graph for this chapter, and it produces just such a slope. If I had not distinguished the black players from the white players, we would be looking at an objective verification of the transparently obvious, and I would leave my readers wondering why I wasted my time putting the evidence together. Players who don't bat much don't play long: big surprise.

But in the light of the preceding chapter and of my initial questions about the rudely handled careers of potential black stars, I *did* distinguish black from white. I expected to find that a greater proportion of black players than of white players tended to receive few at-bats and consequently have short careers. The graph will show that my expectations were not frustrated. Some of its most interesting revelations, however, do not simply leap off the page at a glance. They concern *which* players were getting fewer at-bats. Over and over again, we see black players in the proximity of Caucasians who were clearly not their equals as performers. If two players had 10-year careers, during seven of which they received 200 or more at-bats, a closer look usually suggests that the black player made much better use of his chances than the white player—and yet, both ended up bidding baseball farewell at the same time.

The graph also reveals another, more subtle tendency. The white players are more densely concentrated within the graph's mid-section. Black players either never really got their Major League careers off the ground, or else they soared along for a number of seasons which surpassed what most white players could anticipate. Of course, these are the superstars—Aaron, Mays, and the rest. Race was scarcely a factor at their lofty height: it quickly became a major factor in the middle altitudes. For the Caucasian ballplayer, life in the big leagues was no nine-to-five job with a gold watch waiting after twenty-five years of service—but it *did* promise a degree of predictability greater than the black player would enjoy. This is what the figures indicate, at any rate: it would be shocking if the players themselves were not generally aware of their typical risks at the time.

The following key to players listed on graphs and tables will be used throughout the rest of this section.

<table>
<tr><td><u>*black players*</u></td><td><u>*white players*</u></td></tr>
<tr><td>A Hank Aaron</td><td>A Bob Allison</td></tr>
<tr><td>a Tommie Aaron</td><td>B Ed Bailey</td></tr>
<tr><td>**A** Tommie Agee</td><td>b Steve Bilko</td></tr>
<tr><td>**a** George Altman</td><td>**B** Frank Bolling</td></tr>
<tr><td>B Gene Baker</td><td>**b** Ken Boyer</td></tr>
<tr><td>b Ernie Banks</td><td>*b* Don Buddin</td></tr>
<tr><td>**B** Earl Battey</td><td>C John Callison</td></tr>
<tr><td>**b** Bob Boyd</td><td>c Andy Carey</td></tr>
<tr><td>*B* Lou Brock</td><td>**C** Norm Cash</td></tr>
<tr><td>*b*´ Bill Bruton</td><td>**c** Gino Cimoli</td></tr>
<tr><td>C Joe Caffie</td><td>*C* Doug Clemens</td></tr>
<tr><td>c Ed Charles</td><td>*c* Joe Cunningham</td></tr>
</table>

C Donn Clendenon
c Wes Covington
C George Crowe
D Tommy Davis
d Willie Davis
F Curt Flood
G Joe Gaines
g Jim Gilliam
G Lenny Green
g Pumpsie Green
H Chuck Hinton
h Elston Howard
J Mack Jones
K Willie Kirkland
M Lee Maye
m Willie Mays
M Willie McCovey
m Bubba Morton
N Charlie Neal
P Jim Pendleton
p Vada Pinson
R Larry Raines
r Curt Roberts
R Andre Rodgers
r Floyd Robinson
R Frank Robinson
r John Roseboro
S Ted Savage
s Harry Simpson
S Al Smith
s R. C. Stevens
T Willie Tasby
t Bob Thurman
W Leon Wagner
w Bill White
W Billy Williams
w Maury Wills
W Jake Wood

D Clay Dalrymple
d Jim Davenport
D Don Demeter
E Chuck Essegian
F Ron Fairly
f Tito Francona
G Gary Geiger
g Jim Gentile
H Woodie Held
h Ken Hunt
K Marty Keough
k Ted Kluszewski
K Joe Koppe
k Harvey Kuenn
L Jim Landis
l John Logan
L Sherman Lollar
l Al Luplow
L Jerry Lynch
M Frank Malzone
m Mickey Mantle
M Roger Maris
m Dick McAuliffe
M Wally Moon
P Wally Post
p Boog Powell
R Bobby Richardson
r John Romano
R Pete Runnels
S Ron Santo
s Norm Siebern
S Roy Sievers
s Bob Skinner
S Bill Skowron
s Russ Snyder
<u>S</u> Dick Stuart
T Frank Thomas
W Lee Walls

N.B. *Initials representing black players have been formatted red, but this shade will appear as gray in versions of the text that use only black ink.* The player's initial has been placed uniformly to the left of the point left designates his approximate position on the graph. In cases where several players occupy the same position, the initials have been arranged in alphabetical order and more or less equally on either side of the point. In certain cases where an especially wide letter is being crowded by a nearby point and its initial, these ground rules have been bent a little—but I have very consciously sought to avoid any artificial enhancing of the patterns suggested by the red (black players) and the black initials (white players). The same is true of all subsequent graphs in this section of the book.

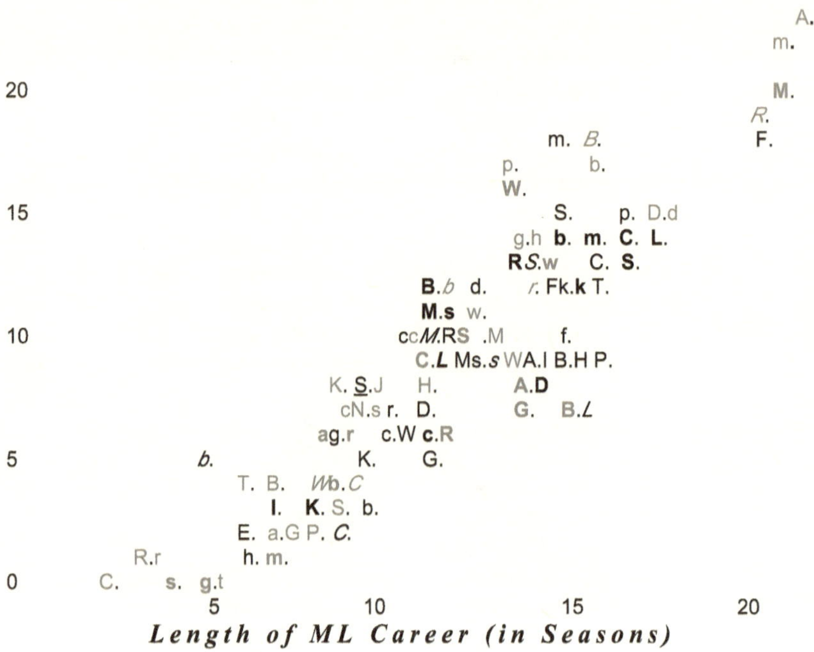

As I remarked in the previous paragraph, the Caucasian players are concentrated in the graph's mid-section. Let us look at that section more closely. Within this central oval, close inspection shows that the black players are more "squared": that is, the total seasons in their career tend to match the total number of 200-and-up-at-bat seasons. This seems like a good thing at first glance, a fair thing. These men were actually being *played* while they remained in the majors. I confess to having been surprised by the discovery. Then I began to consider its implications as I studied the careers of white players in the group. The latter were more likely to enjoy a gradual fall-off of playing time as their powers waned. In some reduced capacity, they might be kept around for two or three seasons, as were Tito Francona (whose last two seasons were sub-200-AB years) and Woodie Held (whose last *four* seasons were so). On the other hand, many black players who had proved themselves year after year continued to post impressive numbers *until* the downward tick. Then they were traded; or, if no one showed an interest, they were released. When Bill White's RBIs dipped under 100 for the first time in four years, he was sent packing to Philadelphia over the winter of 1965—where he promptly posted a 103-RBI season.   Yet the Phillies, for some reason, weren't convinced that Bill could still produce. They halved his playing time over the next two seasons, though still allowing him more than 200 at-bats. Then they traded him back to the Cardinals after 1968, where he was benched and, at last, released. One wonders why the Cards even bothered making the trade.

Al Smith was likewise bundled off by the White Sox after the '62 season, when he hit 12 fewer homers but raised his average to .298 (and hit 8 triples). The Orioles played him for about half a season: then he visited Cleveland and Boston in 1964 long enough to log a few dozen at-bats... and a very fine career was finished. Smith must have been fuming: who wouldn't be? Bill James reports that, upon being released by the Red Sox in 1964, "Smith took a long, thick nail and drove it into a beam in his house, hung his baseball shoes and his glove on that nail, and told his son that if those things ever fell off he would go back and play more ball...."[2] Picture a man who has devoted his life to car-racing or golf making a solemn vow never to look at another gear shift or putter, and you glimpse the depth of Al's frustration.

Contrast the positions on the graph of Bill White, Al Smith, Bill Bruton, and Vic Power (a dark Puerto Rican whose spot would be just to the left of White's at twelve years) to those of Tito Francona, Woodie Held, Gary Geiger, Johnny Logan, and Wally Post. Francona and Logan, especially, were fine all-around players who were able to make themselves useful for years on one team after another. They were not done any favors: they earned their keep. The question I am asking is, why were these very fine black players (potential Hall of Famers, if they had been handled right) not given a similar chance to continue making the kinds of contribution for which they had become known? The discrepancy in this mid-section group is all the more apparent if we omit Earl Battey, who was a catcher and hence more apt to linger in the big leagues   But for Earl, the mid-section's outer rim would consist entirely of Caucasian players. Even in Battey's case, there was only one year of sub-200-AB "lingering": most of his lean years in at-bats (five of them) occurred when he came up with the White Sox. Catcher Ed Bailey's career-high in at-bats, by contrast, was 441 in 1960. After that, he only exceeded 300 AB's twice in six years   Ed was allowed to grow old gracefully.

As we proceed to the graph's upper right, the players are more "squared" on the graph than ever. These men enjoyed long careers for the same reason that they were awarded more than a couple of hundred at-bats throughout their Major League service: they were stars, even superstars. Race seems to have a negligible impact at these rarefied heights. Mickey Mantle sits over Vada Pinson and Ernie Banks. The durable Ron Fairly (whose offensive numbers would have been far more impressive if he had played anywhere but Los Angeles, as Bill James argues convincingly[3]) nestles just below the great Frank Robinson. McCovey, Mays, and Aaron occupy a zenith beyond them all.

Nevertheless, Fairly's apotheosis on the graph does seem sufficient motive for a raised brow. The brow might arch higher as the eye peers slightly farther down the slope, just where the central oval ends. Here we find a small knot of Caucasian players, some of them truly verging on immortality: Ken Boyer and Boog Powell, for instance. Norm Cash and Roy Sievers also came within one or two more superior seasons of being Hall of Fame material, perhaps. The late Ron Santo was recently voted over the Hall's gilded threshold. What, then, are Dick McAuliffe and Bill Skowron doing in this elite company? They were both solid players, but… but McAuliffe batted under .250 in every year from 1967 to 1972 *as a lead-off hitter*, and in two of these years he struck out more than 100 times. What would Floyd Robinson or Jake Wood have done with even half this much indulgence? Skowron was a steady right-handed power-hitter while with the Yankees, a critical member of the Mantle-and-Maris show's supporting cast (and one whose role was poorly filled by the under-achieving Joe Pepitone). But the abysmal season Bill posted with the Dodgers in 1963, when he hit all of 4 home runs and batted .203, would have won any black player a ticket straight out of baseball. Instead, Skowron was traded back into the American League, where he played—and played pretty well—for another four seasons.

Notice one more thing about this liminal section of the graph where high-middle meets upper slope. The Dodgers' sure-handed middle-infielders Jim Gilliam and Maury Wills are here. So is the Yankees' superlative catcher, Elston Howard. The coordinates of these players are perfectly "squared": 14 seasons of play to 14 seasons of over-200 at-bats. Dodger catcher John Roseboro is just a couple of marks below them. I will observe, once again (and not for the last time), that the Dodgers franchise treated its black players with outstanding fairness, as only befitted the team of Jackie Robinson. Charlie Neal played regularly, too, when he was with the squad. As long as they could do the job, these men were put in the line-up, with no nudge being applied to direct them into outfield positions. (We shall see later that exile to the outfield, where positions required less skill and hence carried less job security, was a common strategy for preventing black players from hanging around.) A case could be made for "factoring out" Gilliam and Wills precisely because their organization was so exceptional and because their crucial defensive positions were typically withheld from blacks. We are then left with two more catchers. Howard's career basically ended when his power fell off: Roseboro had a one-year swan song with Washington. Remove these dots, and the circle hovering in the 15/15 area is almost completely Caucasian. That is, unless you were a superstar or played for the Dodgers, being black was a virtual guarantee that you would *not* enjoy more than about a dozen years of full Major League playing time. You certainly wouldn't be coddled with a "gentle letdown".

At last we come to the ignominious bottom, once again. As always, the most dramatic inequities are here. The space is inhabited exclusively (but for the unhappy Chuck Essegian) by black players who would have short careers and would seldom or never see 200 at-bats in a season. The obvious objection to this portrait of "inequity" is also still in force, to be sure: i.e., since my pool of white players is the collection of starters assembled by Post cereals, and since I have admitted black players of the era from every quarter, the low-achievers are bound to be predominantly black. I rebut this challenge in the present circumstances with a couple of observations. First, Willie Tasby *does* appear in the Post cards for the 1961 season—and Tasby is far from having the most impressive stats in the group even though he was allowed to play in about two-thirds of one season's games. (Dark Latino player Pancho Herrera, by the way, would be three years short of Willie on the graph: also featured in the 1961 card collection, Pancho had a lot more holes in his swing than George Crowe or Bob Thurman.)

This brings me to my second point: the career figures for the "at the bottom" black players, although predicated on just a few hundred at-bats, often stack up very well beside those of white players farther up the graph's slope. Consider these lifetime slugging percentages: .394 for Joe Caffie, .379 for Joe Gaines, .444 for Mack Jones, .395 for R. C. Stevens, and a whopping .465 for Bob Thurman (not to mention .430 for Pancho Herrera). Now weigh the same figure for Don Buddin, Al Luplow, and Joe Koppe: .359, .324, and .352, respectively. The highest of these numbers falls well below the lowest for the black players just mentioned (though Bubba Morton, the pinch-hitter *extraordinaire*, logged only a .351 slugging percentage with his propensity for singles). Yet the careers of Buddin, Koppe, and Luplow averaged 7 years: the average career for the six black players (including Herrera) was 4.8 seasons. It doesn't seem too much to ask of a fair system that a Thurman or a Stevens should receive at least one season of 200 at-bats, or that a Joe Caffie should play as many years as a Don Buddin. (The inscrutably durable Doug Clemens, by the way, played more than *all* of the above-named.)

A reader who likes to apply the magnifying glass might think it revealing to study those coordinates which are shared by black and white players. When a black man and a white man have played for exactly the same number of seasons and have enjoyed exactly the same percentage of over-200-at-bat-campaigns in those seasons, do they turn out to be about the same quality of ballplayer? Frankly, I haven't found this kind of exercise very informative. One can hardly avoid being subjective. Personally, I think George Altman and Floyd Robinson stack up well beside Jim Gentile... maybe. But then, Gentile had one monster year (1961, of course—the same as Norm Cash and Roger Maris) which hinted at untapped potential. He may have been handled very poorly: Bill James thinks so.[4] Comparing catchers and other position-players is an apple-and-orange undertaking: I myself would rather have Battey than Logan on a team or Agee than Dalrymple, but both of the former were superior players, and neither of the latter showed great staying power. I certainly think Wes Covington, if given Jim Landis's five straight seasons of around 500 at-bats, would have bettered 67 homers and 319 RBIs by at least 50% (always assuming that Wes's knees had been up to the task); yet Landis may have been the best center fielder in the American League over those same years. I would also take Curt Flood over Harvey Kuenn, though Harvey had more good years than is generally realized. On the other hand, some people might say that Maury Wills, who prospered in the Hollywood spotlight and was no slouch at self-promotion, really didn't deserve to have a career commensurate with Pete Runnels's or Bill Skowron's. Like so many denizens of Tinsel Town, Maury had a complex private life that might rub some observers the wrong way. The fact remains, however—and it surprised me, and will no doubt surprise many of my readers—that Wills far outpaced both Runnels and Skowron in lifetime hits and runs scored.[5]

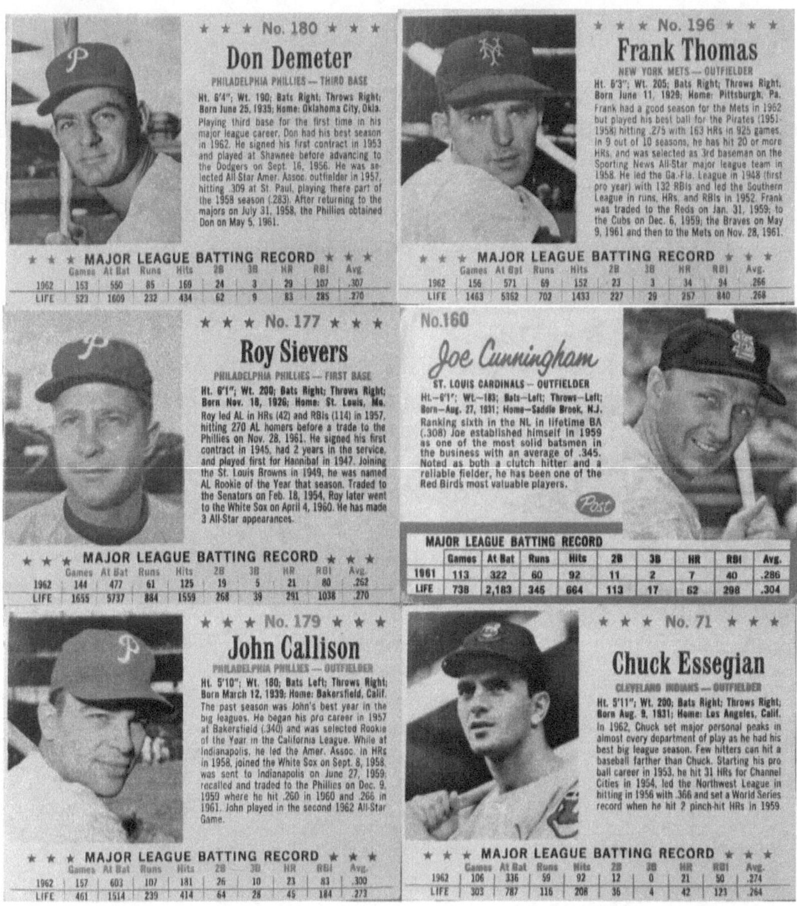

MAJOR LEAGUE BATTING RECORD — Don Demeter

	Games	At Bat	Runs	Hits	2B	3B	HR	RBI	Avg.
1962	153	550	85	169	24	3	29	107	.307
LIFE	523	1609	232	434	62	9	83	285	.270

MAJOR LEAGUE BATTING RECORD — Frank Thomas

	Games	At Bat	Runs	Hits	2B	3B	HR	RBI	Avg.
1962	156	571	69	152	23	3	34	94	.266
LIFE	1463	5352	702	1433	227	29	257	840	.268

MAJOR LEAGUE BATTING RECORD — Roy Sievers

	Games	At Bat	Runs	Hits	2B	3B	HR	RBI	Avg.
1962	144	477	61	125	19	5	21	80	.262
LIFE	1655	5737	884	1559	268	39	291	1036	.270

MAJOR LEAGUE BATTING RECORD — Joe Cunningham

	Games	At Bat	Runs	Hits	2B	3B	HR	RBI	Avg.
1961	113	322	60	92	11	2	7	40	.286
LIFE	738	2,183	345	664	113	17	62	298	.304

MAJOR LEAGUE BATTING RECORD — John Callison

	Games	At Bat	Runs	Hits	2B	3B	HR	RBI	Avg.
1962	157	603	107	181	26	10	23	83	.300
LIFE	461	1514	239	414	64	28	45	184	.273

MAJOR LEAGUE BATTING RECORD — Chuck Essegian

	Games	At Bat	Runs	Hits	2B	3B	HR	RBI	Avg.
1962	106	336	59	92	12	0	21	50	.274
LIFE	303	787	116	208	36	4	42	123	.264

Being Caucasian was no assurance of receiving all the attention one deserved, although five of these six ballplayers had very fine careers. Only Chuck Essegian was virtually ignored despite some solid power numbers. Sievers and Thomas, however, might have flirted with Cooperstown if a single employer had allowed them to settle down and concentrate on their game. (Thomas could have given you an earful about the sainted Branch Rickey's business dealings: he had probably given Rickey one earful too many.) Cunningham might have won a couple of batting crowns, yet he was platooned for all but about three seasons of his career. The same was true of Demeter, whose allegedly ruinous strikeout rate went down whenever he received regular at-bats. Callison was a splendid player in his prime, yet compromised his ability (like so many black players) by trying to stroke home runs with every swing.

1 See *We Played the Game*, ed. Danny Peary (New York: Black Dog and Leventhal, 2002 [originally published by Hyperion, 1994]), 336.

2 Bill James, *op. cit.*, 834. One can only imagine how many times players like Tommy Davis and Lenny Green were tempted to drive that nail.

3 *Ibid.*, 453 .

4 *Ibid.*, 473-474 Gentile seems to have been "stuck" behind Gil Hodges as a first baseman in the Dodgers' farm system, and also to have been beset by poor performances during brief try-outs. There is unquestionably an element of luck in success, whether one plays baseball or trades stocks—and some people, for whatever reason, never catch a break.

5 In continuing to mitigate through footnotes my uncomfortable exclusion of Latino players from these chapters, I will add that Felix Mantilla would share the coordinates of Marty Keough. I don't think most serious observers would consider that pairing very balanced in terms of ability.

III

The Crooked Column: Very Different Opportunities to Hit Producing Roughly Equal Results

It is a perfectly logical expectation that batting average will increase with at-bats. I have discussed the point before: as players play more, most of them get better—and as good hitters hit more big-league pitching, most of them become better big-league hitters. An aberration may occur over the course of a few games, or even a few dozen. Some teams have relatively poor pitching to throw up against a rookie hitter, and some rookie hitters have upside-down approaches to the ball that briefly stump even the best pitchers. (Julio Franco, for instance, liked to drive the low-and-away pitch to the opposite field, and did so with great power. Vladimir Guerrero liked to swing at "bad" pitches, and usually hit them very hard.) To claim, then, that so-and-so's batting averages are inflated year after year because he has so few at-bats is nearly nonsensical. Such a thing might happen only to a very few players, or to any player only for a very short time. By 50 at-bats or so, the rookie is starting to show his true stuff; and if he is never given more than 50 or 100 at-bats per year to improve upon his stuff, he will always be a rookie-level hitter. No important hitting lessons can be absorbed from the bench through the seat of the pants.

Accept all this, and you must admit that it is equally logical to anticipate a steady slope in the graph that plots lifetime batting average with the average number of at-bats per season. The players with fewer at-bats should have lower averages: the players who saw significantly more pitches each year should have distinctly higher averages. As you go upward on the at-bats axis, you should go outward on the batting-average axis. Of course, a few glitches are also predictable. Average isn't everything. Some players have starting roles because of their slick glove work in the field, especially at the most difficult positions: catcher, second baseman, shortstop, and center fielder. Furthermore, some players hit for mediocre average but drive runs home with a steady barrage of doubles and round-trippers. In them, a mediocre average is completely tolerable. We should even make an exception for the weak hitter who roams the comparatively easy terrain of left field, yet is able to draw scores of walks and steal bases. Ron Hunt's (*not* Ken Hunt's) special talent lay in getting himself hit by pitches. His on-base percentage rose so high, as a result, that he often got about as many starts as a potential batting champ.

So let us introduce a few bumps into our ideal slope. Particularly at its higher elevations, we should expect to see a few sluggish averages straying in retrograde fashion back off to the left. These would be the 35-homer guys who hit .260, or maybe the Gold Glove shortstops who hit .256. On the lower ranges, however, we should still expect to see a distinctly rising slope. Utility players tend not to have high averages because they don't see many pitches per week. If they hit better, they would play more. At most, we might find an occasional star in the twilight of his career who is able to log .350 averages pinch-hitting because he has seen so many talented and crafty pitchers already. But then, hitters like that will have recorded lots and lots of full seasons previous to assuming their more modest role. Since the graph proposed here would plot lifetime at-bats, the average total of official trips to the plate might be dropped from 500 to 400 by a perennial star's pinch-hitting exploits—but not from 500 to 200.

The graph below pretty much shreds all of these logical expectations. At every level, we see batting averages spread all over the place: the result looks more like a double helix than a steady slope. It would appear that hitters are *not* reliably played more in response to good hitting—or played less for bad hitting: this, at least, was how things stood in the late Fifties and early Sixties. The kind of graph I predicted isn't even produced if we factor out all the black players and simply study the Caucasians. Guys like Chuck Essegian and Joe Cunningham don't seem to have caught all the breaks they deserved (partially, in Joe's case, because an aging Musial was moved to first base), while Frank Bolling and Dick McAuliffe seem to have been more popular with their managers than their offensive productivity alone would justify. Bolling, at least, was a brilliant second baseman... but might not Al Smith and Ed Charles have been equally so if they had been given a shot at the middle-infield positions where they had excelled in the minors? Was not Felix Mantilla already at about Bolling's defensive level, or close enough that he shouldn't have been limited consistently to half as many at-bats?[1]

For the real imbalance of this shocking column, as you might have guessed by now, shows up best when the black players are viewed beside the white players.

[**N.B.** The numbers I have used are for *official* at-bats: that is, I have not gone to the trouble to figure in how many walks each player drew, how many times he sacrificed, and how many times he was hit by a pitch. This makes my correlation slightly inexact. Yet I would plead that the overall relationships would not change much even with the adjustments mentioned—and we are here trying to see how the players correlate to one another, after all. A very rare few (like Jim Gilliam) drew a great many more walks than the statistical mean—but not so many that a modest 200 at-bats does not continue to define a useful line between sitting on the bench and being used significantly.

I should also note that R.C. Stevens, alas, averaged slightly under 50 at-bats per season (41). I had to award him another nine in order to bring him onto the radar.]

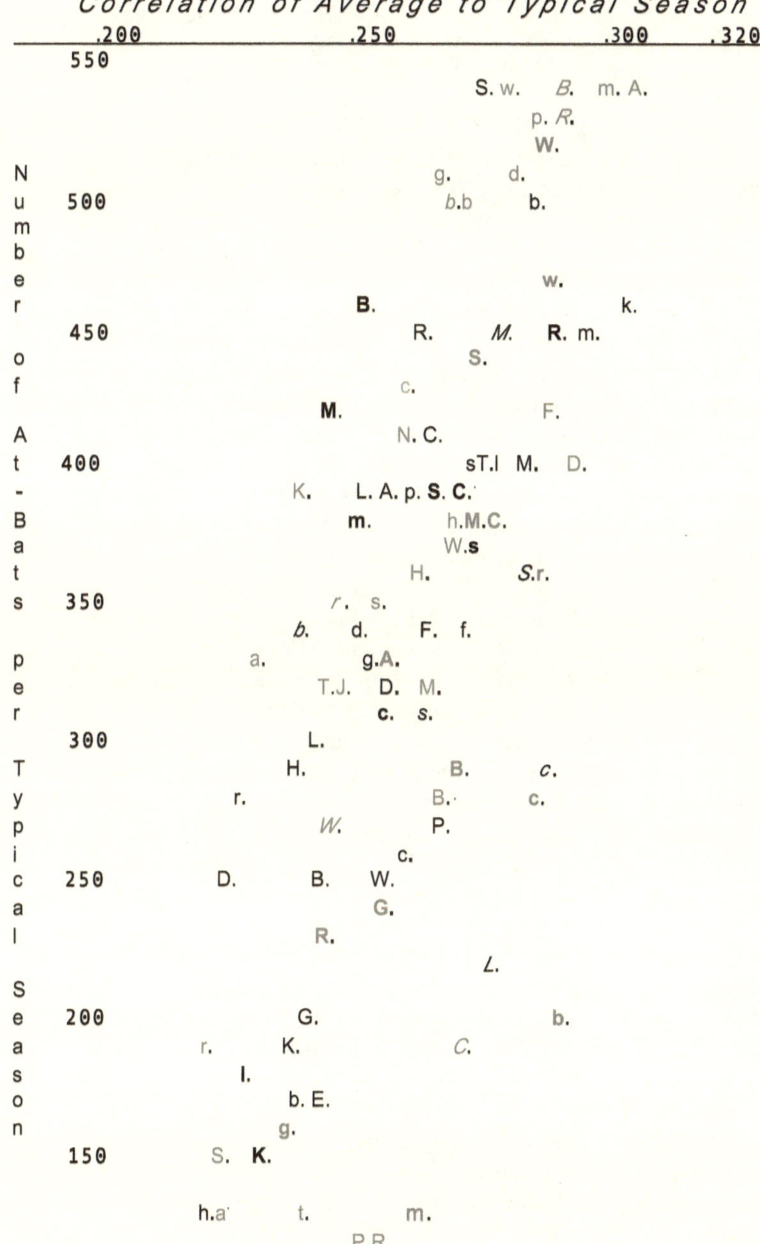

G.

100   C.

s.   C.
   .200   .250   .300   .320
____
           Lifetime Batting Average

Notice first that Bob Boyd, Joe Caffie, George Crowe, and Bubba Morton all ended up with lifetime averages higher than those of white starters like Frank Bolling, Don Buddin, Woodie Held, Jim Landis, Dick McAuliffe, and Bobby Richardson. Yet every one of these latter had more than 380 at-bats in a typical season, and only Boyd among the black players had over 200 (just barely). Since we may reasonably expect that hitters get better with more at-bats, the difference in batting average between the two groups would probably have been more like thirty or forty points than ten or fifteen if all of these men had been played equally. That's a substantial gap in terms of winning potential: starting Buddin instead of Morton at third might well cost you a half-dozen games per season. Of course, Morton was not a third baseman—and therein lies the apparent fallacy of this comparison.

Of the six white players I have listed just above, only Landis was an outfielder. *All* of the blacks played the outfield except Boyd, who was given rather more starts at first (after breaking his arm on an awkward throw from left). On the other hand, only Bolling of the six Caucasians was outstanding at his position. Held might actually have been better off in the outfield. Does anyone really believe that Caffie, Crowe, and Morton couldn't have played first or third with a little coaching, if not up the middle? I shall have further occasion throughout this book to remark the tendency to thrust black talent into the relatively interchangeable—and expendable—positions of the outfield. Here I note in passing how well the strategy served in keeping exceptional hitters from having their day in the sun.

Another objection might be made on behalf of Held and McAuliffe: that their power more than compensated for their low batting averages. This is particularly hard to buy in McAuliffe's case, since he usually batted lead-off. In the critical position of being first to the plate a couple of innings per game (for the pitcher is often the third out—the opposition will walk hitters just to reach him in a crunch), Dick managed to strike out almost one time in six. It's true that he walked almost as often—but the two figures shouldn't be anywhere close in the ideal lead-off hitter. Though Held batted farther down in the order, he struck out almost one in four times, and he drew considerably fewer walks than McAuliffe.

Does this all discredit the importance of the nearly 200 homers which both men stroked in their career? Not exactly: but it forces any impartial observer to wonder why the available talent wasn't better auditioned where the deficiencies were so obvious. In the case of the Tigers, that talent was already on board in the early Sixties: Jake Wood, who led the league in triples in '61. Jake's career average is almost as modest as McAuliffe's—but then, Jake was never given a full season's play after his rookie outing. And Jake—would you believe it—was bumped from second base for McAuliffe *because he struck out too much!* Detroit's decision to remain faithful to Dick throughout a long, up-and-down career is certainly not indefensible. Indeed, such fidelity got spectacular results from Al Kaline, and very good ones from Norm Cash. Yet in the light of Detroit's experience with players who didn't get the "quick hook", the question is more worth asking than ever: why did the jury came in so soon on black players?

While we are busy charging the Fifties establishment with applying a double standard, it's only fair that we scrutinize the case of those black players of the opposite sort: the privileged few who received ample at-bats per season and yet ended their careers with rather poor batting averages. Are there any of this class? Well, yes, a few—but not always a *privileged* few, I think. If we make a kind of box from the .260-lifetime-average vertical line and the 260-at-bat horizontal line, we find the hapless Jake Wood, whose case I have just discussed, in the lower right corner. The *per annum* AB's for Jake's brief career are grossly inflated by his full rookie season and a couple of half-seasons. Having once taught him that a bad month would result in his being benched, Detroit never again managed to get an even performance out of Jake over the long haul—not that he ever saw another long haul. With privilege like this, who needs adversity? Another denizen of the elite upper-left box where you get to play often with a mediocre average is John Roseboro. "Rosey", of course, was a catcher—one of the best in the National League—and also a Dodger. The same pressures were not brought to bear upon him as would have been, say, on Elston Howard if his average had dipped for the Yankees—and both were no doubt better off than a black outfielder. By absorbing the extreme abuse of the catcher's life and handling pitchers adroitly, such players were able to render themselves too valuable to remove from the line-up.

Which leaves a trio of outfielders, precisely: Mack Jones, Willie Kirkland, and Willie Tasby. What are they doing so high up in yearly at-bats and so low in career average? I can answer that question in one word: homers. Kirkland was especially promising. He hit home runs in bunches from 1958 to 1963, during which six years he never received fewer than 418 at-bats. (Twice he surpassed 500.) For three consecutive years over this span, Willie reached the 20's in both homers and doubles. Yet he never hit more than 27 round-trippers (only once did he even get beyond 22), and his .272 batting average of 1959 was his first and last venture beyond the .250's. Kirkland showed promise for a long time without really fulfilling it. How many 100-run seasons would a Ted Savage or a Tommie Aaron have enjoyed if given the same opportunity to do what they did best? How many times might Bubba Morton have hit over .300?

I've made this point before, and it will keep surfacing: the prejudice against black players was rescinded—at least with regard to playing time—if

97

they clobbered home runs, or if they were thought capable of doing so. In my humble opinion, Kirkland really was somewhat privileged. That is, the stats suggest to me that his power won him more playing time than his overall offensive value truly justified. Willie Tasby is a slightly more obscure example of the same phenomenon. (Did these young men catch a break, too, for being called "Willie" in the wake of the great Mays? I'm just kidding... I think.) Tasby had three more-or-less full seasons from 1959 to 1961: these were his career, essentially. In two of the three, he managed double-digit numbers in home runs and doubles (though at no time did any of these figures exceed the teens). His career-high average was .268, not even a match for Willie Kirkland's. Again one must wonder what Joe Caffie or Wes Covington would have done with a chance to play three full seasons in a row (even with a different team every year: at least Tasby stayed in one league). What would Al Smith have done with 400 at-bats in Boston instead of the 51 which the Red Sox allowed him in 1964 before tossing him on the ash heap?

Mack Jones remains. Based purely upon his record and upon the testimonies I have read (I certainly never saw him play), I should say that he was much the best ballplayer of the final three in our 260/260 box. He logged a magnificent 1965 season, hitting 31 home runs—more than either of the Willies ever racked up—in what might be called a time of down-swing for power generally, and a year before the Braves moved to their launching pad in Atlanta. Yet 1965 may have been a curse-in-disguise for Mack. The expectation of other great home run years almost certainly bought him more playing time and a longer career; but I suspect that the pressure to drive the ball over the fence also lowered his average substantially—and probably his doubles and triples, as well, and hence his total offensive output. Mack was a little smaller than Kirkland, and a little larger than Tasby. Yet they (like Aaron, who was also of average size for a ballplayer) batted right-handed, while Mack was a righty who batted left. Such hitters usually have more bat control and less power, since their better hand is on the bottom. Ted Williams actually regretted that he had not grown up swinging right-handed—the same side as he threw from: he was nagged by the suspicion that he might have sacrificed some power in crossing the plate![2]

I am leading up to the claim that Jones's career average might well have been much higher but for the pressure to hit home runs. On the other hand, his oft-visible ability to hit home runs was parleyed into a longer career than even a potential batting champ like Bob Boyd enjoyed. (Boyd actually played for only one season fewer than Mack's ten—but he had well over 1,000 fewer trips to the plate.) The white players in the 260/260 box are mostly "glove men" who were awarded valuable positions in the middle-infield; the black players are mostly potential home run kings who never proved out. It is always a sad time for baseball—real baseball—when the "insiders" who call its shots fail to understand the many facets of the game's offense. We are going through such a time at this moment, as Hall of Famer and professional analyst Joe Morgan maintains.[3] One cannot exactly call the foolish prejudice against bunting, moving runners along, base-stealing, and hitting to the opposite field a *racist* attitude, though it does denigrate skills at which many black players have historically excelled. In the late Fifties and early Sixties, Aaron, Banks, Mays, McCovey, and Robinson were all profiting from home run mania even as Floyd Robinson faced sudden unemployment, Vada Pinson was having an identity crisis, and Tommy Davis was in the process of setting the all-time record for number of uniforms worn. There is most definitely no evidence to suggest that racist owners and GM's deviously nourished a home run craze to keep black players out of Major League baseball. If such a plot had been hatched, it would have been both the most spectacular failure and most dazzling feat of collaboration ever achieved by such a bunch of Keystone Cops.

Nevertheless, an inability to understand the well-balanced offense caused a net loss in opportunities for black talent at the time—as it has, I believe, today. If we reflect that black players as a group were also thought (except by the Dodger organization) to be too slow-witted to handle the shortstop's or second baseman's duties, we may well wonder if—at least half a century ago—the black hitter were thought to be at his best simply hacking at pitches like a coolie with a sledge-hammer.

The graph also shows, naturally, that those great sluggers of African descent who didn't blunder through a disastrous off-year or suffer severe injury were able to claim their 500-or-so at-bats every year. Aaron, Banks, Mays, Pinson, Robinson, and Billy Williams may all be found at the top. Even Bill White and Al Smith, whose career plug was outrageously pulled when, after a whirlwind of trades, their power numbers dropped in limited play, managed to average about 450 at-bats for each season. (White had the further misfortune to come under the magnifying glass during '67 and '68, years when practically everyone's offensive stats suffered because of dominant pitching.) The durable Dodger infielders Gilliam and Wills are also in this elite group, along with their fleet teammate, center fielder Willie Davis; and Lou Brock, representing the next generation of black players who finally forced Jackie Robinson's style of baseball into the mainstream, anticipates the long reign of superstars like Carew, Henderson, and Ozzie Smith. (Yet even Lou, as few recall today, originally reached the big leagues surrounded by a buzz about his tape-measure Minor League clouts.)

The one "oddball" at the top has perhaps the most revealing story to tell: Bill Bruton. Billy was something like the Lou Brock of ten years earlier, a fly-ball hawk in the field and a speedster on the base paths who could reach third on "gappers". The graph may suggest that baseball was grateful to Bruton for his skills, even though they didn't include the potential to hit 20 home runs. This explanation of Bill's numerous seasonal at-bats may be less correct, however, than the "quick hook" theory. That is, as soon as he gave the faintest sign of falling off, Bruton was discarded. (He had misreported his age early on in his career: perhaps rumors had circulated.) The signs of fall-off were indeed faint: in fact, Bill was *not* slowing down toward the end, as is often alleged, if we judge by his rate of stealing bases, which almost doubled in his final year over what it had been during the previous two. He also kept grinding out doubles and triples steadily—but his home runs, alas, were down. So much for the notion that the early Sixties respected Maury Wills as much as Mickey Mantle!

Of course, the Mick is comfortably nestled in the top group (his much-publicized injuries didn't deprive him of nearly as many at-bats as is commonly supposed). Kenny Boyer sits a little above him, and Ron Santo above Ken. It is a bit surprising, though, to find Harvey Kuenn and Pete Runnels in Mantle territory. Both were exceptional hitters: both had won batting titles. But they were not *power* hitters, the apparent requirement of all black players in this highest group who were not employed by the Dodgers. Bob Boyd, Floyd Robinson, Tommy Davis, and Curt Flood might have won batting titles, too. (Actually, Davis won two consecutive ones—ahead of Aaron and Clemente, and Robinson—and came in fifth in 1964.) Neither Kuenn nor Runnels was spectacular on the infield: both were most prized for their singles and doubles. Why, then, could black players—who had made a fine art of stretching singles to doubles in the Negro Leagues—not be prized in the same way?

Why is Leon Wagner, who could hit .300 *and* bang 30 homers, mired down in the range of white players like Russ Snyder and Bob Skinner, having been traded, benched, and released in compensation for averaging one homer about every 20 at-bats? (Leon was actually traded for Snyder in 1968: by this time, Russ was clearly on the downward slope, and had managed only 42 homers and 319 RBIs, in any case, *throughout his entire twelve-year career!*) The coordinates of George Crowe and Harry Simpson are close to Wagner's. We can well imagine that these two, whose talent was a match for Leon's though very differently proportioned, suffered from having entered the Major Leagues in the early Fifties and having been somewhat beyond the stage of tender youth upon entry. To look at Wagner's career, however, one is tempted to conclude that things had not improved much in almost a decade.

To be sure, Daddy Wags had a style which antagonized as many as it delighted, and his clowning has lent a certain plausibility to the rap that he was a careless klutz in the field. I shall be dealing with Leon later, when I come to write at length about particular players. For now, I invite the reader simply to think about what it means to have your career shortened because you are too flamboyant. What, then, would be proper behavior? To keep your mouth shut and your hands to yourself? Orlando Cepeda's clubhouse energy led several teams to post-seasons—and yet, Cepeda kept getting traded. Why, exactly, were people like Wagner and Cepeda supposed to shut up, while Billy Martin's "enthusiasm" was considered an asset before the Copacabana fight?

And what about Wes Covington, who probably could have competed for the Triple Crown in his prime? A brilliant hitter who tore up every Minor League he ever played in, Covington certainly wasn't platooning during these youthful exploits. Indeed, his unforgettable left-handed hitting style—coiled back over his left leg in a crouch, his lithe wrists holding the bat perfectly flat and pointed straight at the umpire's shoulder—would have kept him from flying open against lefty pitchers. Bill James lists Wes (the only mention the

Almanac makes of him) in a table of "players with very balanced offensive skills".[4] Yet Covington's career high in at-bats was 373—little more than half a season—and his average number of at-bats per season is 271. He would be traded five times in eleven years (thrice in 1961). His "swan song" year was a season divided between the Cubs and the Dodgers consisting of 44 at-bats, the Phillies having traded him that winter for... guess who? Doug Clemens.

I might as well add, in conclusion (and in fairness to the unfairly handled), that Joe Cunningham, a Caucasian player who very nearly batted .300 for his career, sits close to Covington on the graph. Joe actually exceeded the .300 mark substantially for three straight years, yet—like Wes—he averaged well under 300 at-bats a season for his career. Also like a great many black players, Cunningham was an outfielder who occasionally filled in around first base. At least he was left-handed (meaning that he really couldn't have been played anywhere else on the infield). He was traded four times in fifteen years—a fairly typical value. Still, Joe Cunningham deserved a better fate. He was a moderately wasted talent. I volunteer him as a reminder that injustice was not always a matter of racial discrimination, even in the late Fifties. Some organizations simply had a genius for finding and stabilizing incompetent management. Some still do.

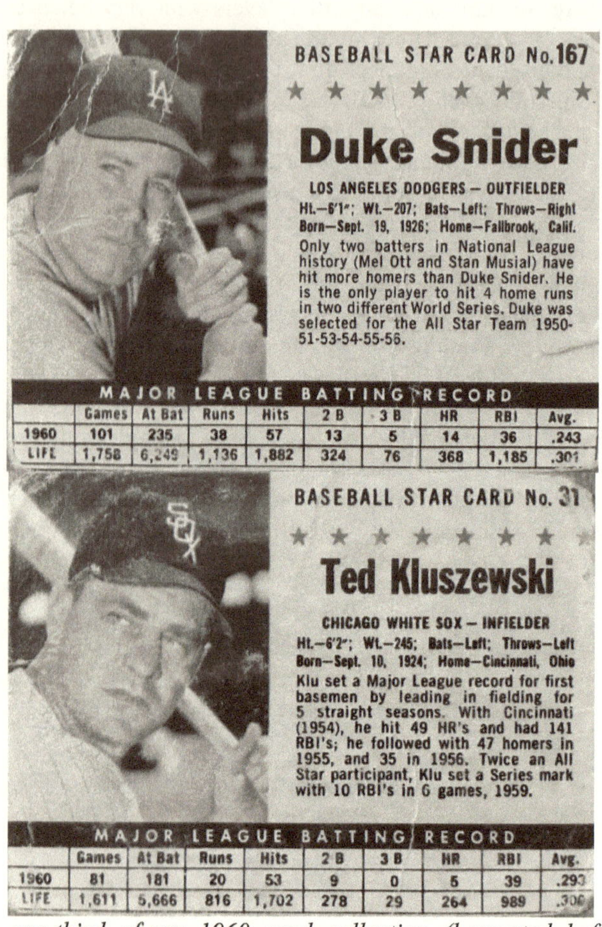

MAJOR LEAGUE BATTING RECORD

	Games	At Bat	Runs	Hits	2 B	3 B	HR	RBI	Avg.
1960	101	235	38	57	13	5	14	36	.243
LIFE	1,758	6,249	1,136	1,882	324	76	368	1,185	.301

MAJOR LEAGUE BATTING RECORD

	Games	At Bat	Runs	Hits	2 B	3 B	HR	RBI	Avg.
1960	81	181	20	53	9	0	5	39	.293
LIFE	1,611	5,666	816	1,702	278	29	264	989	.300

This was one-third of my 1960 card collection (harvested before I had mastered the art of using scissors, apparently). Both the Duke and Big Klu were riding the very long and tolerant tail-end of a vastly popular career. One simply didn't see black players, even superstars, with years like Snider's 1960, and Ted's was little better in terms of power. Once the black slugger's numbers hinted at a downward turn, he was washed up.

1 Mantilla's case is extremely instructive, and I shall be returning to it in my special section on individual players. The very question I have just asked is posed by both Felix and Henry Aaron in the latter's autobiography, *I Had a Hammer*, with Lonnie Wheeler (New York: HarperCollins, 2001), 217-218. Without taking anything away from Bolling, both players are fully aware that the Braves might easily have used Felix to plug the gap up the middle.

2 Cf. *The Science of Hitting* (*op. cit.*), 60"I think I would have been a better hitter if I had also been a left-hand thrower.... If you're right-handed, your chief power source is your right hand, the hand nearer the club head." Of course, Ted was much enamored of power and relatively unimpressed by the number of left-hitting righties who had won batting titles in baseball history.

3 See Morgan's *Long Balls, No Strikes: What Baseball Must Do to Keep the Good Times Rolling*, with Richard Lally (New York: Random House, 1999), especially the third chapter, "Let the Thieves Run Wild!" (39-57). I should add (lest I seem to have implied otherwise above) that Joe is heartened by the recent spate in home runs, attributing to it the resurgence of the game's popularity. Of course, he's right. The truth is that there's absolutely no reason why home run hitters and base-stealers should not coexist symbiotically.

4 Bill James, *op. cit.*, 539. One cannot fault James's relative negligence of Covington: Wes was never given the chance to make much in the way of fireworks. That is precisely my point.

IV

Hot Potatoes: Number of Trades Correlated to Seasons Played

If you and I were pledged to a conspiracy whose objective was the undoing of a certain group of ballplayers, one of the low-down tactics we might employ would surely be the trade. I'm a writer, and I find that I write much better in familiar surroundings. Sometimes I can't write at all in a strange place, even though it may be far more peaceful than my office at home. Ballplayers are the same way. They grow used to hitting against a certain background, to playing a certain infield whose grass grows just so high or roving a certain outfield where the wall is just so far back and the sun at just such an angle over the stands by late afternoon. Have you ever tried imagining yourself at the plate as you take some practice swings in your back yard? Take the swings for five minutes every day throughout the week: then face around and imagine the pitcher against another fence's or tree's background. The change is radically disorienting.

If you and I and a couple of other puppeteers of men were to keep every member of the certain targeted group packing his bags constantly and reporting to a new "home", we would almost inevitably sabotage the group's performance. For, although no ballpark has a tree or rose bush or saguaro cactus growing behind the mound, journeyman ballplayers must adjust to more than slightly altered perceptual settings: they must find new quarters, make new contacts in the community, locate new restaurants whose cuisine doesn't keep them awake half the night, and so forth. If they have families, they must persuade their wives to become, once again, strangers in a strange land. (At least the ballplayer has a couple of dozen teammates: what "team" does his wife join?) They must pry their children away from friends and schools and demand that, once again, they submit to mortifying "new kid on the block" pressures. If we run our detested group through this gauntlet, say, three times in six years, then most of them will surely peel off and seek some less hellish kind of employment. No human being could live this way for a decade—not without incurring some of the miseries from the sad set that includes divorce, loneliness, alcoholism, drug abuse, and suicidal despair.

Believe it or not, Major League baseball never mounted such a conspiracy against its new black recruits. Devices of this subtlety would have required far more coherence—and perhaps a little more intelligence—than the august assembly of front-office movers and shakers could have mustered. What the front-office brotherhood did, instead, was to harrow virtually *all* of its uniformed slaves, black and white, in the manner I have just described. Except for *bona fide* superstars, players who fielded difficult defensive positions brilliantly, or lucky dogs who had somehow ingratiated themselves to management and ownership, no ballplayer of the Fifties and Sixties enjoyed any degree of job security. I was staggered to discover that both the blacks and the whites in my study averaged 4.1 years with each team whose uniform they wore: the figure was identical to the first decimal. (These, remember, are mostly players from Post's limited card collections: i.e., valued starters and proved performers.) Furthermore, there was no significant disparity in the number of times black and white players were traded across league boundaries (a situation where failure is rendered more likely by the hitter's need to learn a whole new array of pitchers). White players were sent to the other league in 31% of their trades, blacks in 34%.

The notorious Reserve Clause which had clung to players' contracts of these years like a ball and chain allowed owners an absolute prerogative to trade a young man whenever and wherever they wanted while his obligation to them lasted. He could not simply rear up and declare, "No, I've made a home in St. Louis and I don't want to move to Philadelphia. Either retain my services for the duration of my contract or allow me to seek employ without hindrance in southern California, where I grew up." This, in effect, is what Curt Flood said to August Busch: he ended up sacrificing the remnant of his career in the gambit. Though salaries were usually negotiated on a yearly basis, the player was "owned" by his team until his contract ran out as a racehorse is owned by a stable.

As a result, it sometimes seems as though certain teams dithered with their players' lives *because they could*. One might be forgiven for recalling the infamous Millburn Experiment, where subjects were allowed to dose an artificial examinee (who was actually not wired up at all—but the subjects didn't know this) with electric shocks when he gave wrong answers. Most of the subjects, insulated behind a one-way window, turned up the voltage without prompting as the session proceeded, simply because they had the power to do so.

Besides sadism, general managers had two reasons for sending players on their merry way. One was the need to appear to be doing something. If you're being paid big money to do a job, you want to be perceived as doing it actively. Make changes: shake things up. If a player performed below expectation last year (whatever that means), shuffle the deck: if he rose to superstardom, keep an eagle-eye on his age and try to deal him at the first sign of decline, while his trade value remains somewhere near the zenith. Many a general manager has ruined a winning combination purely out of the desire to reach in and stir the brew. On the other hand, the sabotage is not always unintended. Some general managers would apparently be happier as managers (or fancy that they would be so). Frank Robinson recounts two clear cases where general managers undercut his efforts as manager because they wanted his job to come vacant: Phil Seghi in Cleveland and Tom Haller in San Francisco. Seghi actually harangued the assembled coaching staff on one occasion about what he would be doing if he were manager.[1] In such cases, trading away vital players was part of the strategy for the siege. Instead of the general manager's being blamed for his own bonehead maneuvers, the manager would take the rap for being unable to work with young talent and unwilling to communicate with the front office.

Who needs to be convinced, besides, that owners were fond of unloading players who stood up too vigorously for better pay and conditions? Frank Thomas (*not* today's Big Frank of White Sox fame) was obviously one such player. Though Thomas might well have ended up in Cooperstown if provided with stability throughout his career, he was an intelligent, vocal, strong-willed man who demanded a fair shake (as his entries in *We Played the Game* reveal).[2] Result: an incredible nine teams in sixteen years! Thomas, of course, was white. Curt Flood, an African-American, probably made himself *persona non grata* to the Cardinals through the same kind of skirmishes over salary, as he implies in his book.[3] Yet Curt, as a black, was also part of baseball's least bigoted team of the Sixties. Flood, Brock, Gibson, White.... Some have wondered if August Busch might have selected the two most dispensable members of this fearless foursome for the block because their protest against the segregated spring-training facilities in Florida (for instance) had made such a clamor.

A less spectacular movement was gaining way on the Milwaukee club before a similar purge was conducted. Henry Aaron makes it clear in his autobiography that he and others had begun to object publicly to the culture of segregation just before Bruton and Covington were sent packing.[4] His book quotes an article which also mentions the newly acquired Andre Rodgers as among the Braves who were demanding more equitable treatment at the spring-training facilities in Florida. Is it entirely an accident that Rodgers was traded away to the Cubs before the 1961 season officially began—before he had played one game in a Milwaukee uniform? Henry never hints that the vocal objections and the sudden trades were related. Perhaps this is because imbecilic trades were routine in the game (he would later watch the heavy hand of Paul Richards deal white superstar Eddie Mathews when the team moved to Atlanta), or perhaps because younger black players like his brother Tommie and Mack Jones were quickly taken on board. These latter, naturally, could be relied upon to raise less of an uproar about salaries, and probably also about segregation, since they were "glad just to be here".

We must not forget that players sometimes changed venue because an admiring coach, himself on the move, wanted to bring them along. Al Lopez quickly traded for black star Al Smith when he became manager of the White Sox; Frank Lane, on the other end of the deal, had grabbed for Minnie Minoso when he left the Sox to become the Indians' general manager. Players in such situations were bound to be happy with their new surroundings. What, after all, is learning a new hitting background beside having a manager who wants to play you every day?

I should also add that we might reasonably expect many players, both black and white, to be traded once or twice early on before some bright coach recognized their potential. Likewise, a solid but aging ballplayer might figure in a couple of deals during his twilight years, especially with young or struggling franchises that needed immediate help to get their head above water. The result might well be a 12-to-15 year career featuring three or four trades, or an average of one trade every four years. This calmly reasoned estimate jibes well with the 4.1-season-per-team average that I reported finding among my study group.

Yet the fact is that the very sensible career plan I have just mapped out does not describe the experience of many black ballplayers. Consider the chart below. Once again, the red (or gray, in some formats) initials represent African-Americans and the black initials Caucasians. A cursory glance shows that the 12-to-17-year range is largely Caucasian territory, while the reds (grays) tend to fall to either side of this island. In other words, the black ballplayers tended to have either exceptionally long or exceptionally short careers—and, *within those lopsided parameters*, they managed to achieve about the same rate of trade as white ballplayers. The next chapter will further break down the nature of the typical black player's career by examining the "longest stint" spent with a single team.

The vertical axis is labeled "team changes" as well as "trades" because a few players were unconditionally released and signed again with a new team. As far as I know, however, this modification of the standard career path was realized in few cases. In any event, the distinction between a trade and a free-agent signing is irrelevant when one is primarily trying to establish that ballplayers led unsettled lives to the whole-hearted indifference of their employers. Leon Wagner signed with the Giants as a free agent toward the end of his career, and Vada Pinson with the Brewers: Wagner received 12 official at-bats in Frisco, Pinson *none* in Milwaukee. (In fact, I did not include the Brewers in the tally of teams for which Vada played.) Tommy Davis was the only player I noticed who significantly lengthened his career through free agency in these times, signing on *four occasions* after a release. Only a former batting champ or All-Star (Davis was both) would have been able to avail himself of this unpromising option. For most, it did not exist.

Excepting Tommy Davis's lonely star, the graph's most remarkable feature must again be the number of black players who were not allowed careers of any great extent—the sad bunch assembled to the lower left. The few whites who penetrate this group were actually traded rather more often. Don Buddin, Al Luplow, and Joe Koppe ride at the top of the "trade wave's" lower slope, and the martyred Chuck Essegian is indeed the only player to sit on the corner of a perfect square: i.e., he was traded six times in six years! Of course, Essegian's fate was not much more lamentable than "Suitcase" Simpson's or Ted Savage's. Everyone seemed to acknowledge that these three players had talent: no one seemed to figure out how to use it. A more common destiny for black ballplayers was to sit on one or two benches for five years (perhaps with jaunts back down to the Minors), unacknowledged and untried, prior to a permanent release.

The ten-year milestone makes an interesting stop. It underscores the surprising conclusion that getting traded was actually a stroke of luck, inasmuch as it postponed complete termination. Six players in my study had ten-year careers on the button. Five were white, and the one black—Mack Jones—was traded the fewest number of times (twice). Of the whites, three were traded five or more times. In the next chapter, we shall see that this enhanced frequency of trades for whites accompanied a tendency to enjoy a longer "longest stint". That is, the one team where a player spent most of his career tended to hold on to him longer if he were white: this, I reiterate, occurred *in tandem with* the white player's being traded more so as to prolong his career.

Correlation of Team Changes to Career Length
(vertical axis represents number of trades and team changes)

```
12
                                                             D.

10


8                                                f.   T.
                               S.
6              E.              c.              H.                    R.
     s.  s.    G.  S.    cW.bS .DL             B.         d.         F.
4                  r.g  W.  K.ARS .ss       S. bC.kP S.p.
            T.         K.P a.bK r. rc.H C.GM .M .w          w.C L.        M.
2           B.h G.lm N. C.    J. c.M  B.s L.  r.R  F.      p.
     s.  g.       W.  B.C      b.BD B.M h.       S. C.m W.      m.  BA.
0    C.R  r.      t.  a.              R.  A.d g.              m.  b.
            5              10              15              20+
     Length of ML Career (in Seasons)
```

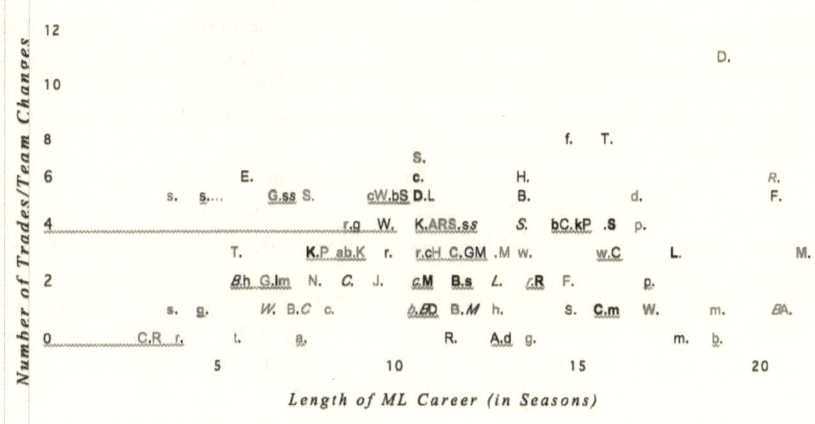

The length of career, then, is really the graph's story. The number of trades turns out to be a means to that end. Consider the region of 15-to-17 seasons played. Fourteen players inhabit this territory. Exactly one of them is black—and he is Curt Flood, whose career was interrupted by a courageous but futile attempt (in terms of saving his own livelihood) to defy the Reserve Clause. In other words, by the fifteenth year, a black superstar would naturally have been identified, and his run in the Major Leagues would last as long as health would permit. Other blacks were washed up—and not for reasons of health. To be sure, this group includes several excellent white players: Ken Boyer, Norm Cash, and Roy Sievers achieved a near-Cooperstown quality of performance (with Ron Santo finally making it through the gate). But why is Bill White not in their midst? Why did Wes Covington never get close?

If I may press the point, consider further the players whose careers reached the 13-to-14-year span: that is, move the cut-off point of our magnification back a couple of years. The racial break-down appears pretty even here: seven blacks and eight Caucasians. Bill White is one of the former. Besides him, we find in this group *all three* of the black catchers who entered the Major Leagues after Roy Campanella and were given a serious shot at success, as well as the Dodger middle-infielders Jim Gilliam and Maury Wills. These men, in other words, survived as long as they did because they were able to hold down key defensive positions. The only member of this cross-section other than Bill White who didn't play "up the middle" defensively was Lee Maye, a veteran outfielder who eked out a few final years by convincing teams that he was a good pinch-hitter (the sort of thing Tommy Davis accomplished to the maximum degree possible).

Once again, too, we see that the white players in this range include stars like Bob Allison and Pete Runnels... but the rest of their bunch is somewhat more dubious. Did Jim Davenport, Woodie Held, and Bill Skowron deserve the same length of career as Bill White, and a longer career than

Covington and Al Smith enjoyed—*substantially* longer than Ed Charles, Charlie Neal, and Floyd Robinson? With the exception of Held, none of the white Major Leaguers I have just named played up the middle on defense (and Woodie was a weaker-than-average shortstop). At least Johnny Logan was solid at short and Ed Bailey a fine catcher. Notice, in fact, that except for Sherman Lollar, none of the white catchers was maintained in active service longer than Howard and Roseboro.

Which just goes to show (if I may harp on an important point) that playing up the middle was as healthy for Major League longevity as getting traded often—and far healthier than multiple trades, we may assume, for general sanity!

To conclude this rather brief chapter, I may as well address an objection to my measurements that isn't very complimentary of black ballplayers, but is sure to be lurking in certain minds. It is this: maybe these young men were sent packing more frequently than their Caucasian counterparts because they couldn't behave themselves as well, undermining their own performance and negatively influencing players around them with their drunkenness and womanizing. I will give this much credit to such rebuttal: other things being equal, poor kids tend to go a little crazier when they make it big than modestly well-off kids. John Roseboro's disarmingly frank account of life before, during, and after the Major Leagues is full of heavily shadowed areas—places in the big-leaguer's experience which the casual fan doesn't know about, and also places in the human soul which too many big-leaguers fail to explore before personal disaster. Rosey specifically mentions black Dodger teammates Lou Johnson and Willie Davis as having neutralized brilliant talent with off-the-field excess. Johnson couldn't control his spending. He was "charging stuff all over town.… Before long, it became bad business for the Dodgers to keep him on the club."[5] As for Willie… "Davis was strange. He didn't drink a lot, but he ran a lot. I think the Dodgers talked him into marrying his girl friend because they thought it would settle him down, but it didn't."[6] At other points in the book, Roseboro expresses his admiration for the orderly personal life of Dodger greats like Gil Hodges and Duke Snider, and he also gives such younger recruits as Don Demeter, Don Sutton, and—of course—the enigmatic Sandy Koufax high marks for keeping their act together. All of these players were white, though Koufax's Jewishness sometimes put his relation to the status quo in doubt.

Yet John praises Roy Campanella in the same vein, as well as Vada Pinson—while he includes white teammates Johnny Podres, Don Zimmer, and Al Ferrara as among Buzzie Bavasi's guys (along with Willie Davis) "who liked to party, who liked to hoist a drink or three, who liked to gamble, who played poker, who followed the horses."[7] Dissipation was clearly one of professional baseball's most triumphantly desegregated activities. And when a general manager like Bavasi was the orgy's master of ceremonies, a player might be forgiven for associating the fast lane with job security.

I have this to add. Most of the black ballplayers in my study could not have carried the rap of being a bad influence on teammates *simply because they came along too soon.* Their spot in the Major Leagues was all too unsteady, and there were all too few of them on a given team: most were narrowly focused on day-to-day survival. The mid-Sixties changed all this. Black players were regular starters, they were making big money, and television had transformed many of them into celebrities. For that matter, the whole of American culture was beginning to melt down: drug use and free sex were the order of the day. None of the black players at my graph's left end ever had World Series money to blow or adoring audiences in Vegas from which to pick concubines. These men could scarcely have run wild with the best (or worst) will in the world.

Finally, there is the geographical factor. When baseball franchises moved west, the big-leaguer's life became at once more stressful and more tedious. The change of several time zones involved in crossing the continent meant that he often didn't know whether to go to sleep or eat lunch when his flight landed in LA—or whether to skip lunch and try a small supper just before the game, or whether to wolf down a huge late breakfast and then nap till four o'clock. Human beings with even the most durable of constitutions are worn ragged by such an existence, week in and week out. Sex, booze, and drugs are three ways that young men with little thought of the long term will predictably seek out to settle themselves down.

Someday, if Major League baseball should ever decide (in a supernatural burst of inspiration) that it wants to offer its public a better product while being more humane to its employees, it may give us four leagues based entirely upon geographical proximity. Then the local rivalries so cherished by advocates of inter-league play would be a routine part of intra-league play (when Brooklyn played at the Polo Grounds, no crowds were bigger). That indispensable portion of the schedule when the Southeastern League played the West Coast League could allow visiting teams two solid weeks of stadium-hopping within the same time zone rather than yo-yoing them back and forth across the Rocky Mountains. In the meantime, expect to see contemporary ballplayers imbibing uppers and downers as the occasion demands while their families fall apart and their children grow up fatherless.

1   See Frank Robinson, *Extra Innings*, with Berry Steinback (New York: McGraw-Hill, 1988), 151-153 for Seghi's tirade before the coaching staff. Frank's experience as the Indians' manager is reported especially in 108-153; the years at the Giants' helm, during most of which Haller was busily dropping wrenches in the machine, are discussed in 169-236.

2   For instance, Frank describes a negotiation with Pirates' General Manager Joe Brown in 1958 (*We Played the Game* [*op. cit.*], 399): "He wanted to split the difference [of a $5000 raise], but I wasn't keen on forgetting about that extra $2500 that could have gone for things for my kids. He said, 'I've never heard a ballplayer say this is what I want and that's it. Well, I can't give you what you want.' I said, 'If that's the case, I'm not signing.'" So Thomas was traded away to the Reds over a $2500 parting of minds.

3   Flood sensed that his $90,000-a-year salary was not made any easier to swallow by his vocal criticism of the system. "I had long been known throughout the league," he writes, "as an agitator against the doubleheader, the 162-game season and, most pointedly, the inequities of the reserve system" (*The Way It Is* [New York: Pocket Books, 1972], 152). He does not suggest, however—despite his typically keen sensitivity to such things—that his eventual trade was an attempt to diffuse any civil rights "agitation".

4   On the same pages of *I Had a Hammer* [*op. cit.*]—210-211—where Aaron discusses the progress that he, Bruton, and Covington made in having the Braves' Florida spring-training facilities desegregated, Henry first mentions the departure of Bill from the team. Wes would follow shortly.

5   *Glory Days with the Dodgers* (*op. cit.*), 169.

6   *Ibid.*, 167.

7   *Ibid.*, 167.

V

Low Crests and Brief Heydays: The Telling Variation in "Longest Stints" with a Single Team

The last chapter established that black and white ballplayers were traded at remarkably even rates. This, however, is not the whole story. The present chapter is intended as an addendum to demonstrate that one must look *within* the figures as well as at them. To be sure, the careers of white players were more often extended by trades than those of black players, as the previous chapter emphasized. An aging player would be more likely to find himself part of a complex deal during two or three of his final four or five years if he were white: he would more likely be viewed by other teams as a good pinch-hitter to call up cold off the bench or a seasoned defender to send in at second base or left field during the late innings. Ponder this situation, though, and see what else it implies. If the rate-of-trade for blacks and whites was equal in the late Fifties and early Sixties, and if whites were more often the object of busy trading activity in their twilight years, *then they must have been traded less often than blacks in their prime.*

The figures-within-the-figures bear out this conclusion (with one or two revealing aberrations). The discovery is significant, because any ballplayer would naturally begin posting his best numbers only after two or three full seasons. If, in that critical mid-career period, he must continue pulling up stakes every second or third year, moving to new cities, adjusting to new bosses and teammates, and possibly learning a new league's pitching, his peak seasons are likely to be hills rather than mountains. It's a little easier to hit .300 when you know that your kids will go to the same elementary school for the next several years than when you're pretty sure that your wife will not follow you for one more move. The more celebrated players also often inaugurated businesses in their communities—restaurants, bars, garages—to capitalize upon their fame. In the days of modest salaries (and, though their pay exceeded the national average, ballplayers were often expected to soak up many of their profession's incidental expenses), such enterprises were a significant source of compensation. They also provided a gateway to the future—to that future which lay beyond a career's final at-bat. Any player who never spent more than three or four years in a given community was greatly disadvantaged in the struggle to survive outside of baseball. He had to know that. It had to be in the back of his mind during a long slump.

In this chapter, I have compiled a series of tables correlating length of career with what I call the "longest stint": i.e., the greatest number of seasons that a player spent consecutively on a single ball club. When the final year with a club was in fact divided between two clubs, I have not counted it. That is, even if Player X was not traded from Detroit to Cleveland until late August, his total with Detroit does not include that final three-quarters of a season. Another factor to be stressed is that a player's return to the team which previously employed him for a generous number of years will not increase that number. Bill White briefly returned to the Cardinals at the end of his career, and Maury Wills to the Dodgers: their "longest stint" with those teams remains unaffected. After all, in a mere two or three years, circumstances can change radically on the club that was once home. The player may have to adjust to a different manager and new teammates. The ballpark may have been redesigned. A certain number of pitchers will be unfamiliar if he has passed the interim period in the other league. Most importantly, the magic of his "peak"—the groove he was in when he had confidently found his professional stride—is gone. Even a relatively simple sport can see the end of a "hot streak" after a brief interruption: many weekend-warriors don't like to be called to the phone while on the golf course. Baseball is not simple, and a span of years is not brief.

I have grouped the players in bunches according to how many seasons their careers lasted, whites on the left and blacks on the right. I didn't include players who appeared in the Majors for fewer than nine seasons because, frankly, almost none of the whites in my study had so brief a tenure. Even at nine years, I have only Doug Clemens and Jim Gentile to compare to six black players. By the same token, I carried the tables no farther than fifteen seasons. The few blacks who played beyond this point were superstars, most of whom naturally had very long runs with a single team (therefore slightly distorting, by the way, the trades/seasons ratio calculated in the previous chapter). Since I deliberately avoided including Musial and Berra and Kaline in the study so as to forestall any suspicion that I was making the typical black career look especially pinched, there are not many white superstars to consider at the over-fifteen-season level.

<u>NINE YEARS</u>

Clemens **4**	Savage **2**
Gentile **4**	Crowe **3**
	Kirkland **3**
	Altman **4**
	Boyd **5**
	Floyd Robinson **7**

<u>TEN YEARS</u>
Cimoli **3**   Mack Jones **6**
Walls **3**
Bilko **5**
Romano **5**
Stuart **5**

<u>ELEVEN YEARS</u>
Demeter **4**   Rodgers **4**
Keough **4**   Covington **6**
Carey **8**   Hinton **4**
Landis **8**

<u>TWELVE YEARS</u>
Bolling **6** Agee **5**
Dalrymple **9**   Bruton **8**
Geiger **7** Clendenon **8**
Malzone **11**   Lenny Green **3**
Maris **7**   Smith **5**
Moon **7**   Wagner **4**
Richardson **12**
Siebern **4**
Skinner **8**
Snyder **7**

<u>THIRTEEN YEARS</u>
Lynch **6**   Battey **8**
Allison **10**   Maye **6**
Logan **10**   White **7**
Davenport **13**

<u>FOURTEEN YEARS</u>
Bailey **8**   Gilliam **14**
Held **6**   Howard **12**
Runnels **7**   Roseboro **11**
Skowron **9**   Wills **8**

<u>FIFTEEN YEARS</u>
Boyer **11**   Flood **12**
Cunningham **7**
Francona **2**
Kluszewski **11**
Kuenn **8**
Santo **14**

The revelations in these tables are pretty stunning. Starting with the nine-season players, we find that only Bob Boyd and Floyd Robinson played for a single team longer than Doug Clemens and Jim Gentile: two men who just might have had Hall-of-Fame careers under different circumstances managed to be more valued by their primary team (barely, in Boyd's case) than a lifetime .229 hitter! (Gentile is better company: Diamond Jim had one stupendous season and a couple of other pretty good forays.) Like Boyd, George Crowe was somewhat impeded by his age from having a longer Major League career—but surely Altman and Kirkland should have found a more loyal employer somewhere. As for Ted Savage, he was never allowed to leave the starting gate.

I commented upon the curious disparity among the ten-year veterans in the previous chapter. All of the white players here (even Lee Walls, who had a brilliant 1958) had shown signs of exceptional ability at one time or another: Mack Jones's ranking in their midst is no disgrace. Jones was actually retained longer by a single team, as well, than any of the whites. What is most conspicuous in this group is the *absence* from it of black players like Altman and Robinson. Why did their careers fall a season short of a decade, while Lee Walls—of whom no team ever thought enough to employ him more than three seasons—was able to celebrate a tenth big-league anniversary on the basis of one big year never again remotely replicated?

In the next four tables, the balance of entries is fairly even: in none of them do we find a lone ballplayer occupying one side of the contrast. All of these men had to be pretty good at what they did to survive more than ten years in the Major Leagues. Andre Rodgers owed his longevity to defense: besides Gene Baker, Ernie Banks, and Pumpsie Green, he was the one non-Dodger in my study to play the middle infield. (Yet he was *not* African-American: Andre hailed from Jamaica, where he grew up playing cricket.) Wes Covington carved out a career with his bat. Even so, he was never allowed even one season of everyday playing-time—unlike Jim Landis, a regular starter for most of his baseball life. Landis and utility man Andy Carey were dependably employed by one franchise (the White Sox and the Yankees, respectively): their eight-year "longest stint" was not far beyond what Covington deserved. For that matter, white player Don Demeter got the benefit of few doubts, either. Don carried a rap of striking out too much (as, indeed, Covington was rumored to be a risk in the outfield), but he never reached three figures in fanning—unlike Landis—and he racked up an impressive tally of extra-base hits. Once again, we see that the raw deal could be an equal-opportunity visitor in baseball.

The twelve-year veterans are perhaps the most shocking group. Bobby Richardson spent his entire career with the Yankees, and Frank Malzone all but his final season with the Red Sox. Both were infielders. So was Al Smith—some of the time. Al had stood out at shortstop in the minors, but "advice" kept nudging him toward third, and thence into the outfield.[1] All the other white players in this group were outfielders except for Frank Bolling, who essentially divided his career between a six-year stint with Detroit and a five-year stint with Milwaukee. Bill Bruton was part of the trade that pried Bolling from the Tigers—which club prized Bill, in turn, almost as much as the Braves had. As far as I know, Bruton and Tommy Agee are the only two of the eleven (or twelve, if you count the oft-shifted Smith) outfielders in the group who consistently patrolled center. Playing up the middle should have made them extraordinarily valuable—and, apparently, it did. (Agee's mere five years with the Mets is not really surprising in light if his emotional instability: like Clendenon, he profited from being part of the '69 Miracle Mets, as well as from being one of this study's youngest subjects.)

That leaves us with Hinton, Smith, and Wagner playing wherever they were put, as against Geiger, Maris, Moon, Siebern, Skinner, and Snyder roving in right and left field. In other words, none of these remaining players held down the most difficult defensive positions on the diamond. One is therefore justified in comparing them largely on the basis of their offensive productivity; and on that basis, it's hard to see why most of the white players should have been employed twice as long by their primary team as the black players. Leon Wagner had the reputation of being a lackadaisical fielder— which he may or may not have deserved more than others.[2] His offensive prowess should clearly have been more coveted; for, let's face it, any player at the Major League level can be successfully coached in handling an outfielder's duties if the coaching staff has the will. Furthermore, Leon was a flamboyant extrovert who kept the team loose, as one can well imagine after reading his entry in Jackie Robinson's anthology.[3]

As for the rest in this bunch, Maris, to be sure, grazed superstardom briefly (one of the reasons this quiet introvert wanted his long stint in New York to end), and Wally Moon had been Rookie of the Year in 1954. But Al Smith *should* have been the American League MVP of 1955, and his subsequent performance surely merited at least as much consideration as Wally's. Why were Green and Hinton, both Red Sox at one point, traded away in about half the time it took Boston to decide that Geiger's .250 bat could be improved upon?

The thirteen-year group was also discussed in the previous chapter, where I again stressed the conspicuously absent. Why Johnny Logan and not Bolling or Maris or Siebern? Among the blacks, why Maye and not Bruton or Smith? Such questions, of course, might be asked endlessly, and their answer often involves a personal component. Bob Allison had absorbed some bad injuries; so had Maris. Al Smith seems simply to have tired of baseball's merry-go-round sooner than Lee Maye. Yet San Francisco's infatuation with Jim Davenport, a career .258 hitter who never logged more than 12 home runs in a season, has something in the nature of objective proof. Why did Davenport deserve a stable environment for almost twice as long as Bill White? (Why over twice as long, for that matter, as white player Jerry Lynch, a smooth outfielder and fine left-handed hitter?) If you had to build a team for one season, would you rather have Jim at third or Al Smith? Yet the Giant franchise continued to be enamored of Davenport even after his retirement.[4]

117

The fourteen-year veterans match four very talented defensive players on the black side against four white players of whom only two have exceptional credentials. Ed Bailey was an excellent catcher, and Pete Runnels a two-time batting champ: Skowron and Held were offensively solid players—Moose, indeed, had occasionally been a stunning run-producing force with the Yankees and fully earned his nine years of tenure with them. I would digress from the main issue if I were to opine that Skowron and Runnels might have posted almost-Cooperstown hitting stats (in different columns) if the Yanks and Red Sox, respectively, had held onto them a little longer. White players are not necessarily any more adept at ingratiating themselves with the front office than black players, as this table shows better than any other. The main point about this group, I think, is precisely that the Dodgers held onto three very good black players and allowed them to show their stuff. There are those who think Maury Wills should be in the Hall of Fame. I myself think a better case could be made for Junior Gilliam—who actually scored 96 more runs in 469 fewer at-bats than Wills (despite Maury's record-breaking base-stealing), had far more extra-base hits, was a model of selflessness, and may have possessed the surest glove (if not the quickest feet) of any Dodger middle-infielder. Perhaps both fall a little short of the requisite credentials. But they got close: like white players Johnny Callison and Norm Cash and Harvey Kuenn, they were *permitted* to get close. What would George Crowe have done with another five years on the team where—all too briefly—he found a home?

A trivia question: who has more extra-base hits in his career, Curt Flood or Junior Gilliam? Flood had 400: Gilliam had 440. (Of course, Jim also had another full season's worth of at-bats, though he played fewer seasons on paper.) Curt is often lionized nowadays because of his heroic challenge to the Reserve Clause and (to a lesser degree) because of his irreverent autobiography. I am not prepared to say, as he often said, that he played a better center field than Willie Mays. Perhaps so. But as the last black player in the study who was not a superstar trickles through our fingers at the fifteen-year cut-off, I think the area of greater interest shifts to the Caucasian side.

Santo eventually reached the Hall of Fame, thanks to the Cubs' loyalty and his later popularity as an announcer. Ken Boyer might well have equaled or surpassed Santo's numbers if the St. Louis franchise had stuck with him as loyally as the Cubs did with their third baseman. Kluszewski had some legendary years, and Kuenn enjoyed one magnificent season among several good ones. It may just be, though, that the best all-around ballplayers in this group—or the players who had the potential of being best all around—were Cunningham and Francona. Left-handed outfielders with speed, occasional power, and a proven ability to hit well over .300 when played regularly, they were nevertheless dealt from team to team like a tennis ball exchanging courts at Wimbledon. One is again very tempted to ask, "What if...?" But the question which should precede this one concerns those who are not here. What if Green, Floyd Robinson, Smith, and White—along with still others of their race who didn't even make the nine-year mark—had been traded enough just to reach fifteen years? Would their career numbers look more like a Francona's, or like a Boyer's?

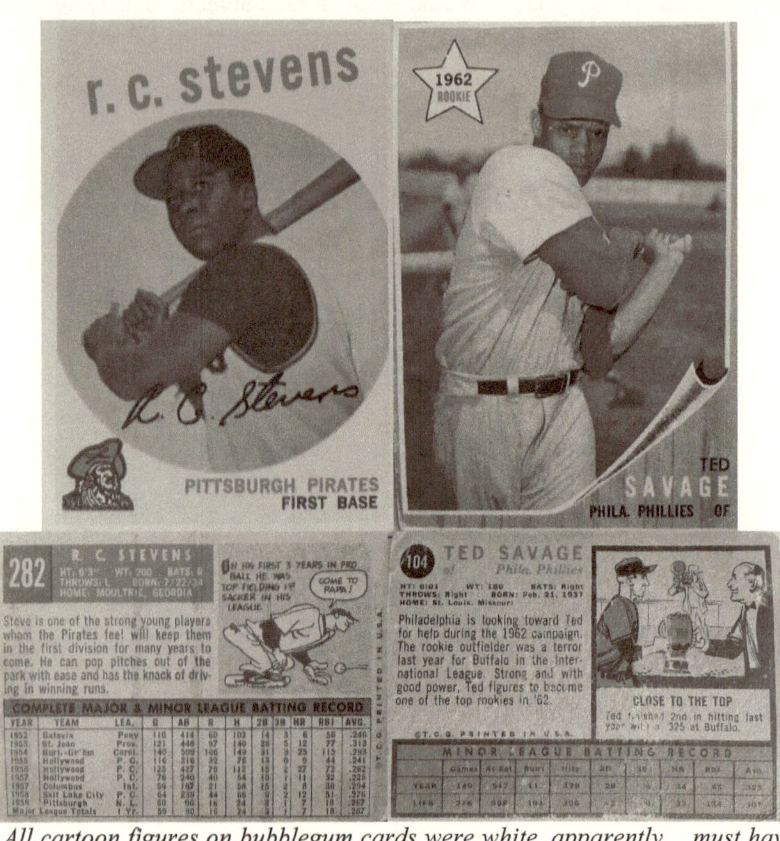

All cartoon figures on bubblegum cards were white, apparently... must have saved on the cost of ink; and it's probably a good thing that caricaturists of the day didn't undertake a representation of African facial features.

1 See Brent Kelley's interview with Smith in *Voices From the Negro Leagues* (Jefferson, NC: McFarland, 1997), 215. Smith was urged by the Cleveland hierarchy to shift from shortstop to the outfield because Al Rosen—who, of course, was a third baseman—would block his ascent to the Majors, otherwise. As we shall see later, a great many young black infielders were told similar things, as if the white establishment really didn't want them learning the crucial infield positions.

2 At various points in his *New Bill James Historical Baseball Abstract* (*op. cit.*), Mr. James accepts the reports about Wagner's fielding at face value, yet defends Norm Siebern (for instance) of similar charges. To be sure, Wagner was probably more deserving of the reputation, as we shall see when I discuss him specifically in Part Two. Yet such things do tend to be magnified, often by those within an organization who wish to get rid of a certain player. In such a case, teaching would be a more benign option than running to the press with criticism.   Ted Williams was a blundering, thoroughly insouciant outfielder when he first appeared on the scene, as well—but coaches worked with him.

3 See Robinson's *Baseball Has Done It* (*op. cit.*), 189-199.

4   The saga of Frank Robinson's efforts to overcome Tom Haller's recalcitrance and sabotage when he was the Giants' manager and Haller their general manger is recounted in the later pages of Robinson's *Extra Innings* (*op. cit.*). Jim Davenport, whom Robinson inherited as a third-base coach and could never seem to pry from that position, was one of the pawns in this struggle. Of course, Davenport and Haller had once been teammates on the Giants. Frank does not accuse Jim of requesting that strings be pulled: the point seems to be (and this is my point, too) simply that Davenport was so well liked by the organization that he received unusually accommodating treatment.

VI

"You Take Mine, I'll Take Yours": Trades Involving Black Players for Black Players

I don't recall when I first began to get suspicious about certain trade activities involving black players. Like so much about this book's subject, the suspicion grew from an invisible seed, and grew so slowly that I noticed its presence only when it was in full bloom. Practically everybody in professional baseball gets traded, of course. In fact, as we have seen, not to be traded very often is usually the kiss of death, for trades allow aging players to hang around for a few more seasons. Superstars were scarcely ever traded in Reserve Clause baseball: Mantle, Kaline, and Banks spent an entire career with a single franchise. Otherwise, however, the lower number of trades among young black players of the late Fifties and early Sixties (not to be confused with a lower *rate* of being traded) put them at a distinct disadvantage compared to white players. They were often done almost before they had started.

I have been over all of this before. What interests me in this chapter is the curious fact—at least I *think* it is a fact—that young black ballplayers were traded extraordinarily often *for other young black ballplayers*. In other words, when these young men were lucky enough to keep a foot in the Majors by being traded to another team, the figure that passed them coming in as they exited was often another player of their race. When you consider how few black ballplayers there were in the Majors, even by 1960, these "same race" swaps seem rather too frequent to be accidental.

One could argue, I suppose, that most black players at this time were necessarily new to the game and young. Major League clubs didn't waste their resources sending twenty-five-year-old Negro Leaguers on the long path of "development" through the Minors. Some of the "kids" just didn't work out—or else appeared to be working out, but were still too much of an unknown quantity to staple into the roster. If other teams which knew of their speed, power, and potential could be persuaded to take one or two of them and one or two old warhorses for an established slugger... well, that's how baseball deals get done.

There are several fallacies in this line of thinking. First, the black players whose trades I have studied were by no means routinely unknown quantities: players who had proved their big-league productivity were as apt to be sent packing as greenhorns. Furthermore, the reasoning is circular. How does *anyone* prove himself if he isn't given a chance to play—and if Player X is dealt to Kansas City after a mere two dozen at-bats, how can you shake your head over him and sigh sententiously, "He's full of talent—but we need someone we can absolutely rely on"? Then, too, what was the explanation for all those years and years that guys like Bob Boyd and Ed Charles were kept in the Minors, if they were to be considered unseasoned when finally brought up? Unseasoned for what, and in comparison to whom?

I will also, very tentatively, advance one more superficially innocent fact in evidence. Starting in 1959—that is, exactly when black players were becoming a substantial presence on every big-league team—a very curious "inter-league trading period" was inaugurated between November 21 and December 15. During this time of Winter Wonderland, ball clubs might swap their players across league boundaries like Christmas gifts without bothering over whether the bundles would clear waivers. I certainly cannot prove that the practice became routine for years just to allow front offices a better chance at keeping their black ballplayers in perpetual motion. In fact, a 1962 story from *The Sporting News* has the faces of five prominent trans-league migrants plastered across the top of the page. All the faces are white.[1] Nobody would ever allege that playing swap was a managerial pastime no older than Jackie Robinson's arrival in Brooklyn. Yet the winter of '62 just happens to have been a relatively peaceful one for black ballplayers: even Leon Wagner would have one more year in Los Angeles. I am not saying, in any case, that the no-holds-barred month was deliberately and exclusively aimed at passing black players around. I'm just saying that such was one of the effects—and I'm also supposing that not all front-office types were utterly blind-sided by this "unforeseen consequence".

The time has come for me to put my cards on the table. What I offer now is not a graph or chart, for trade information from a half-century ago is hard to come by and often incomplete. Besides, not all black players of the time were continually being swapped for other black players. If a graph could somehow be indexed to "race of traded player" and "percentage of Team X belonging to Race X" (a task quite beyond my competence), then many players in this study would turn out to have been treated normally. Yet the number not treated so seems too big. I have a *feeling* that it should be much smaller.

I therefore intend to call as witnesses, one by one, several players whose records I have in something close to entirety, and whose handling appears to me quite lopsided in the manner being discussed. When I have presented my case, I shall revisit certain interesting recurrences in the testimony, such as the names of about half a dozen organizations.

I should warn, finally, that I will count dark-skinned Latino players as black for this exercise, although I have argued elsewhere in the book that their social and cultural situation differed notably from that of African-Americans in many respects. The white establishment put both groups through the same hoops after stealing them from the Negro Leagues. If there was a tendency to pass young black players around like suspect ten-dollar bills, then the Latin players—or certainly the swarthier of them—would have been given the same treatment.

Slugger Willie Kirkland was traded twice in his career. Former batting champ Harvey Kuenn was the objective of the first trade; the second saw Willie switching places (from Cleveland to Baltimore) with black star Al Smith.

Speaking of Smith, he was traded three times over a fairly successful career. The first—and much the most notorious—trade was for the popular Minnie Minoso, whose departure from the White Sox to the Indians created a hostile audience for Al before he ever set foot in Comiskey Park. Hence, with Kirkland added, Smith was swapped for other black players in two of three cases. None of the players concerned, by the way, could have been called an unproved kid at the time.

And who would ever have considered Hall of Famer Frank Robinson an unknown quantity, even in his early years? Actually, question marks did begin to spring up discreetly around Frank after a beaning left him with double vision; but long before that, he was famously (or infamously) dealt by the Reds to Baltimore for the declining hurler Milt Pappas and a couple of small fry, one of whom was black outfielder Dick Simpson. The superstar was traded three more times in the final years of his career despite lingering suspicions about his eyesight, surely a tribute to his legendary ability. On two of these occasions, however (involving the Dodgers, the Angels, and the Indians), Latino players were passed along as discards.

Slugger Leon Wagner, in contrast, was constantly being traded—five times within a decade, to be exact. Yet only twice was another player of dark complexion involved in a deal: first Lou Johnson, who was sent to Toronto (then in the Minors) when Leon was brought up to the Los Angeles Angels, and then a swap between the Angels and Cleveland for Barry Latman (a Jewish player whose swart looks were verged the color boundary: recall that the dark Armenian Chuck Essegian was traded six times in as many years). Johnson's career, especially, has a very different look from Wagner's. He was one of those hapless individuals who spent long years playing at the highest levels of Minor League ball, being bumped up to the Majors at last only to serve, it seemed, as the second or third player in a trade. Lou was swapped *seven times* in an off-and-on career of about a decade. Wagner was the bait in the first trade. Another sent Lou from the Milwaukee Braves to the Tigers for Chico Fernandez, another from the Cubs to the Indians for Willie Smith, and still another—toward the end of his career—from the Indians to the Angels for Chuck Hinton. A black for a black, four out of seven times: this in an era when men of African descent constituted scarcely a quarter of any team's roster.

Hinton was treated to three trades, as well. Before the Johnson trade, he had been sent from the Indians (that's right—the team that would re-acquire him in about a year) to the Angels for José Cardenal. A black for a black, two out of three.

Besides being traded for Hinton, the much-traveled Cardenal was once swapped for Vada Pinson, sending him from Cleveland to St. Louis. Two other deals involved Milwaukee (by this time the Brewers), the Cubs, and—again—the Phillies: Brock Davis was part of one swap, and Manny Seoane the other *quid pro quo*. Two further trades concerned José and various Caucasian players: only two. Black for black, four out of six times.

And Pinson? He was traded four times in a distinguished but troubled career. The Cardenal trade had been preceded by one which sent him to St. Louis from the Reds for Bobby Tolan. It was soon followed by another to the California Angels, which would involve Alex Johnson. Three out of four.

Alex and Lou Johnson should not be confused. Lou possessed an ebullient disposition and was a delight in the clubhouse. Alex had a leaden chip on either shoulder and would confide little more than sullen shrugs to his teammates. "What appeared to be walled-off concentration," wrote Curt Flood of him, "turned out in the heat of battle to be daydreaming, or something undiagnosable."[2] Some of Alex's comments to reporters would probably have tempted even Captain Kangaroo to shred his contract. It should come as no surprise, then, that A.J. was traded five times, including once for Pinson and once for Bill White (involving St. Louis and the Phillies). At least he enjoyed a formidable exchange rate. The previously mentioned Dick Simpson figured in another trade (from the Cardinals to the Reds), and pitcher Pedro Borbon in yet another (from the Reds to the Angels). Four out of five.

Each of the three times Bill White was traded, his ship passed another black player's in the night. The Alex Johnson trade was preceded by one between the Giants and the Cardinals for Sam Jones, and followed—after half a dozen glorious years—by one between the Cards and the Phillies for Jim Hutto, among others. Three for three.

Tommy Davis wore half the uniforms in the Major Leagues at one time or another, but many he assumed as the result of signing as a free agent following a release. In fact, Tommy was traded only four times in his illustrious career. Dark-skinned players were concerned in three of these deals: Tommy Agee, Sandy Valdespino, and Ellie Hendricks. The teams involved were the Mets, the White Sox, the Seattle Pilots, the Astros, the Cubs, and the Orioles. Three for four.

Felix Mantilla was only traded twice during a career of waiting in the wings. The first trade sent him from Milwaukee to the expansion Mets for none other than Pumpsie Green (who had already authored his claim to immortality by being the first black player of the last team to integrate: the Boston Red Sox). Mantilla was a dark-skinned Puerto Rican who was treated to all the adventure of racial pioneering in the Sally League during the Fifties. A teammate of Henry Aaron's for much of his Minor League experience as well as, eventually, on the Milwaukee Braves, Felix was never awarded the special dispensation given to fairer Latin players like Luis Aparicio and Camilo Pascual. The Milwaukee organization was among the more enlightened—bringing it into a head-on collision with a nefarious "gentlemen's agreement" whose boundaries few other teams ran any risk of crossing. Mantilla describes the situation thus:

> A lot of teams had an unwritten rule that you could have five white guys and four black guys on the field, but you crossed the line when you had five black guys and four white guys. I remember one game against the Giants, they had eight black players on the field against us—Jim Davenport was the only white guy— and one of the white players on our team said, "Who are we playing, the Harlem Globetrotters?" [Manager] Fred Haney wouldn't put five black players on the field unless it was an emergency and there was nothing else he could do. If somebody was hurt and I had to fill in at shortstop or second base, that gave us four black guys, and [Juan] Pizarro couldn't pitch….
>
> It was strange, because as long as I was in Milwaukee, we always had a problem at second base, and yet they never gave me the chance to win the job. They would say that I'd get tired if I played all the time, or I was having trouble making the double play. They'd bring in a second baseman and he would come and go, and another one would come and go, and by the time I left, I had been there six years without ever playing more than sixty games at second base.[3]

I reproduce the observations above because they may explain some aspects of the black-for-black trading phenomenon. An astute reader will have noticed that certain organizations recur in my rather haphazard list of oft-traded players: the Dodgers, the Cardinals, the Reds, the Cubs, the Phillies, the White Sox, the Indians, the Angels, the Milwaukee franchises… these were the very teams which had been most receptive to black players from the start.[4] One doesn't see the Red Sox or Yankees or Tigers swapping their black stars back and forth because, quite simply, they had very few to swap. So from a certain perspective, the argument could be made that the clubs which passed black ballplayers like batons in a relay race were at least securing jobs for these young men.

Yet none of this explains *why the relay was being run*. Mantilla's remarks do just that. The teams in question had reached critical mass: a majority of the starting line-up was either going to have to be black, or else they needed to trade a highly qualified starter for a couple of lesser-knowns— one of whom might well be black; that would throw off suspicion of a racial motive, keep a substantial black fandom happy, and satisfy the humanitarian impulses of a faintly conscientious owner. *But it would also obviate a showdown with other baseball owners.* Nobody would wonder why newly acquired Dick Simpson wasn't starting for a departed Frank Robinson, or why José Cardenal wasn't immediately slipped into Vada Pinson's shoes. Think of it: with Aaron, Bruton, and Covington in the outfield and Mantilla at short, the Braves already had four blacks in fair territory. The Dodgers were in an even bigger pickle with the likes of Tommy and Willie Davis, Jim Gilliam, Charlie Neal, John Roseboro, and Maury Wills to juggle years after Jackie had retired. The Giants had several Latino stars to stir in somehow with a mix including Mays and youngsters Willie Kirkland, Leon Wagner, and Bill White—this before Willie McCovey arrived; and Felipe Alou and Orlando Cepeda could not pass for Rickey Ricardo, let alone Rudolf Valentino.

So Swap-Mania was on. A few subjects, like Wes Covington and Leon Wagner, could conveniently be tagged as defensive liabilities so as to explain their limited use. The tag didn't keep them from being traded, but it averted the need to trade for another black. Otherwise, some very creative deals had to be struck, because few teams possessed more than four or six black players. When you are traded 75% of the time for a type of player who represents about 12% of the other squad, you really mustn't take any implied judgment of your abilities too personally. As well as being dark, your skin had better be thick.

Before I leave this mystery, I must propose an even more unpleasant explanation for it than the deplorable "no more than four" rule. Frank Robinson writes in *Extra Innings* that he and other black players on the Reds were suspected of being involved in some kind of clubhouse conspiracy a couple of years before he was bundled off to Baltimore. Here's how he tells it:

> As if I didn't have enough trouble that season [1963], some writers were reporting that Vada Pinson and I had formed a "Negro clique" on the ballclub. One wrote, "They say the two have formed a clique that is gnawing at the morale of the club… and that's why the Reds are not fighting for the flag."[5]

Now, ballplayers form little groups of three or four like any other band of human beings thrown together for long periods of time, from kids in a high school to soldiers in a platoon. Naturally, black players would tend to hang out with other black players after hours; no surprise there, since for a long time they couldn't room with a white player or go to the bars, restaurants, or movie theaters that served white players. Yet this particular kind of clique differed from others, whether it was represented by the Robinson/Pinson duo on the Reds or Aaron, Bruton, Covington, and company on the Braves or Alou, Cepeda, Marichal, and two or three other Latinos on the Giants.[6] It was the *racial clique*. The enduring aspects of segregation had forced it into existence, but it drew the majority's criticism for existing. It must have made a lot of players—and coaches, and reporters, and near observers—feel rather prickly, if not sincerely guilty. It was the kind of thing that wasn't supposed to be too much in evidence: people were supposed to be able to think that a corner had been turned, that long strides had been taken.

It couldn't have helped that Robby was inclined to speak his mind about things. There were a lot of those free-thinkers on the Cardinals during the Sixties, too—one of the National League's great revolving doors for dark-skinned ballplayers. Leon Wagner, George Crowe, George Altman, Ted Savage, Julio Gotay, Bill White, Orlando Cepeda, Alex Johnson, eventually Curt Flood... all of these and more came and went, and they sometimes went or came for each other in a trade. August Busch certainly didn't like some of the "uppity" talk he heard from his athlete-employees, especially those who began to feel their oats during the Civil Rights Movement.[7] I have already discussed (in Chapter Four above) how curious was the sudden disappearance of both Wes Covington and newly acquired shortstop Andre Rodgers from the Braves' roster (the latter before ever having an official at-bat in a Milwaukee uniform) just as their "clique" was starting to sound off about segregated quarters at the team's Florida spring training facility.

Was the desire to keep civil rights off the sports page also a motive force in the swapping of blacks for blacks? That is, did the very franchises which had most willingly accepted dark-skinned players on their squad come to fear that overly visible "cliques" might create the wrong kind of publicity? This fear, of course, could well have worked hand in hand with the "no more than four" rule, or could have worked in parallel fashion with it: one motive might have prevailed over the other during a given trade or on a given team, or both might have combined to persuade an owner that he needed to "shake up" his black talent.

I can't imagine that we will ever know the true reasons behind even a single suspicious pattern of trading. "Home" in baseball is more ephemeral than in real life by a factor of, perhaps, a thousand: everybody is always saying goodbye. History outside of baseball, however, offers many examples of an ambitious chieftain taking advantage of a battle to "arrange" his ally/rival's death in combat. Ganelon did something like this to Roland. As often as not, the manipulator delivers the eulogy over the brave warrior's grave. Some things never change. Beware of friendly fire.

★ ★ ★ No. 28 ★ ★ ★

Leon Wagner

LOS ANGELES ANGELS — OUTFIELDER

Ht. 6'1"; Wt. 194; Bats Left; Throws Right; Born May 13, 1934; Home: San Francisco, Cal. Receiving the Arch Ward Memorial Award for his performance in the second 1962 All-Star Game, highlighted the season for Leon, a season in which he established new major highs for himself in runs, hits, HRs and RBIs. In 1961 he led the Angels in HRs (28), one being a 473½ ft. tape-measure drive at Wrigley Field, then the home of the Angels. Leon was with the Giants in 1958-59 and the Cardinals in 1960.

★ ★ ★ MAJOR LEAGUE BATTING RECORD ★ ★ ★

	Games	At Bat	Runs	Hits	2B	3B	HR	RBI	Avg.
1962	160	612	96	164	21	5	37	107	.268
LIFE	493	1513	233	411	55	10	87	254	.278

★ ★ ★ No. 198 ★ ★ ★

Felix Mantilla

NEW YORK METS — SHORTSTOP

Ht. 6'0"; Wt. 160; Bats Right; Throws Right; Born July 29, 1934; Home: Isabela, P. R. One of the most graceful fielders in pro ball, Felix had his best year in the majors in 1962. Starting his career in 1952 with Evansville (.323) and advancing to Jacksonville (.278) in 1953, he was chosen All-Star shortstop both seasons. Felix played for Toledo in 1954-55 and was with Sacramento in 1956 (.272), before joining the Braves. He was drafted by the Mets in the NL expansion on Oct. 10, 1961.

★ ★ ★ MAJOR LEAGUE BATTING RECORD ★ ★ ★

	Games	At Bat	Runs	Hits	2B	3B	HR	RBI	Avg.
1962	142	466	54	128	17	4	11	60	.275
LIFE	546	1419	188	348	47	7	29	138	.245

★ ★ ★ No. 87 ★ ★ ★

Manny Jimenez

KANSAS CITY ATHLETICS — OUTFIELDER

Ht. 6'1"; Wt. 185; Bats Left; Throws Right; Born..................November 19, 1938 Home..........San Pedro de Macoris, D. R. One of the leading hitters in AL in 1962(.301), his rookie season in majors, Manny continued to hit at about the pace he did in minors, (batting .316 in 468 games). Hit .444 in 1957 in 3 games at Juarez and was released. Led Northern League in batting (.340) and received All-Star honors in 1958. Selected to 1959 South Atlantic All-Star team. Obtained by A's from Braves on Dec. 15, 1961.

★ ★ ★ MAJOR LEAGUE BATTING RECORD ★ ★ ★

	Games	At Bat	Runs	Hits	2B	3B	HR	RBI	Avg.
1962	139	479	48	144	24	2	11	69	.301
LIFE	139	479	48	144	24	2	11	69	.301

★ ★ ★ No. 197 ★ ★ ★

Richie Ashburn

NEW YORK METS — OUTFIELDER

Ht. 5'10"; Wt. 170; Bats Left; Throws Right; Born March 19, 1927; Home: Tilden, Nebraska Richie has twice led the NL in batting (1955 with .338 and 1958 with .350); 3 times in hits, 4 times in singles and 4 times (once tied) in walks. He holds the record for most years (9) with 400 or more putouts as an outfielder. After a year in military service, Richie came back for his second year with Utica in 1947, joined the Phillies in 1948 and was selected by the Sporting News as Rookie of the Year. The Cubs acquired him in a trade on Jan. 11, 1960 and he was later sold to the Mets on Dec. 8, 1961.

★ ★ ★ MAJOR LEAGUE BATTING RECORD ★ ★ ★

	Games	At Bat	Runs	Hits	2B	3B	HR	RBI	Avg.
1962	135	389	60	119	7	3	7	29	.306
LIFE	2189	8365	1322	2574	317	109	29	587	.308

A contrast in employer devotion: the oft-traded Wagner had a longest stint of four years in Cleveland   Mantilla warmed a Braves bench for years, then played five seasons for three clubs. Jiménezr received almost half his big-league at-bats in 1962. Ashburn's tour of duty in New York punctuated a Hall-of-Fame career with the Phillies and Cubs.

Note that the three players whose hands are visible have spaced them apart on the handle—Wagner very dramatically, Ashburn by about a quarter-inch. Leon and Felix hold the bottom hand loose so as to turn fast on an inside pitch, while Richie's top hand is looser, allowing him to reach for the outside pitch: a high-power versus a high-average strategy. Such ingenious eclecticism of technique was common in the Negro Leagues but often scoffed at by Major League hitting "experts". Negro League veterans often remarked that Ashburn played ball as they were taught to play it.

Manny's card, by the way, throws the quartet's symmetry off ever so slightly because I clipped it from the back of a Jell-o box, where the promotion was also being run. (Such cards were narrower and the stars flanking the serial number on top slightly smaller.) Willie Davis's card, reproduced later in this volume, was one of only three or four others that I so harvested.

1 The five players are (in order of their photos) Billy Pierce, Frank Bolling, Gene Freese, Joe Cunningham, and Roy Sievers. See Frederick Lieb, "Inter-League Swaps Produce Flags, Duds," *The Sporting News*, 17 November 1962: 3-4.

2 *The Way It Is* (*op. cit.*), 77. Curt goes on to recount that, during the 1967 World Series, Johnson could not be found to pinch-hit because he had retired to the clubhouse to make a sandwich.

3 From Henry Aaron's autobiography, *I Had a Hammer* (*op. cit.*), 216-218.

4 The Philadelphia Phllies were in fact among the last National League franchises to integrate. By 1961, however, the Phils had a particularly high percentage of Latino players in their starting line-up: Ruben Amaro, Tony Gonzalez, Pancho Herrera, and Tony Taylor.

5 *Extra Innings* (*op. cit.*), 54.

6 Leo Cardenas would probably have been tossed in with Robinson and Pinson: he had sided with them in a clubhouse shouting match with sportswriter Earl Lawson—an unfortunate situation which at last evolved into Pinson's smacking Lawson in the face and being charged with assault. The racial angle of the exchange would not have played well with the status quo, and the "clique" story might well have had its origin here.

7 Curt Flood gives the full text of Busch's very public rebuke of the team in 1969 (before dozens of specially invited reporters and outsiders) as Appendix B in his *The Way It Is* (New York: Pocket Books, 1972), 195-204. The dressing down is bombastically replete with trusting fans, the game's wholesomeness, and the good of the nation—all because Flood and others were insisting on raises. Curt does not suggest a racial side to this incident and the subsequent tension it fueled, but one can scarcely believe that such a perspective didn't occur to him. After all, the same Busch had made Stan Musial a "$100,000 man" toward the end of his career more than a decade earlier, and most of the "trouble-makers" now were rather darker than Stan.

VII

Black and White Lead-Off Men: Different Abilities or Contrastive Philosophies?

I confess that I had little idea where this chapter would lead me when I jotted down a kind of proposal for its parameters. No doubt, as I sought to ferret out statistically verifiable ways in which black ballplayers were especially valuable yet plainly undervalued, I followed a hunch that the category of the lead-off man would be promising. We all know about the sluggers: Hank Aaron, Willie Mays, Frank Robinson, Ernie Banks, and Willie McCovey. If Luke Easter and George Crowe had broken into the Majors earlier, we would probably be adding their names to the same elite group without hesitation. (Luke hit 83 homers in three seasons: George hit 31 over the one season when he played very nearly full-time.) All sluggers were household names, and big drawing cards at the ballpark. In the latter capacity, they were able to wring huge contracts from stingy, autocratic owners. Race seemed to make little difference here: in fact, the number of Caucasian bombers whose income matched Henry Aaron's by the mid-Sixties was quite modest. White sluggers were in relatively short supply. The list included Mickey Mantle and Eddie Mathews, of course… but after those two, the late Fifties and early Sixties ran dry of strong men who would one day top 500 home runs. Ted Williams, naturally… but Ted was strangely faraway to those of us who were born around 1955, as was DiMaggio. The Korean War had left a lacuna in his career, and he was practically done by 1960. So for Musial: he belonged more to the Forties and early Fifties. Stan was not primarily a home run machine, in any case: some of his doubles just happened to clear the fence.

Harmon Killebrew appeared on the scene at the very end of the Fifties. A one-dimensional slugger so unlike Williams and Musial, he offered little to dazzle the crowd *except* home runs. He had sprung straight from the mold of Adcock, Colavito, Kluszewski, Sauer, Sievers… all of whom had some very good "power" years, but not enough strung together for deification. Duke Snider barely managed to stagger across the then-magical 400-homer border of Hall of Fame country after his Dodgers departed Ebbets Field—and then had to wait years and years to be crowned an immortal.

Yes, the black sluggers are much the most recognizable members of the group. What this proves about racial discrimination in baseball is that home runs trump any social stigma. (Apparently they still do: all but the most blatant steroid-abusers from the Nineties are likely to be ushered into Cooperstown shortly: Joe Jackson and Pete Rose never had it so good!) Mays, Banks, Aaron, *et al.* had figured out the equation, though others who might have joined them either "wasted" their time trying to produce RBIs however possible (e.g., Bill White—and one might add Roger Maris) or just never quite found the properly demure, "aw, shucks" style in public (e.g., Leon Wagner, and later Dick Allen).

The lead-off men, frankly, intrigue me far more. Baseball is really about scoring runs, and these are the "table-setters" for the sluggers; yet surprisingly little consensus seems to exist about how a table should be set, so analyzing the lead-off job is immensely more complicated than tallying up home runs. Of course, I expected to find that black lead-off hitters stole more bases than their white counterparts... and so I did. This was true, in fact, by a laughable margin. Yet the consequence was not necessarily that they scored more runs, and hence were better lead-off men: the puzzle had far more pieces than that.

I think it is clearly true, even today, that good lead-off hitters are undervalued, whatever their race. The legendary post-season home runs of Bobby Thompson and Kirk Gibson were both preceded by walks, and Paul Molitor had singled ahead of the Joe Carter homer that ended the 1993 Series. Long balls mean much more if preceded by "small ball", and the lead-off man is the key to multiplying the slugger's contribution. Yet he never gets his due of respect. If a black man were first up in the early Sixties, did he get even less respect than a white man?

I would prefer to toss out some numbers before attempting to answer such a question. Let me say a few words in explanation of the following tables, first of all. They contain the stats that most people consider important when evaluating lead-off men. Without doubt, runs are the "bottom line"— but to score them you have to reach base, which makes on-base percentage (OBP) a high priority. Batting average (BA) is a major component of the OBP, but far from the whole story. Another significant factor here is walks received—and I included strikeouts along with walks because their pairing is a kind of baseball convention, though I'm not sure that striking out matters much at the top of the order. The lead-off man rarely has any base-runners to advance or drive in (remember: we're well before the Designated Hitter era), so strikeouts are scarcely different from any other kind of out. (The *way* the game's first hitter strikes out may indeed be consequential—e.g., swinging wildly at three offerings in a row versus taking a lot of pitches to let your guys see just what the opposing hurler's got; but I have no statistics to measure such variant styles.) Stolen bases, too, may be overrated for lead-off men, especially if a high number of steals is matched with a high number of "caught stealing's" (CS). I suspect that steals are most useful as an indicator of speed—for speed is the key outside the batter's box. It gets the runner from first to third on a single to center (or even a bunt down the third-base line), it brings him home from second on a bloop hit, and it even forces errors when an infielder momentarily bobbles a routine ground ball (a factor not reflected in the OBP, which excludes reaching on errors).

Naturally, we also have to know how many trips to the plate the hitter enjoyed; for if these are not roughly equal, we have no basis of comparison. They are rarely equal in my sample below, so I have provided a final index: Runs per Plate Appearance (RPA). For some reason, accurate figures for plate appearances (official at-bats plus walks, sacrifices, and the rest) are not always easily obtained, but I believe my figures to be accurate with the possible exception of a few overlooked safeties-on-errors. The EPA is a calculation of runs scored as a percentage of these inclusive trips to the plate. The measure has clear flaws: the best lead-off man in the world cannot make the hitters behind him do their job. But he would be the best in the world, surely, at making it home in an imperfect world, whether by steal or induced error or trick slide or lucky star.

In keeping with my method, I selected all the names below from my card collection (with the single exception of Lou Brock). I divided the players into two groups corresponding to the two seasons for which I had very nearly a complete set of cards: 1961 and 1962. Of course, my reason for doing this was not only to track the players' performance a little longer, but also to take into account the longer baseball season which 1962 inaugurated (an additional eight games). In some cases, I am certain that the players I chose regularly topped the line-up (e.g., Bobby Richardson and Lenny Green). In many others, however, I found myself having to select a player who seemed to have spent more of the season leading off than his teammates, yet spent far from the entirety of his at-bats occupying the top spot in the line-up. In fact, I quickly realized in combing through data that teams half a century ago juggled their line-ups to a degree which seems astonishing now. Trying to name a lead-off hitter for the Milwaukee Braves, the Baltimore Orioles, the Kansas City Athletics, or the Boston Red Sox was like throwing darts at a rotating board. Even Henry Aaron occasionally led off for the Braves, the Orioles auditioned a young Brooks Robinson for the spot in '61, and the Red Sox had far less luck with Chuck Schilling than they would with Curt four decades later. Where are Felix Mantilla, Bob Boyd, and Pumpsie Green when you need them? (Answer: waiting for the phone to ring.)

1961

	AB	R	SB	CS	BB	SO	BA	OBP	RPA
<u>Caucasian</u>									
G. Geiger	399	67	9	4	36	63	.263	.327	.154
D. Howser	611	108	37	9	92	38	.280	.377	.154
H. Kuenn	471	60	5	4	47	34	.265	.329	.116
R. McMillan	505	42	2	4	61	86	.220	.305	.074
A. Pearson	427	92	11	3	96	40	.288	.420	.176

	AB	R	SB	CS	BB	SO	BA	OBP	RPA
B. Richardson	662	80	9	7	30	23	.261	.295	.116
B. Robinson	668	89	1	3	47	57	.287	.334	.124
B. Virdon	599	81	5	8	49	45	.260	.313	.125
<u>African-Am.</u>									
Curt Flood	335	53	6	2	35	33	.322	.391	.143
Lenny Green	600	92	17	11	81	50	.285	.374	.135
Maury Wills	613	105	35	15	59	50	.282	.346	.158
Jake Wood	663	96	30	9	58	141	.258	.320	.133

1962

	AB	R	SB	CS	BB	SO	BA	OBP	RPA
<u>Caucasian</u>									
J. Adair	538	67	7	7	27	77	.284	.319	.119
R. Ashburn	307	49	7	6	55	27	.257	.373	.185
B. Lillis	457	38	7	3	28	23	.249	.292	.078
R. McMillan	468	66	2	2	60	53	.246	.336	.125
A. Pearson	614	115	15	6	95	36	.261	.360	.162
B. Richardson	692	99	11	9	37	24	.302	.337	.136
C. Schilling	413	48	1	0	29	48	.230	.286	.109
B. Virdon	663	82	5	13	36	65	.247	.286	.117
<u>African-Am.</u>									
Curt Flood	635	99	8	6	42	57	.296	.346	.146
Lenny Green	619	97	8	4	88	36	.271	.347	.139
Tony Taylor	625	87	20	9	68	82	.259	.336	.174
Maury Wills	695	130	104	13	51	57	.299	.347	.156

Several observations leap to the eyes (as the French say). One is that the black lead-off men overwhelmingly tend to score more runs than their white counterparts (with Albie Pearson providing the only real competition over both seasons). This impression, of course, is somewhat skewed because the black hitters in this small sample also tend to have more at-bats: we can straighten the matter out later by using the Runs per Plate Appearance. A cursory glance will also reveal that the black players are both more prolific base-stealers and that their base-stealing percentage is better. Speedsters Gary Geiger and Dick Howser, light-hitting Bob ("The Flea") Lillis, and tiny Albie Pearson had some feel for the sport: the other white players were lucky to break even at it (Richie Ashburn having slowed down in his final years). The black players do not necessarily have a better walk-to-strikeout ratio, a higher batting average, or a superior on-base percentage. There seems to be a very vague tendency in that direction—but we are also comparing eight players to four in both years, and several among the eight were trying out for the lead-off man's part on their way to settling into another niche. At most, we might say preliminarily that, if a black player were penciled into the top of the line-up, he had already given the manager clear reason to believe that he would perform well there. His promotion to so important a role might well be less casual than a white player's.

134

It seems to me that the black players' assets stand out most plainly in the stat which I have generated specially for lead-off men: the RPA, or runs scored per official at-bats *and* walks. Consider these benchmarks first. An RPA of .125 would mean that a hitter is scoring one run per eight plate appearances, or about every two games. A lead-off man would average closer to nine—or even ten—appearances per two games, yet this would still leave him unlikely to cross the plate more than once every couple of games with his .125. That's not very impressive.

We should to see something in the neighborhood of .140 or .150 as an RPA for a hitter in the lead-off position. (This would yield a total of around 85 or 90 runs over a full season.) If the RPA were in the vicinity of .200, then the hitter—especially a lead-off man—would be scoring very nearly one run per game. This has seldom been done, and very seldom indeed by the batter atop the line-up. Babe Ruth and Lou Gehrig own several of the highest single-season run totals ever posted (with Ruth's 177 at the top). Slap-and-run hitter Kiki Cuyler once scored 155 in one year, and Ty Cobb 147. Rickey Henderson and Craig Biggio both made it to 146 in one season's campaign.

Realistically, then, we would expect an exceptional lead-off man post a figure of around .150, and a superb one to arrive in the neighborhood of .175. On the tables above, the black lead-off hitters *are above the .140 mark five out of eight times* (with Lenny Green's .139 RPA for 1962 barely missing). In contrast, only five out of 16 figures for the white lead-off men break this barrier. Two of the five marks belong to the Los Angeles Angels' diminutive superman Albie Pearson (who stood an explosive 5'5" tall). One was posted by Boston's Gary Geiger, who frequently batted farther down in the line-up. The identical mark (.154) was achieved in a more legitimate lead-off role by the Athletics' rookie sensation (the AL's only rookie in the All-Star Game that year), Dick Howser. A broken hand limited Dick's 1962 season, but he could clearly have developed into a superstar: his 37 stolen bases more than doubled Lou Brock's rookie total!

In a kind of poetic justice, the highest RPA of all—black and white players together—was a whopping .185 that aging star Richie Ashburn eked out of a .257 batting average and a wealth of experience. A number like this is Aaronesque: Hammering Hank had a .193 RPA in 1962, when he scored a career-high 127 runs.

The other white players were mediocre to pitiful. If .125 were to be considered about average, they failed to reach this mark exactly half the time, and twice hit the nail of mediocrity right on its head. Bob Lillis and Roy McMillan floundered around the .075 range in 1961. In Lillis's defense, it should be said that the expansion Colt .45's had few big bats working farther down the line-up: Román Mejías did most of the club's heavy lifting that inaugural year. McMillan, on the other hand, had the likes of Aaron, Mathews, Joe Adcock, and Frank Thomas behind him. The big guys couldn't pick him up very often when he was hardly on base three times out of ten.

Which brings us to on-base percentage, the stat most often used to evaluate lead-off men. Albie Pearson reached base a stunning two times out of five to lead the pack. Elder statesman Richie Ashburn, with his shrunken .257 batting average, still managed to soar in the lofty .400 OBP region, and the upstart Dick Howser actually threw a bit of a shadow on the quondam batting champ. Harvey Kuenn, also the owner of a batting title but also on the decline, would better his .329 on-base mark over the next two seasons. In 1961, however, Harvey and the remaining Caucasian lead-off men were again flirting with mediocrity. In four spots, their OBP has failed even to reach .300 (and remember, this number includes drawing walks and being hit by pitches). The fleet Gary Geiger's figure is a mere .327.

Very near Geiger and Kuenn's level, we find the *lowest* values for the black lead-off men: .319 for the young Lou Brock (officially still a rookie in 1962) and .320 for Jake Wood (also a rookie in 1961). The remaining six figures never descend more than a few points below .350, with Curt Flood coming very close to .400 in 1961.

Time for the million-dollar question: *why* did black lead-off hitters so obviously tend to out-perform their white counterparts by all meaningful measures? Was it speed? Well, yes… but not necessarily stolen bases *per se*. Richie Ashburn could still swipe a base—but he didn't try much any more, and Jerry Adair or Bill Virdon would probably have left him behind in a foot race by 1962. I suspect it was more a matter of knowing when to use speed: how to tell instantly that a low liner would fall for a hit, how to see instantly that a fielder was taking his time collecting it… how to calculate instantly that a bad pitch had bounded far enough from the catcher to advance a base, how to reckon instantly that the third-baseman was charging a bunt hard enough that he couldn't get back to cover his sack…. Old-timers like Ashburn and Kuenn were smart base-runners. Somehow, youngsters like Howser and Pearson— and all of the black players named—had learned the same lessons, had listened to the more experienced ballplayers talk. Or maybe, in the case of the black players, they had learned by taking chances on "unorganized" teams where play was much less structured than in the white Minor Leagues. Yet none of this group had played in the Negro Leagues—and, of course, neither had Ashburn, Howser, or Pearson. One must assume, finally, that they had been encouraged in base-path daring by coaches black *and* white—by ballplayers of the old school—while other lead-off hitters like Adair, Geiger, McMillan, and Richardson played for franchises that wanted their runners to stay put and wait for a long ball.

For this informative irony must not be overlooked: most of the oft-scoring players (i.e., the ones with the high RPAs: a high OBP gets you on base but not around the bases) did not have All-Star sluggers batting behind them. Their impressive run totals are not the result of ensuing home runs. Bobby Richardson actually scored more frequently per at-bat in 1962 than in the previous year, when Mantle and Maris homered a combined 115 times. Mays and Cepeda had belted 86 homers over that same fateful Season of '61, yet Harvey Kuenn had crossed the plate only 60 times. To be sure, Lenny Green had Harmon Killebrew behind him, Jake Wood had Kaline and Colavito and Cash, Lou Brock (who was leading off when Ashburn wasn't) had Banks and Santo and Williams... but Maury Wills with the new-look, light-hitting Dodgers? Curt Flood with the Cardinals? Albie Pearson with the Angels? On whose bat were *they* coasting?

There is one more piece to the puzzle: walks—or walks and strikeouts, if we must honor the custom and take them together. And, upon reflection, I think we must. I think strikeouts in a lead-off man say much about his ability to get walks. You want your first hitter to reach base ahead of the sluggers, naturally, and a walk's as good as a hit; but working a pitcher for a walk requires taking a lot of pitches, and a close pitch on a full count can be called either way. In other words, by seeking walks, lead-off men are also leaving themselves somewhat open to strikeouts. It is the very rare hitter who can draw walks in three digits while striking out only a couple of dozen times over a season. Jim Gilliam could do it, and so could Nellie Fox—and so, in this group, could Albie Pearson and Dick Howser, or very nearly. Like Fox, Pearson and Howser were both of short stature. Their reduced strike zone helped them to get on base without having to take a lot of third strikes, in the process. Otherwise, the only reliable way for mere mortals (i.e., men less pesky with a bat than Gilliam and Ashburn) to avoid strikeouts on a full count was to put the ball in play, no matter where it was pitched: to get a small piece of it and hope that someone threw it away on the peg to first. Such was Bobby Richardson's approach—and, apparently, Bob Lillis's. Looking at their other numbers as lead-off hitters, one has to wonder if they wouldn't have been better advised to take more close pitches, pumping up their strikeout totals *but also their walks*. Jake Wood is said to have lost his place in the starting line-up—and this would quickly mean his place in the Major Leagues—because of his 141 whiffs in 1961. That tally, to be sure, was huge by the day's standard: but Jake also drew almost 60 walks, and he ended up scoring 96 times. Would the Richardson approach have served him better? If Jake had halved both his strikeouts and his walks to send dribblers to the pitcher, would the result not probably have been 80 runs scored?

Rookie Lou Brock's walk-to-strikeout ratio was about the same as Jake's, Lou being punched out very nearly 100 times, as well. His speed soon allowed him to correct the imbalance quite satisfactorily. Why did no one in Detroit put the same trust in Jake's speed, when he had stolen 30 bases during his first season in contrast to Brock's 16? For the fact is that these young men were not Bobby Richardson: either one of them could probably have legged out one dribbler back to the pitcher per three or four shots at it.

Discrimination? Young black players unduly penalized for their strikeouts? Adair, Geiger, McMillan, and Schilling all posted strikeout totals that more or less doubled up on their walks. Yes... but these totals never quite made it into triple digits. What I conclude from studying a very murky picture of a very complicated task—batting lead-off—is that black ballplayers were not cheated of recognition in this role *because they were black*. Instead, I think they tended to be prized well below their real value *because they played with a subtlety that the white establishment no longer understood*. Most white managers and coaches to this day do not perceive the latent contradiction in the battle cry, "Get plenty of walks, but don't strike out!" Even the players who magically manage to walk four or five times as often as they fan are not considered as good as gold: on the contrary, much of the baseball world seems actually to value the free swinger who belts lead-off home runs, going one-for-five with a solo bomb, over the little guy who goes oh-for-two with three walks. Just a few short years ago, how many Scott Podsedniks would Alfonso Soriano's annual salary have paid for?

How long did Richie Ashburn have to wait to be admitted into the Hall of Fame? How eagerly did Major League baseball work to create a home for Albie Pearson and Dick Howser? Both were released for good after approximately 3,000 official at-bats, both had swiped about 100 bases in that brief span, both played excellent defense, both had consistently walked about twice as often as they struck out, and both had an RPA of about .140 (i.e., they scored about once every seven plate appearances)—this despite being traded hither and yon toward the end of their squeezed careers and relegated to bit parts. Why the lack of esteem? Because they were scrappy—because they were not big bruisers who could batter down outfield fences.

Again, the prejudice here is by no means directly racial—but it does victimize those whose special aptitude is swift, creative play. In the Fifties and Sixties, the Nellie Foxes and Richie Ashburns were quickly vanishing: the players who bore the brunt of this prejudice against resourceful, dynamic play were black ballplayers. If they walked... well, anybody could walk! Eddie Gaedel walked in his one plate appearance, too (the dwarf hired for one at-bat by Bill Veeck). If they struck out... well, they needed more seasoning in the minors. If they led the team in steals... well, why take all those risks in front of Kaline, and why distract Colavito by scrambling around in the background?

The prejudice against "small ball" wasn't aimed at blacks—but it wasn't *not* aimed at them, either. The Major Leagues seemed already to be headed in the other direction when Jackie Robinson broke in—but they seemed to accelerate in that direction after his arrival. The lead-off man, who would exhibit Jackie's style *par excellence*, dramatized the shift in taste. Yes, Maury Wills and Lou Brock would become the toast of their towns... but Lenny Green was discarded far too soon, Jim Gilliam was nudged into obscurity, and Al Smith was forced to try to re-invent himself (not very successfully) as a power-hitter. Tony Taylor, the dark Cuban lead-off man for the Phillies, was known to almost no one outside of Philadelphia despite being for years an accomplished get-on-base-and-score type of hitter. And Tommie Aaron, who drew smirks for riding brother Hank's coattails onto the big club, had an RPA of .145 in 1962—the same year that poor Roy McMillan finally achieved something like mediocrity in the lead-off position.

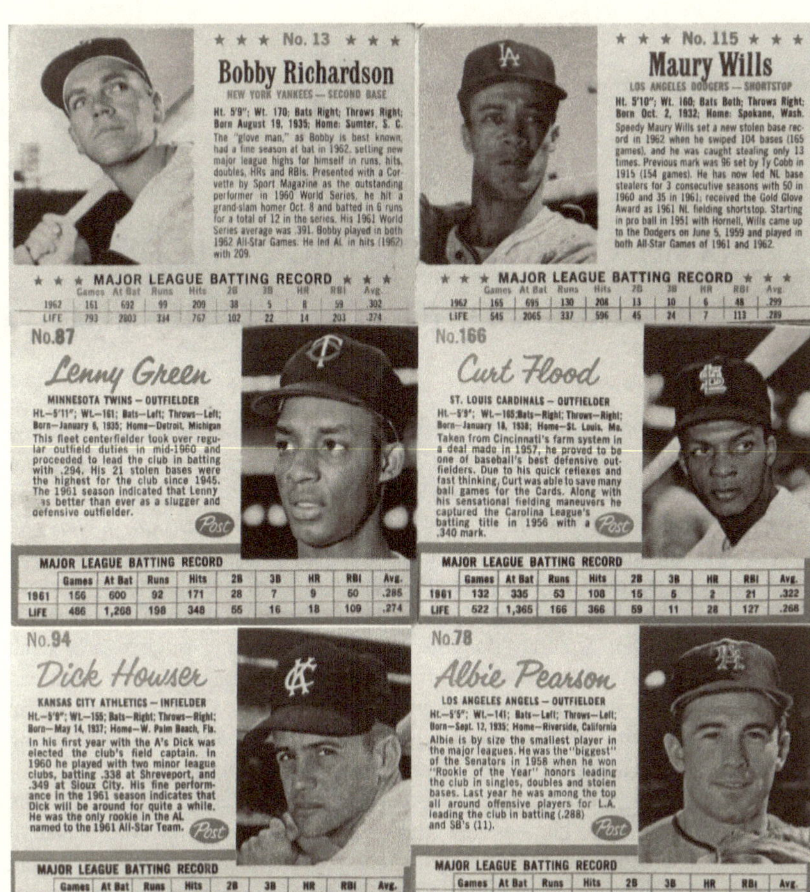

Richardson and Wills encapsulated the contrast between Yankees and Dodgers, National and American League: station-to-station versus punch-and-run baseball. Did Howser and Pearson, with their astonishing run totals for cellar-dwelling teams, play too much like black ballplayers for American League tastes? They vanished in a hurry.

VIII

The Careers of Black Pitchers: Close Calls Going the Wrong Way

For several reasons, the treatment of black ballplayers who entered the Major Leagues in the mid-Fifties and early Sixties as pitchers is harder to evaluate than that of black position players. For one thing, of course, the group of pitchers was much smaller than the group of position players, so conclusions must be based on a much narrower sampling and run a greater risk of being exaggerated. For another, the very nature of pitching is mysterious even to those who have worked at it all their professional lives. What makes a good pitcher—what qualities do you look for in a young pitcher, and what qualities do you assume will come along with time? Coaches and scouts can honestly disagree about a prospect's ability or potential—rather more so than in the case of a hitter. Charges of bigotry should not be made lightly... and with pitchers, we always seem to be feeling our way through a mist.

Consider the uniquely severe, usually suppressed strains on the pitcher's spirit. His choices are the center of activity on the baseball diamond—and often of the crowd's cheers or howls. How will a young pitcher respond as he is moved up to higher levels of play and larger audiences? How severely will he take a setback to heart? A rookie hitter who nervously swings and misses three times in his first at-bat has, in the worst-case scenario, squandered a relatively promising chance for his team to score. Other shoulders besides his will have to bear some of the burden in the event of a loss. If a young pitcher, however, nervously walks several hitters and then grooves several fastballs in his first outing, the game may well be out of reach for good, and the experience may well hang over him for days or months. It could conceivably end his career, especially if some important person already has doubts about him.

At least the scenario above involves real culpability, though perhaps assigned with an unfair emphasis. Throughout the twentieth century, pitchers were largely evaluated, even by the game's insiders, on the basis of wins and losses—statistics that can quickly descend into absurdity. If the young pitcher of the previous paragraph walks no one in his first three outings and allows no solid contact, he may still go 0-and-3. Maybe a lazy or over-aged or near-sighted (or personally hostile) outfielder keeps allowing bloopers to fall in, never incurring an error and thus leaving the pitcher responsible for the safeties on the scorecard. The youngster can acquire a bad rap that dogs him for the rest of his brief journey through the big leagues and lethally sabotages his self-confidence, even though his work was almost flawless.

No baseball card can quantify how such reactions have affected a pitcher's career. Only if he enjoyed a long run of fully occupied seasons can we be sure that, in his day, he possessed the focus and courage to endure the typical game's crises. Even a personal testimony from a well-placed source can seldom account for all the circumstances behind a celebrated arm's being traded or banished to the bullpen. Not only must we doubt our knowledge of the pitcher's emotional condition in such cases—we can't be sure, especially of decades-old cases, that we know his physical condition. Teams did not (and do not) want their competition to guess that the man on the mound wouldn't last long if he had to throw a lot of pitches, or that he wouldn't be torturing his elbow with a breaking ball any more than was absolutely necessary. In the Fifties, pitchers were even known to withhold such information from their own coaches and managers. Why give the organization another reason to replace you with somebody else? Some managers openly groused that they didn't like to hear about pitchers' aches and pains: the agony went with the turf, and putting up with it was part of pulling your weight. Here, too, the situation was different with position players. An adept base-stealer might hobble around before the game to lull the opposition to sleep; and if a hitter has a bandage on his wrist at the big-league level, you can be sure that he wants it to be a magnet for inside pitches.

For these reasons and still others, then, one can't simply glance at a sheet of stats half a century after the fact and be confident of having all the relevant details. I shall be looking at the statistics in this chapter, all right—but with diminished confidence. The best I can do is try to find trends; and, as I have already emphasized, I lack a sufficient number of subjects even to present any trend confidently.

I can make my number of subjects a little less insufficient, however, by beefing it up with the names of some pitchers not in my card set, but fairly well known to students of Fifties baseball. From my almost-complete collection, I drew all the black pitchers I could find—a total of merely four, since I was not including Latino hurlers: Bob Gibson, Sam Jones, Al McBean, and Earl Wilson. (McBean hailed from the Virgin Islands, as I have already noted, and hence was trailed by a slightly different bundle of prejudices— probably a more flattering one; but I needed all the recruits I could get at this point.) To this group I added Frank Barnes, Norm Bass, Marshall Bridges, Benny Daniels, Jim Grant, and Brooks Lawrence. That made an even ten: still paltry, but a starting point.

I was already surprised at this juncture that some of the names with which I supplemented my Post cereal honorees did not appear in the cards. To be sure, a few of the lot had departed the Majors by 1961; Frank Barnes had finished a brief career the previous year. Yet Marshall Bridges went 8 and 4 with the Yankees in '62, and Bennie Daniels 12 and 11 with Washington in

'61. Perhaps one can understand a middle reliever like Bridges not being able to find a place among the pen-striped heroics of Mantle, Maris, Ford, and Ralph Terry (who went 16 and 3 that season). But the Senators didn't employ very many winning pitchers the previous year (none in double digits besides Daniels). Post chose to recognize Dick Donovan for winning the ERA title with a 2.40 mark (and a record of 10 and 10—shades of Nolan Ryan with the Astros). That, too, is perhaps understandable... but why did light-pecking infielders Coot Veal and Billy Klaus, who hit a combined .215 in a combined 469 at-bats, deserve to grace America's breakfasts with their mugs more than Bennie, who worked over 200 innings? My suspicions were beginning to stir.

Then I discovered the most egregious oversight of all: Jim "Mudcat" Grant had been omitted from the nine players selected to represent the best of the 1961 Cleveland Indians. Post's designers had not allotted space symmetrically: the first-place Yankees occupied Numbers 1-13, the fourth-place Indians only Numbers 37-45. Vic Power and Willie Kirkland were featured, so one could not argue that black faces were being denied admittance. Would a third black have been one too many, however? Why else would Jim Perry have been chosen to be the only pitcher in the group, with his 10-and-17 record and an ERA of almost 5.00? Was it so important to find space for Johnny Temple, Bubba Phillips, and Chuck Essegian when Grant had posted a 15-and-9 record, leading the staff in wins while pitching almost 245 innings?[1] (Grant, by the way, did appear in Post's 1960 run of cards, so the ground of exclusion couldn't have been too personal.)

I decided after a little such rumination to cast this entire chapter in a kind of narrative form similar to what I have just used above, talking over each pitcher's numbers and his fate while jumping around among Caucasian pitchers who seemed to have about the same numbers but—sometimes—very different fates. I couldn't think of a better way to map a tricky passage through so much complexity. We all know that comparing wins and losses can be pretty unenlightening in the study of pitchers: the best pitcher in the world can't win if his offense produces no runs. The Earned Run Average (ERA), which is a ratio of how many runs score per nine innings pitched *without* the contributing factor of defensive errors, is more often consulted by analysts. Yet this index, too, has its flaws. We must not forget that in the Fifties and Sixties, starters were expected to stay in the game a full nine innings: most managers were happier to win 10-8 with a single pitcher than to use two or three pitchers in a less nerve-racking 10-4 victory. Pitchers in these circumstances might groove fastballs with a big lead just to spare their arm and let the outfield get some exercise. Several of the long flies might not be caught... well, big deal!

I tried to develop my own stat, which I called the BPI (Base-runners Per Innings), by dividing the total innings pitched into the sum of walks and hits. (This is essentially the same as what "sabermetricians" now call WHIP, or Walks and Hits per Innings Pitched.) I reasoned that the best pitcher is he who does not allow runners on base by any means, and that even the fearless aggressor who gives up three solo homers in an 8-6 victory knows what he is doing—arguably—better than the lucky stiff who wins 8-3 but walks ten hitters. Yet this stat really didn't tell me much, either, I found. Ralph Terry's BPI was an extremely low 1.19 (his number of runners per typical inning), exactly the same as Bob Gibson's... but what different pitchers! There is something to be said, after all, for pitching on or around the corners in certain situations and risking a walk—not that Gibson ever walked very many batsmen. Terry, however, seems to have thrown altogether too many pitches over too much of the plate, given what he was able to put on a ball. The *real* measure of a great pitcher, it turns out, is when he allows base-runners (with no outs? with two outs?) and how coolly he operates after having let them reach. Satchel Paige is said to have drawn the seven defenders behind him in around the mound on one occasion, bases loaded with no outs, and then to have struck out the side.

I simply don't know how to create a statistic for that kind of poise under fire. And so, in its absence, I shall proceed to offer a series of observations as we flip through baseball cards together: not the most objective method in the world, but the best I can do.

***

I shall begin with the pitchers who logged the most innings in their career and work down. Basically, we find three tiers: the hurlers who worked until they wanted to stop, protracting their success into the 15-year range (always a very small group); the players who hung around for a decade or maybe a dozen years, meeting with success in their heyday but usually having to wait long for their big chance and then—after a brief golden noon—having to accept bit parts wherever they could find them; and finally, the unfortunates who lasted a mere two or three years in the Majors. There are plenty of white pitchers as well as blacks, of course, in these latter categories.

If Hall-of-Famer Bob Gibson's career is compared with Hall-of-Famer Jim Bunning's, no suggestion that Gibson walked a rougher road in the Majors leaps to the eye purely from statistics. Indeed, it was Gibson, not Bunning, who was able to spend all of a 17-season career on one team. Bunning's 17 years were divided almost evenly between the two leagues, allowing him to become the only pitcher to win 100 games in both (which is really another way of saying that Detroit made a monumentally bad trade). It must be said, of course, that while Bunning had earned more loyalty from the Tigers than he received, Gibson had made himself simply indispensable. He was *the* dominant pitcher of the Sixties, taking them from end to end (i.e., considering that Koufax fell by the wayside after 1966). In his autobiography, Bob insists that he was never taken very seriously by player/manager Solly Hemus, no matter how compellingly he staked his claim to a starting role by excelling in spot starts.[2] There is no reason to think that Gibson was showing a thin skin in this matter, or that other young black pitchers were not similarly exhorted at pre-game strategy sessions, "You don't have to listen to this. Just try to get the ball over the plate."[3] Nevertheless, merit prevailed in Bob's case. Whatever inroads bigotry made into his early career soon met with dead-ends.

143

It seems to me very likely that Jim Grant's career was an entirely different story—the kind we would like to believe is just a fantasy in the minds of the over-sensitive. I mentioned just above the curious absence of Jim's face and stats from my Post baseball cards of 1961. I don't know why "Mudcat" would have been a target for cold-shouldering, unless for the very reason that he was a "threateningly good" black ballplayer. In *The Neyer/James Guide to Pitchers*, about the only comment listed under "Mudcat Grant" is the following remark by one Bob Swift, Washington Senators pitching coach: "… his curve isn't much and that Mudcat has trouble throwing his change-up."[4] This sort of inane disparagement from a has-been (or a never-was) nursing his plug from a fold-out chair in the bullpen is highly reminiscent of the insightful advice which Bob Gibson reported having heard so often on Solly Hemus's Cardinals. A major difference is that Grant never played for the Washington Senators: Hemus at least saw Gibson on a daily basis (even if he couldn't remember Bob's name). Unwittingly, James and Neyer have documented a rather widely circulated contempt for Jim Grant in the American League's tightly closed coaching fraternity. "That Mudcat", apparently, was that good.

As with Gibson, Grant's career suffices to show that his "isn't much" curves were usually more than enough. By 1964, Jim had won 67 games and lost 63 for the Cleveland Indians while working over 200 innings in half of his six complete seasons there. The Tribe had steadily drifted toward mediocrity following manager Al Lopez's departure after the 1956 campaign. In the first five years of the Sixties, only Dick Donovan had managed to better Grant's 15-win season of 1961. Nevertheless, the Indians hoisted Jim to the trade winds at the end of '64—and gale-force they were, taking him to seven other teams over the remaining seven seasons of his career. Yet despite being bumped to the bullpen, trotted out for spot starts, and thrust back and forth across league lines and into new surroundings, Jim always succeeded in pitching around .500. His 145 career victories were 26 games over the break-even mark. He struck out more than one hitter per two innings, and his walks-per-inning ratio was very nearly the same as Bob Gibson's. Mudcat might not have ended up in Cooperstown… but if used properly, he would likely have won 200 games.

How can I write such a thing so confidently? Well, of course, anyone can speculate. But if we compare Grant's 14-season career with that of the very fine Caucasian lefty Larry Jackson, we find that Jackson received half again as much mound time while struggling much harder to break even. Larry's 194 wins were only 11 games over .500. Yet the Cardinals and the Cubs stayed very faithful to him for most of his career, even though—like Mudcat—he posted only one 20-win season. He was always being given chances to come back and do it again (in fact, he *lost* 21 games the year after his banner season). While Jim Grant spent the second half of his career mopping up other pitchers' messes, starting no games at all in his final two seasons, Jackson averaged about 35 starts in each of his last three seasons.

Then there was Bob Purkey, a Caucasian righty who fiddled around with Pittsburgh for four seasons (logging under 100 innings per year), then became a workhorse in Cincinnati over the next seven seasons. Bob, too, had one great year: 1962, when he went 23 and 5. Otherwise, he seesawed between winning and losing years, finishing 14 victories above the break-even line with 129. Purkey walked few and struck out few. He gave his team innings—and the Reds teams of the early Sixties always had a chance to thump out a win with their heavy bats.

Was Mudcat Grant the best pitcher of these three? I cannot competently answer such questions, and my intent is not to make the attempt—but Grant was most certainly the only one of the three to be so quickly relegated to a supporting role after showing unmistakable signs of rare ability. Larry Jackson started over two-thirds of the games he appeared in, and Bob Purkey very nearly achieved that ratio. Of the 579 games in which Grant had some part, just over half were starts, the vast majority of these coming *before* his 21-and-7 season! Something's very wrong about the numbers here.

What to make of Earl Wilson and Al McBean, two of the period's best-known black pitchers after Gibson and Grant? Both lasted about a decade as Major Leaguers and both consistently posted winning records, but Wilson almost doubled the number of innings pitched by McBean over that stretch. This seems especially ironic in that Earl's Boston Red Sox had not exactly earned themselves a reputation for extending opportunities to young black players. Indeed, Wilson was rather famously traded by the Red Sox following a spring-training incident in which a Florida bartender vocally, abusively refused him service. Howard Bryant offers a thorough account of the events:

> His [Wilson's] mind was made up. For a redneck at the Cloud Nine bar to call him a nigger and refuse him service was degrading. For the Red Sox to tell him to cover up the story was cowardly. For him to lie to protect both was not only immoral, Earl Wilson thought, but also made him something he never wanted to be, the willing agent of a segregated order.
>
> The choice was clear. He would tell the press the story in its entirety. The Red Sox would now have to respond.
>
> The end for Earl Wilson in Boston came quickly. All it took was a hot Florida night during spring training in 1966. Wilson learned that the Red Sox weren't about to defend a black ballplayer against the customs of the South. The culture of the organization, from the front office down to the clubhouse, was not merely conservative, but was also still uneasy about the racial transformation in the game. Instead of the issue being one of racial fairness, Red Sox manager Billy Herman labeled Wilson a drinker and a troublemaker.[5]

So the Boston franchise had not changed its stripes… yet the record prior to this "misunderstanding" (as owner Tom Yawkey would have styled it) does not indicate that Wilson was denied playing time once he had logged what might be called a couple of "feet-wetting" years (the first of which involved being Pumpsie Green's roommate, since Pumpsie had to be paired with another black on the road). Earl may not have been happy in Bean Town, but he didn't want for work. By 1966, when he was dealt to Detroit, he had gone 56 and 58 over seven seasons, so one can hardly charge that he had been denied the permanent spot accorded to staff aces. After the Cloud Nine incident, trouble-maker or not, Wilson was also a workhorse. His new surroundings seemed to energize him, not surprisingly, and he proceeded to string together four winning seasons with the Tigers, including a 22-11 record in 1967.

Earl seems to me to have been handled approximately like many Caucasian pitchers of his day. Frank Lary and Ralph Terry broke into baseball a little earlier and stayed with it for about the same length of time. Both saw very limited action as rookies. Terry, whose inaugural outings were particularly unpromising, was "farmed out" by the Yankees to the Kansas City Athletics in order to mature (a common occurrence between these oddly associated franchises).[6] The Yanks brought him back in 1960 to post the first of four winning seasons with them, including a banner 1962 at 23 and 12. At the first sign of recidivism in '64, however, Terry was again discarded. "Yogi was the manager," confided Ralph later in an interview, "and he didn't think much of me."[7] He pitched well for Cleveland in '65—where GM Gabe Paul snared him in an unethical contract—but not so well for Kansas City and the Mets in '66.[8] I have no idea if his post-baseball life (as a golf instructor) was happier than Earl Wilson's: his pro baseball road certainly wasn't much smoother.

Frank Lary probably fared the best of the three in that regard: ten full seasons in Detroit, including a final two when the Tigers were very patient about his injured arm. Lary started 14 games in both '62 and '63 after having enjoyed more than 30 starts for each of the preceding seven years. Over those seven seasons, Frank won 15 or more games five times (over 20 twice) and never failed to log well over 200 innings (294 in '56). One could certainly argue that Lary had earned the 22 starts he received with five different teams over his final two seasons. His knuckler, curiously added to a brisk fastball and slider, made him a very rare commodity, and a resourceful pitcher always enjoys a little more longevity than the flame-thrower whose arm has aged.

In comparison, Ralph Terry received 11 starts after his last winning season, Earl Wilson 25. It's hard to find any sadder story here than the one where the old warrior doesn't know when to hang up his sword.

Earlier I mentioned Al McBean as impinging upon this group of unusually successful pitchers. To be sure, Al played for slightly fewer seasons (10) and pitched considerably fewer innings (just over 1,000) than the pitchers named above; but the stats suggest that he *could* have kept up with most of them, pitch for pitch—and also, I think, that he *should* have. I find strong reason to believe that Al McBean was not given the kind of playing time he deserved. Maybe it had something to do with his hailing from the Virgin Islands (a Caribbean, pseudo-Latin connection which often created better vibes in the States than being a native black). Maybe the feeling was that Al had more to learn than youngsters reared around America's asphalt jungles and semi-rural sandlots. If so, however, the prejudice persisted for a decade of proof to the contrary; and, in any case, such a theory can't account for Al's having started more games in his sophomore season than at any other time. McBean went 15 and 10 that year (1962). He would never have a losing season until 1968, when he finished a respectable 9 and 12 (ERA 3.59) for a Pirate team which was floundering about in the second division. That was enough for the Bucs. Two years, three trades, and exactly one start later, Al was out of a job. His career win/loss percentage stood at .573—24 points above Jim Bunning's and just 18 below Bob Gibson's.

In Part 3, Chapter 5 of this book, I muse upon the notion that certain organizations set their young black players up to do poorly. On the whole, such conspiracy theories strike me as too thin-skinned to muscle the reality of bigotry beyond the appearance of whining that it has to some. Charges like these are unprovable, and they also make no sense. Why cut off your nose to spite your face—why under-utilize good talent and lose possible Series money just to smirk at someone of another race? All the same, the Pittsburgh Pirates can frequently be found through the Fifties and early Sixties making very doubtful decisions about their black players. Al McBean's clearly reluctant deployment as a starter after his brilliant success in the role is one of these decisions. In fact, Al's 15-and-10 campaign was rewarded by only seven more starts the following season (which he parleyed into a 13-and-3 record by looking sharp out of the bullpen). The fatal 1968 season was his next—and last—modest crack at the starting rotation. How—tell me, *how*—does one justify sending to the pen a young gun who went 15 and 10 in his second year to make room for a newly acquired Don Schwall, owner of a 9 and 15 sophomore record?

By way of contrast, I might point out that Caucasian lefty Jim O'Toole started his career much less auspiciously than McBean, yet ended up having pitched 60% more innings than Al when his career, too, wound down after a decade. Jim's break-through year was his fourth (1961), when he went 19 and 9. He had only once reached the .500 mark before; and of his next three seasons, all featuring wins in the high teens, only one was not somewhat tarnished by an almost equal number of losses. O'Toole finished his career with three distinctly declining seasons, going a total of 12 and 20 over that period despite receiving 56 starts (i.e., having no decision about 60% of the time). His career 98 victories bettered his losses by 14—he was, overall, a successful Major League pitcher; but he did not win at Al McBean's rate (despite playing with a powerhouse offense), he did not mature as fast as McBean, and his downward slope was much more lengthy and charitable than Al's.

Am I saying that McBean was a better pitcher than O'Toole? No. Am I saying that he would have been better, given an equal chance? No, I cannot even say that much without being arbitrary. I am merely saying a) that Al was clearly not given an equal chance, and b) that his early career would have justified better than O'Toole's the granting of an indulgent chance. And by the way, the Reds stuck with Jim all the way through the ninth season of his career.

Sam Jones appears to belong somewhere in this group. His career of 12 seasons saw him complete about 30 more innings than Jim O'Toole, and Jim had only 16 more starts than "Sad Sam" (a sobriquet bequeathed by an earlier Sam Jones—but it seemed to fit Sam's meditative face). Yet Jones is actually unique among the black pitchers featured by my Post baseball cards in that he arguably should be classed with the first wave of African-Americans to break the color barrier. In looking at cases like his (which, strictly speaking, lie just beyond this study's parameters), I have often been struck by the suspicion that the "first wave" may indeed have had smoother rolling in some ways. These players were novelties, sometimes even legends, recruited (or rather purchased—or even heisted) directly from the Negro League teams where they had established themselves. Larry Doby, Monte Irvin, Hank Thompson, Luke Easter… the black fans who had thronged to see them play on the Kansas City Monarchs or the Homestead Grays now filled Major League parks to watch them play integrated ball. Owners were happy to put them on display, especially since there were as yet too few of them to make white dominance of the game seem in any way jeopardized.

Jones was also a very fair-skinned black man, which probably didn't hurt his Major League marketability. In 1955, after two years of rehabilitating an exhausted arm in the Minors, he became the first African-American besides Don Newcombe to pitch more than 200 innings (almost 242), a feat which he would accomplish three more times and for two other teams. His ability was of the intimidating kind (a lively fastball complemented by a legendary knee-buckling curve) which more reliably translated into high strikeout totals than wins. "Toothpick" (so called because of his favorite chew rather than his bodily frame) fanned almost a hitter per inning throughout his career, but also served up a lot of long balls. Bob Gibson allowed fewer than a third as many homers in well over twice the innings, Ralph Terry about a fourth as many in just a little more mound time.

Make no mistake: Sam was a fine pitcher. Though he finished his career only a game over .500, he went 39 and 19 in the combined seasons of 1959 and 1960. One could find Caucasian pitchers like John Buzhardt who lasted about as long (actually a season longer, in Buzhardt's case, though for fewer innings) while displaying less ability. In two seasons with Philadelphia, John went a disheartening 11 and 34, his losses tripling his victories during either campaign! It is true that the five seasons (two consisting of 200 innings pitched) granted to Buzhardt before his three modest winning years with the White Sox would have been awarded to few young black pitchers of the day, if any. But this does nothing to indicate that Sad Sam, in comparison, had much to be sad about professionally: it merely sets the stage, rather, for our final group of hurlers—those with careers of less than a decade.

These hapless might-have-beens may be subdivided into those who managed to struggle along for a handful of seasons and those who imbibed the proverbial cup of coffee. Benny Daniels and Brooks Lawrence both pitched about 1,000 innings in careers that included the last years of the Fifties. They broke in making few starts (very few in Daniels' case), worked their way into the regular rotation for a few seasons, and then tailed off and were cut loose. Daniels seems to have been given a thoroughly fair shake on paper. Despite showing no particular promise in four seasons of bullpen duty for Pittsburgh, he was obtained by the expansion Senators in 1961 and thrust into a starting role for his career's remaining five years. Only the first found him breaking the .500 mark, at 12 and 11. (As has already been noted, this was the highest victory total of any Senators pitcher, though not good enough to win Daniels a spot among Post's baseball cards.) Bennie tended to walk about as many men as he struck out (around one of each every other inning) and gave up an above-average number of home runs. Sportswriter Bob Addie opined that the one-time Senator ace "baffled his bosses with his often brilliant and then mediocre performances," as one can well imagine after viewing the stats.[9] It would be hard to contend that the Major League's discriminatory practices cheated Daniels: he would, at any rate, have to stand far back in line to lodge a complaint.

Brooks Lawrence was both an earlier pitcher and a better one. The truth is that he was rapidly worked into a starting role, going 15 and 6 in his rookie season. His sophomore year was as curiously curtailed by the Cardinals after this scintillating debut as was Al McBean's third year with the Pirates. Over the next two seasons, having been traded to the Reds, Brooks logged records of 19 and 10 and then 16 and 13 while working well over 200 innings in either case. Thereafter he never again approached either the .500 mark or the 200-inning milestone, though the Reds kept him around for two more seasons and part of a third (1960).

I confess that I cannot quite make Lawrence out. His three stellar years certainly lead one to wonder if the tank was truly empty when the Reds shifted him to the bullpen (in which function he saved 10 games during 1959). His career ERA stood at an unimpressive 4.25—but then, the Reds put up lots of runs in those days, and Brooks is the prototype of the Fifties pitcher who, cushioned by a big lead, would be left out after 100 pitches on a hot day to give innings. Was Lawrence, perhaps, troublesome off the field? Pitcher/chronicler and novelist-wannabe Jim Brosnan represents him as taciturn and somewhat distant. The Cincinnati squad was not without racial tensions, and Lawrence seems to have suspected that his victory-total stalled at 19 in 1956 because "Birdie Tebbetts didn't want a black man winning twenty games."[10] Tebbetts, by the way, was Cleveland's manager when Ralph Terry was suckered into an incentives-laden contract by Gabe Paul and then benched as he approached his magic number. "I'm the manager, and I'll pitch who I want," replied Birdie to Ralph's protests.[11] In other words, there's corroborating testimony that Tebbetts was capable of such conduct.

On the other hand, Lawrence's stats do not imply that he was overpowering, and evidence of an outrage done to him is not crystal-clear by any means. The case on paper is best made by emphasizing the cold shoulder turned to him in St. Louis after his rookie season (a stunningly rude payback for a job well done) and his obvious competence when pitching out of Cincinnati's bullpen during his "decline". His sweet-and-sour career could simply be the result of talent poorly assessed and managed—a practice which is quite color-blind in baseball.

What kind of career characterized the Caucasian pitcher of this period who worked in the Majors for just under a decade and racked up about 1,000 innings? Art Mahaffey finished just one inning shy of that round total, most of it during six seasons with the Phillies. Despite Philadelphia's perennial mediocrity, Art had a fine 19 and 14 season in 1962, and a decent 12 and 9 campaign in '64. At the peak of his career, his strikeout tallies consistently doubled his walks allowed, though he also gave up 36 homers in his golden 1962. Reviewing Mahaffey's stats, one readily discerns the portrait of a young man gradually groomed to start in his rookie year, mauled on the firing line as a sophomore (when the number 19 attached to his losses), modestly successful at last for about three seasons, and thereafter unable to sustain the confidence of his employers over two fragmentary seasons. The portrait might be titled, "The Average Career of an Average Starter". (Braves fans like me may notice the name "Steve Avery" scrolling through the back of their mind.)

Daniels, Lawrence, and Mahaffey all registered career ERAs of over 4.00. Don Elston and Carlton Willey finished under that mark by at least 24 points, though only Daniels' win/loss percentage was lower than theirs. Willey was used with a strangely sparing caution by the Braves for five years, then by the Mets for three. In only three seasons did he receive more than 20 starts, yet he recorded exactly one save throughout his career. James and Neyer quote a Fifties sports magazine as insisting that he possessed "a terrific fastball".[12] Perhaps this explains why he was held in reserve as something of a secret weapon; but then, the laser fastball doesn't seem to have vanquished many adversaries, for only Carl's rookie season would turn out to be a winning one (by the smallest of margins).

Don Elston, in contrast, spent most of his career as a bullpen specialist long before the role was widely recognized. In fact, the term "save" was first coined to credit him for his valuable contributions to the Cubs.[13] Only in 1957 was Don ever employed as a starter. His saves entered double digits for three straight years. Mr. Wrigley thought enough of him to keep him on the payroll for almost the entirety of his nine-year career.

Is there an instructive contrast here between the blacks and the whites? Well, a couple of oddities do spring out, as a matter of fact. Brooks Lawrence's case for having been dealt an unfair hand grows stronger when we view him in this company. Only Mahaffey had a career as brief—and Mahaffey simply never was the same caliber of pitcher as Lawrence, by any measure. One could protest that these two were starters and lived or died by a different set of rules than, say, a Don Elston; but the reliever was not a specialist in the late Fifties, only a failed starter, so the rules at issue had not yet been written. Or let us grant that Elston was used in an extraordinary role: why was his special contribution recognized while similar efforts on Lawrence's part went unrewarded? And what, by the way, was Carlton

Willey's role—Surprise Starter Deployed Every Other Week? The Caucasian pitchers in this group may or may not have been inferior mound artists to the black pitchers. My intent, once again, is not to argue either side of this question. It is merely to highlight what the record shows: that the white pitchers tended to have longer careers while throwing fewer innings, as if the test of fire to which they were professionally submitted had been allowed to cool a few degrees. In fact, Lawrence, like Al McBean, appears to have been allowed fewer innings *only after having proved that he could handle more.* The bullpen, in his case and Al's, became less of a hiding place than a dusty, stifling closet.

Marshall Bridges perhaps belongs on the fringe of this subset, a step away from the "short-termers". Like Lawrence, he posted seven Major League seasons—but they amounted only to 345 innings, about a third of Brooks' total. In a very peculiar career, Marshall never pitched more than 76 innings over a season, yet only once was he clearly employed as what would be called a closer today. At the same time, he was no Carlton Willey (who, though rarely seen, logged about two and a half times as many innings). The four starts given to Bridges by the Cardinals during his rookie season were an all-time high—he would start only once more in the remnant of his career! Apparently his having gone 6 and 3 in that initial campaign did not convince St. Louis's coaches or anyone else that he could do the job. Marshall may have been the Ted Savage of the mound, to judge by his stats: a universally recognized talent involved in a trade at least every other year (four teams in seven seasons) who nevertheless watched most games from the sidelines. The Yankees used him wisely as a reliever in '62, when he went 8 and 4 out of the bullpen with 18 saves, a respectable tally even by today's standards. Yet no team—including the Yankees—ever made the long-term investment in him which the Cubs had made in Don Elston. Bridges won over 60% of his decisions, but he stirred little interest anywhere. No black pitcher's handling in this era appears to me more suspect.

Don Schwall, on the other hand (he who displaced Al McBean from a starting role in Pittsburgh), was a Caucasian whose stellar rookie effort sustained at least a faint interest in his starting abilities for five years thereafter, though real trust wavered early. In fact, once Schwall's 9-and-15 sophomore season had reversed his 15-and-7 rookie adventure, Boston handed him off to the Pirates, where his 6-and-12 record in 1963 permanently tarnished his image. He never again received either starts on a regular basis or as many as 100 innings of work in a season. Ironically, Don dramatically improved his strikeout-to-walk ratio as he matured, and his modest seasonal records began to surpass the .500 mark routinely after his "demotion". The shot at a big-time role, however, had lasted exactly three seasons.

Why Ed Rakow was allowed to pitch sub-.500 ball as a starter for all four of his over-100-inning seasons is a baseball enigma. Rakow consistently gave up as many hits as innings, though he wasn't wild and usually had good strikeout numbers. The Kansas City Athletics, thanks to Charlie Finley's meddling, had little by way of offense during Ed's tenure with them: he would surely have fared better elsewhere. Yet if one views his seven years of Major League service (filled out by two seasons of barely hanging on) beside Schwall's, one cannot help but conclude that the wrong man got the greater chance.

And if one views both Don and Ed beside Marshall Bridges, one must wonder why the last never got an audition as a regular starter at all. Schwall was abandoned too early, while Rakow was trotted out to take lumps for an inferior team: neither of these brief careers gleams with the labors of balanced, competent grooming. Yet both men ended up having pitched almost twice as many innings as Bridges. Marshall was never sufficiently among the elect to fall from grace, never sufficiently pressured by a second-rate franchise for his mettle to have been properly tested. Perhaps unfairness is typical of Major League life. The undermining of Marshall Bridges' seven-year non-career, however, looks more like a work of sheer stupidity—of unoffered rather than unequal opportunity.

Rakow appears in my 1961 card collection. Why he, and not black pitcher Norm Bass, who in his Major League debut season had become the only member of Kansas City's staff with wins in double digits (11 and 11)? Unfortunately, Norm had no further occasion to take bows. The Athletics rewarded his team-leading performance (in what has become to me a familiar pattern as I review this era) by more than halving his starts in '62, no doubt disrupting his rhythm enough to make his paltry 10 starts ineffectual. At 2 and 6, Bass could be relegated to yet more restricted duty the following season. Having surrendered 10 earned runs in just under 7 innings to inaugurate his 1963, he was released. Another small chapter in the baseball tome, *How to Sidetrack a Promising Pitcher*, had been written.

Post's denying Bass a baseball card may well have been connected to race—but the game's negligence of him, surprisingly, was not uncommon in the careers of white players, either. Dave Stenhouse also pitched three seasons for a struggling franchise: the Washington Senators. One nearly break-even season (11 and 12) was followed by a reduction of starts and less than half the mound time, as in Norm Bass's case. Dave actually had somewhat better control than Norm. Was this why his third and final season included 14 starts to Norm's one, 88 innings to Norm's 6 and two-thirds? Both men probably deserved more instructive care and more foresightful patience. The fact remains, however, that Stenhouse's final shot consisted of something like half a season, Bass's essentially of one bad outing.

An even shallower cup of Java went to the Cardinals' black hurler Frank Barnes, who had one start apiece in '57, '58, and '60, and racked up a grand total of 36 and two-thirds Major League innings. It is virtually impossible to say anything responsible about Frank's potential, given such a dearth of evidence. His career ERA was almost 6.00 because, in 1958, he had endured a couple of rough, brief outings. His strikeouts and walks were almost even at approximately one per inning, and he allowed homers at no more than the average rate. If Barnes became another invisible man for reasons relating to his off-field behavior, then this, too, is invisible in retrospect.

We can return to the miserably operated Kansas City Athletics for an example of a Caucasian pitcher who was similarly jettisoned after two seasons. Jim Archer worked over 200 innings as a rookie in 1961, displaying extraordinary poise by striking out almost twice as many hitters as he walked. In fact, Jim's 3.20 ERA that year did not deserve to be matched with a 9-and-15 record. If the Athletics' deranged leadership realized this, the 1962 season betrays no sign of it. Archer received just one start, appeared in just 18 games, and worked just 27 and a third innings. He was the right man in the wrong place.

There is more evidence to argue that Archer was a fine pitcher than that Barnes was. Again, I insist that my purpose is not to say otherwise. The question I raise is this: when Major League baseball made dubious judgments about the talents of its pitchers, why did it do so while merely ignoring Archer's obvious merits *but denying Barnes a chance to demonstrate any merit*? Jim doesn't seem to me to have been wisely judged: why was a basis for judging Frank never created?

To recapitulate: Bob Gibson is on everybody's short list of great pitchers after World War II, and Sam Jones and Earl Wilson had pretty good Major League careers. Bennie Daniels suffered the hard luck of pitching for a miserable team in his brief heyday, and both he and Norm Bass were suspiciously snubbed by Post cereals when, despite leading their sorry clubs in victories, they were not selected to appear on baseball cards. But all the signs suggest that Daniels was no better than an average pitcher over the long haul. The cases of pitchers like Bass, Frank Barnes, and Marshall Bridges are more disturbing not so much because these young men offered more evidence of greatness than Bennie, but because they were given virtually no chance to testify to their talent through playing time. Bass's break-even rookie year impinges upon the patently "quick hook" cases of Jim Grant, Al McBean, and Brooks Lawrence. These men were indeed given a chance to show their stuff—and they showed it to great advantage. In all three of their careers, success was punished by demotion. Grant was nudged from the starting rotation very shortly after a 20-win season: he had dipped to .500 in the ensuing year, but his ERA actually dropped five points to 3.25. McBean was given only one more chance as a regular starter after his sophomore 15-and-10 performance—six years later—and he, too, was then saddled with a mediocre record only because of a weak offense and a poor bullpen. It's difficult to say why Brooks Lawrence's ERA was mildly inflated over 4.00 in 1958 after two powerful years as a starter—but, once again, this proven star was essentially put out to pasture for one season of indifferent success.

I have demonstrated every step of the way that white pitchers often suffered from the similarly arbitrary decisions of the ruling class—*but their suffering was rarely so abrupt*. A year of logging twice as many victories as defeats typically earned the Caucasian starter two or three more shots at replicating the feat. As for those like Marshall Bridges who were neither fish nor fowl—who were allowed to excel neither as starters nor as relievers—one has to wonder if they were not being paid so that black fans in the bleachers, scanning field and dugout for evidence of integration, could see dark faces spectating in uniform. The customers were no doubt somewhat satisfied by the prospect because it superficially hinted at progress. Strictly in terms of getting to play ball, however, the likes of Bass and Barnes and Bridges would have been better off if the Negro Leagues were still around.

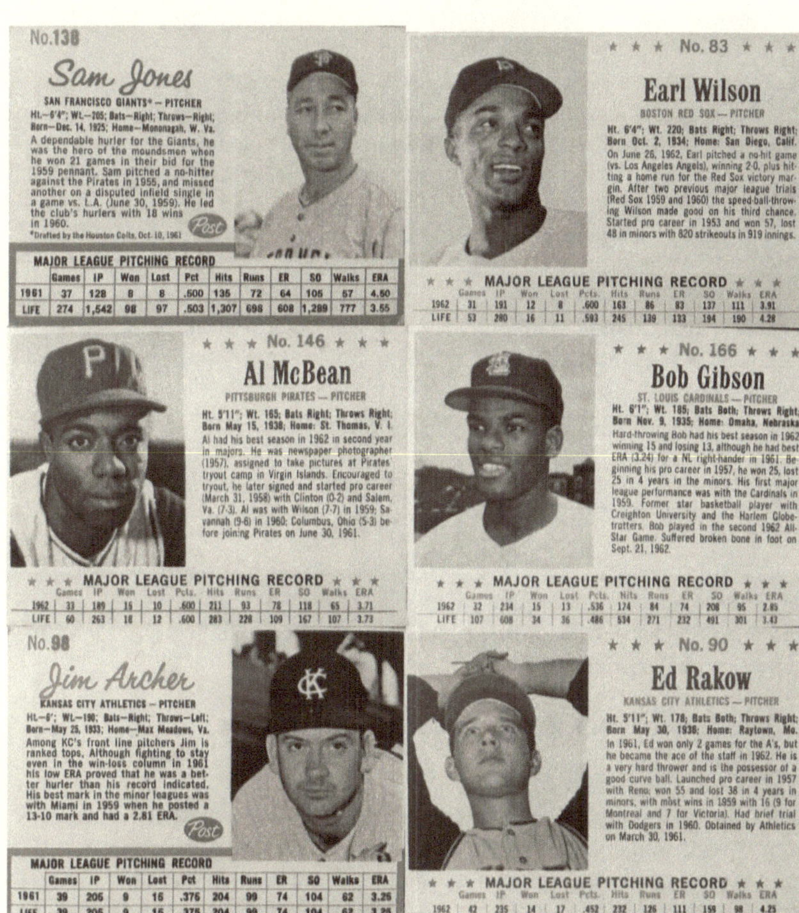

No.138
Sam Jones
SAN FRANCISCO GIANTS* — PITCHER
Ht.—6'4"; Wt.—205; Bats—Right; Throws—Right; Born—Dec. 14, 1925; Home—Mononagah, W. Va.
A dependable hurler for the Giants, he was the hero of the moundsmen when he won 21 games in their bid for the 1959 pennant. Sam pitched a no-hitter against the Pirates in 1955, and missed another on a disputed infield single in a game vs. L.A. (June 30, 1959). He led the club's hurlers with 18 wins in 1960.
*Drafted by the Houston Colts, Oct. 10, 1961

MAJOR LEAGUE PITCHING RECORD	Games	IP	Won	Lost	Pct	Hits	Runs	ER	SO	Walks	ERA
1961	37	128	8	8	.500	135	72	64	105	57	4.50
LIFE	274	1,542	98	97	.503	1,307	698	608	1,289	777	3.55

★ ★ ★ No. 83 ★ ★ ★
Earl Wilson
BOSTON RED SOX — PITCHER
Ht. 6'4"; Wt. 220; Bats Right; Throws Right; Born Oct. 2, 1934; Home: San Diego, Calif.
On June 26, 1962, Earl pitched a no-hit game (vs. Los Angeles Angels), winning 2-0, plus hitting a home run for the Red Sox victory margin. After two previous major league trials (Red Sox 1959 and 1960) the speed-ball-throwing Wilson made good on his third chance. Started pro career in 1953 and won 57, lost 48 in minors with 820 strikeouts in 919 innings.

★ ★ ★ MAJOR LEAGUE PITCHING RECORD ★ ★ ★	Games	IP	Won	Lost	Pcts.	Hits	Runs	ER	SO	Walks	ERA
1962	31	191	12	8	.600	163	86	83	137	111	3.91
LIFE	53	280	16	11	.593	245	139	123	194	190	4.28

★ ★ ★ No. 146 ★ ★ ★
Al McBean
PITTSBURGH PIRATES — PITCHER
Ht. 5'11"; Wt. 165; Bats Right; Throws Right; Born May 15, 1938; Home: St. Thomas, V. I.
Al had his best season in 1962 in second year in majors. He was newspaper photographer (1957), assigned to take pictures at Pirates' tryout camp in Virgin Islands. Encouraged to tryout, he later signed and started pro career (March 31, 1958) with Clinton (0-2) and Salem, Va. (7-3). Al was with Wilson (7-7) in 1959; Savannah (9-6) in 1960; Columbus, Ohio (5-3) before joining Pirates on June 30, 1961.

★ ★ ★ MAJOR LEAGUE PITCHING RECORD ★ ★ ★	Games	IP	Won	Lost	Pcts.	Hits	Runs	ER	SO	Walks	ERA
1962	33	189	16	10	.600	211	93	78	118	65	3.71
LIFE	60	263	18	12	.600	283	228	109	167	107	3.73

★ ★ ★ No. 166 ★ ★ ★
Bob Gibson
ST. LOUIS CARDINALS — PITCHER
Ht. 6'1"; Wt. 185; Bats Both; Throws Right; Born Nov. 9, 1935; Home: Omaha, Nebraska
Hard-throwing Bob had his best season in 1962 winning 15 and losing 13, although he had best ERA (3.24) for a NL right-hander in 1961. Beginning his pro career in 1957, he won 25, lost 25 in 4 years in the minors. His first major league performance was with the Cardinals in 1959. Former star basketball player with Creighton University and the Harlem Globetrotters. Bob played in the second 1962 All-Star Game. Suffered broken bone in foot on Sept. 21, 1962.

★ ★ ★ MAJOR LEAGUE PITCHING RECORD ★ ★ ★	Games	IP	Won	Lost	Pcts.	Hits	Runs	ER	SO	Walks	ERA
1962	32	234	15	13	.536	174	84	74	208	95	2.85
LIFE	107	608	34	36	.486	534	271	232	491	301	3.43

No.98
Jim Archer
KANSAS CITY ATHLETICS — PITCHER
Ht.—6'; Wt.—190; Bats—Right; Throws—Left; Born—May 25, 1933; Home—Max Meadows, Va.
Among KC's front line pitchers Jim is ranked tops. Although fighting to stay even in the win-loss column in 1961 his low ERA proved that he was a better hurler than his record indicated. His best mark in the minor leagues was with Miami in 1959 when he posted a 13-10 mark and had a 2.81 ERA.

MAJOR LEAGUE PITCHING RECORD	Games	IP	Won	Lost	Pct	Hits	Runs	ER	SO	Walks	ERA
1961	39	205	9	16	.375	204	99	74	104	62	3.26
LIFE	39	205	9	16	.375	204	99	74	104	62	3.26

★ ★ ★ No. 90 ★ ★ ★
Ed Rakow
KANSAS CITY ATHLETICS — PITCHER
Ht. 5'11"; Wt. 178; Bats Both; Throws Right; Born May 30, 1936; Home: Raytown, Mo.
In 1961, Ed won only 2 games for the A's, but he became the ace of the staff in 1962. He is a very hard thrower and is the possessor of a good curve ball. Launched pro career in 1957 with Reno; won 55 and lost 38 in 4 years in minors, with most wins in 1959 with 16 (9 for Montreal and 7 for Victoria). Had brief trial with Dodgers in 1960. Obtained by Athletics on March 30, 1961.

★ ★ ★ MAJOR LEAGUE PITCHING RECORD ★ ★ ★	Games	IP	Won	Lost	Pcts.	Hits	Runs	ER	SO	Walks	ERA
1962	42	235	14	17	.452	232	126	111	159	98	4.25
LIFE	96	382	16	26	.381	393	225	195	249	158	4.59

Same Jones was so fair-skinned that he was able to pass for white when the big team went south for spring training. Wilson was not so lucky: after complaining when a Florida bartender called him every name in the book for entering a white tavern, Wilson was traded from the Red Sox, who preferred to pretend that the incident had never happened. Gibson was among the Cardinal group—which included white players like Stan Musial and Ken Boyer as well as Curt Flood and Bill White—which successfully integrated training facilities in Florida. McBean, the Virgin Islander, settled in his happy-go-lucky way toward obscurity in the Pirate bullpen, one of the most underemployed pitchers of his era. But then, Jim Archer's talent was also poorly handled, while the less gifted Rakow made out relatively well. In some organizations, bigotry grew invisible behind incompetence.

1 Barry Latman was the only other Indian in double-digit wins to break the .500 mark. Latman's winning percentage was actually superior to Grant's (at 13 and 5), but he pitched far fewer innings and his ERA was twenty points higher. In any case, Barry—who was of Hispanic extraction—didn't beat Jim Perry out for Post's honors, either.

2 See *Stranger to the Game* (*op. cit.*), especially 52-65. Gibson writes, for instance, that Hemus constantly ran down young black players on the Cardinals, that he hurled racial epithets at black players on opposition teams, and that he once lifted pitcher Frank Barnes (see below) from a no-hitter as soon as Frank surrendered a walk in the fifth inning.

3 Hemus's typical remark to a young Gibson, repeated often and usually in front of many teammates; see *ibid.*, 53.

4 See Bill James and Rob Neyer, *The Neyer/James Guide to Pitchers* (New York and London: Simon and Schuster, 2004), 221. I leave the reader to determine what sort of authority should be attributed to an observation labeled with the verbal sneer, "that Mudcat".

5 The fullest account I have found is in Howard Bryant's *Shut Out* (*op. cit.*), 70-80. .

6 Wrote Bill Veeck in reference to the Athletics' first owner after their move from Philadelphia, "Until Arnold Johnson died, Kansas City was not an independent major-league team at all, it was nothing more than a loosely controlled Yankee farm club" (*op. cit.*, 280). Yankee co-owner Del Webb actually held the mortgage to the Athletics' new park when Johnson selected Webb's construction company to upgrade the facility! Commissioner Ford Frick seems not to have had the slightest concern about or interest in any of these dealings.

7 Tony Kubek and Terry Pluto, *Sixty-One: The Team, the Record, the Men* (New York: Macmillan, 1987), 190.

8 *Ibid.*, 191. Terry actually says he "signed a performance contract, which was illegal in those days"; i.e., he would get paid on the basis of how many games he won. He believes this led to his being benched.

9 Cited in Moffi and Kronstadt, *Crossing the Line* (*op. cit.*), 165.

10 See Henry Aaron, *I Had a Hammer* (*op. cit.*), 157. I discuss this allegation further in Part 2, Chapter 5. I do not believe it to be true, by the way—but that

Brooks thought it so already suggests a serious problem of communication on the Reds, probably undergirded by several racially-tinged incidents.

11 *Sixty-One* (*op. cit.*), 191.

12 *The Neyer/James Guide to Pitchers* (*op. cit.*), 426.

13 *Ibid.*, 196: "Jerome Holtzman, who was covering the Cubs in Elston's heyday, developed "saves" as a way of tracking Elston's contribution to the team.

IX

The Careers of Black Catchers:
Slow Beginnings, Uncertain Middles,
and Sudden Ends

It seems almost miraculous that any African-American ever started in the position of catcher during these years. Blacks were supposed to run like gazelles, suiting them perfectly for outfield work but not for squatting behind the plate. In fact, many a fine black shortstop or second baseman was transplanted to third base and thence to the outfield because... well, because the middle-infield positions required that one respond quick-wittedly to complex situations. A kid who performed the shortstop's duties tolerably well in the Negro Leagues (after all, *someone* had to play short on those teams) could hardly be expected to meet with the same success in the Majors. And if shortstop was out of bounds due to its intellectual demands, catcher should have been considered banned to black players *a fortiori*. The catcher has to do more thinking than anyone else on the field. He calls pitches based on the pitcher's ability, the scouting report about the hitter, the positioning of the fielders, the particular situation on the base paths and the scoreboard, the pitches seen previously by the hitter that day... a lot to remember, even for a white man!

Of course, Roy Campanella, the forerunner of all black catchers, wasn't exactly—or wasn't entirely—black. His name was Italian, and his skin was relatively light. (His mother was actually Caucasian, and his father's Roman surname clearly was neither imported from Africa nor adopted from some plantation-owner of yesteryear.) Roy was also a lively sparkplug, not a brooding, surly introvert or a heel-dragging farm boy from deep down South. He was born and raised in Philadelphia, and endowed with an urban Yankee's humor, savvy, and fire. No one had to worry about his raising delicate issues of race: he was "just another guy playing baseball."[1]

For other black catchers, however, playing baseball like any other guy proved extremely difficult. I discuss in this chapter the three black catchers—Earl Battey, Elston Howard, and John Roseboro—who appear in my Post cereal cards from the 1961-62 collections. Other than this trio and Campanella, I have managed to unearth only five dark-skinned catchers (i.e., including Latinos who were treated like American blacks) on the rosters of Major League ball clubs during the Fifties: Sam Hairston, Ray Noble, Valmy Thomas, Quincy Trouppe, and Charlie White. (Noble was from Cuba, Thomas from the Virgin Islands.) If one subtracts Thomas's whopping total of 626 career at-bats, the remaining four of this group garnered a sum of 381 official trips to the plate in their combined big-league experience. Hairston visited the plate five times, Trouppe 10. (Not that it matters... but Sam collected a single and a double, for an average of .400.) As tough as it was to break into the Majors as a young black outfielder in the Fifties, catchers obviously had a much longer shot at success. Even Valmy Thomas's 600+ at-bats were stretched out over five years: 88 was his highest total during any single season—meaning that he spent a lot of time playing the late innings of relatively secure or unimportant games in order to give the first-stringer a break.

In fact, this profile of the catcher who logs only about twice as many at-bats as games-appeared-in is widespread among the five obscure figures mentioned just above, as well as being reflected in the early big-league careers of Battey, Howard, and Roseboro. In his rookie season (and only real year in the Majors), Charlie White had just 93 plate appearances in 50 games. Sam Hairston collected his five at-bats in four games, and Quincy Trouppe his 10 at-bats in six games! Catchers, of course, tend to hit at the bottom of the order, and hence normally bat less often per game than other players. They typically spend more time on defensive drills (and so less in the batting cage) than their teammates, they are usually slower than other players, and they also tend to grow wearier than anyone except—just maybe—the pitcher as the game wears on. All of these factors render them less effective hitters who bat seventh or eighth in the line-up. Nevertheless, I regard it as very symptomatic that the young Earl Battey received seven at-bats over five games in 1955, whereas rookie Caucasian catcher Ed Bailey had eight official plate trips during a mere two games in 1953. (Both drew one walk.) It looks very much as though Ed started the two games in which he appeared, while Earl was squeezed into the final innings of his five games without a single start.

The truth is that a catcher can be sandbagged by a manager who doesn't really want to play him a lot easier than any other position-player. Warming up pitchers before and during games is a thankless, arduous chore in which the *persona non grata* can be employed day after day, week after week, under the pretext of getting him accustomed to the way various members of the staff throw. The position really does require a great deal of study—more than any other on the field. Even a young pitcher can explode upon the Major League scene if he has an extraordinary fastball (though these rising stars usually turn into comets, vanishing after a season or two of brilliance). Valmy Thomas played for a different team over each of his five seasons, always as a back-up to the starting catcher—and no one could ever compellingly challenge his treatment, because that's what a great many Major League catchers do: back up other catchers. Earl Battey might well have passed most of his career playing second fiddle to Sherman Lollar if the White Sox had not traded him to the Twins. John Roseboro would probably have spent two or three more years being Campanella's understudy but for Roy's paralyzing car wreck over the 1957-58 off-season. Elston Howard, having passed several years in the Minors as the Yankees dragged their heels toward integration, was actually the exception in receiving about half the big team's starts at catcher when finally called up. That Yogi Berra was that rarest of creatures, a good-hitting catcher, and was hence too valuable to wear out behind the plate may have had much to do with Howard's intense baptism of fire: Yogi was playing a lot of left field by this time.

Yet the steep learning curve notwithstanding, it does seem as though Caucasian catchers of the day were able to graduate to a starting position rather more quickly than black catchers. I have also found evidence that the former were more likely to linger in the big leagues than the latter. An aging white receiver, his knees aching and his fingers arthritic from years of abuse, might well be thought a worthwhile investment during his twilight years. He could spell the new young star every third or fourth day behind the plate, he could work with youngsters in the bullpen, and he could take the occasional pinch-hitting assignment. Black catchers, in contrast, did not enjoy much of a dusk, no matter how glorious their career. Once they couldn't catch about half the season's games, they were cleaning out their locker.

The statistical evidence I have is admittedly slender, based on a necessarily small sampling: Battey, Howard, and Roseboro. The Forgettable Five I mentioned would perhaps not be fair witnesses: because their careers were indeed so extremely brief, we know in advance that their entrances were humble and their exits sudden. As in the previous chapter about pitchers, then, I propose to develop the point by selecting a few Caucasian catchers from among the Post baseball cards for 1961 and 1962 and contrasting these with the three black catchers enrolled in those cards. I shied away from choosing obscure candidates like Dick Brown or Haywood Sullivan or Joe Pignatano, since Battey, Howard, and Roseboro were exceptional both defensively and offensively. (They would indeed be Hall-of-Fame material, in my opinion, if the Committee properly acknowledged defensive contributions.)

I emerged, then, with five white catchers who were all considered good hitters as well as excellent receivers, and whose careers typically ran about a dozen seasons, never a mere three or four: Ed Bailey, Smoky Burgess, Clay Dalrymple, Sherman Lollar, and Johnny Romano. This is already a pretty disparate group. Dalrymple rarely hit for high average, Romano actually managed only 10 seasons, and Burgess and Lollar played a stunning 18 seasons in some capacity or other. Yet perhaps disparity in this context is desirable: that is, having found five non-black catchers who were respected in their day, perhaps I have groped my way closer to the consequences of their *not being black* if their careers have certain similarities within such difference.

The table below contrasts the first two seasons and the last two seasons played by my group of black catchers and white catchers. I have added Valmy Thomas and Charlie White to the group of blacks, though Charlie's big-league career only included two seasons and Valmy (like Ray

Noble) is open to the suspicion of having been treated or viewed a little differently because of his Caribbean connection. I have created columns for games played and for at-bats because, as I have already explained, a catcher can be used rather extensively on defense without being given many occasions to hit (and a paucity of plate appearances, besides, strongly implies that the catcher was not usually a starter, but an insertion during the late innings). I've also provided batting averages and slugging percentages just to substantiate that the white catchers don't seem to have received more playing time earlier—or to have been granted a few at-bats well into their decline—because they were better or more powerful hitters.

In the final column, which is perhaps the most meaningful, I have listed the players' plate appearances per game. (Plate appearances [PA] include all official at-bats as well as walks, reaching on errors, sacrifices, and every other possible result of standing in a batter's box.) This brings the fact to which I hearkened earlier in parentheses out in the open: that is, the figure confronts us with something like objective evidence that black and white catchers tended not to be starters at corresponding points in their careers. Black catchers often "filled in around the edges" for two or three years; if they survived beyond that point, they might well receive about 300 at-bats per season right up until their final year. White catchers, in contrast, often found their way into the starting role more quickly; and upon aging, they might well be kept around in some scaled-down capacity for a couple of years beyond their last full campaign.

Relatively subtle stats like plate appearances, by the way, were often unavailable for more obscure players when I began this study. I have updated my figures, but I sometimes emphasize at-bats because, half a century ago (and perhaps twenty years ago), reaching base through a walk was considered a pitcher's failure rather than a hitter's success. Yet dividing the number of games played into the number of at-bats alone produces a much less revealing statistic than my PAG (Plate Appearances per Game). For one thing, some have argued that the first black ballplayers were frequently hit by pitches (see Part 3, Chapter 5, under "beanball"); and for another, catchers often bat eighth in the line-up so that they have more time to rest their legs during the game. In pre-DH baseball, this means that they hit just before the pitcher... which means, in turn, that they may often have been pitched around. To ignore the tally of walks that the eighth-slot hitter draws would be to deflate his activity at the plate by perhaps fifteen or twenty percent.

I also realize that a heavy hitter in a rather light-hitting line-up is likely to bat farther up and hence have more trips to the plate per game. In a season when both started regularly, Elston Howard would amass dozens more plate appearances than Clay Dalrymple just because Elston would often bat in the heart of the order. Excepting him, however—and John Romano at his peak—none of these catchers remotely approached the Yogi Berra or Johnny Bench caliber of slugger. In very practical terms, a catcher who starts a good bit of the time should have around three plate-appearances per game—the minimal number of times any player in the line-up can bat unless he is lifted.

The distance above or below 3.00 of the PAG number should therefore reliably indicate to what degree a given catcher was allowed to play full-time or to what degree he was slipped in for a couple of innings here and there. I think my figures are sufficiently sound to support a few generalizations of this sort.

FIRST SEASON

	GAMES	PA	B. AVG	SLG.%	PA/G
black catchers					
Earl Battey	5	9	.286	.286	1.80
Elston Howard	97	306	.290	.477	3.15
John Roseboro	35	79	.145	.261	2.26
Valmy Thomas	88	262	.249	.390	2.98
Charlie White	50	93	.237	.312	1.86
white catchers					
Ed Bailey	2	9	.375	.500	4.50
Smoky Burgess	22	60	.268	.321	2.73
Clay Dalrymple	84	180	.272	.411	2.14
Sherman Lollar	28	70	.233	.288	2.50
John Romano	4	8	.286	.286	2.00

SECOND SEASON

	GAMES	PA	B. AVG	SLG.%	PA/G
black catchers					
Earl Battey	4	5	.250	.250	1.25
Elston Howard	98	316	.262	.362	3.22
John Roseboro	114	431	.271	.456	3.78
Valmy Thomas	63	160	.259	.357	2.54
Charlie White	12	30	.233	.267	2.50
white catchers					
Ed Bailey	73	223	.197	.388	3.04
Smoky Burgess	94	238	.251	.315	2.53
Clay Dalrymple	129	432	.220	.294	3.35
Sherman Lollar	11	33	.219	.375	3.00
John Romano	53	153	.294	.468	2.89

PENULTIMATE SEASON

	GAMES	PA	B. AVG	SLG.%	PA/G
black catchers					
Earl Battey	115	412	.255	.327	3.58
Elston Howard	108	129	.178	.244	1.19
John Roseboro	115	406	.263	.321	3.53
Valmy Thomas	8	18	.063	.063	2.25
Charlie White	--	--	--	--	--

<u>white catchers</u>

	GAMES	PA	B. AVG	SLG.%	PA/G
Ed Bailey	90	187	.230	.348	2.08
Smoky Burgess	79	80	.313	.388	1.01
Clay Dalrymple	13	40	.219	.344	3.08
Sherman Lollar	84	256	.268	.350	3.05
John Romano	122	395	.231	.404	3.24

L A S T   S E A S O N

	GAMES	PA	B. AVG	SLG.%	PA/G
<u>black catchers</u>					
Earl Battey	48	123	.165	.211	2.56
Elston Howard	71	229	.241	.335	3.23
John Roseboro	46	104	.233	.314	2.26
Valmy Thomas	27	92	.209	.314	3.41
Charlie White	--	--	--	--	--
<u>white catchers</u>					
Ed Bailey	5	4	.000	.000	0.80
Smoky Burgess	77	76	.133	.250	0.99
Clay Dalrymple	23	67	.204	.286	2.91
Sherman Lollar	35	83	.233	.288	2.37
John Romano	24	71	.121	.138	2.96

First of all, let's get the hitting out of the way. Whatever we are going to find out in these tables is *not* that weaker hitters were justly punished with demotion or dismissal. Elston Howard and Earl Battey, at the end of distinguished careers which saw them appearing in several All-Star Games, slipped below the dreaded Mendoza Line (a .200 batting average) one time apiece (.178 and .163): otherwise, no black catcher in this group with at least 100 plate appearances ever failed to hit above .200. The same is not quite true of the white catchers: Ed Bailey once hit .197 in well over 200 plate appearances—and this in his sophomore season! Of course, Ed was an exceptional catcher defensively, and would also bounce back to be a formidable offensive producer. If a black player, however, had made such a stumble in his sophomore year, it might well have been his last miscue. Charlie White's second-season .233, in only 30 trips to the plate (remember: these figures above include walks, sacrifices, and hits-by-pitches), was apparently part of what motivated his permanent exile from the Major Leagues.

Nor were the black catchers deficient in slugging ability (i.e., the manufacture of extra-base hits). Of first-year catchers with more than 100 plate trips, only Elston Howard and Clay Dalrymple achieved a .400 slugging percentage—and Howard excelled Dalrymple by a large margin while also having about half again as many turns at bat. (N.B.: a high proportion of extra-base hits is often the somewhat artificial result of few plate appearances, though more appearances favor a finer batting eye and higher average. The argument for discounting R.C. Stevens' 7 homer in 92 at-bats, for instance,

163

would be that he caught fire for a short span.) Among sophomore seasons, John Roseboro's and John Romano's stand out for surpassing the .400 slugging mark. This time the white player edges out the black player; but Rosey's plate appearances more than doubled Johnny's total. Romano would eventually come into his own as one of his day's sluggingest catchers (if you'll excuse the odd superlative). His next-to-last season shows him still plugging away at slugging, all alone in the .400 range. Yet his fall-off in his final season was precipitous—so much so, indeed, that it gave him the shortest career of any of my list's regularly starting catchers.

So the bat was never really a problem in this group unless it combined with the additional problems of age... or let us say, rather, that when these catchers were young, a concern about offense would have been raised only as a fulcrum upon which to pry an unwanted player loose. The catcher's first and last duty is to his defensive work, and these men were all polished receivers. How carefully were they rehearsed for the role? Very carefully indeed, in Earl Battey's case. Battey appeared in just nine games over his first two seasons. The truly odd thing about his situation was that Earl was supposed to have been Sherman Lollar's understudy—yet the White Sox proceeded to call up John Romano in 1958, two seasons prior to trading both Earl and Johnny! Bill Veeck loved a trade, and he had apparently decided (rightly, as it turned out) that Sherm was good for a few more years. It should be stressed that Veeck's wheeling and dealing wrenched both younger men free of a log jam in which their careers were stagnating. Pitcher Barry Latman recalled of his White Sox days, "Battey and Romano had to get all their signs from [Manager Al] Lopez, but Lollar was on his own and called a good game."[2] It was clearly time to break loose: Battey, especially, might have remained a marionette behind the plate for another two or three years.

To be sure, Lollar himself was brought along slowly: such was the norm in the Forties and early Fifties. His 11 sophomore games are the lowest total for any white catcher in the group. Yet the other four catchers more than make up for his employer's diffidence. In the second year of Major League service, Caucasian receivers in my sample appeared in 360 games; black catchers appeared in only 291. Recall that the black sample is already distorted by the peculiar situations of Elston Howard and Johnny Roseboro. Howard, having logged a great many Minor League seasons, came to a Yankee club which a) wanted to placate the public outcry against its segregation, and b) desperately needed the aging Yogi Berra's bat in its ever more lightweight line-up. Roseboro was catapulted into the starting role by Roy Campanella's career-ending crash into a telephone pole. But for these anomalous circumstances, both players might have followed a path of development much more like Battey's—or even like Charlie White's, if not Sam Hairston's and Quincy Trouppe's.[3] Dalrymple was not replacing any superstar when he caught most of the Phillies' games in his second season; neither were Bailey and Burgess when they appeared, as sophomores, in about half of their club's games. The disparity in second-year playing time is real, and its size in spite of Howard's and Roseboro's special circumstances seems to preclude pure accident.

I find it fascinating that the proportions are completely reversed as the players near the end of their career. In the next-to-last season, only Valmy Thomas did not appear in at least 100 games among the black catchers (Charlie White having already made his exit). Among the Caucasian catchers, all are embarked upon a much more gradual descent to retirement except for John Romano—whose career, frankly, looks like a black player's from several standpoints. During the last season of active duty, the disparity in playing time grows even more remarkable. Despite the absence of Charlie White from their midst, the black catchers still surpass the white catchers in number of games appeared in by a count of 192 to 164—about a 20% difference. The gap in plate appearances is yet more striking. None of the white catchers would come near the 100 mark over that final season—but only the hapless Thomas failed to sail past a century of plate appearances among the black catchers, and Elston Howard surpassed 200.

This, you might say to yourself, is a good sign: it took the black players a while to achieve equal recognition, but at last—as receivers, anyway—they are being prized even more than white players. Well... I doubt that Battey, Howard, and Roseboro would take quite that view if you could question them. (You can no longer do so in this life: all have completed their final earthly season.) A ballplayer, like anyone else, wants to work as long as he can: a paycheck is a paycheck. The white catchers tended to be considered valuable members of the team even when they could rarely start a game because of injury and age. Their wealth of expertise was a treasure trove whose riches could be lavished on young pitchers and upcoming catchers. The black receivers, in contrast, were not good for much of anything when they could no longer take a beating behind the plate every other day. Old white warhorses were put out to stud: old black warhorses were packed off to the glue factory. I know that my apothegmatic verdict isn't quite fair based on a small sample... but that's the direction in which this hazy evidence points.

That the black catchers were in fact starting a good many games late in their career—just as they were *not* starting as often as whites early on—is suggested by the final statistic, the plate appearances per game. Let us go back to the first-season record of each player. Among the Caucasian catchers, only John Romano almost drops below 2.00 PAGs on average; among the black catchers, two fall short of this mark. Things even out in the sophomore campaign; indeed, only Earl Battey is not well into the range above two plate trips per game. Even the ill-starred Charlie White was averaging exactly two and a half plate appearances per game now, which implies that he was starting a healthy number of the games.

Of course, Charlie's second season was also his last, so the generous allotment of playing time during this year may have been the kiss of death. The total of games in which White appeared also shows a stiff drop now over the rookie season. That is, Charlie seems to have started more often in his second year but also to have played far less, as if management were preparing to say to the public, "There, you see? We let the guy start 10 games, and he's still poking around in the .230's. He's just not going to make it."

Whether Valmy Thomas had "made it" as he approached his penultimate season (only one removed from his second season), his plate trips per game were very curtailed by that point, and in none of his big-league years did he appear in fewer games. Valmy visited a new team every year: perhaps the Orioles simply had nothing for him to do but take towels to the bullpen. Battey and Roseboro are both comfortably over the 3.00-PAG mark at this stage and batting above .250; it's the explosive Howard who appears to have hit the skids. The same two (Battey and Roseboro) easily surpass all the white catchers in trips to the plate per game; the fast-fading Elston Howard even beats out Smoky Burgess in that category. The white catchers, in short, are now clearly starting rather few games behind the plate, perhaps enjoying a semi-official stint as player/coach.

By the final season, the reverend Smoky Burgess is not even averaging one turn at bat per game. (Neither is Ed Bailey—but Ed scarcely played a month into the 1966 season, having never managed a single hit in his last brief tour of duty.) At the spectrum's far end, the resurgent Elston Howard (who must surely have been injured the previous year) is trudging to the plate an average of three and one-quarter times per game as he helps the Yankees' arch-rival Boston win a trip to the World Series. His black cohorts are still active, too, though not to such a degree. Earl Battey, legendary for his ability to absorb punishment, is at last allowed to leave the occasional game in the seventh inning. Roseboro, now a Washington Senator, is starting regularly until he and manager Ted Williams have a disagreement about how to handle a young pitcher, resulting in Rosey's permanent sidelining.[4] Williams was no bigot—just one of baseball's standard dugout despots. (A crying shame: Roseboro did, after all, catch each of Sandy Koufax's four no-hitters. Pitcher Johnny Klippstein once said of him, "He was an excellent receiver with quick hands and feet and was the best in baseball at blocking the plate."[5]) Yet despite their relenting activity, Battey and Roseboro still produced a PAG around the 2.50 mark. The indefatigable Sherman Lollar, finally running low on fuel, sat out games almost exactly at Roseboro's rate (though presumably under less duress).

White catchers Dalrymple and Romano, in contrast, are playing almost as much as Howard *when they do play* ... but the trouble is that their batting averages have gone flat. Nevertheless, both will make it all the way through the season. Valmy Thomas is another story. Occupying the same leaky boat as Clay and Johnny, he also boasts a high PAG (3.41)—implying that he starts more games now than he ever has—but paradoxically sustains a miserable batting average of around .200. Yet Thomas will be put out of his misery in mid-April, while Dalrymple and Romano will catch their final game in the fall. Remarkably, all three play in almost exactly the same number of games before their professional plug is pulled. The difference is that two white catchers are drawing a year's pay while waiting for two dozen starts. For Valmy as for Charlie White, a close succession of starts behind the plate signals a kind of "See there?" flourish of self-justification on the part of his employers before they cut him loose.

An aging catcher starts a lot of games for only two reasons. One is that he's a legend in his time and inspires everyone around him—a Howard, a Bench, or a Carlton Fisk. The other is that he's fighting for his professional life—trying to convince a skeptical management that his off-and-on career is about to switch back on, that he can still do a young man's work. The stats say that Clay Dalrymple and Johnny Romano ended up in this latter mode, as most catchers—and most players—eventually do. Valmy Thomas *might* be compared with them, except for one thing: it took baseball's decision-makers only half as long to conclude that his vital spark had been extinguished.

Yet what about the black success stories: Battey, Howard, and Roseboro? Shouldn't the legend-in-his-time have a different set of stats for his final season than theirs—shouldn't his swan song be the year where he has barely two plate appearances per game? Perhaps Earl Battey was just as happy to go out on a more active note, despite all the bruises he had endured. Yet Jim Grant had said of Earl, "He could settle down any pitcher. I thought he was like a granddaddy."[6] Doesn't that sound like the perfect pitching coach? John Roseboro's retirement, too, was as voluntary as Mother Nature allows such things to be without any help from well-wishers. He would write later that admitting he could no longer perform physically "was the hardest thing I have had to do in my life."[7] Rosey most definitely wanted to manage after his playing days. What he got, instead, was three years as a lowly bullpen coach (sandwiching a brief stint at first base) with an Angels team in complete disarray. Elston Howard fared a little better: he became the Yankees' first black coach in 1969, apparently a primary motive for his withdrawal from active duty… but his forward motion was stalled there for the next 11 years, until he decided to give up the fight. Howard longed to manage, as well.[8]

These three men lasted well over a decade in baseball's most dangerous position, so one can scarcely question the wisdom of their decision to stop playing the game when they did. As for the bilking of black candidates for manager… that, in a way, is a separate story. Maybe the proper conclusion to the present tale is really Valmy Thomas's strange career. Wouldn't it have been nice to clean out one's locker quietly as the autumn leaves fell, like Dalrymple and Romano, rather than be cut before the azaleas bloomed for a couple of bad weeks at the plate? Wouldn't it have been nice if a solid rookie season had led to increased playing time, as it did for Clay and Johnny, rather than to ever-diminishing roles? Howard and Roseboro would both have made superlative managers, yes—and so would Battey; but Thomas could have been a very fine big-league catcher for years to come. Bigotry and all, the latter job still had a lot more specific openings year to year than the former. It is there that the absence of black men for any length of time is more conspicuous, in my opinion.

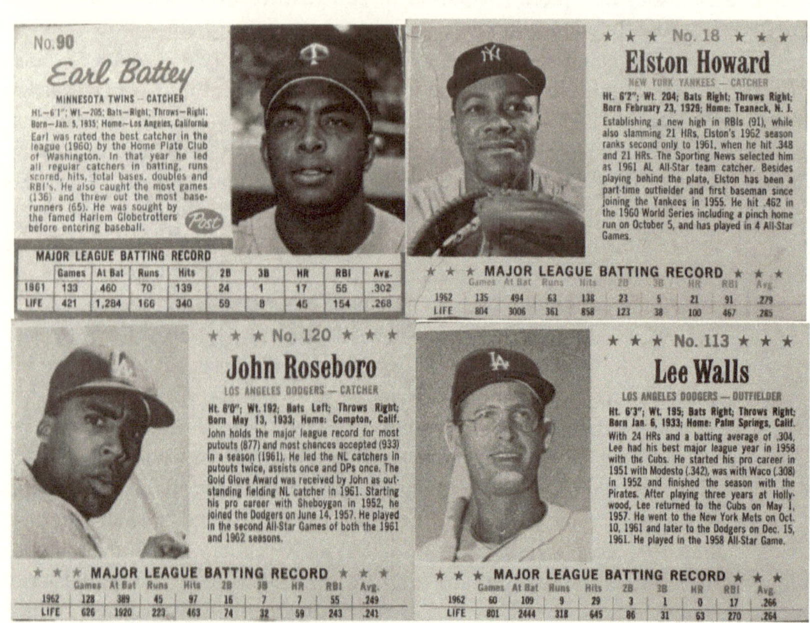

No. 90

Earl Battey

MINNESOTA TWINS — CATCHER

Ht.—6'1"; Wt.—205; Bats—Right; Throws—Right; Born—Jan. 5, 1935; Home—Los Angeles, California

Earl was rated the best catcher in the league (1960) by the Home Plate Club of Washington. In that year he led all regular catchers in batting, runs scored, hits, total bases, doubles and RBI's. He also caught the most games (136) and threw out the most base-runners (65). He was sought by the famed Harlem Globetrotters before entering baseball.

MAJOR LEAGUE BATTING RECORD

	Games	At Bat	Runs	Hits	2B	3B	HR	RBI	Avg.
1961	133	460	70	139	24	1	17	55	.302
LIFE	421	1,284	166	340	59	8	45	154	.268

★ ★ ★ **No. 18** ★ ★ ★

Elston Howard

NEW YORK YANKEES — CATCHER

Ht. 6'2"; Wt. 204; Bats Right; Throws Right; Born February 23, 1929; Home: Teaneck, N. J.

Establishing a new high in RBIs (91), while also slamming 21 HRs, Elston's 1962 season ranks second only to 1961, when he hit .348 and 21 HRs. The Sporting News selected him as 1961 AL All-Star team catcher. Besides playing behind the plate, Elston has been a part-time outfielder and first baseman since joining the Yankees in 1955. He hit .462 in the 1960 World Series including a pinch home run on October 5, and has played in 4 All-Star Games.

★ ★ MAJOR LEAGUE BATTING RECORD ★ ★

	Games	At Bat	Runs	Hits	2B	3B	HR	RBI	Avg.
1962	135	494	63	138	23	5	21	91	.279
LIFE	804	3006	361	858	123	38	100	467	.285

★ ★ ★ No. 120 ★ ★ ★

John Roseboro

LOS ANGELES DODGERS — CATCHER

Ht. 6'0"; Wt. 192; Bats Left; Throws Right; Born May 13, 1933; Home: Compton, Calif.

John holds the major league record for most putouts (877) and most chances accepted (933) in a season (1961). He led the NL catchers in putouts twice, assists once and DPs once. The Gold Glove Award was received by John as outstanding fielding NL catcher in 1961. Starting his pro career with Sheboygan in 1952, he joined the Dodgers on June 14, 1957. He played in the second All-Star Games of both the 1961 and 1962 seasons.

★ ★ ★ MAJOR LEAGUE BATTING RECORD ★ ★ ★

	Games	At Bat	Runs	Hits	2B	3B	HR	RBI	Avg.
1962	128	389	45	97	16	7	7	55	.249
LIFE	626	1920	223	463	74	32	59	243	.241

★ ★ ★ No. 113 ★ ★ ★

Lee Walls

LOS ANGELES DODGERS — OUTFIELDER

Ht. 6'3"; Wt. 195; Bats Right; Throws Right; Born Jan. 6, 1933; Home: Palm Springs, Calif.

With 24 HRs and a batting average of .304, Lee had his best major league year in 1958 with the Cubs. He started his pro career in 1951 with Modesto (.342), was with Waco (.308) in 1952 and finished the season with the Pirates. After playing three years at Hollywood, Lee returned to the Cubs on May 1, 1957. He went to the New York Mets on Oct. 10, 1961 and later to the Dodgers on Dec. 15, 1961. He played in the 1958 All-Star Game.

★ ★ ★ MAJOR LEAGUE BATTING RECORD ★ ★ ★

	Games	At Bat	Runs	Hits	2B	3B	HR	RBI	Avg.
1962	60	109	9	29	3	1	0	17	.266
LIFE	801	2444	318	645	86	31	63	270	.264

Battey had perhaps his best offensive year in 1961, when he surpassed .300 for the only time in his career. Catchers were always absorbing physical abuse, and New York took care to give Howard some time off in the outfield. Roseboro was closer to Battey in the amount of punishment he took: besides getting famously clubbed by Juan Marichal, he lost most of his front teeth in a bullpen accident (after which, he said, the dentist made him look better than ever). Lee Walls, a manager's delight in his eagerness to volunteer for hard duty, was supposed to be LA's third-string backstop, but was seldom pressed into service. Query: why could a utility player like Lee extend his career by practicing a little with mask and mitt while a born-and-bred catcher like Valmy Thomas was considered incapable of subbing at another position?

1 See Moffi and Kronstadt (*op. cit.*), 27. This is the second half of Roy's famous salute to Jackie Robinson, who "made things easy for us" in his view.

2 Danny Peary, *We Played the Game* (*op. cit.*), 453.

3 In all honesty, I think Trouppe's age was probably the primary factor working against him in Cleveland, an organization which pioneered integration in the American League and whose arbiters in Qunicy's case, Al Lopez and Hank Greenberg, were anything but bigoted. Qunicy makes a convincing case for himself in his book (*20 Years Too Soon* [*op. cit.*], 111-112); and Jim Hegan and Birdie Tebbetts, the team's preferred catchers, couldn't hit a lick compared to him. Baseball rarely makes a long investment in 38-year-old rookies, however.

4 See John Roseboro (with Bill Libby), *Glory Days with the Dodgers, and Other Days with Others* (New York: Atheneum, 1978), 243. Roseboro claims that Williams ordered him to have young pitcher Joe Coleman throw nothing but curves in a regular-season game until he mastered the pitch. Roseboro was appalled at this tactical use of humiliation before a large crowd: hence his benching. "Ted took that away from me," John records gloomily, referring to the satisfaction of ending his career in active service.

5 Danny Peary (*op. cit.*), 394

6 Danny Peary (*ibid.*), 617.

7 John Roseboro (*op. cit.*), 246. The ensuing chapter (247-257) details Roseboro's rough, brief ride as a coach, which left him destitute and suicidal.

8 Elston's wife confided that "his dream was to manage the Yankees. We always thought that since they acted like great white liberals, they might give Elston a chance." (Quoted in Moffi and Kronstadt [*op. cit.*], 135.)

Part Three

Lost Narratives:
Reconstructing Fragmentary
Careers from Stray Details

I

Not Always in the Cards: The Original Quandaries of Individual Players Reconsidered

In Chapter 3 of Part 1, I offered at face value several cases of careers that seemed to be shot full of holes—or perhaps in a few instances (e.g., Frank Robinson) aimed at and missed—by a malicious establishment. With the exceptions of Joe Caffie, Valmy Thomas, and Bob Thurman, they were all drawn from a study of my Post cereal cards covering the 1961 and 1962 seasons; and with the exception of Manny Jiménez and Felix Mantilla, all players involved were of African descent without having any Latin blood that I knew of. They seemed to me, at first glance, very good candidates for victimization by bigotry. I'm sure that few of them have ever harbored any desire to claim such a distinction: Major League ballplayers are high achievers, by definition, and the "victim" mindset doesn't mix well with the kind of energy required to bust your tail day after day, year after year. The "can do" attitude, though, may blur first-hand testimony with wishful thinking—and it very well explains why so few players have volunteered to testify before me. I wanted at the beginning of this book, as I want now, to know the bedrock truth—not the perceived truth of any concerned party (though more perceptions would certainly have helped me to get to the bottom). All of the cases I listed smelled fishy to me, and I have since tried to examine the merits of every one very closely.

Some turn out to have much more merit than others. A foul smell is not always a rotting fish: it can be plain bad luck or simple bad timing. In this chapter, I propose to review the case of every player mentioned at the beginning of Part 1 and share a more mature, considered verdict. I will say at the outset that I see no monolithic conspiracy on the part of white owners and managers to cheat black players of time on the field. The mission of a ball club is to win; and while the very occasional leader might be stupid enough to sabotage his own job or investment just to vent a primitive hatred, I find it wholly implausible that large numbers of successful people would do so.

What does emerge from this scrutiny of individual cases, instead, is a more nuanced understanding of the obstacles facing black ballplayers in the later Fifties and early Sixties: not outright hostility, most often, but very narrow windows of opportunity placing extraordinary pressure on these players to explode like a firecracker at the plate whenever they were penciled into the starting line-up. Such pressure did not always bring out the best in them: it would be the ruination of most normal human beings. The second and third chapters of Part 3, indeed, will emphasize just how destructive the pressure to play long ball became for many very fine black ballplayers. I should never have stumbled on that insight, however, had I not first put the magnifying glass up to individual careers.

George Altman

The mystery of George Altman became less opaque to me (though it did not disappear) after a discovery. First the mystery, then the discovery. George spent his first four Major League seasons with the Cubs, and his batting average improved with each year, climaxing in a sixth-place finish for the batting crown after the 1962 campaign at .318. His power numbers observed almost the same glorious ascent, peaking a year earlier with 27 home runs and 96 RBIs—and, by the way, a league-leading 12 triples. Not that '62 witnessed a sudden power-outage: Altman's 22 home runs and 74 RBIs were easily the second-best marks of his career, and his 27 doubles fell just one shy of the previous year's mark.

Nevertheless, the Cubs decided to unload their All-Star outfielder to the Cardinals after the 1962 season. In return, they essentially received pitchers Larry Jackson and Lindy McDaniel. These two starters were a fine acquisition for a team perennially troubled by weak pitching—and, of course, the starting-rotation omelet could only be fried up by breaking a fat egg, such as a potential batting champ. That's how trades work: teams cripple one aspect of their game to fortify another (often, alas, with a zero-sum result). In retrospect, this particular trade was about as fruitless as most—but it was more defensible than a great many.

Too bad for George Altman that he got packed off to a pitcher's paradise (which had probably made Jackson and McDaniel look a little better than they were). His average and power figures both took a beating in 1963 (though .274 is not to be scoffed at in any ballpark). The Cardinals had apparently expected Wrigley Field numbers out of their new star, so George was again shipped out in the winter of '63—this time in a two-for-one deal to the New York Mets, with Roger Craig being the one worth two. Craig had posted 15 wins *and 46 losses* during his two previous seasons with the Mets: August Busch must have taken George's 9 homers pretty hard. It probably hadn't helped Altman's concentration, either, that he had been trying to fill Stan Musial's shoes, or that Stan had announced his impending retirement in plenty of time for fans to ride George.

In any case, the bad luck didn't wear off in New York. Though Altman saw over 400 at-bats in 1964, he batted an anemic .230, and his home runs and RBIs were ironically identical to the previous year's tallies—which, of course, was a slight upswing if pegged to the reduced at-bats. Yet the statistics show that Altman was pressing by this point. He had always managed to draw about half as many walks as he logged strike-outs: in '64, the ratio plummeted to 18/70. The Cubs, surely remembering his glory days with them, re-acquired him in a trade after the '64 season, and for three miserable years George struggled to catch fire again (now, however, spending well over half his time on the bench). There was no combustion left. In 1967 he was released after appearing in only fifteen games.

In the light of my research, the mystery is not why the Cubs traded Altman, to begin with, but why some players rebound so much better than others to having the rug pulled out from under them. On paper, George's case anticipates that of Leon Durham, another black slugger from the left side whom the Cubs rendered thunderstruck when they traded him to Cincinnati for reliever Pat Perry. Durham—would you believe it?—shortly ended up in St. Louis, where his hot bat turned to ice. He, too, never recovered from the gaping wound of being unloaded after a six year stint over which he hit 20 or more home runs five times. There was nothing ostensibly race-indexed about either of these deals, to be sure (though one may observe that neither Ron Santo nor, in 1988, Ryne Sandberg was made the sacrificial lamb to the Cubs' ever-deficient pitching staff). Once the Cubs had recovered Altman at a discount, however, why didn't they at least give him something like a full season to locate his missing confidence? Why obtain the former All-Star a mere two years later just to put him out to pasture?

I could muse, once again, upon the many sub-.250 seasons that Detroit tolerated from Norm Cash and Dick McAuliffe en route to letting them fulfill splendid careers. On the other hand, I could meditate a little further on the resilience that allowed a Frank Robinson or a Tommy Davis to keep floating to the top after every trade. Race was not unconnected to the enormous pressures placed upon young athletes at this time, but neither, I think, was it the primary source of pressure. The mystery of what George Altman might have been had Chicago not disrupted his productive rhythm in his prime, like all mysteries of squandered potential, is at last insoluble.

In Altman's case, though, a surprising epilogue seems to reinforce the notion that the Cubs wasted a rare opportunity. I recently discovered that George went on to have a very fine career playing ball in Japan. From 1969-1975, he hit 205 home runs for his new employers and batted a combined .309. Though insider's wisdom has it that Japanese baseball presented less of a challenge to American-bred hitters than what they encountered in the States, one might adjust for inflation and still suppose that Altman could have posted 20 annual homers and an average around .280 in the friendly confines of Wrigley Field for quite some time if he had been handled with greater care. The Cub's loss was Japan's gain and, for once, a happy ending in those chronicles of neglect where the careers of so many black ballplayers may be found.

***

<u>Postscript</u>: Mr. Altman very kindly responded after I had sent him a copy of my remarks above. Below I reproduce this response in its entirety:

175

Your pressure theory concerning power was partly right in my St. Louis experience. I was batting over .350 three weeks into the 1963 season. Busch Stadium in St. Louis had a short porch [in right field]. Someone from the front office came to me saying Mr. Rickey, the GM or VP, wanted me (a straight-away hitter) to pull the ball to take advantage of the short porch. I mistakenly tried to heed this advice and started "stepping in the bucket" and pulling off the ball. I was pulling the ball a lot but wasn't getting the loft needed to clear the high stands in right. I started to drop my hands and upper-cut. I also was fouling a lot of balls off my right foot. This caused me to have to wear a shin guard. This led to groin problems in trying to beat out grounders. As my average declined I developed pressure in the back of my eyes causing blurred vision. I tried glasses for a while. Finally, after my average dropped to .230, I abandoned the pull-hitter experiment and got back into the line-up on a regular basis. I was a part of the team surge in late August when we won 18 out of 19 games. I played against left-handers and righties. I had a 19-game hitting streak going when the Dodgers came to St. Louis and pitched four left-handers in the series to beat us four straight. I was benched for that series and used only sparingly as a pinch-hitter.

In 1964 I was traded to the New York Mets. I dove for a ball on the last day of spring training and dislocated my shoulder. I should have been out a month or more. Casey Stengel came to me a week later on opening day and asked me to play. It was too early and the shoulder bothered me all year.

In 1965 I returned to Chicago. I started well, batting .300. Then my groin muscle separated from the bone while I was beating out a bunt. Again I was pressured to return to the line-up too soon and had groin trouble all year.

In 1966 Leo Durocher signed to manage the Cubs. We opened in San Francisco. I hit well in that series, including a home run. I was benched for the next series in Los Angeles. Leo was officially on a youth movement. Regardless of how well I played, I was relegated to part-time duty.

In 1967, I went to the Pacific Coast League and did very well there, playing full time. When I was recalled to the Cubs, I sat for two weeks before getting a chance to play. After one or two games, back on the bench. I knew I could still play, so when the Japan offer came I took it.

I found out in Japan that I wasn't ever in tip-top shape while playing in the Major Leagues. Even though I worked harder than most players, it wasn't enough for me. 1961 was probably the only year that I was injury-free in the Major Leagues. I was able to play virtually injury-free in Japan due to their hard training methods.

Obviously, there must be many such cases as George's in this section's following thumb-nail sketches where a player's somewhat irregular career was impacted by injuries far more than I could ever know. Ballplayers would not have thought it wise in this era to complain about an injury or to refuse the manager's request that they start. [Stengel, by the way, was notorious for badgering injured players to get back on the field.] In the case of black players, especially, who were routinely cut during a "youth movement" or were instantly assumed to have their best years behind them as soon as they hit a slump, the pressure to play in mangled condition must have been considerable.

I continue to believe that the identification of home runs with job security altered a great many swings besides George's in 1963, and that theme shall recur throughout this and subsequent chapters. Branch Rickey was actually employed by the Cardinals as a senior advisor at this time (he would be carried away by a stroke within a couple of years). Rickey had always liked the pulling, slightly upper-cutting swing, and he had directed his scouts to look for it in previous years. Anyone can understand why the young George, trying hard to please his new bosses and slipped a word of advice from a living legend, would want to oblige... but the DiMaggio/Williams swing was not his style, and it certainly contributed to short-circuiting his Major League career.

An even broader theme, however, is simply that lurking sense of not being likely to receive the benefit of any doubt—a sense which might, for instance, have made George dive for a ball in a spring-training game. The hunger to silence one's critics utterly can be almost suicidal when those critics are not susceptible to reasonable proof. Is there another case in baseball history, I wonder, of a player's being benched after a 19-game hitting streak? I, at least, have never heard of such a thing. Any remotely thoughtful person would be bound to grow a little paranoid in such circumstances.

Earl Battey

Larry Moffi and Jonathan Kronstadt produce a very helpful section on Earl Battey.[1] These pages explain what I at first took to be a slighting of Battey's talents during his five years of tenure with the White Sox. Battey did not prosper offensively from being benched somewhere between 30% and 98% of the time over those seasons: not many young hitters would. He was backing up the older, well-established catcher Sherman Lollar—a Caucasian, to be sure, but also a darned fine ballplayer. As far as racial issues are concerned, one might indeed argue that Chicago was ahead of many other organizations in allowing a young black player to spend so much time on the bench. The usual drill for blacks was that you either started or departed.

When the Washington Senators packed up and moved to Minnesota in 1960 (something the United States Senate should seriously consider doing), Battey went with them and became a local legend. He absorbed staggering amounts of abuse behind the plate (since there was apparently no young Earl to back *him* up) for about a decade, blossoming offensively even as his defense made him an All-Star. When he retired, the only duress which seems to have influenced the decision was that of a body submitted to as much punishment as was humanly endurable. No story here, except the one of across-the-board success.

Bob Boyd

I have no personal recollection whatever of the late Bob Boyd as a ballplayer. Somehow I had acquired one of his baseball cards—*not* off the back of a cereal box. He had a pleasant face that stuck in my mind... but by the time I was peering with little comprehension at black-and-white images on the Saturday *Game of the Week*, Boyd had already retired. My curiosity about his career, therefore, did not begin in a childhood daydream, but in a middle-aged review of statistics. I was surprised to find that Boyd hadn't hit more home runs, for I recollected that my baseball card reported him to be a first baseman—the infield position which is most readily associated with strapping hulks who crush hanging sliders. It would appear that Bob was played out of position for most of his all-too-limited career in the Majors. Standing at 5'10", he had no transparent qualifications for being a target on the first sack, though he was indeed left-handed. The Orioles, with whom he logged his best years (hitting over .300 in four of his five Baltimore seasons), presumably wanted to work his bat into the line-up however possible. The raw stats also show something rather rare in an eager black player given a chance in the newly desegregated Major Leagues: Bob did not swing out of his shoes trying to prove himself. His career walks-to-strikeouts ratio is almost three to two.

The first of Brent Kelley's excellent books offering interviews of former Negro Leaguers suggested to me that my indignation on Bob's behalf may have been unfounded. Boyd apparently didn't throw well enough to play the outfield: in fact, he seems to have broken his arm trying to hurl a bullet from left field while with the White Sox. The result was a fracture that required surgical wiring. The wire later came loose while Bob was playing the infield, and had to be surgically retrieved from the now-healed bone! One can hardly blame a manager for not wanting to roll the dice with a player who is apt to wrench his body apart when, in the heat of the action, he attempts to burn one in.

I can only marvel at how poor the coaching must have been half a century ago. Pitchers sometimes shatter their arms trying to snap off an especially sharp breaking ball... but an outfielder incurring a fracture on a brisk throw? That's a new one on me. It bespeaks a flawed throwing motion, such as would usually be corrected at the high-school level nowadays, if not sooner. If we needed one more indication that yesteryear's managers and coaches often owed their positions more to cronyism than to teaching ability, this would be it. Of course, nothing in such an indictment is immediately connected to racism.

Yet some of Bob's comments to Kelley are extremely revealing in a manner less removed from race, or at least from prejudice against the eccentric. Boyd tells Kelley, in defending his performance as a first baseman, "I had speed and was a good fielder."[2] These are two important qualities often sacrificed when a man is planted at first just because of his size. In any case, ballplayers were not as tall in the Fifties as they are now, and Boyd's height was not unduly short for the position. Moose Skowron was only an inch taller, and was right-handed into the bargain. Yet Boyd substantially surpassed 400 at-bats only once in his career—the 1957 season, when his batting average ranked fourth in the American League. These facts were enough to start me wondering all over again after I had pondered them.

And then there is this most interesting exchange earlier on the same page:

Boyd: I was hittin' the ball hard, straight on a line. I wasn't a large man, you know, and I just couldn't hit no home runs, but everything I hit it looked like it was on a line….

Kelley: Someone said you'd have had a little more home run power if you had not had such a level swing. You had the most level swing in the league and maybe if you had a slight uppercut you'd have driven more balls out.

Boyd: Well, I don't know. I wasn't worried about home runs at the time because I was fast and all I wanna do is get the ball between somebody.

Kelley: When you played, stolen bases were not emphasized, so your speed wasn't used to advantage.

Boyd: They never would let me steal. I don't know why. The most stolen bases I had was 42 [Sacramento, 1951], I believe; that was in the Pacific Coast League. I think I led the league in stolen bases. That's the most I ever did any runnin'. Paul Richards never would let me go. I don't know why.

And I don't know why, either—other than that the white baseball establishment mistrusted base-stealing (and still does, in some measure), although the Negro Leagues had brought it to a refined art. The home run was far more secure in this view: money in the bank—put the ball out of play where the speed of a Lou Brock is not needed to score and the arm of a Willie Mays cannot compromise the outcome. Boyd didn't hit home runs: he stole bases. That was probably enough for Paul Richards, Bob's manager in Baltimore. Richards would later be general manager for a Houston organization over which charges of racism often drifted. (Joe Morgan took strong exception to former Astros skipper Harry Walker: see Chapter Five below.) Richards would move on to occupy the same position in Atlanta, where he had several run-ins with Henry Aaron. The Hammer writes that Richards tactlessly announced to the whole team that everyone was "trade bait", and that he quickly made good on his threats. "He was the kind of guy who would call you into his office and talk to you as he looked out the window, as if you weren't really there."[3] These are not accusations of outright racism; Aaron stresses, rather, that Richards possessed an imperious attitude, wholly unreceptive to suggestions from others.

Boyd, I hasten to add, gratefully remarks, "Paul was a baseball man," after describing how, after his anguishing arm troubles, Richards would have him and an outfielder temporarily swap places on defense whenever a force play at second was impending.[4] That's pretty accommodating—and I am certainly not floating any allegation, once again, that Richards cheated black players of time on the field strictly because of their skin color. But Bob's most famous manager did not appreciate new ideas unless they were his own, and he may have felt that the recent imports from the Negro Leagues were bringing in some bad habits. Curiously, Minnie Minoso lavished praise upon Richards specifically because he "allowed me to make my own decisions on the bases."[5] Maybe Paul simply decided that Minoso was a better base-runner than Boyd... but that, of course, begs the question, since Boyd had proved his running abilities. Did it matter that Minnie was a Cuban? Richards himself was a Texan—as am I; so I can affirm with some authority that in Texas of half a century ago, a Latino would generally have received more respect than a black man.

In remarks beyond the interview in Kelley's book, Boyd was sometimes more forthcoming about the situation's friction. He once observed that Richards "never broke his word... but he didn't like blacks. I was in enough team meetings where he talked about the black players on the team... and he didn't say very nice things about them."[6]

Paul Richards was unarguably a very "by the book" figure, and rather domineering. He did not take inordinate risks, and he did not appreciate ingenuity on the field. His own testimony in a book published half a century ago shows him to have been almost neurotic about controlling his players: "We actually went seven years in Baltimore when I was managing without ever having a player doubled [up] with the bases full and nobody out.... You can't hit a ballplayer over the head, but you've got to get his attention and stamp the lessons into him.... It's up to the man in charge to see that his players are always drilled in and constantly alert to these things [the 'small details that add up to the winning of a ball game']."[7]

Paul Richards, I suspect, was quite typical of the kind of manager who used his young black players' special talents less than he might have. Rigidity was the roadblock; and it was not thrown up against blacks for having dark skin, but for not playing by that unwritten book. Richards didn't calculate all the tight games he might have won by letting players *of demonstrated base-stealing ability* take off at their discretion: he was too busy patting himself on the back for keeping every runner so near his bag that he couldn't be doubled up on a line drive. And if you *did* give a particular runner the green light, would it be some crazy black kid from the crazy Negro Leagues? The manager holds the team's consignment of brains... and one has the feeling that black players, especially, were to present their skulls for a

180

salutary beating with the Big Man's lessons.

Bill Bruton

It is my considered belief now that Bill Bruton had a fine Major League career and was highly valued by both the franchises that entrusted their center fields to his patrolling for several years. For three consecutive seasons (1953-1955), Bruton led the National League in stolen bases, and twice he was the same league's triples champ. Billy also ended up being the only National Leaguer of the twentieth century to triple three times in one game, and he later tied another record by doubling four times in a nine-inning show. He was a hustler *par excellence*, surely one of the best lead-off men of his day.

And it didn't stop there. An exceptionally intelligent man (Bill had prepared to be a chemist in school) who was eloquent both in speech and in writing, he was well liked in his adopted home up north. The Milwaukee fans worshiped him, as well they might have. He had won the first-ever Major League game played in their city with a walk-off home run, and his contributions were key to the Braves' pennant-winning years. His eight seasons at Milwaukee always found him starting regularly except in the aftermath of a very badly broken leg.

He was equally respected during his four years in Detroit, as far as I can tell. I admit to feeling a little suspicious that his last season with the Tigers—really a half season, consisting of only 296 at-bats—should not have won him a contract for the following year. All he managed to do was bat .277 and score 42 runs while legging out 5 triples and 14 stolen bases, so any suggestion that the leg had never healed completely or that he was simply growing too long in the tooth should not have been taken seriously. A white player who had posted such numbers would probably at least have been allowed to sit on the bench for another season, going in to pinch-run or to rove the outfield in the late innings of a close game. Bruton was released at the season's end. The oracle at Wikipedia, I have noticed, blandly asserts that he "called it quits". I suppose, facing the bleak opportunities of free agency, any sane adult pushing forty would indeed call it quits. This is also known as yielding to the inevitable.

Of course, there is little reason to suppose that Bill still had great baseball deeds in him. He was most certainly not a potential member of the 3,000- hit club or the 400-homer club who had been passed around like a bad penny and then ousted for no plausible reason. Billy was too old to have played much longer, even if he might have contributed for another season or two. (He had actually been born four years before the date claimed by his 1961 Post cereal card, a subterfuge which had been inaugurated early in his career to keep the scouts interested.) The real tragedy in his case is that he got such a late start at the Major League level—as well as (we should add) that he was never offered any sort of coaching, managerial, or administrative position after retirement. His intellect would have thrown an immense shadow over baseball's front-office Land of Lilliput.

Joe Caffie

I have happened upon nothing—absolutely nothing—that furthers my understanding of Caffie's Major League experience except the brief account of his career in Moffi and Kronstadt—and this account really begs the question of bigoted motives more than ever, though the authors (as is their wont) do not float any explicit charges.[8] They begin, "Had Joe Caffie reached the major leagues about 10 years later, he probably could have made a career on his speed alone." Yet stealing bases certainly wasn't held against Luis Aparicio during these same years—and Luis, no better a hitter than Joe for average, clearly lacked his ability to switch on shows of power. No doubt, lack of consistent power was *alleged* as Caffie's weakness by the white establishment, which frequently reined in its inheritance of base-stealers from the Negro Leagues (for reasons about which we can only speculate). Since Joe played the outfield rather than—like Aparicio—the middle infield, his *mere* speed and solid batting average were accounted a liability. The absurd brevity of his big-league auditions strongly suggests that the deck may have been stacked from the start.

Bill Veeck was no longer in Cleveland by this time, but the Indians continued to employ comparatively many black ballplayers while extending to them comparatively fair treatment. Maybe Joe just couldn't break into the Indians' outfield... but this is why the baseball gods invented trades. Why did Caffie not catch on somewhere else? Cases like this do little to convince today's onlooker that baseball of the Fifties was generally serious about promoting the highest caliber of player, regardless of his race.

Ed Charles

In Bill James's slightly facetious ruminations on a comically inept franchise, Ed Charles comes off as one of the best things the short-lived Kansas City Athletics would ever offer the baseball public:

> Ed Charles was perhaps the best player in the history of the Kansas City Athletics... [at least] you can make an argument for him. Charles played 726 games for the A's, which is (and will always be) the franchise record, and also holds the franchise records for total bases (1,065) and power/speed number (68.8). He is second all-time among KC A's in runs scored (344), hits (703), and RBI (319).[9]

Ed was one fine ballplayer. He showed up in my 1962 card collection as a rookie, during which freshman campaign he legged out 7 triples to go with 17 homers—proving him a member of that rare species, the slugger with speed. My card's artless prose adds that Charles was acquired by Kansas City "after hitting .314 in nine years in the Braves' farm system." What it doesn't note is that Ed was a *second baseman* in those days. Remember the curse of the black non-Latino middle infielder? Either move to one of the corners or the outfield, or languish in the Minors until your knees die. And to think that they were making such a fuss in Milwaukee about needing a second sacker during these very years! As we have seen (Part 2, Chapter 6), the Braves under Fred Haney were committed to abiding by the unwritten law that no more than four blacks should be on the field at any given moment. It was Charles's bad luck to be owned by the organization that employed Aaron, Bruton, Covington, and Mantilla.

This is a fairly undiluted form of racism, though it does not involve the deliberate oppression of a specific player in specific circumstances because of his skin color. Charles was already twenty-nine years old when he got his big break. What I had initially perceived in his stats as a very quick hook at the end of over half a dozen solid seasons was probably a judgment against Ed's mounting years, not against his baseball ability. Playing only about two-thirds of the 1968 season (The Year of the Pitcher) for the Mets, Ed had mustered 15 homers and 53 RBIs while sustaining a .276 average—this in an unfamiliar league with better pitching. When the Mets cut him loose after a slow start the following year, they demonstrated very little patience... but, by that time, Charles was pushing thirty-seven. To receive much consideration at that age in baseball, you have to be Mays or Musial. Race most likely had nothing to do with it.

So, yes, I think that Ed Charles would have and should have enjoyed a longer career: he *would have* in a system devoid of racial bigotry, and he *should have* because the system was grossly hypocritical in thus secretly preserving the "abolished" color barrier. But Ed's release was not in itself a bigoted act. No doubt, it is such chains of events as his career which render the past very hard for his generation of players to discuss. You can't say much to challenge the verdict passed on your actual performance: you can only brood, obsessively and pointlessly, on why you weren't allowed to perform earlier... and what's the point of that?

Wes Covington

Wes Covington has often been perceived as having enjoyed a good Major League career. Of course, in a way, that is all very true. Tommy Davis holds up Wes as the epitome of a player who "established himself" as a solid hitter and was able to hang around for years as a pinch-hitter deluxe.[10] What I continue to find wanting in this view, however, is a recognition that Wes had earned the right to do much more than come off the bench in the late innings. The redoubtable Bill James mentions him almost unwittingly—doesn't really mention him, in fact, so much as pulls his name out of a database when compiling a list of hitters whose hits were most evenly distributed.[11] Wes Covington ranks seventh (or did when James's book was published) among the *all-time leaders* in garnering doubles and triples to go with their handfuls of home runs and armloads of singles. This is not a mean-nothing statistic—unlike, say, hitting for the cycle. The cycle is a haphazard, one-day affair: to spread out varieties of hit smoothly over the course of a career signifies several important qualities in the hitter. It strongly implies, at any rate, that he made solid contact, stroked the ball to all fields, and exhibited speed and "hustle". Personally, I would draft such a player before a monolithic home run hitter seven days a week—and *not* to sit on my bench.

My original discomfort with Covington's handling has therefore stayed with me throughout my researching of this book. When I look at that frayed baseball card clipped half a century ago from the back of a cereal box, I still mutter to myself, "This guy should have been given more of a chance." To be sure, for most of his Major League career, Wes had bad pins beneath him: a knee injury in spring of 1959, later an ankle injury, and a host of nagging pains that wouldn't go away. Was there ever a veteran outfielder before the arthroscope, however, who did *not* have bad knees? I suppose it's possible that Covington never had more than 373 at-bats in a season because his agonies required "down" time... possible, but unlikely. In those days, ballplayers lived with pain and were expected to *play* with pain. Furthermore, the picture of a hobbling Wes who staggers to the plate every other game for a pinch-hit appearance (*à la* Kirk Gibson) hardly jibes with all those doubles and triples in Bill James's database. If his legs were always in danger of collapse, why not bring him in from the outfield and start him at first base, where his ailing joints would endure minimal strain?

Wes's teammate on the Milwaukee Braves, pitcher Bob Buhl, has quipped of his defensive abilities, "he'd have to hit .400 to help a club because he wasn't that good in left field."[12] Well, maybe not. Covington made some spectacular catches in the 1957 World Series, yet he seems to be fitted with the collar of defensive ineptitude in many quarters.[13] Hearsay estimates of fielding proficiency are notorious for their bias. I have seen Josh Gibson rated by various eye-witness observers as better than Campanella and, then again, barely adequate. The word among some players about Willie Mays, no less, was that you could always take second on him if a runner was headed for third, because he would routinely ignore his cut-off man. Covington, I would guess, probably played his position well enough. I ask again, if he was something of a liability in the outfield yet could consistently bat .300 with power, why wasn't he brought in to play first base? Granted, the Braves had already imported Joe Adcock to first for this very reason; but by 1962, there were ten teams in either league, and few would have had Covington competing against an Adcock.

So am I alleging that Wes was seldom a regular starter because of his race? That doesn't seem entirely plausible to me. As I have demonstrated already (see Part 2, Chapter 3), the invidious pattern of the day was less to assign reduced roles to black players than to cut them at the first hint of a downward tick in their productivity. Pinch-hitting, inasmuch as it provided a means to hang around for years after one's prime, tended to be reserved for Caucasian veterans who had lost a step in the field or a split second with the bat. Compared to the sudden exits of some black players, Wes's swan song was graceful.

I have three points of rebuttal to argue, however. The first two were suggested to me by Henry Aaron's autobiography, and one of them is not assessed at its full significance even by Aaron, I think. Hank discusses the unwritten law in force throughout the Fifties that no team should field more than four black players at any given moment (i.e., that whites should compose over 50% of the nine on the grass).[14] With Aaron in right field, Bill Bruton in center, and Covington in left, one space was left over for someone like Felix Mantilla or pitcher Juan Pizarro. This opprobrious "gentlemen's agreement" may well have cut Wes's playing time short even in his early days at Milwaukee, when he presumably had two good legs under him. It could have done so, as well, in Philadelphia, where dark-skinned Latinos like Rubén Amaro, Tony González, Pancho Herrera, and Tony Taylor were making a splash. The knees would be a good pretext for enforcing a practice unmentionable in public. Tommy Davis had his broken ankle that never fully healed, and Wes had his knees.

The second item has already been brought up in another context: Aaron's proud recollection of the stir which he and his fellow black Braves raised about segregated spring training facilities in 1961. It doesn't seem to bother Hank that Andre Rodgers was gone from the Braves' roster before their first official game that season, and that Wes appeared in all of nine games before following Andre to the Cubs. "I wasn't any more of an activist than Bruton," recalls Henry, "but I could stand my ground and let guys like Wes Covington stir things up."[15] The more confident Covington, being also less of a star than Aaron, would have been an easy bomb to defuse through a trade. As for Bruton, he had been dealt to Detroit in December of the previous year: maybe discontent was rumbling before February, or maybe the whole smelly business is a series of coincidences. Maybe. Those in a position to know certainly wouldn't be players like Aaron and Covington, nor could they be relied upon even now (if they were alive) to acknowledge a large dose of unflattering truth. I only note that when vultures circle, a corpse usually lies somewhere below.

The most tendentious point for last. Readers may smile... but I wonder if Wes's very odd batting stance may have cost him playing time? I don't remember much from the grainy black-and-white televisions of my childhood—but I remember the gap between Leon Wagner's hands, and I remember Wes Covington's exotic backward coil. He always made me think of a scorpion with its tail smoothed out. The bottom hand's wrist curling beside his cheekbone, Wes somehow held his bat straight out toward the backstop and parallel to the ground. He was the quintessence of poised energy. I tried to imitate him in childish enthusiasm, but couldn't come close. Speaking of childishness... would a manager really shy away from playing a guy because his stance made solid citizens smirk? Who could believe such a thing? But then, who could believe that the Majors didn't want Henry Aaron until he started pulling the ball, or that Paul Richards ordered Bob Boyd—a base-stealing champ in the minors—to stay put? Wes was different, as so many of the new black stars were different. I keep saying that the palace guards didn't appreciate this difference—that it made them nervous. Picking on a slugger for refusing to model a stance out of the mold seems ludicrously petty... yes, and pettiness is precisely what appears most transparently in the double standard of this era.

***

Postscript: Without much success, I have been casting about for a way to ascertain if some of the black outfielders—such as Wes and Leon Wagner—saddled with a reputation for sloppy glove work may have been near-sighted. In my Post Cereal card collection, five white players and two Latinos (Julian Javier and Zoilo Versalles) were photographed wearing spectacles. Not a single black player of my group had corrective lenses—though George Altman (see above) confesses that he briefly tried them out. Fly-hawks like Dom DiMaggio and sluggers like Del Ennis had made glasses fully acceptable years earlier; and, in fact, George Crowe wore a pair in his day (as did black pitcher Norm Bass in the early Sixties). For the most part, however, black players seemed to shun specs. Teammates felt that Sam Jethroe's defensive foibles bespoke weak eyes, yet he had no correction (see Leon Wagner below). Though Bob Gibson was more than a little myopic (hence his fierce scowl when staring in to get his sign), he would seldom don glasses even as a hitter. Perhaps this generation's aspiring stars didn't want to offer white decision-makers another reason to reject them—or perhaps, as I tend to believe, the vision of most had simply not been properly tested at any point in their lives, even if they had served in the armed forces (where such things as physicals could be very slap-dash). A person who has never worn glasses doesn't know that he needs them, usually, until the optometrist demonstrates the difference they make. The outfield positions, furthermore (as I can aver from personal experience), magnify minor visual problems more than any other spot in the ball park—including the batter's box. Paul Waner was both myopic and alcoholic, yet somehow managed to amass 3,000 hits. So hitting with blurry vision is faintly possible: tracking high drives through tiers of spectators from 300 feet away... no.

Tommy Davis

The word "irrepressible" springs to mind when I think of Tommy Davis. The very fact that Tommy's autobiography is primarily a chronicle of the Dodgers' infancy and first glory days in Los Angeles (as the title announces) rather than of his own career says much about the man.[16] Davis has been a "team player" in baseball and in life. He heartily enjoys people and relishes the humor of situations that many of us would find unsavory. He is no fool, and was no ingénue as a young rookie: but he seems constitutionally averse to dwelling upon details that nail his fellow beings red-handed in a posture of vengeful bigotry or ruthless injustice. It should also be said that Tommy immensely enjoyed hob-nobbing with the likes of Sammy Davis, Jr., and Bob Hope, that the kid from Brooklyn understandably had his head turned by being invited to romp on the Vegas stage and to do skits on national television, and that—for two years under the famous hillside which reads

186

"Hollywood"—he was the best hitter in baseball. No man would lightly sweep aside such gilding to brood upon the tarnish beneath it. *Fulsere quondam candid tibi soles*: Catullus might just have written Tommy's epitaph—"Once upon a time, your suns shone brightly."

I therefore found that I was wasting my ink in my epistolary attempts to get Davis to talk about the legend of a broken leg ruining his career and forcing the Dodgers to trade him. It was one of many occasions in trying to assemble first-hand testimony for this book that I felt like a kill-joy detective hinting to a forgotten celebrity that his brightest trophy was a plastic rip-off, and that those who had awarded it were con artists. Who wants to listen to a line like that? Besides, who am I to suggest to Tommy Davis that his badly shattered leg did *not* affect his subsequent performance even after it ostensibly healed? It was his leg, not mine. Every time he pushed off of it while striding toward a pitch (for the injured pin was his right), he may well have sensed a twinge of pain, or have discovered that the old thrust just wasn't there any more.

At the very least, though, the statistics leave me perplexed. Tommy had about 900 hits as a Dodger; he would collect about 1200 more after departing LA. In 1969, four years after the horrendous fracture of his leg, he would post a career high in stolen bases with 20 (most of them in a Seattle Pilots uniform). Wherever he was sent—and Tommy Davis set a Major League record for being sent places—he performed exceptionally well. (For instance, in 1973 he batted in 89 runs for Baltimore while hitting .306.) Over the course of his staccato career, he managed to hold onto a .294 average. If his bad leg continued to nag him all this time, he certainly wouldn't have been the first ballplayer in history to have pain as a constant companion: Mickey Mantle had *two* bad ankles for much of his tenure. The baseball world's concern over Tommy Davis's right tibia seems to me very like a ready-made excuse to give up on him the instant his performance dipped slightly below his stellar precedent—or a ready-made pretext, maybe, to package him up the instant another organization offered younger players in a deal.

Nobody stuck by Tommy the way the Tigers stuck by Dick McAuliffe, say, or the Red Sox by Frank Malzone. Of course, ball clubs did not and do not exist to model loyalty; but the record shows precisely that Davis *helped teams win* wherever he traveled. He posted averages at or near .300 in an era when practically no one could reach that ceiling. (1968 was the *annus mirabilis* when Carl Yazstrzemski led the American League with a .301 mark.) He was playing for second-division teams that needed someone to carry their offensive game on his shoulders—a pressure which, by the way, is seldom conducive to peak performance. No doubt, Tommy would have incurred more gratitude with his numerous employers if he had cracked more homers, for it is the home run above all else that makes shoulders look broad. McAuliffe and Malzone both excelled in this department, though they played infield positions where less power was expected than from outfielders like Tommy. Davis's 27 round-trippers in his superman year of 1962 probably paved the way, furthermore, for disparagement when baseball's monomaniacal overlords figured out, at last, that he wasn't the next Aaron, or even the next Willie Kirkland.

I am not implying that straight, stark racism is the answer to the Davis conundrum. For every Frank Malzone, there is an unhappy Frank Thomas—the *white* Frank Thomas of yesteryear. Dumping fine players for no apparent reason has long been a favorite pastime of baseball brain trusts, and to posit bigotry as the motive in the case of fine black players would be redundant.

But the true motive is not necessarily untinged with racism, either. When the Dodgers shipped Gil Hodges and Duke Snider back east to the expansion Mets, it was because of their age *as reflected in* their severely curtailed home run output. The white occupants of front offices didn't seem to understand that home runs are bedeviled by unproductive outs, and that a walk, a steal, a bunt, and a ground-out could also win a game. This obstinate ignorance always tended to work against black players more than white players. After all, Hodges and Snider *were* home run hitters, so to judge them by that standard was at least not unfair. But why had the Dodger organization moved to trade Jackie Robinson and, later, Jim Gilliam, effectively ending both their careers when neither wished to build a new life in a strange city? Yes, their power—which had never been phenomenal—was falling off; but nobody has ever known more about how to eke out a victory in a tight ball game than these two men. For all that, they had apparently failed to earn the esteem which (for example) Al Lopez held for Al Smith—and this was the "enlightened" Dodger organization!

I have a suspicion that Davis met with the same lack of esteem based upon ignorance of the game's anatomy. His teammates Willie Davis (no relation, though also black) and Ron Fairly were able to survive much longer in Dodger blue because they showed consistent power (an emphasis which may actually have diminished Willie's game, for he was arguably the fastest player of his generation and could surely have parleyed a less ambitious swing into twenty or thirty more points on his average). The Braves had Aaron, the Giants had Mays, and the Reds had Robinson: Tommy had briefly looked as though he might just be flirting with such high-power company. Then the leg… and there goes his power. Nobody cared that he could hit to all fields— or nobody who mattered.

Two or three passages in Tommy's delightful little book are especially revealing—perhaps more so than he realizes. Of his leg injury, he has this to say:

> Dr. Kerlan told the Dodgers to give me two years to recuperate because I had a real bad injury and it would take that long to get me back at full strength. They traded me after one year. So I was determined to come back after they traded me. That's why I tell everybody that the best year I ever had was 1967 with the Mets. I hit .302 for a last-place club and that enabled me to play until 1976 because I hit the ball on a bad ankle. Forget all the statistics. That

was survival.[17]

I interpret the cryptic final sentence to mean that Davis regards the second half of his career as a monument to sheer determination triumphing over constant pain—that his brilliance was, from 1967 on, no longer attributable to explosive talent so much as to courageous concentration. Well, and so it was for DiMaggio, Mantle, Koufax, Gibson... great players inevitably play hard, and players who play hard play hurt. The baseball establishment surely knows this. In fact, in Tommy's day general managers were renowned for the veiled-threat bromides they dished out to keep their players taking the field as their bodies fell to pieces. The broken leg was in itself no reason to give up on Tommy, or not much of one. It was the little bit of a reason that allowed general mangers to do what they do best: tinker with the machine instead of standing back and letting it work out its kinks.

Buzzie Bavasi was the Dodgers' GM. Most of his brotherhood simply built up and defended unto death a brick wall during contract negotiations.[18] Buzzie was more creative. Before his tactics became widely known, he would wave in a player for a session, suddenly be called from the office, and abandon his guest to pace the empty room until "chancing" upon other players' contracts left in full view on his desk. The indiscretion, however, was illusory, for the contracts were bogus. They would couple a superstar's name to some exiguous figure, and the nervous young man awaiting the audience would be pounded into submission upon discovering what his "betters" earned. Davis relates an incident involving Ron Fairly where Bavasi physically brandished various stars' contracts in his face before the mysterious call to another room. "Buzzie did that kind of stuff all the time. He did it to me by leaving Maury [Wills]'s fake contract out there for me."[19] Stunningly, these anecdotes appear in a chapter of the book called "A Walk on the Lighter Side" and in a section which Tommy labels "Buzzie the Prankster". Not all of his Dodger teammates viewed such lubricious mendacity as a prank.[20] After all, many had families to feed and few ways of feeding them besides playing ball.

Less jocular is Tommy's recollection of how he managed to get the axe in Oakland. It seems that he had innocently recommended an agent to Vida Blue in 1971, when Blue, fresh from winning a Cy Young Award, was bombarded with requests for endorsements. Tommy, a two-time batting champ himself and a veteran of the Hollywood scene, knew the ropes. So pleased was Blue with his legal representation that he allowed the attorney to intrude upon contract negotiations the following spring. A's owner Charlie Finley, furious that he could not underpay the day's best pitcher by several thousand dollars, asked questions until he learned that Tommy had made the original introductions. Tommy was released on the spot.[21]

I am not about to write the sentence, "If Tommy had been white, Finley would have swallowed his anger," even though I suspect it of holding some truth. May I venture to say, instead, that black players seemed disproportionately mauled in the day's sanguinary contract disputes? Koufax and Drysdale famously held out for more money, mounting a two-man boycott in 1966. Mantle refused to appear for spring training on at least one occasion. It was Curt Flood, however, who probably got himself traded by extorting what he was worth from August Busch—an event which, of course, ended his career when he refused to pull up stakes and head for Philadelphia. And it was Tommy Davis who had both legs broken, one might say figuratively, for innocently sharing an attorney's acquaintance.

You weren't supposed to enter the boss's office with representation: that wasn't how the game was played—the *other* game which ultimately fed your children.[22] The Finleys of the baseball world no doubt felt that Tommy should have known better; and maybe they felt, in addition, that such a bad apple needed removing from the barrel fast before his corrupting influence spread to others of his race. Bill Dewitt reacted similarly to Frank Robinson's palling around with Vada Pinson. When a small clique of guys does something the management doesn't like and all the guys have an unusual skin color, acting up a little becomes hatching a conspiracy.

Manny Jiménez

Manny was one of the dark-skinned Latinos (like Felix Mantilla, discussed immediately below) whom I did not include in my statistical comparisons because I detected possible differences in the treatment of black and Latin players—but whose Post cereal baseball card, nevertheless, was among the first to get me thinking about racial issues. When I reconsidered Jiménez's rookie card from 1962, I was astonished to reflect that this young man virtually disappeared almost at once. Had he died? No. Had he suffered serious injury? Possibly… but not according to any evidence that I could find. In my search for answers, I found the following information at baseballlibrary.com, posted by one Jesus Cabrera:

> Jimenez looked promising when he hit .301 with 11 HR and 69 RBI in his rookie 1962 season. But he lost his power in reduced playing time in 1963 and, regaining it in 1964, saw his BA plummet to .225. He resurfaced with the Pirates, leading the NL in pinch hits in 1967 and in pinch at-bats the following year, when he went 10-for-53 in that role. He hit .303 overall that year by going 10-for-13 in his only non-pinch at-bats.

Now, I am sincerely grateful to Mr. Cabrera for this posting, and I understand that a site such as Baseball Library does not desire speculative discussions such as mine in this book. For that matter, anyone can look at Jiménez's stat sheet and tell that his power faded during his sophomore season, and that his batting average plummeted during his third season. If the Kansas City franchise were second-guessed by reporters about benching Manny (and he *was* benched: fewer than a third of his rookie at-bats in the second year, well under half in his third year), then these explanations would be the obvious on-the-record response. And they're true: the figures don't lie. Manny's home run bat vanished in '63, and his average tanked in '64.

But this is also utter folderol—preposterous, in the word's literal sense. That is, the consequences have been slipped up front as premises. Manny wasn't benched because he didn't hit better: he didn't hit better because he was benched. How do I know this? Because the figures (which don't lie) show that he had never really lost his hitting savvy—that he was being undermined by his employers. His on-base percentage for 1963 actually exceeded his rookie number. He was still striking out fewer than once per ten at-bats and walking above that ratio (unlike his rookie season, when he walked under 7% of the time). In other words, Jiménez was doing just fine as a sophomore. The missing homers may have been attributable to his being batted farther down in the line-up, where he could be pitched around. That would also explain the walks. To chastise him for responding to this situation as any good hitter ought to smells of a set-up: i.e., "Let's put him where he won't get good pitches. Then either his average will go down or he'll take walks and not rack up homers." If you had a player who reached base twice every five at-bats, wouldn't you play him more than every third or fourth game, whether or not he hit the ball out of the park?

But the fix was in, and Manny seems to have gotten the message. In 1964 he selected the second option: swing hard at everything to pump up the homers, but watch your average go down as the pitchers work your aggressive style just off the corners. Sure enough, Jiménez "regained" his power—but now the lower average was an unpardonable sin. In four more Major League seasons, he never saw more than 66 at-bats per season. The team that took him on as a pinch-hitter deluxe, by the way, was the Pirates. As we shall see (Chapter Five below), Pittsburgh had a knack for snapping up dark-skinned players obviously on their way out and allowing them to play a token role briefly. That Manny hit .303 *and* logged three extra-base hits in his final five dozen Pirate at-bats—during the Year of the Pitcher, no less—didn't impress the organization enough to keep him around.

I have yet to see that explanation of Manny Jiménez's mutilated career which would convince me that his treatment by Major League baseball was other than deplorably biased, nor does the nature of the bias seem very much in question.

***

Postscript: I had given up on finding out more about Manny Jiménez and was proceeding—on a hunch—to research Charlie Finley, the cocksure, irascible owner of the Athletics who soon bundled them off to Oakland. Was "Charlie-O", perhaps, a bigoted autocrat who had engineered the eventual expulsion from the franchise of such extraordinary talents as Jiménez and Ed Charles? Well, yes and no. I found, to be exact, that Finley was an equal-opportunity persecutor of order, common sense, and baseball acumen. He would create the A's juggernaut of the Seventies—and then, quite as suddenly, dismantle it in whimsical pique.

As far as Manny Jiménez is concerned... see for yourself. My source, I should say, was again Baseball Library:

> Finley's first of many feuds with players and managers commenced at the 1962 All-Star break when he ordered Manny Jimenez, who was leading the AL with a .350 average, to start hitting home runs. Manager Hank Bauer took Jimenez's side and was fired after the season. Jimenez slumped and was sent down in 1963.

"Jiménez slumped." We know now that this isn't quite the whole story, either. Manny's home run production slumped in 1963—whether in defiance of Finley, in the self-defeating struggle to crank out more homers, or in response to a batting-order demotion, I still have not discovered. When he started to pop four-baggers in 1964, his average clearly tumbled: we have established that much, as well. What is of extreme interest to me here is that we now have a second documented case (George Altman's being the first) of a black player's being put under great pressure by the front office to hit home runs. Manny had sense enough to take bad pitches and keep his on-base percentage up even in the worst of times: he could have been one of the great hitters of his generation. Instead, a dictatorial fool of an owner was sold on the notion that "dumb outfielders" were best employed swinging for the fences, and his brilliant idea cleft Manny's career like a wedge.

Did Finley actually think of Jiménez, more specifically, as a "dumb black outfielder"? I have no evidence of that... not really. But the following state of events in 1963, when Manny was suffering from royal disfavor, should be noted. The starting outfield for the third-from-last 1963 Kansas City Athletics consisted of Gino Cimoli, Bobby Del Greco, and José Tartabul, none of whom came close to equaling Manny's batting average that year and *all three of whom managed 13 home runs in almost 1100 at-bats*! Tartabull, of course, was himself a Latin player, and was soon put on the bench to make room for such Caucasian sluggers as Mike Hershberger and Jim Gosger. I repeat: where vultures circle, can a carcass be far away?

A short article from a 1962 *Sports Illustrated* has also lately come into my hands which sings some slightly condescending praises of Manny.[23] It is replete with references to his broken English and "squeaky, toothy giggle", employing the vein in which it had reported the young Bob Gibson as saying, "I don't do no thinkin' about pitchin'. I just hum dat pea."[24] The local fans apparently never watched The Bill Dana Show ("My name... Hos-Say He-MAIN-ez," Bill used to sulk in one commercial), so they call him "jim-en-ez, as in jiminez cricket. His teammates just call him mayonnaise, which sounds about right." The only reason I append this doubtful venture into humor is that the reporter also—finally—gets around to noting that "since 1957... [Jiménez] has been hit by 55 pitched balls, six of them this year. (The one that broke his wrist was supposed to go into his ear but he blocked it.)" Manny's manager, Hank Bauer, adds that the youngster's big leg-kick leaves him exposed to pitches riding too far inside, since it's hard to retreat on one leg.

It sounds very much as though Manny hit rather as Harold Baines did and Ichiro Susuki does—two other artist-batsmen with scores of doubles and occasional home run power. The broken wrist would have been on Manny's more dominant right hand (he batted left but threw right), and it was probably still tender in 1962. I would also not be surprised if Jiménez had not backed off the plate an inch after his experiences to make of himself a less inviting target. Both of these conditions—a tender "power hand" and a somewhat lunging, front-foot swing—would tend to detract from Manny's ability to belt homers, though they might also cause him to focus on the ball more and hit low line-drives. (Hence the league-leading average.)

If I have to spell it out… I am reiterating, in different terms and for different reasons, that Charlie Finley ruined a terrific talent.

Felix Mantilla

Mantilla had a very solid year for the expansion New York Mets in 1962. He batted .275, hit 11 home runs, and knocked 21 other extra-base safeties while scoring 54 runs and driving home another 59—all of this from the bottom half of the order. He was promptly traded to Boston, which franchise manifested no very great desire to play him in '63. The next year, however, the Red Sox gave Felix 425 at-bats—almost as many as he had enjoyed with New York. Mantilla responded with his best season ever, belting a noisy 30 home runs to go with a .289 average. As a reward, Felix received another hundred at-bats in 1965 (his first and last total of over 500). The homers settled back into his more typical range at 18, but his average remained fairly static at .275—and his RBI tally, most impressively, swelled to 92.

And then Felix Mantilla was done. Dealt to Houston (where Paul Richards was GM), he logged 151 at-bats, flirted with the Mendoza Line (a .200 batting average), was ruled no longer capable of Major League levels of performance, and haunted the big leagues no further.

I begin with the second half of Mantilla's career and speak of his experience as ghostly because, in Milwaukee for his career's first half, he was indeed something very like a waif drifting between the bench and various infield positions, never very substantial to decision-making eyes that peered right through him in search of answers to the Braves' second-base and shortstop problems. In Chapter 6 of Part 2, I reproduced Mantilla's disheartening observations about the "gentlemen's agreement" that precluded teams from having more than four dark-skinned players on the field at once. Felix was the odd man out, more often than not. Although the Braves' front office let on that his fielding was suspect, he had always been one of the smoothest-fielding shortstops at every level of ball he had played.[25] (The throwing error to end a forced play-off which sent the Dodgers to the '59 World Series was in fact a superb pick-up behind second base, followed by a flick to first rather poorly played by Frank Torre. Felix always received the blame for the miscue, though he arguably deserved little or none at all.) When slurs against his fielding proved to have little carry, press releases picked on his hitting—and it *is* pretty hard to hit Major League pitching if your greatest exposure to it, week in and week out, is from the dugout. Yet even the often gullible Ed Walton could see through the smoke screen: "One of the most versatile fielders ever to play the majors was making a 35-game appearance with the Braves [in 1956]. That was Felix 'The Cat' Mantilla. They said he was a good field, no hit player, but after 11 seasons this appeared to be only half correct."[26]

One would have thought that liberation from the sorry state of affairs in Milwaukee would have launched Mantilla's career… but he could achieve escape velocity neither in New York nor, of course, with the racially retrograde Red Sox.

I have a feeling that Felix would not have remained invisible in Chicago or on the West Coast. He was in the wrong place at the wrong time. A victim of racial prejudice? That conclusion seems to me clearly beyond question.

Al McBean

Cleveland-area sportswriter Morris Eckhouse offers the following helpful and succinct account of McBean's baseball career at www.baseballlibrary.com:

> Born in St. Thomas, Virgin Islands, McBean was photographing a Pirates tryout camp in 1957, tried out himself, and earned a ticket to professional baseball. He graduated to the big leagues in 1961 and fashioned Pittsburgh's second-best record (15-10) in 1962. Thin, loose-jointed, and cat-like on the mound, he found even more success as a reliever. He was TSN NL Fireman of the Year in 1964, when he had 22 saves and led the league with eight relief wins. Known for his flashy attire and expensive wardrobe, he returned to starting in 1968 and went to the Padres in the expansion draft after the season

I'm sorry… but I didn't understand the shifting of Al to the bullpen when I wrote about pitchers (Part 2, Chapter 8) and I *still* don't understand it. The reliever had not yet come into his own in the early Sixties: relegation to such duties from the starting rotation continued to be viewed widely as a demotion. Perhaps Danny Murtaugh and the Pirates' brain trust had no such denigration in mind—perhaps they were ahead of their time. The career of the Pirates' Caucasian pitcher Elroy Face would seem to justify a charitable interpretation of McBean's re-deployment after a brilliantly successful sophomore season in a starter's role. But Face had always been used primarily in such a manner (going an incredible 18 and 1 out of the bullpen in 1959). Al, on the other hand, had proved himself a highly competent starter for a team where break-even starters were in short supply. I suppose it's possible that Murtaugh was anticipating Face's final days and grooming a replacement. At the very least, however, transferring a 15-and-10 starter to the bullpen on a team that could only beat out the expansion Colt .45s and Mets in 1963 seems an unpromising path to managerial longevity.

As Mr. Eckhouse's sketch intimates, Al McBean was certainly no clubhouse grouch. On the contrary, Red Schoendienst seems to have dubbed him the funniest man he ever saw, and the fans loved his routine-rupturing antics (such as crawling over the foul line when taking the field and mopping sweat from his forehead with a bright red bandana). Al was the very antithesis of a trouble-maker. That his less frequent use, therefore, may have been chastisement for disruptive behavior seems completely implausible.

Of course, Danny Murtaugh did *not* keep his job for very long: he was dismissed after the '64 season. Maybe his slightly but sincerely nutty approach to the allotment of pitching duties was an honest experiment with unhappy results. The approach was continued, though—at least as far as McBean was concerned—when Harry "The Hat" Walker succeeded Murtaugh as skipper; and Walker has been indicted by Joe Morgan as an overt bigot (see Chapter 5 below). Murtaugh had given Al almost as many innings in relief as he had pitched in 1962 out of a starting spot: Walker reduced his mound time dramatically. As I have already said, I find McBean's handling over these years extremely suspect.

But would pure, unadulterated bigotry (viz., "I'm not going to play that black blankety-blank!") account for the benching of a potential ace? I prefer to avoid such propositions. They seem extravagant to me: a manager wants to keep his job as much as anyone else, and only a vindictive lunatic would sabotage his team to carry forward a private race war. What, then, might have been in the mind of someone like Harry Walker? I have written elsewhere of the put-downs that Bob Gibson described receiving under skipper Solly Hemus. It appears that not a few managers during this era fully believed their black pitchers mentally incapable of undertaking a several-inning effort: they could throw bullets for an inning or two (hence their effectiveness as relievers), but their minds could not embrace the kind of long-term strategy and retain the kind of minute detail needed to navigate a tough line-up for nine complete frames. Jim Grant (who would certainly appear in this chapter if Post had awarded him a much-deserved place among its 1961 cards) spelled out the presumptions about black pitchers very clearly after his retirement:

Except when baseball brought in Jackie Robinson and Larry Doby, it went along with the slow, general transition in society instead of taking the initiative. A lot of us who came along after Jackie and Larry broke in were justifiably angry at our treatment. We had to go along with much that was humiliating. For instance, because I was black, it was generally accepted by the powers that be that I wasn't smart enough to both pitch and call my own game—it was infuriating that the white manager and his white catcher called my games. The reason I didn't succumb to my anger is that I understood that racism is inbred. People don't just become bigots. It has to be taught.[27]

These remarks may actually explain more about Grant's rude handling than McBean's, for Mudcat would have to be superhuman to have kept such simmering indignation entirely bottled up—whereas Al, as we have established, was extraordinarily easy-going by nature. But then, I am not suggesting that McBean was exiled to the bullpen for chafing at the guidance of his "betters": I am suggesting that the shift of roles may have been perceived by its engineers as beneficial both for him and for the team. As a reliever, he would work shorter stints. He wouldn't have to think so much, to remember so much. In fact, it is entirely possible that a young man could be the victim of such patronizing "favors" and not even know it. All he would ever hear would be, after a loud clap on the back, "Al, my boy, I think you've got real talent as a reliever. We need you down there in the pen, kid."

No, I have not a shred of hard evidence that McBean ever received that clap on the back. I could swear, though, that I hear its echoes as I look over his career stats.

Charlie Neal

About Charlie, the amiable Ed Walton, who seems to have gobbled up everything the sports page fed him, has this to say: "Neal was characterized as temperamental, no hustler, and needing to pull the ball to hit over .250, but was rated as a good fielder."[28] I cannot for the life of me understand how anyone could associate pulling the ball with pumping up a batting average—how any paid mouthpiece would be so arrogant as to release such a claim to the general public, or how any scribe would be so gullible as to reproduce it. Young black ballplayers, as we have seen and shall continue to see, were often exhorted to pull in order to achieve more power. Those experienced hitters who dished out such advice (i.e., excluding Branch Rickey and Charlie Finley) appear to have had no illusions about its leading the apt pupil to a batting title. White baseball didn't want batting champs in the late Fifties and early Sixties: it wanted sluggers. In his classic instructional videos and book, Ted Williams made no bones about preferring the style that sacrifices a few points off the batting average for enhanced power. Ironically, Ted was the last man to hit .400. One wonders what he could have hit if he'd really tried!

As a second baseman, Charlie Neal showed no dearth of power. Maybe the lessons on pulling the ball worked, and maybe not. He tied none other than Gil Hodges for the team lead in home runs in 1958, the first year the Dodgers played in Los Angeles. Both belted 22—stunning for a middle infielder, but not for Gil: the LA Coliseum, a converted football field, spelled death to the Dodgers' traditionally formidable long-ball attack. Charlie, however, slammed two homers *over the right-field wall* that season, the only Dodger to reach those distant seats all year. He certainly wasn't pulling in those at-bats.

The 22 home runs were a new record for Dodger second basemen, as well; and the following year, Charlie almost equaled that tally with 19 four-baggers. In fact, his slugging percentage from 1957 to 1959 was comfortably above .400, and he drove in an average of 70 runs per season over the same period from a spot in the line-up where such production is not expected. To have found such a potent bat at second base, of all places, must have been a godsend for the Bums as they made their West Coast transition while awakening to the age of their once-mighty bombers and the inefficacy of Hodges and Snider in the new confines.

But batting average… well, if you wanted to hammer Charlie for something, it might well be his average. Not that he had much trouble staying above .250 until his playing time was reduced: his only journeys beneath that measure of mediocrity occurred during his last season in Los Angeles and his last in the big leagues (split between the Mets and the Reds), both of which seasons saw him taking little more than 300 official trips to the plate. Seldom did he hit much above .260, seldom much below it: he was constant in that regard, and such constancy is itself highly prized. (If you're not going to hit .300, the next-best thing is to be *dependable* at .265 so that your manager can pencil you into the line-up accordingly.)

If Neal was supposed to hit .290, he shouldn't have been urged to pull the ball (though it seems that this might have worked against his power, too). If he was supposed to collect 35 extra-base hits per season (something Yankee second baseman Bobby Richardson managed twice in twelve years), he shouldn't have been nagged about his average. The only problem with Charlie's offense, speaking realistically, was that he always struck out about half again as much as he walked. The ratio was fairly steady. It seems that his power was discovered early (and it would be hard to hide power at Ebbets Field), lauded, and fixed in his mind as one of his great assets. Then, when the Dodgers had to make room for other black infielders (Junior Gilliam was already being shoved all over the diamond), Charlie's batting average became an issue. Catch-22.

Frankly, I don't feel that I have found my way anywhere near the bottom of Neal's case. Ballplayers both black and white have been caught in these contradictory expectations many a time. At least Charlie could say that when power was demanded of him, he found it in abundance. Other black players destroyed their swings in its fruitless pursuit. Yet this rare versatility earned Neal only eight seasons in the big leagues, with the miserable '62 Mets discarding him after a solid year and the Reds scarcely giving him a try-out. Walton noted something about Charlie's being "temperamental, no hustler". Evidently, "hustle" factors out such feats as being among the team leaders in stolen bases year after year. Criticisms of character are often code for "doesn't instantly execute manager's desires"… but I have nothing substantial to say on that score. Dodger teammate John Roseboro remarks cryptically at one point, without further elucidation, that "Neal screwed up with management and got traded."[29] The gaffe doesn't seem to have been of the sort that left towns painted red or otherwise caused a public relations problem, for the Dodgers handled dozens of those routinely, and Roseboro also writes quite bluntly about his acquaintances' lives off the field. Too vocal at the wrong time, perhaps? Too willing to speculate about Buzzie Bavasi's lineage to his face?

More likely, Neal was just awkward verbally. His appearance was not prepossessing (his severe buck teeth should have been straightened when he was a child, but of course were not); and in the relatively abundant newsreel footage of the '59 World Series and its heroes, he generally seems to hang back and glare uneasily at the camera. People who have trouble finding the right words under pressure often grow a little withdrawn and surly. It's a natural response to being dragged out of one's element.

Moffi and Kronstadt are confident that Neal's rather sudden exit from the Dodger organization had racial undercurrents: "According to New York sportswriter Dick Young, baseball was not yet ready for a team with seven or eight black ballplayers."[30] That may well be. But Hodges and Snider shifted their waning careers back to New York, as well: the Mets were bad, all right, but they had come home. The question that lingers in my mind is, *why didn't the Mets hang onto Charlie?* Or the Reds? Who would go so far as to see bigotry in those cases? If it was there, I suspect it had something to do with that "temperamental" odor. The Cincinnati press and the Reds' front office (in some indecipherable combination) were already grumbling about the "Negro clique" in the clubhouse (see Part 2, Chapter 6). Charlie may have walked through the wrong door at the wrong moment. If he wasn't temperamental before, he would have been after a month in Cincinnati.

Vada Pinson

In the so-called Year of the Pitcher (1968), Vada Pinson hit a puny 5 home runs in almost 500 at-bats. His .271 average was nothing to sniff at... or wouldn't have been for anyone else. For Vada, it was his lowest mark since 1964, when he batted .266 *but also* clubbed 23 home runs and 11 triples. The homers ascended into double-digits again in '69—but the average went farther south, wintering at a frigid .255 (Vada's lowest mark ever in a full season of at-bats).

To put these two miserable seasons into perspective, Pinson had, over the nine previous years stretching back to his sophomore campaign in 1959, typically hit about 21 home runs *per annum*, 34 doubles, and 10 triples, while batting an even .300, knocking in 84 runs, and scoring 100. Perhaps the most stupendous aspect of Vada's "typical season" (the like of which most players would be happy to log a single time, even those who profit from today's offensive inflation) is its consistency. Year after year, the lines across the stat sheet show figures varying by minuscule margins. Over his inaugural decade, Pinson led the National League (i.e., the more offensively dynamic league) once in games played, twice in at-bats, once in runs, twice in hits, once in singles, twice in doubles, and twice in triples. Four times he was among the top ten in batting average, three times in slugging, seven times in total bases, and seven *consecutive* times in runs scored. From 1959 to 1971, he failed to place among the top ten in stolen bases only three times (once because of a fractured leg—which did not, however, immediately sideline him[31]).

Add to these tallies a Golden Glove which Vada managed to wrest away from rival center fielder Willie Mays in 1961, and you have one of the most complete players of a very distinguished generation. Pinson's RBIs may have been a bit beneath the spectacular; but for the first half of his career, Vada played for a Cincinnati team where most of the mopping up was done by Frank Robinson.

Curiously, though, after Frank departed the Reds at the end of the '65 season, Vada proceeded to reel off three of his four worst RBI years for the franchise, no doubt sealing his own trade at the end of that disappointing run. When I read in Bill James's *Baseball Almanac* that Pinson had felt compelled by Robby's example to show more power, I was confident that the mystery was solved. To be exact, James cites sports reporter Earl Lawson: "I have to think that during the winter of 1961 Pinson came to the conclusion that the top awards and big bucks came with home runs." He would naturally have figured this out: anyone could have, with far less cause to brood over the fact than Vada. It is a small step from here to the supposition that Pinson began to press for the long ball.[32]

Reading Lawson's own account of Pinson's attacks upon him—full-blown incidents of the worst sort, ending in Lawson's filing an assault charge after Vada physically bullied him a second time—I grew more convinced than ever that Pinson was a man under heavy pressure. Not only were the confrontations themselves wholly out of character: more than that, Lawson's criticism was surgically precise, and it must have pierced Vada like a lancet. In his summary of the story he originally printed, the Hall of Fame sportswriter recalls the relevant details:

> In the story I said Pinson's stubborn refusal to capitalize on his tremendous speed by dragging an occasional bunt probably would cost him the National League batting crown. At the time, Pinson trailed Pittsburgh's Dick Groat, the league leader, by only seven points. I wrote if one were to tack 10 bunt singles onto Pinson's hit total for the same number of at bats, he'd be hitting 20 points higher than his current average. I pointed out that the Reds' Don Blasingame had beaten out twice that many bunts in 1962 and he didn't even have Pinson's speed.[33]

Why would these have been fighting words, unless a) Pinson knew that their advice was very sound, and b) he felt compelled to ignore the advice? Why would he have felt so compelled? Well, because of the laurels showered upon Robinson, to be sure... but who knows what other hints and nudges were passed his way, quite unknown to Lawson, from a front office that had long wanted to unload Frank? Imagine yourself facing a very probable promotion into an enviable job for which, however, you fully realize yourself to be unqualified. The last thing you need is for some well-meaning and keen-witted but politically naïve observer to hound you about being unqualified. Perhaps Vada should have done just what Lawson recommended… but perhaps a batting title with only a dozen homers to go with it would have gotten him traded just as fast as his disastrous over-swinging.

Let us stipulate, then, that Vada Pinson's career veered off track just at the brink of superstardom because he began to press at the plate, trying to drive pitches out of the park which were not particularly "drivable". Indeed, if Jim Brosnan is to be believed in his iconoclastic exposé, *The Long Season*, Frank Robinson once remarked in 1959 after a Pinson home run, alluding to the speedster's overly fast circling of the bases, "Little man, you just better stick to singles and leave the long ones to us cats who know how to act 'em out."[34] Good-humored ribbing has been the prick of ambition many times in human history. Vada would have been aware from his first full Major League season that he *could* hit home runs and that those around him did not think him *best suited* to hitting them. Messieurs Muffi and Kronstadt offer the clearest kind of confirmation that such thoughts were already fluttering about Pinson's head in his rookie season. They quote Vada as saying only a year later, recollecting the grand slam he hit in his second big-league game, "Probably the worst thing that happened to me was hitting a homer against Pittsburgh last year in the second game of the season. It won the game but it didn't do me any good. I started thinking of myself as a slugger."[35]

Of course, during the mid- to late-Sixties, a lot of hitters were apparently just as ill-suited to playing long ball yet apparently as keen to play it as Vada. I personally cannot find enough Koufaxes, Gibsons, and Marichals to account for across-the-board twenty- and thirty-point drops in batting averages during the very years when both leagues should have been recovering from expansion's ravages of pitching staffs. (The Angels and Twins debuted in 1961, the latter moving from Washington and forcing the nation's capital to throw together a new team hurriedly; the Colt .45s and Mets raised anchor the following year.) When Major League hitters swing from the heels, however, Major League pitchers—even merely "ordinary" pitchers—allow them to retire themselves.

In this section of the book, I find myself floating the suggestion over and over (nor will Vada be my last occasion to do so) that pressing hitters were themselves being pressed—and not in a manner wholly unrelated to racial prejudice. If ever there was a guy who shouldn't have been thinking about the fences, it was Vada Pinson. For almost a decade, he stretched doubles into triples at an astounding rate and racked up steals when they were still largely discouraged. In short, Vada played like the Ghost of the Negro Leagues. His game was multi-dimensional—and some of his liners, to be sure, cleared the fence. Yet few line-drive hitters have Aaron's ability to ratchet their shots consciously up a notch to clear the wall. Aaron made the adjustment because he was convinced that white baseball would never recognize him (or the race of players he represented) at full value any other way. If Pinson was responding to the same pressures, then he probably pulled his career off its 3,000-hit, Hall of Fame trajectory by so doing. In that case, the motive for his unfortunate gambit can be attributed, not to some greenhorn infatuation with power which really makes no sense in a ten-year veteran, but to an anxiety about his livelihood as he plied his craft before ignorant (or grudging) eyes.

Are there signs of racism in Pinson's treatment beyond this point (which itself would be considered a stretch by some)? I no longer think so. My original amazement that Vada Pinson should have become a distant memory while his '61 and '62 baseball cards showed every promise of immortality is, most of all, a response to something very like Greek tragedy. One often registers that crushing disappointment over grand potential pulled awry by its very richness of options when one studies retrospectively the careers of ballplayers. Vada should probably be in the Hall of Fame.[36] He will not be—not tomorrow or next year or ever. He died years ago (in 1995), he was never a flamboyant extrovert who could mobilize virtual strangers in his behalf (unlike Orlando Cepeda), he actually got himself into physical confrontations with a very popular gentleman of the press (not wise for Hall of Fame aspirants), and he forged no placatory ties with the indispensable Fourth Estate after his career (unlike Phil Rizzuto).   Earl Lawson's chain of reasoning—or wishing—is irresistible in retrospect: if only…. If only Vada had ground out one more stellar season while in the American League (his 1970 with Cleveland was pretty darn good, but not stellar), his Cooperstown credentials would have been far more compelling than those of others who have made it past the gates of Olympus. If only he had spread the "peak" and "trough" years of his later career more evenly (as did Willie McCovey), or if only his superb defensive play hadn't been eclipsed by a beloved superstar's (as Bill Mazeroski's was not), or if only he had hung up the cleats before a final season dragged down his average while adding very few hits (as Ron Santo managed to do)… *if only*.

Beyond question, Vada's best claim to Cooperstown ended up being his hit total of 2757. If, over the last decade of his career (that is, after he visited .300 for the final time in 1965), he had chalked up a mere 15 more hits per season, relying on speed and bat control instead of power, nobody could have refused him a place on the podium. He took his maturing career in the wrong direction, probably under pressure from ownership and management as well as from his own desire for recognition. If only he had taken Earl Lawson's advice to heart after leaving Cincinnati… if only Oedipus had taken a different path at the crossroads…

Floyd Robinson

When I began this study with a short narrative about collecting baseball cards in my childhood, Floyd Robinson was one of the names I pointedly mentioned as having awed me with his numbers only to have disappeared off the game's radar when I looked back much later. In reviewing those old cards, I singled out Floyd as a possible victim of residual racism—a player who certainly had his chance, but who may have enjoyed far less of a chance than others of a lighter complexion.

I no longer believe that this is true in any obvious sense, based upon what evidence I have been able to scrape together. Floyd's 1962 season was a smaller version of the monster '62 Tommy Davis put together in the National League, with scintillating offensive statistics spread out evenly across the board. Robinson's .312 batting average ranked third, his 45 doubles led the league, his 10 triples took second place, and he also added 11 home runs on his way to batting in 109. It's hard to imagine that a season like that could just be a flash in the pan.

And it wasn't. Floyd had other very fine years. His .301 average was fifth in 1964's American League, and his home run totals actually climbed for two out of the next three years. Nonetheless, something was gradually going wrong. By 1965, Robinson's average had dropped to .265, and it would continue to plummet for the remaining three years of his career. The White Sox can scarcely be faulted for dealing him to Cincinnati after his '66 performance at a .237 clip, or for cutting his playing time in half over that season. Unlike George Altman, he was not interrupted amid a string of stellar campaigns—but like George Altman, he never found his old footing again on American turf. As far as I know, Floyd did not follow George's (and Willie Kirkland's) example and re-invent himself in Japan.

Well, these things happen. A guy has a great year—even a great two or three years—and then can't seem to find the old magic. Oakland and Boston even offered Robinson an opportunity to hang around in 1968 (which he could not successfully exploit). In many ways, Floyd reminds me more of Caucasian outfielder Norm Siebern than of George Altman. In 1962, you would have sworn that Norm was a young man bound straight for Cooperstown. His .308 average and 117 RBIs were very close to Floyd's numbers, and his home run output more than doubled Floyd's. But Siebern would never again crack the 20-homer bracket or bat .300. In four of his remaining six years, his average dipped below .250. Boston gave him his final two dozen or so at-bats, just as it had Floyd: in fact, they both made their brief stop in Fenway during the baleful year (for hitters) of 1968. I don't know if they were able to exchange words or glances before slipping under the waves. Neither wore the Red Sox uniform for very long.

Beneath all this circumstantial melodrama, the statistics tell a tale whose deeper meaning, I suspect, has never been appreciated. The mid-Sixties witnessed the fizzling out of a great many promising offensive players. Some of those who had already clearly established themselves, like Ron Fairly and Vada Pinson, were able to cling to life as Major Leaguers until their swing grew healthier. Others like Robinson were casualties of their age, since they would almost certainly have lit up the pitching of the late Fifties. Siebern batted .300 in 1958 as a virtual rookie—and this, rather than any race-based motive, is probably why his descent was allowed to last a little longer than Robinson's.

But was the pitching really so dominant in the mid-Sixties? We've all been told so: the statistics speak for themselves, do they not? Actually, I believe the stats to be whispering a subtly different message. To stick with

Robinson and Siebern, both elicited vast tallies of walks in their early years—usually more than their strikeout total. Giving away walks is not a mark of superlative pitching; and in "old-fashioned" baseball—pre-Ruth baseball, or the baseball of the Negro Leagues—the hated tribe of pitchers would have been cruelly punished by highly efficient offenses everywhere for free passes. But not in the mid-Sixties. Why not? Because hitters were not bunting or looping in opposite-field singles: *they were swinging for the fences*. This suggests why Robinson and Siebern may have steadily struck out with greater frequency until their walk/whiff ratio was about an even balance. That is, they were looking for a fat pitch to drive, and they ended up hitting behind in the count too often—or perhaps their homer-hungry eyes persuaded them that every pitch looked fat, which is even worse. Junior Gilliam, in contrast, typically drew two or three times as many walks as he posted strikeouts, and he most certainly wasn't accomplishing that unsung but impressive feat of discipline by trying to emulate Frank Howard.[37]

As I have already said many times, the mid-Sixties obsession with home runs also explains why *so few home runs were hit*—and so few doubles, and triples. Hitters were pressing. The few who didn't press—Aaron, McCovey, Billy Williams—made out just fine. But a great many other black players, having seen that the plums went to the sluggers, were not making solid contact with their hefty cuts: they were turning good pitchers into great pitchers. The expansion years of 1961 and 1962 must still have been sending faint ripples through big-league pitching staffs in '66 or '67. Think of it: how many truly outstanding pitchers flourished in these years? Koufax retired after 1966, and Whitey Ford was essentially done much sooner. Drysdale was not particularly effective on his own. Gibson, Marichal... and then a handful of fire-ballers like Bob Veale who profited from the epidemic of home run fever to post one or two red-letter years, and a host of breaking-ball artists who were the true beneficiaries of the high mound. (Pitchers with high leg kicks like Gibson and Marichal could throw a bullet in a parking lot: rather fewer actually pushed off the rubber for velocity, as did Koufax.) The plight of Robinson and Siebern is especially telling, it seems to me, in that both were right-handed throwers who batted left: i.e., their better hand was on the bottom of the bat, where it could steer with greater finesse, and the majority of pitchers they faced (righties) could not buckle their knees with breaking balls. Such hitters do not normally reach .300 and then never visit the mark again. Richie Asburn, Bill Bruton, and Pete Runnels were tough outs as long as they wore spikes—and Robinson and Siebern, like Ashburn and Bruton, were generously endowed with speed. Something had gotten into the heads of many very fine players, I am convinced, to make them forget their virtuous habits—and I believe that something to have been the home run.

This theory is vaguely supported by a brief testimonial from the 1963 American League Rookie of the Year, Gary Peters, who was Floyd's teammate on the White Sox. I found a passage where Peters describes Robinson as "a good low-ball hitter. He hit a lot of line drives for extra bases."[38] Such a hitter would meet with disaster if he attempted to elevate his drives by flying open: he would pull off the lower pitches and chase the higher ones fruitlessly (in a caricature of Ted Williams' patented power-hitting formula). For a batting average to tumble as sharply as Floyd's did in 1965 while his home runs (but *not* his doubles) actually increased, he would surely have to have been swinging more aggressively.

A bit of hearsay renders this theory even more persuasive, in Floyd's case. I cannot recall the precise source, but a television baseball analyst once remarked that Robinson posted one of his best seasons while complaining of an injury—a strained muscle, I believe. Such a handicap would be a blessing if Floyd were indeed over-swinging: it would force him to shorten up his stroke and concentrate on simple contact. Home run fever, a far more debilitating ailment, would have had the opposite effect.

I have mentioned the reports suggesting that Vada Pinson was chagrined over Frank Robinson's overshadowing him with really no more of an advantage than his home run power. Aaron, of course, openly testifies that he dedicated himself to the long ball at various points in his career when he saw how it was honored in Major League baseball. (The following chapter will offer specific references.) I don't know how much of this unstated but rigid insistence on the part of management and ownership may have been inspired by dread of the Negro Leagues' more improvisational style of play— dread, I mean, that limited managerial skills would drown in a sudden flood tide of player resourcefulness—and how much may have been fueled by the advent of television and the highlight reel. But if the former motive was indeed significant, as I suspect, and if Floyd Robinson did indeed alter his approach to the ball like so many young black talents who were not true power-hitters, then Floyd's somewhat short-circuited career was not, after all, completely unaffected by racism. That players like Norm Siebern vanished into the same chasm merely illustrates—brilliantly illustrates—that the prejudice against the Negro Leagues' "eccentric" play wrought a lot of collateral damage among talented white players.

Frank Robinson

If Robby ever endured any raw deals in his career on account of his race, one would have to say that he sand-blasted the rough spots right back in the faces of his detractors. If his magnificent career was cut short in any way, the culprit was a beaning that left him with double vision—not the malice of bigots. The concussion and its aftermath were typical of his style: stand right on top of the plate, claiming it all for yourself—and if anyone tries to scare you off, stand a little closer next time. Indeed, Frank had such a pugnacious reputation as a player that I was amazed to discover in him, through the help of *Extra Innings*, one of the keenest minds in the game—and also (perhaps after years of learning the hard way) one of the most mature emotional constitutions.

But let's acknowledge the elephant shifting its hefty weight about our armchairs: the trade of Frank Robinson by Reds' owner Bill DeWitt to

Baltimore in 1965 for Milt Pappas, Jack Baldschun, and Dick Simpson may well be among the three least defensible deals in baseball history. Pappas's best years on the mound were behind him: he would end his career as little better than a .500 pitcher. Baldschun was obscurity itself, and Simpson was another black face to diminish the impression that the Reds were going white. In a way, the trade remains as incomprehensible now as on the day it was announced; and in another way, nobody ever really had much doubt that its motive was a deeply personal animosity. Earl Lawson (the recipient of Vada Pinson's pugilistic self-assertion, and no stranger to animosity as a sportswriter) has this to say:

> DeWitt took a lot of static for trading Robinson. And Robby never missed an opportunity to shoot verbal barrages at DeWitt. The Reds' owner never did reveal publicly his real reasons for trading Robinson.
>
> Obviously, though, DeWitt was candid with Bob Howsam, who took over as Reds' general manager after the sale of the club. When asked if he would have dealt Robinson as DeWitt had, Howsam replied, "Knowing what I now know about him I probably would have. I think, though, I would have gotten more for him than Jack Baldshun, Milt Pappas, and Dick Simpson."
>
> Actually, there was no doubt in DeWitt's mind about Robinson's playing ability. The Reds' owner had confided to me that he had tired of the on-field, off-field aggravations Robinson had presented.[39]

Of course, it would be perfectly idiotic to attempt to justify the trade on the basis of playing ability when Robinson proceeded, the very next year, to win the American League Triple Crown and MVP Award and to lead Baltimore to the World Series. In fact, speaking of "off-field aggravations" in the teeth of such evidence is close to overweening arrogance. Most franchises would give out free tickets half the season to be so aggravated. Lawson implies above that Howsam's utterance sheds some kind of light on the situation. I see two possibilities: a) that Howsam swallowed DeWitt's version of events hook, line, and sinker; or b) that Howsam joined DeWitt in deploring the infamous "concealed weapon" incident as absolutely beyond endurance. A young Robinson had unwisely pulled a handgun once upon a time at spring training in Florida to punctuate an argument with some "good old boys" who took exception to their local diner's new black clientele. The occurrence was a one-of-a-kind fracas without any injuries. Yet Mr. DeWitt refused to make bail when the police took Frank downtown; and, for his part, Frank never forgot his owner's instant desertion at a critical moment. "To Bill DeWitt," he would write in *Extra Innings*, "players were just chattel."[40]

The incident was certainly not devoid of racial tension. Robinson had been psychologically scarred by his years of Minor League ball down South: the gun was a response, immature but understandable, to those painful memories. Bill DeWitt's sprint to judgment, however, and the tenacity with which he would cling to that judgment for years until unloading Robinson, suggest the influence of race, as well. Frank immediately and forever became a hoodlum to DeWitt once he produced his pea-shooter in a café. The impression was so repellant to the Reds' owner that he could at last set it to rest only by discarding one of the game's greatest players at a fire sale.

It was not entirely unheard-of for white players to fall afoul of the law. One has to wonder if Mr. DeWitt would have been so perturbed by Mickey and Billy's midnight antics. Of course, Robinson's white teammate Johnny Temple (by whom Earl Lawson also had the distinction of being punched) would eventually have major legal problems, and old comrades didn't exactly rally around. Johnny was too blue-collar—not that Mickey Mantle was otherwise; but Mick was straight out of *Li'l Abner*, while Johnny could have been the vagabond in *The Postman Always Rings Twice*. Stereotypes certainly include race, but they do not end with it.

Speaking of blue-collar white men who run afoul of stereotypes and, eventually, the law… John Roseboro wrote that part of what made the Reds' front office nervous about Frank Robinson's "black clique" was its apparent adoption of a young Pete Rose:

> The story we got out of Cincinnati was that when Pete first came up he got close to Frank Robinson and Vada Pinson. The Reds' brass thought he got too close and got rid of Robinson and Pinson to break it up. It was a black-white thing, the story goes, and also a matter of Frank being hard to handle and outspoken and maybe being a bad influence on Pete.[41]

Now, trading away two perennial All-Stars to safeguard one yet-unproven (and not entirely promising) kid seems a little excessive. There were no reports that Robinson and Pinson were skirt-chasers, hard drinkers, or drug-abusers. On the contrary, Roseboro speaks glowingly of Vada's character several times in his book—and about Frank I have never read anything more damning than the arrest for possessing a firearm. The scuttlebutt that Rosey recounts was probably justified, then, in considering the troublesome—for management—aspect of this trio to be the "black-white thing". Whatever your estimate of such gossip, the mere fact of its existence is already reason to believe that the Cincinnati clubhouse was not free of racial hostility. The authors of this "story" may well have gotten the primary motive for Frank's trade entirely wrong; but if the thought process of DeWitt and his lieutenants could be perceived (or misperceived) in such a manner by Reds players, the franchise clearly had long-standing trouble.

Ted Savage

I originally selected Ted Savage for the mix because I needed a few more players to round out my study group, and Ted's 1962 Topps rookie card impressed me. The card was clearly printed before the '62 season, for it contains only Minor League stats. Ted performed quite well enough in 335 at-bats that year, however, for Post cereals to have stamped his mug and numbers on a few million boxes: a .266 average, 54 runs, and 20 extra-base hits (along with 16 steals). It was an expansion year, unfortunately, and the cereal moguls allotted rather few places to a hapless Phillie team that could finish ahead of no one but the Colt .45s and the Mets. After that campaign, Ted spent years shuttling back and forth between the Minors and various big-league teams. His potential was obviously recognized around baseball—but it was exploited, just as obviously, to sweeten the pot in one multi-player deal after another.

The back burner notwithstanding, Ted continued to play hard wherever he was given a uniform. On May 20, 1967, during his less-than-full-season with the Cubs, he stole home. Three years and three trades later (i.e., in 1970), on a young Milwaukee Brewers team, he batted an impressive .279, walloping 12 homers, 5 triples, and 10 doubles en route to driving home 50 runs and scoring 43—this in 276 at-bats! Multiply all of these numbers by two, and you have a probable All-Star season (especially by 1970 standards)... but Ted was rewarded early the next year with a trade to Kansas City—where the also young Royals, apparently in a building mode, quickly put him out to pasture. End of career.

And end of story... or beginning? Is there not a real story here, a very persuasive morality tale about a young black multi-tool player being just good enough to lubricate trades, but scarcely getting a chance to play and never being rewarded properly when he played well? The evidence remains sketchy, precisely because Ted Savage's whole career was suffocated in obscurity. But the following summary that I found on the Internet certainly looks more like whitewash than hard fact:

> His speed and power made eight big league teams give this 6'1" 185-lb right-handed hitter a chance. Only in his rookie year with the Phillies in 1962 was he a regular, because he never became a consistent hitter. His best season came with the 1970 Brewers, when he had career highs of 12 HR, 50 RBI, and a .279 average in 274 at-bats.[42]

Pardon the redundancy of my producing those 1970 stats again—but I can never resist holding up for common enjoyment a self-contradictory piece of writing. If Ted never established himself as a consistent hitter, then why did his career's third and final approach to a half-season of Major League ball achieve All-Star quality? His fielding percentage was often close to Leon Wagner's (see below) until he was put at first base (as Leon never was). Should we use that explanation, instead? Maybe his fielding was just too much of a liability. But then, when you are palmed off on a new team every year, and actually get to play for that team in only a few dozen games, you might possibly be pressing while in the field. You might even be pressing at the plate. The possibility is substantial enough that you might expect some eminently professional coach to pull you aside at some point, settle you down, and assure you of your bright future… all the things that were clearly never done for Ted Savage. His baseball legacy, rather, was to enable a lot of long-forgotten trades.

Ted Savage could be the poster-child for everything that made me write this book. The back of my 1962 Topps baseball card shows him, in cartoon caricature, accepting a trophy from a gent-in-tux (also in cartoon style) for having the runner-up batting average while in Buffalo. Both figures are Caucasian. Exactly. Ted Savage spent a decade representing promise among the wrangles of wheeler-dealers. The man himself never got to step out of front-office fantasies.

Al Smith

Al should probably have been the 1955 Most Valuable Player in the American League. Batting .305, he led the league in runs scored (123) from his lead-off position in the Indians' line-up, and also managed 22 home runs and 31 other extra-base hits. Yogi Berra got the nod from the sportswriters, instead; but as Al pointed out much later in an interview reproduced by Brent Kelley, the home run totals of the two were practically even, Yogi's superior RBI numbers were owed to his batting clean-up, and Al was his clear superior in every other offensive category. (Since Smith was an outfielder, let us grant, he could hardly assert equal defensive value to Berra as a catcher). "They claimed that because they [the Yankees] won the pennant—they beat us out—that's how come he got it. That's what they say." Just before these summary remarks, Al had devoted some words specifically to the writers in Cleveland:

> I never got a first place vote [for the 1955 MVP] out of neither one of the sports writers there [in Cleveland]. And I could've won that thing. If one of 'em had given me a first place or second place vote, I could've won it. Look at the record. Kaline and I were right together and Yogi had a point or so more. Look back on the record and you'll find out that I don't think I got a sixth place vote from the Cleveland writers.[43]

If these appear bitter remarks, they surely had every right to be so. Al relates that his 22-game hitting streak during the same glorious season had been snapped when, after he had beaten out a "push-bunt", the hometown Indians' scorekeeper had charged an error to Allie Reynolds for not covering first base! Not only do scorekeepers very rarely assign "errors of omission", but a player can typically expect to be lavished with a few generous hits per season in his own park. It most certainly looks as though the sportswriters of Cleveland gave Smith a working over (he went on to have a 12-game streak after that: the "charitably" scored total would have been 35 games.). Al does not come right out and charge the harrier hacks with bigotry… but he scarcely needs to. That supposition is what literary scholars call nowadays the "subtext" of the interview.

And Al Smith was just the sort of black man whom bigots would have targeted, frankly. He didn't look almost white, like Bill Bruton. His very dark skin, in fact, was exaggerated by a sandpaper beard which kept peeking through, no matter how closely he shaved. (His teammates nicknamed him "Fuzzy" on this account.) His features were broad and thick, and his brow was heavy, creasing his forehead with wrinkles that might have been mistaken for a scowl. His face was not the smiling invocation of warm-heartedness, photographed *ad infinitum* on Willie Mays and Ernie Banks, that might have reassured mainstream white America about the desegregation of baseball. Of course, Yogi was no Rock Hudson... but that, after all, is the point. Unequal treatment for equally rugged looks.

Muffi and Kronstadt quote Al as saying, "I'm a laughing ballplayer. I gotta keep it up. That's me. No sense in being moody."[44] And Smith was a pleasant, even inspiring teammate, by all accounts. The question I raise here is, did this decidedly warm heart fail to win over a predominantly white public because the residue of bigotry demanded a more photogenic warmth? Who knows—who could possibly know for sure? (Pardon the analogy... but Richard Nixon would surely have beaten out John F. Kennedy in the presidential election five years later if their degree of photogeneity had been reversed.)

That Al Smith was a "laughing ballplayer" after his retirement seems dubious to me. Indeed, perhaps that remark was drawn from him because journalist Hal Lebovitz had observed that he had much to pout about. I have seen reports that Al remained bitter about his Major League experience throughout his later life. I cited much earlier (in Part 2, Chapter 1) a vignette related in Bill James's *Baseball Almanac*: that Smith went home after being released by the Red Sox at the end of the 1964 season, hung his cleats and glove from a nail, and vowed never to play again until the nail let its burden drop. To be sure, Al suffered from a degree of bad luck that might have left anyone a little grumpy. When Cleveland swapped him for Minnie Minoso, the White Sox fans took an instant disliking to him, for Minnie had become a Windy City favorite. Owner Bill Veeck's bid to rehabilitate Al's image has become legendary: the "Al Smith Day" on which everyone named Smith or some variant thereof was admitted free. Al, alas, hit into two double plays and committed an error that led to the winning run's scoring.

Anyone can have that kind of bad luck—anyone good enough to make it to the Majors. What might have eaten at Al far more was the frequency with which he was traded after productive years, and even—just maybe—the awareness that he tended to be exchanged for other black players (viz., Minnie Minoso and Willie Kirkland). I, at least, find this latter tendency a bit malodorous, since I have observed it in the careers of other black players of the era. Al had certainly encountered prejudice in his professional life: we can all well imagine that frustration with racial bigotry was part of the force behind the hammer pounding that famous nail into a wall of his home.

Yet, to be ruthlessly honest, Smith's release by the Red Sox, tainted though that franchise surely was by a history of bigotry, makes poor evidence of racial discrimination. The man who had once regularly drawn 80 walks a season with Cleveland and legged out a total of doubles in the high Twenties had steadily begun to walk much less from year to year while apparently dedicating himself to pursuit of the long ball. Most importantly for a ballplayer like Al Smith, the runs scored described a fairly steep fall-off throughout most of his Sixties seasons. Batting average and on-base percentage also trended downward, although not so decisively. (In fact, these numbers were always respectable: Al's 1960 average of .315 was his highest ever.)

Al Smith's case cries out to be discussed in my next chapter, where I speculate that "home run mania" pulled a great many fine young black stars disastrously off their game, sometimes ending what might have been Hall of Fame careers. Smith, I believe, was pressing. Even when he succeeded at hitting his way on base in later years, he wasn't drawing walks as of old. He seemed to have grown preoccupied with pumping up his power numbers rather than scurrying into scoring position. Occasionally the numbers did indeed climb (his 28 homers in 1961 was a career best)—but there were times, too, especially in his final three seasons, when the ball didn't fly off his bat, his cleats didn't wear out home plate, and his average was... well, average. Veteran pitchers can find a lot more ways to get a hitter out who wants to pull and elevate every offering than one who is willing to smack the pitch wherever its vector is already tending.

I have a notion (less than a suspicion—just a hunch) that, deep down, Al may have recognized his departure from the formula of his early successes. He must have sensed that he had betrayed his special talents by letting Yogi's extra six homers in 1955 gnaw away at him—an MVP award for six more lousy home runs! That could have been a large part of his grudge against big-league baseball: i.e., that he had let it make a less effective ballplayer of him. No villain is so detestable as the one who wins you over.

Or maybe I over-dramatize. Maybe Al did not see his altered approach to the game as a betrayal so much as a necessary but almost certainly doomed adjustment. Having watched baseball make rich men of Mays and Banks and Aaron while turning up its nose at his walks, bunts, steals, and runs scored, maybe he felt forced to be less of Al Smith and more of Willie Kirkland (for whom he was swapped in his career's last trade). That is, maybe he divined that, without the long ball, his livelihood might dry up very abruptly—more abruptly than it in fact did. Perhaps those 28 homers in 1961 had won him his three final years; perhaps leading the league in runs scored again wouldn't have secured him a single new contract. Either change yourself into something you simply cannot remain for very long, or find another job: the black ballplayer's version of Hobson's Choice. That would be enough, it seems to me, to sour a man's retirement.

R.C. Stevens

Like Ted Savage, R.C. Stevens was enlisted into this study in order to round out my numbers. Post cereals printed no baseball card for him in 1961 (his last big-league tour of duty), but I did happen to possess a Topps baseball card detailing his career through 1958—his first Major League season, played with Pittsburgh. (We called these "bubblegum cards": you couldn't purchase one without the other.) "Steve" had toiled in the Minors since 1952, where his batting average fluctuated but his power numbers were always formidable. The .267 he posted during his rookie year with the Pirates was perfectly respectable, especially considering that he had only 90 at-bats spread out over 59 games. No doubt, he was often slipped in at first base during the late innings, for his baseball card reveals that he was the leading fielder at that position in three of his Minor League seasons. Yet perhaps the most impressive thing about the rookie was his ability to hit with power immediately in the big leagues: with 7 homers in 1958, he was belting a long ball once every 13 trips to the plate. Sluggers who carry such a ratio through a full season of at-bats are usually in the running for the home run crown.

Yet R.C.'s career was essentially finished after this promising start. I have found very, very few references to him, and no explanation whatever of his early demise. Moffi and Kronstadt report that, invited to the Pirates' spring training in 1955, Stevens "showed up 20 pounds overweight, which excited the wrath of [Branch] Rickey."[45] Clearly, however, this explains only why R.C. didn't make the big team a little sooner, if even that much. Defense cannot have been the problem: to go with his distinguished Minor League credentials, he made all of two errors at first base in 104 Major League games. I would hazard a guess that his batting right while throwing left did not endear him to big-league brain trusts, where the image of the powerful left-handed hitting first sacker is quite cogent. Very few players have ever managed to sell the bats-right-throws-left combination. Those that do, like Rickey Henderson, are usually outfielders rather than first basemen. Caucasian outfielder Carl Warwick began a modest Major League career in 1962: I can recall no other right-hitting lefty from that era. All the same, the Pirate first baseman to whom Stevens played second-fiddle in the late Fifties—Dick Stuart—was a right-handed slugger (lifetime average: .264).

By the time Stevens was traded to the Senators in 1961, his power seemed to have deserted him: one extra-base hit in 62 at-bats, and 2 RBI. Sitting around as somebody's understudy isn't beneficial to the timing of *any* performer. That Washington should have released "Steve" is therefore scarcely a surprise. The mystery is why Pittsburgh had done so little to exploit his talent over the previous two years. I haven't enough clues to suggest an answer. Sometimes players just don't work out, especially young ones who start pressing. One can certainly not affirm that R.C.'s race was responsible for his being rewarded with so little playing time after 1958. One can probably speculate, however, that it didn't help.

Bob Thurman

My best guess is that two things deprived Bob Thurman of the big-league career he deserved: his age and the "gentlemen's agreement" that precluded Major League teams from fielding more than four black players at once. The latter situation naturally brought the former more and more into play. The year when Vada Pinson became ensconced in the Reds' center field—1959—was by no accident Thurman's last brief hurrah with the big team. With George Crowe, Jim Pendleton, and Frank Robinson already on board and Brooks Lawrence, Don Newcombe, or Orlando Peña likely to appear on the mound from day to day, an aging slugger whose skin color forced a quick review of the starting line-up became an unaffordable luxury. Naïve to the last, Big Swish told manager Birdie Tebbetts, "I know I'll be back, and when I am I'll make you play me."[46] Bob was losing a race with time, and he had already lost a race, as a younger man in the mid-Fifties, with The Times.

It is this former race, of course, whose rigging is the more scandalous. (The latter race is invariably rigged against us all.) Why didn't the Reds play Thurman when their squad was still very sparsely populated with black players? He had given them ample reason to. On a late-summer game in 1956, he homered in three consecutive at-bats against Milwaukee. He batted .295 that year—but with only 139 trips to the plate, which represents about a quarter-season. At this time, of course, he had already surpassed his thirty-fifth birthday (and frowning at age was a favorite sandbagging maneuver used against a great many black players: it could scarcely be challenged, because the game has always treated players in their mid-Thirrties as one hard day away from a stroke). Thurman would perhaps have fared better if he had not become stalled in the Yankees' organization for five years. Feeling among New York's African-American fans that players like Bob were merely on display here and there in the farm system would eventually grow quite vocal—too late, however, to win Bob the chance he merited.

Thurman's case is certainly not one of failure. He eked out a five-season big-league career (though it amounted to only 663 at-bats), and he had a devoted following among the Cincinnati public. One could well grow more outraged by looking elsewhere... but one could not very successfully quell the impression that Bob's performance was the brilliant tip of a never-to-be revealed iceberg.

Leon Wagner

Perhaps I have a soft spot for Leon Wagner because I can actually remember, as a small child, watching him play ball in grainy black-and-white televised images. It may be mostly imagination... but I could swear that I saw him hit the game-winning home run in the second All-Star Game of 1962. What I really remember is the wide gap between his hands as he held the bat in readiness. *Omne ignotum pro magnifico est*, observed the Roman historian Tacitus—"everything unfamiliar assumes an aura of magnificence." Leon's unique grip had mystique. Boys who grow up with baseball have always wasted hours, days, and even years trying to replicate the exotic batting style of some flashy star, usually to the consternation of their coaches. I tried the "Wagner gap" for a brief while, but didn't stick with it—probably because (like most fine baseball minds today) I did not comprehend that one of the two hands must remain loose enough to rotate and slide during the swing. Now that aluminum bats are a fixture in youth baseball, and now that the wooden bats of professionals mimic the aluminum models of their childhood, the virtues of "hand-spreading" are inconceivable to players and coaches alike.[47]

Leon died a year too soon for me to interview (to be exact, on January 3, 2004). I had written him before I began any other work on this book: the letter came back marked with his date of decease, informing me without being opened that I had missed my chance to ask about his grip. I can now only hope that he didn't end his days embittered—a licensed hope, for bitterness would have been quite out-of-character. Wagner's testimonial in Jackie Robinson's anthology, *Baseball Has Done It*, from which I have cited often, is full of irrepressible spirit and ebullient personality. (In Chapter Six of this section, I have occasion to quote his views about dugout humor.) Today we would say that such a player is a real asset in the clubhouse. In Leon's time, self-assertive horsing around may not have been highly prized, especially in a black man. It may account for why he was traded so often, despite his invincible bat. He would eventually leave baseball for Hollywood, becoming a rather successful bit-actor for several years. The question that occupies us here, however, is why baseball did not write him into larger parts.

Consider this: with 211 career home runs in 4426 at-bats, Leon was on a pace to break 400 homers at the end of an 8,000 at-bat lifespan in baseball—the duration which sluggers of that caliber usually enjoy. Of course, such projections can be very presumptuous. Ted Kluszewski never approached so many trips to the plate, although he was among the most feared bombers of the mid-Fifties. The plane ran short of fuel. Batting average may actually climb with age and experience: power numbers inevitably go down as reactions slow and injuries pile up (all performance-enhancing wonder-drugs having been factored out). The reason why this argument fails to resolve the mystery of Leon's curtailed career is the *frequency with which he was traded*: four times over twelve years, his longest stint with one team (Cleveland) being four years. I am doubtful that even Mantle or Mays could have bested Wagner's long-ball numbers under such unsettled circumstances. Except in Cleveland, he was never regarded as part of his team's nucleus. Why not?

Defense is invariably cited: sometimes lack of speed is tossed in. Bill James offers both explanations. At one point in his delightful *Baseball Almanac*, he brands Leon as slow afoot; at another he impugns Leon's basic ability to judge a fly ball, writing, "Some guys... can run and maybe even throw OK, but are just bad outfielders." At yet another point, Bill trots out his figures and notes that Wagner shows up as Number Six in all baseball history when one prioritizes "lowest range factors compared to league norms among listed outfielders."[48] In other words, besides being slow afoot, Leon got a late read on hits.

Now, I don't begin to understand how Mr. James arrives at his ratings in this last case, though I am sure the method is very ingenious. The discovery that, just below Wagner on the same infamous list, Tommy Davis made his entry among history's most range-challenged outfielders gave me pause. Tommy Davis stole 136 bases in his career—not stellar, but a long way from plodding. Maybe some of these grounded albatrosses played in parks where they couldn't pick the ball up very quickly... would James's figures alert us to that? (The "wedding cake" bleachers in the new Dodger Stadium at Chavez Ravine were an outfielder's nightmare.) Maybe both Davis and Wagner were actually a little near-sighted (see postscript to Wes Covington). Davis is wearing glasses at the plate in one photo I possess of his late Dodger years, though I never saw photos or footage of his doing so in the outfield. Warren Spahn insists that Sam Jethroe, the Boston Braves' fleet-footed black outfielder, "couldn't see.... I saw that guy run right by fly balls... [that] it took them ten minutes to retrieve."[49] Those of us who coach kids are all too familiar with this particular cause of getting bad jumps on flies, even though public schools are required to test children's eyes routinely. Half a century ago, nobody would ever have thought to include an eye exam as part of a spring-training physical. How likely is it that a black kid growing up in the segregated South would ever have been sat down before an eye chart? Big Frank Howard, a popular Caucasian slugger, realized that he needed specs at the plate only in the mid-Sixties, having already played big-league ball almost a decade.

Whatever the cause of Leon's miseries, there is plenty of testimony— first-hand, ballplayer testimony—that he was not pretty to watch on defense. Said Carl Long, his teammate in the Negro Leagues, "Wagner was a butcher outfielder. He could *hit* that ball, but he wasn't a good outfielder. He didn't have the arm and he misjudged a lot of balls."[50] Sometimes a bad rap follows players around unfairly, but the word of well-disposed observers like Mr. Long must be awarded a great deal of credence. So let it stand that Leon played a lousy left field in more ways than one. Two questions should immediately follow: given his phenomenal hitting ability, why wasn't he coached to do better on defense... or why wasn't he moved to first base?

These are indeed two distinct questions. A player with the coordination required to bat .300 (Leon topped .290 in 1963 and 1965) should certainly be redeemable in the catching of routine fly balls: all it takes is practice. If, however, speed is required to roam the large outfields in certain ballparks, the slow-footed slugger is typically moved to first base. Ted Williams was a ghastly fielder when he was called up to the big leagues: he spent more time in left field practicing his swing than following the action around the plate. With practice and forceful persuasion, however, he became a very competent fly-shagger. Fenway Park forgave his lumbering gait. Leaden-footed slugger Joe Adcock could not be thus rehabilitated on the Milwaukee Braves, so he was stood on first base to be the infield's common target. Both of these worthies posted fielding percentages roughly equal to

Leon's during their early outfield years, and Wagner's did improve whenever he was given time to get to know a new park and pitching staff. (His fielding percentage during his last two years in Cleveland was a bit above the league average.) Yet the bad rap always clung to him—and no team seems ever to have risked putting him on first for a single game.

I realize that a first sacker needs good hands, if not good feet—and I realize that Leon Wagner is credited not only with being deficient in all aspects of his defensive game, but also with dogging it during practices and making flippant remarks when exhorted to try harder. I can't rebut the criticisms of attitude. I wasn't around, and I don't have the ear or the address of anyone who was posted at Ground Zero. But my ample experience of human organizations emboldens me to say this much: a reason can *always* be found for demoting or dismissing someone. Rumors can be created *ex nihilo* when, on rare occasions, they do not snowball around a grain of truth. Particularly when a person has already built up an equivocal record, the blunt fact that he has failed in some way becomes a kind of magnet for every uncharitable remark ever made about him. From 1961 to 1965, Leon Wagner hit 150 home runs, batted in 455, and scored—by the way, heavy feet and all—428. His average season over this period, spent with two teams, consisted of about 30 homers, 91 RBI, and 85 runs scored. Not very many players in either league could boast such figures over this same period. It is hardly the profile of a big, clumsy, lazy, back-talking klutz. In the middle of this period, the Los Angeles Angels traded Wagner to the Indians for Barry Latman and the previously mentioned Joe Adcock—a nobody and a has-been for a man who had batted in 197 over the past two years. In 1968, the Indians traded Wagner to the White Sox for Russ Snyder—a speedy, scrappy outfielder, to be sure, but one without any power to compensate for the 97 homers Leon had clubbed in a Cleveland uniform over the past four years (and this in the middle of the homer-obsessed Sixties). Misjudged fly balls, bad throws, no speed... was that really all there was to it?

I remain deeply skeptical about all the explanations of Leon Wagner's somewhat disappointing career. If he overran flies, why didn't a coach work with him? If he was slow, why wasn't he moved to first base? If he shirked hard labor, how did he ever fight his way up through the Negro Leagues and the minors, to begin with? None of this makes very much sense to me: all of it put together doesn't make *enough* sense.

I find it far more plausible that Leon's penchant for not being anyone's silent punching-bag made some of his teammates and coaches "uncomfortable". Despite the good humor with which he repaid a prank or jibe right back, he was probably resented. I suspect that his brand of tit-for-tat equality in such exchanges was "before its time". But his big feet, of course, were a lot easier to talk about to the press—and Leon himself, being Leon, was immediately ready to walk away from baseball without looking back once doors started to slam in his face regularly.

Rest in peace, Daddy Wags.

Bill White came to bat officially about 1500 more times in his career than Leon Wagner, and stroked just over 200 home runs (202) compared to Leon's 211. Yet the figures that count most directly in the winning or losing of a ball game—runs and RBIs—show the two as almost identical producers. Once adjustments are made to the disparity of at-bats, the two knocked in runs at virtually the same clip and crossed the plate with virtually the same frequency. White, to be sure, enjoyed more stability in his career and played with more offensively resourceful teams. Nevertheless, Bill White was consistently one of the most reliable run-producers of his generation. He was true to form even in 1966, just after a stunningly abrupt trade had uprooted him from St. Louis and in the very midst of the fabled Drysdale-Gibson-Koufax-Marichal reign of terror over offenses everywhere. That year saw Bill drive home 103 runs, score 85, and—for the sixth straight season—reach the 20-homer plateau.

And then White suffered the fatal blow for a black player in mid-career: he got injured. A damaged foot (I do not know the details) sidelined him in 1967. The following year, his bid to make a comeback was unimpressive (.239 in 365 at-bats). Those previous seasons of 100+ runs-batted-in, one of them in Philadelphia, would not buy him a longer trial: he was traded back to the Cardinals, where he appeared in 15 games (about two weeks of on-the-field duty) before being released. It was a very unceremonious exit for a perennial All-Star.

As is so often the case, however, one can find white players who received just as little consideration when they fell on lean times (though it's hard to find any black player from this era who was nursed through bad stretches as was, say, Andy Carey or Jim Landis or Dick McAuliffe). If race had nothing whatever to do with White's treatment, then he certainly suffered from a succession of mind-numbed bosses—a very tenable proposition if one accepts the testimony of Curt Flood and Bob Gibson. Yet players are often the last to know what's going on in such circumstances. Even Flood, who represents himself as full of street-smarts and absolutely anything but gullible, repeatedly mentions Tom Haller and Robin Roberts with admiration in *The Way It Is* for their determination as player-representatives. Frank Robinson has quite a different opinion of Haller's fair-mindedness in *Extra Innings*, while about the amiable Roberts he confesses to harbor nagging memories of a slur shouted during a brawl.[51]

Who can know what's really in any human being's mind? What is a GM thinking when he crafts a trade, an owner when he orders a release, a manager when he imposes a platoon? The fact remains that White was exceptionally intelligent and eloquent as a player-spokesman (he would later become president of the National League, of course, and then resign when he felt himself being manipulated). Another fact: the Cardinal "family", so highly—and rightly—praised by Flood and Gibson for its immunity to racism and its solidarity before issues like spring-training segregation, was broken up not once, but twice, in the very midst of the franchise's brilliant mid-Sixties successes. Both times, the departure of minorities was masked by the acquisition of more minorities. Exit George Altman, enter Lou Brock; exit Bill White, enter Orlando Cepeda; exit Cepeda, enter Dick Allen. I have already devoted a chapter to the delicate technique of such juggling. Blacks were by no means always traded directly for other blacks, nor were their "substitutes" necessarily acquired in trades at all. (Recall that youngsters Mack Jones and Tommie Aaron were brought up just after the Braves had jettisoned Bruton, Covington, and a bypassing Andre Rodgers.) A charge of racial bias is difficult to maintain when the team at issue remains racially mixed in about the same proportions… and the influx of "new blood", at the same time, would allow such delicate issues to settle to a depth where only the sharpest eyes might have found them.

Bill White indeed possessed a sharp pair of intellectual eyes—and he was very curiously handled in the mid-Sixties. Of course, players do not like to attribute their misfortunes to racial prejudice or anything else beyond their control: their motivation as players requires that they believe in their ability to fight their way into the starting line-up. But the rest of us can wonder… and, at some point, we *must* wonder.

***

Postscript: I, for one, will now wonder more than ever. With the help of the MLB Players' Association office in Denver, I had originally forwarded a kind of form letter to White and over a dozen other former players announcing the nature of my intended research. Only one player eventually responded. At least one had very recently died. Others, I suspect, receive requests like mine routinely and have better things to do than straighten out some unknown hack. I sent follow-up letters to the group but obtained the same results—with one exception. Bill White (or someone of his household), rather than simply chuck my nuisance-mail into the bin with a pile of sale papers and gadget catalogues, took the trouble to write "refused" upon it and to have it returned. Why? To communicate two words to me in code, the second of which would be "off"? Why go to such effort to underscore before my eyes that no further queries of mine would be read, and that the whole undertaking was not appreciated?

In the unlikely event that Mr. White should ever read these words, I sincerely apologize for any discomfort I may have caused him. But for the sake of my study, I note that my asking a few obvious questions about his career appears to have provoked severe discomfort. Here is a man, I believe, who was treated very badly and who ended up feeling it very keenly.

Jake Wood

Ed Walton, an East Coast academic who seems to have made a loving hobby out of chronicling the arrival of big-league rookies, writes of Jake Wood that he "showed the poise of a veteran despite setting several strikeout records."[52] I could find no other meaningful reference to Wood in any

217

source—no testimony, that is, suggesting why his career consisted essentially of one full season in which he led the American League in triples. Walton's few words probably tell the only story needed to justify Jake's demotion to oblivion, at least for the casual observer: the strikeouts. To fan 141 times in 663 at-bats might be tolerable in a young Pete Incaviglia, but Jake was no home run machine. Throughout six more fragmentary seasons, as well, the Detroit second-sacker continued to average about one strikeout per five trips to the plate—or once a game. Sorry, Jake… move over for Dick McAuliffe, who at least would compensate for his whiffs by leading the league's second basemen in homers. Of course, the Tiger brass couldn't have known that in spring of '62; and as for smoothness at the keystone sack, McAuliffe had practically never played second at the time![53]

But Jake, most likely, was trying precisely to be what McAuliffe would become: an unlikely slugger fielding a position not known for its power-hitters. This was sheer folly: simply glancing at the stats is enough to reveal that Wood had blazing speed. Besides legging out triples consistently, he stole 79 bases in his very brief Major League career—and that without the benefit of many free passes. Jake Wood walked once for every two strikeouts—a huge gap for anyone hitting first or second in the order—nor did he ever bat much above .250. Despite the mediocre average, he sustained a 10-game hitting streak in 1962: an indication, perhaps, that he was "hacking" all the time, and that pitchers had difficulty keeping balls out of his reach even when they were well shy of the strike zone. Streak or not, Jake made it safely to first with comparative infrequency, especially for a lead-off hitter. Whenever he did, he must have been swiping second with amazing regularity. He would continue to be the third-ranking base-stealer in the American League for the two seasons following his full year in 1961, even though those two seasons *together* surpassed his at-bats in '61 by a count of only 55.

Now sit back and figure out how a kid with blinding speed who is officially said to have "the poise of a veteran" could end up on the shelf when the least competent coach in the business could have told him—*should* have told him—what any comparable little-leaguer would hear: "Take more pitches. Cut down on your swing. Drop some bunts." Walton's naiveté in wedging "poise" and "several strikeout records" into the same sentence is disarming in an amateur. When one further reflects that the comments must have originated in some press release, however, one is struck by the cynicism of the men who manipulated these young talents—who engineered for them an almost inevitable professional failure. In Chapter Five of this section, I shall review certain charges that managers like Harry Walker and Solly Hemus were setting their black players up to fail by *reining in* their home run cuts. This may be so: I suppose it depends upon whether or not the player in question in fact possessed home run power. In Jake's case, such tutelage might have transformed him into a forerunner of Lou Brock, or perhaps an American League version of Maury Wills. Jake was set up by being *ignored* (assuming that no malign counselor actually prodded him to swing for the fences). Or perhaps the Tigers' coaches really were more incompetent than a little-league volunteer… but the beneficial adjustments available in his case were so obvious and so easily mastered that the scent of malice hangs in the air, even half a century later.

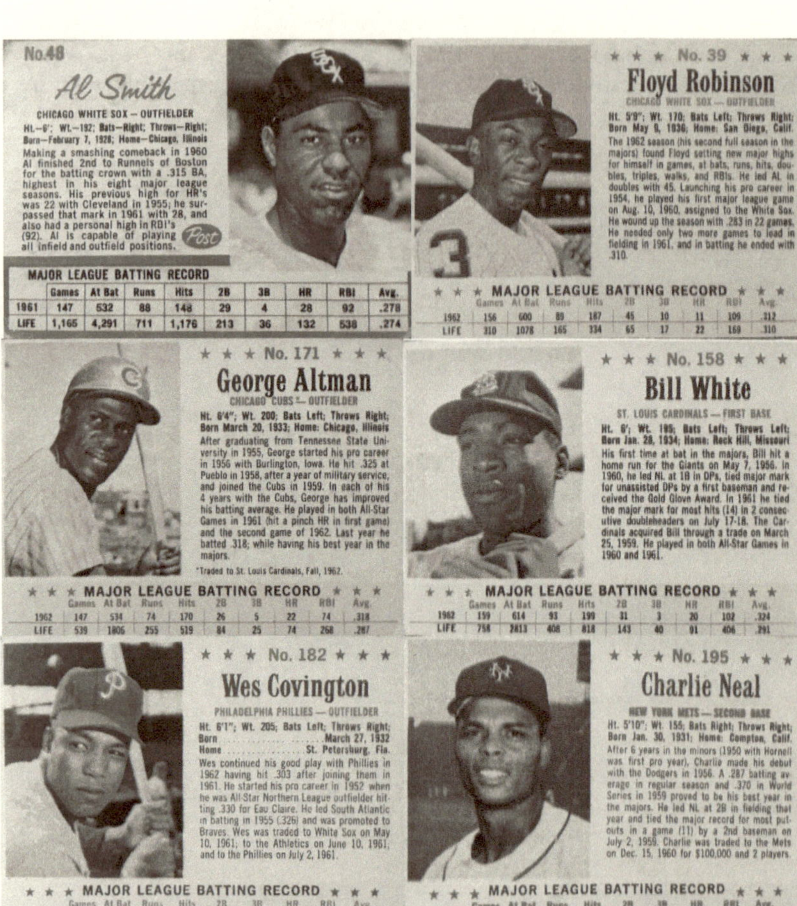

MAJOR LEAGUE BATTING RECORD	Games	At Bat	Runs	Hits	2B	3B	HR	RBI	Avg.
1961	147	532	88	148	29	4	28	92	.278
LIFE	1,165	4,291	711	1,176	213	36	132	538	.274

MAJOR LEAGUE BATTING RECORD	Games	At Bat	Runs	Hits	2B	3B	HR	RBI	Avg.
1962	156	600	89	187	45	10	11	109	.312
LIFE	310	1078	165	334	65	17	22	169	.310

MAJOR LEAGUE BATTING RECORD	Games	At Bat	Runs	Hits	2B	3B	HR	RBI	Avg.
1962	147	534	74	170	26	5	22	74	.318
LIFE	539	1806	255	519	84	25	74	268	.287

MAJOR LEAGUE BATTING RECORD	Games	At Bat	Runs	Hits	2B	3B	HR	RBI	Avg.
1962	159	614	93	199	31	3	20	102	.324
LIFE	758	2813	408	818	143	40	91	406	.291

MAJOR LEAGUE BATTING RECORD	Games	At Bat	Runs	Hits	2B	3B	HR	RBI	Avg.
1962	116	304	36	86	12	1	9	44	.283
LIFE	680	2007	244	567	76	14	85	326	.283

MAJOR LEAGUE BATTING RECORD	Games	At Bat	Runs	Hits	2B	3B	HR	RBI	Avg.
1962	136	508	59	132	14	9	11	57	.260
LIFE	864	2999	433	791	100	37	84	369	.264

The best years of these men would be worthy of the game's greatest stars. Their "bad" years were few enough—and good enough—that their quick exit makes little sense.

Notes

1 Larry Moffi and Jonathan Kronstadt, *Crossing the Line: Black Major Leaguers, 1947-1959* (University of Iowa Press: Iowa City, 1994),125-126.

2 Brent Kelley, *Voices From the Negro Leagues* (Jefferson, NC: McFarland, 1997), 186.

3 *I Had a Hammer* (*op. cit.*), 258.

4 Kelley, *op. cit.*, 187. Boyd also acknowledges on 184, by the way, that Richards platooned him—a strategy that makes little baseball sense with a potential batting champ who bunts well and hits low line drives. For that matter, what sense does it make to tip off the opposition that you have no faith in your first baseman's arm? Every time an easy grounder was flipped over to first, a runner on second would go home—unless, I suppose, he were playing for a skipper in the Richards tradition.

5 Minnie Minoso (with Herb Fagen), *Just Call Me Minnie: My Six Decades in Baseball* (Champaign, IL: Sagamore, 1994), 67.

6 Larry Moffi and Jonathan Kronstadt, *Crossing the Line: Black Major Leaguers, 1947-1959* (University of Iowa Press: Iowa City, 1994), 54.

7 From Donald Honig, *The Man in the Dugout* (Chicago: Follett, 1977), 122, 123, and 142, respectively. Richards also remarked in his interview that he intensely disliked having players' children in the locker room(130). This is the side of him that rubbed Aaron the wrong way.

8 See *Crossing the Line* (*op. cit.*), 144-145.

9 *The New Bill James Historical Baseball Abstract* (*op. cit.*), 586.

10 See p. 127 in Davis's autobiographical reminiscences, *Tommy Davis' Tales From the Dodger Dugout*, with Paul Guttierez (Champaign, IL: Sports Publishing L.L.C., 2005): "Wes Covington established himself, and then he became a good pinch hitter. But there weren't too many black players who sat on the bench. Either you started or you went back down to the minors or moved on to another organization or went home." This, as I shall point out shortly, is part of the anomaly in Covington's case. Why *did* he sit on the bench? Had he established himself to such a degree... or did managers intend to play him more, and then mysteriously hold back?

11 I have previously mentioned this short table of players with "very balanced offensive skills" to be found in *The New Bill James Historical Baseball Almanac* (*op. cit.*, 539).

12 See *We Played the Game* (*op. cit.*), 353-354.

13 Cf. Larry Moffi and Jonathan Kronstadt (*op. cit.*), 146. The authors report Covington as having responded, "They don't pay outfielders for what they do with the glove." This happens to be entirely true, especially of the Fifties. Ted Williams and Mickey Mantle were both nursed along through very unpromising freshman adventures in the outfield. Wes's bat was not of their caliber, to be sure—but some of the outfielders auditioned by the Braves in Wes's day (e.g., Gino Cimoli) were not of *his* caliber, either.

14 Henry Aaron, *I Had a Hammer* (*op. cit.*), 216-218. Much of this passage is actually in the words of Felix Mantilla, whose case I discuss below.

15 *Ibid.,* 211. Aaron is not implying, by the way, that he allowed others to spearhead protests while he sat back; he is simply acknowledging that, as a less-than-outgoing young man, he had little talent for playing the spokesman in such a delicate operation.

16 I refer to *Tommy Davis' Tales From the Dodger Dugout* (*op. cit.*).

17 *Ibid.*, 147.

18 George Weiss, for instance, once attempted to bully Mickey Mantle during a contract negotiation by waving before him a manila folder alleged to contain details of Mickey's after-hour antics, meticulously collected by a detective. "I wouldn't want this to get into Merlyn's hands," sniffed Weiss, referring to Mrs. Mantle. See *The Mick* (New York: Jove, 1986), 150.

19 *Ibid.*, 173.

20 Jane Leavy uses Tommy's case to exemplify Bavasi's methods and then summarizes, "Ploys like this left a bitter aftertaste. Players would mutter under their collective breath, but that was the limit of collectivism" (*Sandy Koufax* [*op. cit.*], 202).

21 See Davis's *Tales From the Dodger dugout* (*op. cit.*), 151-152.

22 Leavy (*op. cit.*) offers an instructive example of defective etiquette: "When Roger Maris tried to take his brother, the businessman, with him to talk money after hitting 61 home runs, the Yankee brass kicked him out. Contract negotiations were, in fact, not negotiations at all. 'Negotiation by ultimatum,' Koufax called it" (202).

23   See Horn Huston, "Nobody Knows Mayonnaise Except the Pitcher," *Sports Illustrated* 16:23 (June 11, 1962)::84-86, 89.

24   Gibson, of course, had never said any such thing—he was from Nebraska, and possessed nothing of the stereotypical Deep South accent. He relates this tasteless literary flourish in *Stranger to the Game* (*op. cit.*), 51.

25   See Mantilla's comments in Henry Aaron's *I Had a Hammer* (*op. cit.*), 218: "They would say that I'd get tired if I played all the time, or I was having trouble making the double play." Felix had been an All-Star at shortstop more than once during his Minor League experience. The error that sent the Dodgers to the World Series in a 1959 play-off game occurred on a grounder that was headed sharply for center field, and that frankly might not have been touched by Johnny Logan, whom Felix had replaced late in the game after an injury.

26   From *The Rookies* (New York: Stein and Day, 1982), 132-133.

27   See Danny Peary, *We Played the Game* (*op. cit.*), 440.

28   From *The Rookies* (*op. cit.*), 132.

29   See *Glory Days with the Dodgers* (*op. cit.*), 192.

30   Larry Moffi and Jonathan Kronstadt, *Crossing the Line* (*op. cit.*), 154.

31   Curt Flood records in *The Way It Is* (*op. cit.*, 67) that Pinson was playing on a broken leg when he came over to St. Louis: "The pain was fearful, but neither the team's trainer nor its physician could find anything wrong. So he played, rather than be a jaker. I finally persuaded him to get an X-ray, which revealed the broken bone and torn tissue." This incident, by the way, gives a very fair idea of what pressure the players of the time were placed under to ignore their injuries and play on.

32   *Op. cit*, 736. In the same section, by the way, James relates an uncharacteristic and briefly physical confrontation which Vada had with Mr. Lawson. I may as well say here (since I shall not do so elsewhere) that Pinson's bid for the Hall of Fame could not have been helped by the encounter. Duke Snider was denied admittance to the Hall for years because of one or two trivial run-ins with sportswriters, and Jim Rice continues to be cold-shouldered in the voting thanks to his less than cordial relationship with the Boston press a long time ago. Being voted an immortal turns out to be highly political, like so much in life.

33 Earl Lawson, *Cincinnati Seasons* (South Bend, IN: Diamond Communications, 1987), 124-125.

34 Jim Brosnan, *The Long Season* (New York: Harper, 1960), 183.

35 *Crossing the Line* (*op. cit.*), 191.

36 Consider that Pinson's .286 career batting average is actually one point higher than Yastrzemski's, his career slugging percentage just twenty points below Yaz's, and his double/triple total only 93 behind Yaz's though he had 2343 fewer at-bats—about five season's worth, *none* of them in a hitter's park like Fenway.

37 Yet it must be added that Los Angeles effectively ended Gilliam's career after the '66 season by inaugurating a trade which he declined. Even the Dodgers' front office hadn't learned to estimate such a contribution at its true worth.

38 *We Played the Game* (*op. cit.*), 619.

39 *Cincinnati Seasons* (*op. cit.*), 152.

40 *Op. cit.*, 51.

41 From Roseboro's *Glory Days with the Dodgers* (*op. cit.*), 175. Rosey later writes that, when he was coaching for the California Angels and Frank was brought over in a trade, the legendary slugger came across as "bodacious, a braggart, loud and crude, and [he] disrupted the team" (253). Maybe this was the aspect of Robinson's character which DeWitt and Howsam discussed in private—but why all the secrecy? And isn't it the manager's job to hold aggressive natures in check? Indeed, Roseboro continues by saying that Frank's trouble-making on the Angels arose mostly because manager Bobby Winkles couldn't control the team, even before Robby arrived. Likewise, the tension in Cincinnati had climaxed in Frank's being traded only after Fred Hutchinson, a forceful, imposing manager, retired due to failing health.

42 The passage is drawn from www.baseballlibrary.com. I have no idea who wrote it, but the author was almost certainly merely repeating judgments which he had heard or read elsewhere—for this is the kind of blandly nonsensical justification which public relations types always offer for a dubious decision.

43 See *Voices From the Negro Leagues* (*op. cit.*), 215.

44 *Crossing the Line* (*op. cit.*), 102.

45 See *Crossing the Line* (*op. cit.*), 193.

46 See Moffi and Kronstadt (*ibid.*), 141.

47 The aluminum bat is so light, and the wooden bat patterned after it so toothpick-thin in the handle, that choking up or spreading the hands apart makes no sense with it. Both varieties of stick are designed solely to be held down on the knob, allowing the hitter to whip a bloated barrel through the strike zone in a split second. Some hitters claim that a whip-like bending of the thin handle literally occurs, accelerating the barrel's transit through the zone. Whatever the truth of such theories, bats today simply do not have the dimensions necessary for judging whether Leon's stunning grip possessed more assets or liabilities.

48 *Op. Cit.*, 815 for slowness, 676 for bad fielding, and 821 for poor range in the outfield.

49 From the transcript of an interview with Spahn in *The Only Game in Town*, ed. Fay Vincent (New York: Simon and Schuster, 2006), 155.

50 See *The Negro Leagues Revisited* (*op. cit.*), 305.

51 For Robinson's ordeal as the Giants' manager under General Manager Tom Haller, see his fifteenth chapter, "A GM for No Season," in *Extra Innings* (*op. cit.*), 182-199. The incident with Roberts is briefly described on 45. Frank adds that Roberts later apologized for a word blurted in the heat of a brawl, but "what had come out of Roberts's mouth during the scuffle, I felt, had come from his heart." It occurs to me, if I may plead Robin's case, that epithets growled during a fracas come off the top of an overheated head, not the bottom of an opened soul. Frank's judgment here is pretty harsh.

52 Ed Walton, *The Rookies* (New York: Stein and Day, 1982), 172. This is Walton's first and last mention of Jake.

53 John Skipper, *Charlie Gehringer* (Jefferson, NC: McFarland, 2008), 168, reports that Hall of Famer Charlie Gehringer was enlisted by the Detroit front office to work with McAuliffe, regularly a shortstop, at second base during spring of 1963. It can therefore not be claimed that Wood was simply edged out at the end of 1961 by a superior candidate in the wings.

II

Round Trip or One Way: The Suspicious Influence of the Home run Over Unsteady Careers

Home run hitters fared better among the first generation of black ballplayers to whom all Major League teams' doors were actually open. I remarked this so often in the previous chapter's review of individual players that I fear I may seem to pound on a loud, dull drum. The fact of the matter is unmistakable. Which players in my study enjoyed the longest stints with a single team, the highest-paying contracts, the greatest prestige, and the most durable careers? Aaron, Banks, Mays, McCovey, Robinson, and Billy Williams. What high-average, low-power players enjoyed any of the same advantages? Not Bob Boyd, or George Crowe, or Jim Gilliam, or Al Smith. Gilliam had a good run with the Dodgers, to be sure—but the franchise also tired of him a lot sooner than it did of Ron Fairly's moderately powerful bat. Lou Brock and Curt Flood are the exceptions that prove the rule: the former's career was among the most recent to be admitted into the study, and the latter's was in fact cut short long before Curt showed any clear sign of irreversible decline. Would Mr. Busch have traded away Aaron or Mays in his pique over a whopping contract? He certainly dealt Altman and Pinson after little more than an audition, both of whom had come very close to being batting champions before but apparently disappointed him with their mere handfuls of homers. The Yankees fell in love with Elston Howard's home run production even more than with his fine catching, and the Giants and other teams kept penciling slugger Willie Kirkland into the line-up even though his average crept cautiously out of the .250's for only a single season of his nine.

Promising black players were often ordered, exhorted, nudged, or otherwise influenced in their early development to go for the downs. Ernie Banks relates in his interview for Jackie Robinson's anthology, "During spring training [of 1954] the Cubs went all out to coach me in long hitting. My teacher was none other than Ralph Kiner. Like me, Ralph was not a natural long hitter. He had taught himself how to pull and get distance."[1] In other cases—probably far more frequent cases—aspiring black ballplayers were simply left to infer from the circumstances that without the long ball, their repertoire of skills held little interest for Major League scouts. The anecdotal evidence I have seen suggests that, if they were told anything at all by a shaking head or a retreating figure, it was to forget about the big time because they could *only* bunt, run, and hit line drives to all fields—because they weren't pulling enough, or because they didn't have the physical size to pull with authority. Ron "Bunny" Warren sums up a frustration that many must have shared:

> I'll tell you something else that was really discouraging to a lot of black ballplayers. At that point, the major leagues, they were looking for bulk, like football players—the Kluszewskis, the Big Swishes [Bill Nicholson], the big guys who could get the ball out of the park. The guy 165 pounds, 158 pounds—they wasn't looking for these type of guys too much because they were going for the power stroke. Now baseball has come to the point where they're looking for speed.[2]

Mr. Warren goes on to praise Ozzie Smith in his interview—so we know that "now" was probably in the mid- or late-Eighties, before baseball again turned away from speed and versatility to worship at power's dull altar. His comment is doubly interesting in that we also know well (and he must have realized) that not all white rookies of late-Fifties/early-Sixties vintage, by any means, were strapping hulks. In particular, middle infielders were permitted to be quite small: Bob "The Flea" Lillis and Bill Moran spring to mind. We have already seen that middle infielders from the Negro Leagues tended to be nudged to third and first or into the outfield, where—what do you know!—the matter of size and its connection to homering ability becomes much more important.

Henry Aaron was one of the shortstops who was thus finessed into a defensive position where his glove would be of less value to the team and his offensive power consequently the basis, for the most part, of whatever success he might have. Aaron's case is especially instructive, both because he has given us such a very thorough account of his career and because the all-time leader in home runs (of the "unjuiced" variety) was so transparently *not* built primarily to hit them. No hulking Kluszewski or towering McCovey, but a bean-pole of a kid who barely topped six feet, the young Aaron could hit the ball on a line wherever it was pitched. Mickey Owen once lamented, "If he hadn't started thinking about home runs later on, he would have had some years when he batted .400, just like Hornsby."[3] But Aaron *did* think about them, and early on, if not with deliberate resolve at that stage. "Maybe subconsciously, I was affected by the fact that the home run hitters like Mathews and Mays got more publicity than I did—and more money—but I felt like I was swinging the bat the same way I'd always swung it."[4] This comment refers to the years of the late Fifties. It is extremely fortunate, perhaps, that a young Henry did not become too eager at an age before experience could have checked his excesses, for the baseball graveyard is littered with potential stars who were destroyed by the discovery that they had occasional power (e.g., Odibe McDowell and Eric Anthony).

For the dismal truth is that, besides ruining your average, swinging for home runs also proves to be a surefire way *not to hit home runs*. In a rare moment of talkativeness, Charlie Gehringer once lamented to an interviewer that he had allowed an early burst of home runs in 1932 to corrupt his hitting style. This caused his safeties of all varieties, big and small, to stall. "I believe I still had eight when Ruth had 34. I kept going for the distance and had only my third year under .300 in all my years of playing," recalled the Hall of Famer.[5] Mature hitters will sometimes enter the batter's box with the intent of trying to score big in one blow, it's true: but this only happens in specific situations (e.g., team behind with two out in the ninth inning and a strictly fastball pitcher on the mound), nor are its results typically positive, even then. Great home run hitters universally agree that the best plan is to see the ball well and make solid contact. Mike Schmidt puts it as well as anyone:

> … When you're not taking the healthy kind of swing at home plate that fans want to see, they get angry, because you don't seem to be the aggressive hitter you're supposed to be. They like to see you spin around in the batter's box, with your helmet flying off.
>
> Home runs aren't like that. I can't emphasize enough that home runs result from *technique*.[6]

The spectacular home run swing to which Mike refers is something else again. Mickey Mantle made it famous, and Ted Williams preached it in one book and several instructional films (though in a more graceful form than Mike's caricature of it). The front hip flies open, clearing the way for the hands to drive through like a lumberjack's who intends to make short work of a sapling. Since the opening front hip requires that the body's weight be shifted backward just before the stride (through a coil more often than a leg lift in those days), the swing can acquire an upward slope if you work hard to "stay back", as so many young hitters were advised to do. This slope, Ted reassures us, merely puts the bat in the ball's plane of flight. Yet overemphasizing the "stay back" directive leads to making the back leg the exclusive axis of a very circular swing—what hitting coaches call "rolling over". The front shoulder flies open too soon, and the eyes almost inevitably pull off the ball as the neck arches back. Such a hitter will strike out a lot if his adversaries can pitch him consistently on the outside corner, which his stroke's tight circle can scarcely touch. Even Ted basically gave up on that corner, not offering at pitches in its vicinity unless he had two strikes; and Ted, need I say, was not apt to stress excessively the "pull swing's" riskier tendencies.

Many of the great Caucasian power-hitters of the Fifties and Sixties hit in precisely this manner. (A significant minority also held the bat high over their shoulder, rear elbow cocked upward, and threw steeply down on the ball like a contemporary slugger to create backspin; yet a lot of these, like Kiner and Kluzewski, encountered career-shortening spinal problems thanks to the era's heavy bats) Of those I have seen on film, I might name Johnny Mize and Duke Snider as modeling the Williams paideia; of those I dimly recollect seeing on television, Mantle and Killebrew are clear examples. Ted was right: the opening front hip produced a dead-pull hitter who murdered everything from the middle of the plate in.

But this was far from a flawless strategy for the slender-framed. Almost every black slugger who successfully cranked out home runs year after year either ignored it or "beat the odds" through some adroit variation of the formula. Frank Robinson stood on top of the plate to give him better coverage of the outside corner. Willie Mays and Roberto Clemente had a stride that often took them from one end of the batter's box to the other. What this did, to look at the swing again as a geometry problem, was to make the focus of the bat's circle forwardly mobile so that its outer arc "flattened" into the side of an ellipse. The result looked more like saturation- than precision-bombing: it could be pretty wild. Yet it allowed more of the bat to stay in more of the strike zone for a longer time. These two collected plenty of hits off of their stick's less promising spots.

Aaron, of course, was the master of what is called "front foot" hitting (as Babe Ruth—no featherweight by any standard—had been before him). The front hip still opens up, but not as dramatically. The front leg is closer to the upright as contact is made, for most of the stride's weight shift is collected there. The back foot, rather than being dug firmly into the ground as the bat cracks, is often dragging its toe (or even lifting clear of the ground). Compare a baseball card of Barry Bonds to one of Frank Thomas (the *contemporary* Frank Thomas) featuring the two as they follow through with their stroke. The former is a prototypical "Williams hitter", the latter a front-foot hitter. Many hitters (like Mays, I suspect) manage to work somewhere between the two extremes. Obviously, there's more than one way to skin a cat.

Ruth, Aaron, the "new" Frank Thomas… these are among the most redoubtable power-hitters in baseball history. How could anyone argue that they didn't have a "home run swing"? Well, baseball gurus of the Fifties certainly did. For some reason which I shall not venture to explore, African-American and Latino players seemed more likely in this era to be more upright on their front leg when they made contact. Since the same was true of white players in "dead ball" times—and even of Ruth—the difference must clearly be attributed to habits rather than genetics. Stan Musial, with his bizarre crouch (very similar to Wes Covington's, by the way), finished fairly upright on his front leg. The same is generally true of any hitter with a big hitch (a pump of the hands before swinging: e.g., Jimmie Foxx and Hank Greenberg) or a big leg lift (e.g., Mel Ott or Paul Waner). These styles had lost popularity in big-league ball of the Fifties. By the same token, some black hitters did indeed seem to rock back and take ferocious "Williams" swings with the kind of result that made white GM's happy. Roy Campanella, Larry Doby, Monte

Irvin, and Hank Thompson are all stellar examples. Is it mere accident, I wonder, that they were among the first Negro Leaguers to be admitted into the Majors? Recall George Altman's testimony in this section's first chapter: none other than Branch Rickey had urged him to "stay back and elevate".

I know of one case, in particular, where a white instructor—with the best of intentions—was trying to teach a young black prospect of the late Fifties to "stay back" on the ball: Dixie Walker, who said proudly of Mack Jones, "I'm going to try to make him into another Henry Aaron." Walker directly preceded this surge of optimism with the remark, "He [Jones] murdered the ball in batting practice this season. But in a game he still leaned forward with his body ahead of his bat, and lost power."[7] This is actually a pretty good dozen-word description of the front-foot swing. Dixie clearly thought that flying open off the back foot was the key to home run paradise. I suspect that this sort of thing went on all the time. The young Aaron himself was once scouted by a certain Billy Fisher who complained, echoing the prejudice of the day, that "he didn't pull the ball."[8] Jim Cohen reports this incident in more detail than does Henry's autobiography, but without changing its substance (except for a variant recollection of Fisher's first name), from the days when he played for the Kansas City Monarchs and Aaron for the Indianapolis Clowns (of the Negro League):

> Hank Aaron hit a home run over the right field fence and he hit *another* home run over the right field fence. I thought sure Ted [Fisher] would have notice of that, but he was still working for Branch Rickey—he was working for Pittsburgh then—and he said, "He's fine, but they like for you to pull the ball up there [in the Majors]."
>
> He didn't like him because Hank wasn't pulling the ball. If they don't throw you something to pull, they can't pull it. He said, "I'll talk to Rickey," and I said, "You better hurry up, 'cause the others are after him real bad."[9]

Cohen makes it quite plain that Mr. Fisher was only honoring the expectations of his big-league white employers. The privileging of the hit pulled hard down the line was obviously a value embedded in his entire organization, ascending all the way to Branch Rickey.

Let me be unequivocal: I am *not* proposing that the Secret Order of White Hitting Instructors and Scouts agreed in the winter of 1950 to short-circuit the integration of baseball by tearing apart their black prospects' strokes. I should not be surprised, however, if many such grizzled veterans smiled at how Jackie Robinson swung out of his shoes (for Jackie, too, ended up on his front foot, despite being Mr. Rickey's hand-picked standard-bearer for integration… another hint, perhaps, that Rickey wanted his trial balloon to have an escape hatch?). The same old plough horses no doubt elbowed each other over Musial's stance: the press certainly cracked no end of jokes at Stan's expense. This crowd honestly thought that such a style was "goofy";

and they could prove by anecdote over a few beers—if not by photograph and documentation—that their understudies or the golden-haired boys of the past had hit more homers when they "stayed back". One such hitting ideologue, Joe Gordon (formerly of the Red Sox, whose list of dead-pull hitters featured many older than Ted Williams), was credited by a young white lad from Georgia named Coot Veal with undermining his stroke. Claimed Veal,

> I was a front-foot hitter, but they [the Tiger coaches] were teaching me to swing off my back foot. Meanwhile, Harvey Kuenn was hitting line drives off his front foot. He was the best front-foot hitter I ever saw. They didn't try to change him, and he went on to be a batting champion. But they tried to change me, and I think that hurt me.[10]

Kuenn, a Tiger All Star (and also white), belonged to the previous decade's beginnings; and indeed, I suspect that he may have copied the stroke of Tiger Hall of Famer George Kell (to judge by newsreel footage). That was then: this was now. Scrappy pre-war play had been replaced by the ballistic missile.

The post-war period in American society, after all, was not known for its resourceful experimentation. This was the era of Eisenhower stability and The Man in the Gray Flannel Suit. Baseball reflected the trend. No less an innovator than Bill Veeck had the following choice words for baseball's ruling class in the Fifties:

> In baseball, it gets back to the baseball moguls' preoccupation with dignity and control. The businessman has taken over the game. The businessman, quite naturally, has an organization manager. The organization manager's slogan is, "We don't have no stars on this team. They're all just one of twenty-five." You don't have no stars, Managers, and you don't have no pennants.
>
> Color is the thing they have done everything in their power to get rid of. As soon as a boy is signed, a carefully planned program of brainwashing sets in.[11]

An organizational mindset like this would not be predisposed to look kindly upon mavericks and individualists who dangled their bat down their shoulder in an odd poise, lunged at the pitch with a yard-long stride, stole bases in tight ballgames with no one out, laid a bunt down in tied ballgames with two out, caught fly balls at the belt, flipped the ball from the hip, etc., etc. The brain trust of which Veeck speaks knowingly would want its performers to roll reliably off the assembly line like the latest station wagon from Detroit. If the man at the top didn't bring much understanding to the game, the men below him certainly wouldn't risk their jobs to educate him.

The sabotage of integration, in other words, lay in the home run itself—in the mindless inflexibility with which the "moguls" clung to that sublime image of a pale speck arching toward the upper deck. Who knows what degree of deliberate short-circuiting went into this "conspiracy"? Not much, probably... but probably more than not any. I am a white Southerner myself, and I haven't spent all my life in an ivory tower. It would only have been par for the course if the less "quiet", more "lunging" swing not uncommon in the Negro Leagues came in for some bluntly barbed wit—the "Cadillac swing", all flash and fins. Vic Power complained bitterly of being harassed merely for his "showboat" style of fielding (a style which, in fact, contributed to his being one of the best first basemen in baseball.)

> When I was coming up in the minors pitchers they throw at me every day and I was fighting every day to make them know I not afraid, but in the big league they don't throw at me much, maybe only when they get mad at me for my way of playing, catching the ball with one hand, grabbing hits away from them, they don't like it too much. But I think they don't throw at me because I'm colored. It's because I play my way, catch the ball with one hand, not to show off, I catch it so because it come natural with me, it's the way I feel. When I catch the ball with two hand I feel tied up. With one hand I catch the ball better, stretch better. If I catch with two hand and make no error I don't see why I should catch with two hand because a lot of sportswriter want me to. That's the censor around baseball, the sportswriter who want me to play their way and not the way that come natural to me. I don't showboat or things like that. I notice the people, the crowd, they like it when I play my way.[12]

White all-star teams had played black all-star teams in exhibition games for years before Jackie ever put on a Dodger uniform. The black teams won at least as often as they lost. They did things that nobody (or few white players, at any rate) had ever seen or heard of, stealing bases, throwing behind runners, and dropping bunts in the most unlikely spots. They were scary; and when word got out that they would be infiltrating the Major Leagues, some of the white players must have gotten very scared, indeed.

I believe the word also got out—and very quickly, starting from dozens or hundreds of sources at once—that this excellent free-style play was to be squelched as young black players were "trained" to be big-leaguers. Ira McKnight, Satchel Paige's last catcher with the Kansas City Monarchs, described himself as "mostly a line-drive hitter. I didn't hit for power.... I had some power but I didn't like to strike out too much, so I hit mostly line drives—a contact hitter. I'd bat two sometimes and I'd bat three and then I batted four and five. I had good speed for a catcher."[13] The same kind of self-portrayal—and it was almost always a very accurate one—could be heard from most stars of the Negro Leagues. Josh Gibson and Bill Wright could slam home runs with the best anywhere. Their feats did not generate a lack of esteem, however, for the lighter hitter who managed to reach base and scurry to scoring position before they came to the plate. In the white-dominated

Major Leagues of the late Fifties, such contributions definitely conferred upon their authors a second-class citizenship in most organizations.

Tommy Davis tells of an incident that occurred when he was batting in the heart of the order for Bobby Bragan's Triple A team in Spokane. Davis successfully beat out a bunt late in a close game. This stirred Bragan to lecture the whole team afterward in the locker room—mentioning no names—about the importance of three, four, and five hitters swinging for the fences. When Tommy tried to justify himself to the manager privately, he was scratched from the next day's line-up.[14] It doesn't sound as though Bragan would have appreciated having Ira McKnight stroke low liners in the heart of his order, either. Davis actually expresses a good-humored gratitude for the lesson... but what lesson, precisely, was he taught? Why swing for Bragan's "double or better" when you have the ability to beat out a bunt and steal second? What's the difference, other than that the double is more of a long shot? Is it that fewer white players could bunt and steal—or is it that most white coaches couldn't teach such tactics effectively and most white managers not employ them cannily?

If young black prospects wanted to stick around, they were to accept as gospel the dubious proposition that home runs win ball games, and so learn to win games accordingly.[15] How many, like young Mack Jones, were actually encouraged to adopt the "home run swing"? I don't know—but it doesn't really matter. *Any* swing can be ruined by a preoccupation with home runs. I mentioned the Ted Williams swing earlier merely because it so clearly implies the kinds of vice into which hard-hackers might have plunged themselves: giving up the outside corner, lengthening the stroke (i.e., "being long to the ball"), and pulling the eye off the pitch. An overly aggressive young hitter could learn to do this all on his own.[16]

In the last year of the Fifties, Henry Aaron was beginning to get the message loud and clear. He writes that his "career goal at the time was to get 3,000 hits"—but that the substantial stride he made toward that goal in 1959 was subordinated by MVP voters to the home run production of Eddie Mathews and Ernie Banks (the latter of whom, as we have seen, had successfully converted to long-ball hitting under the Cubs' tutelage).[17] During the off-season, Hank had an experience which must have dismissed any lingering doubts. "If anything finally changed me, it might have been *Home run Derby*, a made-for-television competition held in Los Angeles after the 1959 season."[18] Aaron won a series-record $30,000, which went quite a long way in those days. I might add that in the reruns of the show which I've seen, a great many *bona fide* back-foot sluggers did very poorly (e.g., Rocky Colavito and Gus Triandos): more proof that most hitters cannot just dial up a long ball at will. Aaron and Mantle were the best at it.

Again, let me clarify: the white establishment obviously failed if it hoped to denigrate the black player's contribution to baseball by emphasizing the home run. But there was never any such denigration intended. First Mays, then Robinson and Aaron, emerged into the game's elite group of six-figure salary-kings as their homers stacked up. ("Hitting home runs paid off," concludes Aaron after describing his 1967 contract.[19]) The establishment was only too glad that these young men from "across the line" had beaten straight-laced baseball at its own game. For the fact remained—at least temporarily—that baseball *was* straight-laced, not the no-holds-barred scramble it had been in the days before Ruth (Nap Lajoie had once stolen first base from second) or that it had continued to be in the Negro Leagues until they expired. For every Mays or Aaron who was crowned king, there were dozens of Jake Woods whose one promising season was not thought promising enough (triples... who cares?) and hundreds, perhaps, of Ted Savages whose special qualities were filtered out after blunt review.

In this light, the Aaron story is bittersweet. Henry was prepared to pursue Ty Cobb's record, but white baseball worshipped Ruth's far more... so he conquered Ruth, forcing a nation to recognize that his race was the equal of any other. Yet perhaps he also postponed the triumph that the feats of Maury Wills and Lou Brock logically demanded—a triumph of speed and creativity which, unlike his home runs, translated into pennant after pennant; and perhaps he made it that much more tempting for Vada Pinson to remodel himself disastrously.

At the time, of course, Aaron was primarily trying to keep his job, like all of us. I am observing an irony, not insinuating a betrayal. And perhaps the final word on this matter should be that the age of speed and creativity was itself short-lived. Barry Bonds would fairly soon wrest the home run crown away from Henry (after treading down those who had just stepped over Roget Maris) amid the game's dirtiest scandal in almost a century... and Major League baseball has not numbered so few African-Americans among its players since I wound a rubber band around my first card collection.

Notes

1 From *Baseball Has Done It* (*op. cit.*), 147. Memory gilds the past, of course, and by the time Ernie got around to writing his autobiography, *Mr. Cub* (with Jim Enright; Chicago: Follett, 1971), he recalled Kiner as merely encouraging him to keep pulling the ball rather than showing him how to do it. In fact, Ernie's fourth chapter represents everyone in the Chicago organization as applauding his pull-hitting. That much is probably completely true.

2 See Brent Kelley's interview of Warren in *Voices from the Negro Leagues* (Jefferson, NC: McFarland, 1998), 272-273.

3 Quoted in Henry Aaron's *I Had a Hammer* (*op. cit.*), 110.

4 *Ibid*, 167.

5 From *The Sporting News*, 8 Jan. 1966.

6 *Always on the Offense* (*op. cit.*), 76.

7 See Jackie Robinson's *Baseball Has Done It* (*op. cit.*), 46-47.

8 *I Had a Hammer* (*op. cit.*), 48.

9 See *Voices from the Negro Leagues* (*op. cit.*), 196.

10 *We Played the Game* (*op. cit.*), 238-239.

11 From Bill Veeck (with Ed Linn), *Veeck—As in Wreck* (New York: Bantam, 1962), 122.

12 From Jackie Robinson's collection of testimonials, *Baseball Has Done It* (*op. cit.*), 170.

13 *Voices From the Negro Leagues* (*op. cit.*), 302.

14 *Tommy Davis' Tales From the Dodger Dugout* (*op. cit.*), 21.

15 The figures I have collected for the twentieth century indicate that teams with a home run champ tend to go to the World Series slightly more often than teams with a batting champ, by a ratio of 34 to 26. (This does not include those rare teams with both laureates, which would vex the issue.) Yet the ratio is almost dead-even (15 to 13) since 1950, and would indeed lean the other way but for Mickey Mantle's influence. In other words, the Steroid Era has

not witnessed a steady stream of clubs borne to the Series on the unnatural shoulders of big boppers. Furthermore, home run hitters usually command enormous salaries, so their presence often indicates an owner's ability to buy other advantages; and if we also factor in the anomaly that home run stats say more about foot-speed than raw power before Babe Ruth (Lajoie, Cobb, and Speaker all won home run titles in the century's early years), then high-average hitters seem to me to have a competitive edge.

16 I do not contest that Ted Williams actually helped a great many struggling hitters—but consider this. When a hitter struggles in baseball, *any* change in his swing is apt to produce temporary improvement, first because it crosses up the opposition's "book" on him, and second because it may modify in an unknown way whatever unknown habit is undermining his performance. It is also true that today's home run mania has essentially thrown out Ted's book to embrace the fundamentally less sound theory (for achieving high averages) of swinging down on the ball. I would be inexcusably arrogant if I were ridiculing the advice of perhaps baseball's greatest hitter ever. What I am trying to do, instead, is to protest the ridiculing of other methods which other hitters, arguably about as great, chose to use.

17 *I Had a Hammer* (*op. cit.*), 202.

18 *Ibid.*, 203.

19 *Ibid.*, 260.

III

The Night of the Pressing Hitter: More on How Home Run Mania Undercut Young Black Ballplayers

Since I have dedicated the present section of the book to evidence more anecdotal than statistical and more inductive than deductive, this chapter may seem out of place. I am going to crunch some numbers again. I shall not, however, volunteer any more graphs or tables. I don't really think that the method I propose here is sufficiently objective to justify a big spread: a competent statistician could probably make it so, but the task is well beyond me. All I want to do is pair off three groups, one of whose members broke into the big leagues in the first half of the Fifties and one either in the very late Fifties or the early Sixties. What I propose to demonstrate by this is that the later arrivals from white baseball's farm system (for such was the route they traveled) "pressed" at the plate more than their slightly older brethren who matured in the Negro Leagues. The culture of the home run had not quite dominated white baseball when George Crowe, Jim Gilliam, and Harry Simpson came on the scene—or not nearly so much, at any rate, as it would when Ed Charles, Curt Flood, and Willie Tasby made their entrance. The former three players learned to diminish their rate of striking out and to balance punch-outs satisfactorily with walks. The latter three players, I suggest, were typical of their period in feeling compelled to play long ball. The result was that, despite the lessons of experience, their strikeout levels, instead of mildly tapering off, began to rise with time.

I have sought to pair players who seemed to me roughly the same kind of hitter. Crowe and Charles could hit for both average and power; Gilliam and Flood batted at the top of the order and reached base however they could; Simpson and Tasby appear to have been above-the-mean hitters in most regards but not outstanding. The genesis of this chapter, frankly, was its predecessor. I was only struck by the possibility of arranging such comparisons when, while writing about the home run, I marveled that so many beneficiaries of black baseball's tradition—taking what you're given, making things happen, staying alive to have another cut—even if they were not in fact Negro League veterans, should have struck out so often. How could someone with Jake Wood's speed (to take an extreme example) have fanned 141 times in his only full season? Why wasn't Jake being directed to cut down on his swing, and to bunt more often? Surely he wasn't batting clean-up in a murderer's row which featured Cash, Colavito, and Kaline—the Killer Kappas!

It seems, rather, that Wood wasn't getting any direction at all, or else was being lured along with his other young contemporaries to emulate Aaron and Mays. He certainly didn't receive any positive feedback for leading the league in triples: that feat essentially ended his career. Does anyone doubt that, if 10 of those 14 three-baggers had left the yard to give Jake 21 home runs in 1961, he would have been a fixture in the '62 Tiger line-up, strikeouts and all?

Strikeouts. They were no stranger to George Crowe, but neither did they haunt him. George consistently fanned about once every eight or nine official trips to the plate: the ratio was 12% when he began with the Boston Braves in 1952, 13% when he smacked 31 homers and 92 RBIs for Cincinnati in 1957, and 14% for his entire career. He usually drew at least half as many walks as he suffered punch-outs: in 1955 he actually had 45 free passes to go with 44 whiffs. The career ratio is 65%, almost exactly two-to-three.

Now contrast Crowe with a stillborn star of the early Sixties, Ed Charles. The Kansas City third baseman only struck out 15% of the time during his career—but the problem got distinctly worse as he became more seasoned. In his rookie year, the ratio was 13% along with 17 home runs and a .288 batting average. The latter two figures proved to be career highs. Ed's power numbers hovered in the same area for two more seasons, but by 1964 he was fanning 17% of the time, very nearly reaching three digits in strikeouts— and his average had plummeted to .241. He did record a career high in walks, as well; yet their proportion to his whiffs was now 70%, whereas it had been 77% and 73% in the two preceding years. Ed's figures were not following a healthy growth curve. He rebounded with the Mets in 1968 to hit 15 homers—but he had just over twice as many strikeouts as walks; and his extra-base hit total *other than* home runs was a puny twelve, worse then the previous season's and far worse than any of his marks before 1967. Bear in mind that Ed had suffocated for years in the Braves' farm system: he was no youthful "phenom" brought along before he could learn the strike zone.

Jim Gilliam and the strikeout were scarcely on speaking terms. Junior's career strikeout-to-at-bat ratio is an exiguous 5.8%. At no point of his career did he fan more often than walk: typically he walked two or even three times more often. Even his career-high in home runs—13, posted during a 1954 campaign in homer-friendly Ebbets Field—saw him walking two-and-a-half times more often than striking out. Jim knew his limitations, and stayed within them.

One would be tempted to say as much of Curt Flood, especially after reading his own account in *The Way It Is* of how he was persuaded to stop swinging for the fences early on.[1] Interestingly, Curt had his first taste of the Majors a full five years before Jake Wood and six before Ed Charles. Home run fever had not yet won over even the young Henry Aaron. In his first true season of big-league duty, Curt's strikeout total was a little less than twice his number of walks and at a ratio of 13% to his official at-bats—not at all bad stats for a rookie. His batting average dipped for the next couple of years; but in 1961, he logged the first of five consecutive stand-out seasons, during only one of which did he bat under .300 (.296 in 1962) and over which his BB-to-SO ratio leveled off almost to the even. Then, in 1966, the strikeouts suddenly doubled up on the walks, and the ratio would stay more-or-less lopsided for the rest of Curt's career. Significantly, I think, 1965-1966 were the only consecutive years when Flood posted home run figures in double digits. Only twice in his previous seven full seasons had he done so. It is difficult to resist the conclusion that he had at last succumbed to the general mania for long balls. Also significantly, his extra-base hits *besides* home runs gradually declined until 1969, when he forsook the homer and rediscovered the double.

Is this not the signature of a pressing hitter? How do you explain the general diminution in doubles and triples around baseball even as individual players post relatively healthy home run figures if the pitcher's mound was just too high and the strike zone too generous? On the other hand, if players were starting to swing harder but with less control, one would expect precisely to see lower averages, fewer low line drives carrying to the wall (i.e., doubles and triples), and *both more and fewer* home runs on a case-by-case basis (depending on whether the player could get his abundance of "big flies" actually to sail over an obliging home-field wall). Flood just wasn't created for such spectacles. Like Gilliam, he was a run-scorer: crossing the plate was his strong suit and his destiny in baseball. Yet Curt's totals in runs scored plunged from 1966 through 1968, despite his having over 600 at-bats in two of those three seasons. Gilliam's career ended in '66 with a mere 235 at-bats, but he managed to reach home plate at a rate which would almost have tripled Curt's total for that year. Flood had veered under the gravitational influence of that binary star, Aaron-Mays.

The most obscure for the last. Harry "Suitcase" Simpson won his sobriquet by being packed off to a different team almost yearly. Such circumstances are not amenable to low strikeout totals, yet Harry's career ratio of K's to at-bats is a respectable 15%. It was at precisely this level in the banner year of 1956, when Simpson clubbed 21 home runs and batted in 105. Though traded a sum of five times (and across leagues) in his final two seasons, The Suitcase nevertheless maintained his walk-to-strikeout ratio at almost 60%--*and* he continued to rack up homers, extra-base hits, and RBIs (10, 19, and 50, respectively, over a two-season span amounting to half a season of at-bats).

In a similarly brief and trade-torn career beginning in 1958, Willie Tasby also had one stand-out year: 1961, when he homered 17 times and batted in 63 runs with fewer than 500 at-bats for an offensively challenged Senators team. Willie's 1959 campaign had been almost as impressive. Like Simpson, Tasby tended to hit a bit above .260 in his prime and to leg out a goodly number of extra-base hits. Yet strikeouts were much more of a nemesis in his case. Having logged 80 of them in '59 (his first real season) while walking only 30 times, he appeared to bring the problem somewhat under control the next year, and came within a half-dozen of evening the walks/strikeouts ratio. Then, tarnishing the brilliance of his '61 season, he drew within the same half-dozen of posting 100 whiffs. The trend continued in his final two years. Not that striking out about twice as often as one walks is unacceptable in a power-hitter… but the point is that Willie seemed to have mastered his problem for one year early on—and in Boston, where the temptation for right-handers to swing out of their shoes is often irresistible.

The reader may protest that the pressure to belt homers was felt no less severely by white players than by black players. Everyone knew that Mantle, Mays, and Musial hadn't been paid big bucks for their good looks, everyone knew that expectations were higher once Maris had shattered Ruth's record, and everyone knew that the pitching following the 1961-62 expansions would be "easy pickings". Well, yes… but black players knew something else, as well. They knew that the outfield positions into which they tended to be channeled were low-security investments, and that no outfielder could stabilize his future very much merely by winning a batting title if he didn't add 15 or 20 homers. (Consider the obscurity of Roberto Clemente relative to Aaron, Mays, and Robinson; or consider Richie Ashburn, a white player whose 2,574 hits, mostly singles, and two dozen "firsts" in offensive categories over the years got him to Cooperstown only after thirty years.) A white outfielder might just survive if he hit .300 and knocked 6 homers a year: a black player would find himself relegated to the role of a utility player or pinch-hitter deluxe *if* he were lucky. So the young black players swung hard, and freely. Many of them, I suspect, swung too hard, and too freely.

I have already written several times that I believe The Year of the Pitcher (1968) and its accompanying argument (that great pitching dominated the mid- and late-Sixties) to be a myth. Yes, the period was characterized by several overpowering fastballers: Bunning, Drysdale, Gibson, Koufax, Marichal, McLain, and (briefly) Bob Veale, as well as the little-known and much-abused Mudcat Grant and Earl Wilson. But there were at least as many off-speed and "junk ball" artists tormenting hitters of the day: Mike Cuellar, Tommy John, Jim Kaat, Frank Lary, Mickey Lolich, Mike McCormick, Gaylord Perry, Sonny Siebert, a young Don Sutton… nor is this to say that there weren't some great curves and change-ups among the fire-ballers. In that respect, the lowering of the mound, advertised as a response to the Gibson fastball, was either utterly absurd or else a cynical gimmick. Bob has written, "Among all the modifications… that one [the lower mound] probably had the least effect. It affected *me* the least, anyway, because, unlike other pitchers, I relied very little on an overhanded curveball. Those who did, such as Nelson Briles, found that they were less able to bring down the curveball from on high and drop it vertically through most of the hitter's latitudes. My fast slider wasn't bothered much."[2]

Baseball's overlords probably didn't quite know what they were doing or why they were doing it, from the perspective purely of playing the game. Theirs was a marketing decision. Attendance had been falling off, and they wanted to titillate the public's desire to see offense hopping and buzzing. Ironically, no such result appeared immediately. Walks were up in coming years, as Gibson's remark above seems to foreshadow; but the obsession with homering apparently continued to pull many hitters away from their natural game. The Roses and Carews proceeded to leave most of the pack behind in average until "small ball" returned in the mid-Seventies… and the heyday of the black ballplayer in the Majors was thereby ushered in.

Yet even before the mound was lowered, disciplined hitters had made out just fine. They fell into two groups, essentially: not black and white, but far line-drive hitters and medium line-drive hitters. Scarcely a one of them came to own any ball-park records for distance by the time his career ended. Black ballplayers are heavily represented among the far line-drivers: Aaron and Mays (if not Billy Williams) are certainly more recognized and celebrated to this day than Al Kaline. When one descends to the medium line-drivers, however—the hitters who kept racking up doubles and triples rather than strikeouts—one discovers a bewildering absence of African-Americans from the very slot which Jackie Robinson and other Negro League veterans had filled so brilliantly a decade and a half earlier. The young Pete Rose is here. So are Latino stars like Clemente, Tony Oliva, and Zoilo Versalles. Yastrzemski probably belonged in this group early on. The enigmatic Johnny Callison also deserves membership, unless we disqualify him for striking out 419 times over a four-year period when his slugging percentage never dipped below .491. I have a hunch, just from the stats, that Johnny must have been a bad-ball hitter. How else could you fan that many times while still peppering the walls with doubles and triples (242 over a six-year stretch, a Mays-like feat that Mickey Mantle never came close to accomplishing)?

I'll bet, too, that players like George Altman and Floyd Robinson were Callisons who could *not* hit bad pitches. For the mosaic composed by the stats portrays, once again, a pressing hitter—and a pressing hitter has forgotten Ted Williams' cardinal rule, without which the patented Williams swing is suicide: "Get a good pitch." A Cuellar, a Lolich, or a Perry wouldn't give you a good pitch; and it was the like of these as much as Gibson and Marichal who created The Year of the Pitcher. The mid-to-late Sixties were The Night of the Pressing Hitter.

All of the line-drive hitters I named above (with the exception of Callison, apparently) knew how to wait the pitcher out. I'm sure they were looking for the perfect pitch in the perfect spot early in the count—and, of course, they didn't always get it. I don't pretend to know how they managed when behind in the count. Some must have adjusted, cutting down on their stroke, and some must have guessed with consistent success just what "pitcher's pitch" they were about to see. But here's the real point: the black players among them knew, or thought they knew, that they couldn't afford too many bloop hits to the opposite field. They knew that there was a white player waiting to take their place in the starting line-up if they couldn't crank one over the fence every third or fourth game. And so Al Smith piled up almost as many strikeouts as Henry Aaron in 1963 during scarcely more than half as many at-bats, and George Altman's K's sailed past both Aaron and Mays that same year—one year after a period of four-team expansion in the Majors.

Look at it this way: is something highly peculiar not going on when a great hitter has to hear that he's over-swinging, not from a manager or a coach, but from a sportswriter? You'd think it might work the other way around: you'd think some populist cheerleader from the broadcaster's booth like Harry Caray would bellow, "This big kid needs to start yanking a few out of here," while cooler heads in the dugout would impress upon the player in question the importance of hitting the ball low, hard, and often. In Altman's case, the whisper from the front office was of much the same content as the insipient cheerleader's, and no coach filtered its harmful "advice". Ty Cobb had once expressed delight at George's "ability to hit to all fields and his level swing."[3] We have seen from George's own description of his St. Louis days, however, that he was persuaded to suppress these cardinal virtues at a critical point in his career. Manny Jiménez received the same "advice" in the form of an order from His Majesty, Charlie Finley. Iago would have given Othello similar counsel if the two had played baseball.

In Vada Pinson's case, the hack with the typewriter actually seems to have had more sense than anyone. In his introduction to Earl Lawson's book, Pete Rose writes, "Earl was so close to Hutch [manager Fred Hutchinson]— and to other managers that followed him—that he was almost like a coach or a team captain is today. If the manager wanted to get a message across to a player or if a player wanted to get a message to the manager, they could do it through Earl.... I really think this was behind his fight with Vada Pinson."[4] I might be missing something here... but shouldn't a manager communicate a desire to see a player bunt more often *directly* to that player? What was Hutchinson afraid of—the tall, rugged man whom Gordy Coleman said he would bet on against a bear in a cage? Was he torn between his hope of seeing the team win as an extraordinary athlete blossomed and his fear—that fear of unpaid bills which can undermine the most virile man—of not giving owner and public another Frank Robinson? Mr. DeWitt, the Reds owner, had quickly and overtly fallen out of love with Frank, and he is bound to have made known to his manager a desire to see another heavy slugger emerge. Did Hutchinson sense that he might lose his job if he did it too well?

Pinson, at least, feared losing *his* job if he didn't morph into Robby: of that we can have little doubt. It was a common fear, and not unjustified. Though Lawson represents Vada's craving for home runs as largely ego-driven, the short-lived careers of .300 singles-hitters like Bob Boyd and Joe Caffie tell their own story. Lawson was right about Vada's over-aggressiveness—but Vada was probably right, too, in thinking that he didn't have a lot of options. Such a dilemma would be enough to give a hair-trigger to an altar boy.

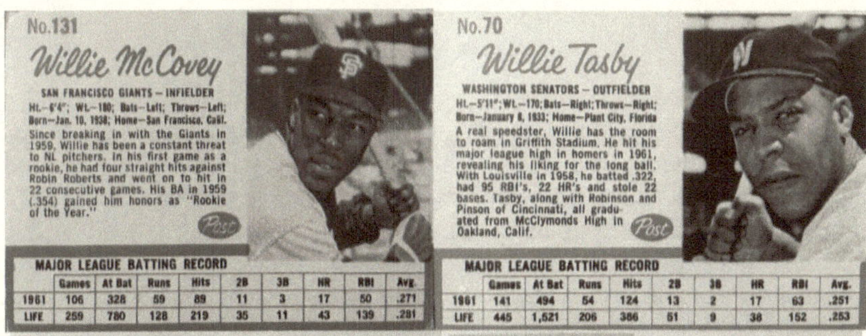

No.131

Willie McCovey

SAN FRANCISCO GIANTS — INFIELDER

Ht.—6'4"; Wt.—180; Bats—Left; Throws—Left;
Born—Jan. 10, 1938; Home—San Francisco, Calif.
Since breaking in with the Giants in 1959, Willie has been a constant threat to NL pitchers. In his first game as a rookie, he had four straight hits against Robin Roberts and went on to hit in 22 consecutive games. His BA in 1959 (.354) gained him honors as "Rookie of the Year."

MAJOR LEAGUE BATTING RECORD

	Games	At Bat	Runs	Hits	2B	3B	HR	RBI	Avg.
1961	106	328	59	89	11	3	17	50	.271
LIFE	259	780	128	219	35	11	43	139	.281

No.70

Willie Tasby

WASHINGTON SENATORS — OUTFIELDER

Ht.—5'11"; Wt.—170; Bats—Right; Throws—Right;
Born—January 8, 1933; Home—Plant City, Florida
A real speedster, Willie has the room to roam in Griffith Stadium. He hit his major league high in homers in 1961, revealing his liking for the long ball. With Louisville in 1958, he batted .322, had 95 RBI's, 22 HR's and stole 22 bases. Tasby, along with Robinson and Pinson of Cincinnati, all graduated from McClymonds High in Oakland, Calif.

MAJOR LEAGUE BATTING RECORD

	Games	At Bat	Runs	Hits	2B	3B	HR	RBI	Avg.
1961	141	494	54	124	13	2	17	63	.251
LIFE	445	1,521	206	386	51	9	38	152	.253

★ ★ ★ No. 93 ★ ★ ★

Chuck Hinton

WASHINGTON SENATORS — OUTFIELDER

Ht. 6'1"; Wt. 180; Bats Right; Throws Right; Born May 3, 1936; Home: Rocky Mount, N. C.
In 1962, Chuck, in his second big league season, was one of the best hitters in the AL (.310). He launched his career with Phoenix in 1956 and after 2 years in service, was the leading hitter in the Northern League in 1959 (.358) and the California League in 1960 (.369). Was selected by Senators in AL expansion on Dec. 14, 1960 from Baltimore. Hit .260 in 1961 for Senators.

★ ★ ★ MAJOR LEAGUE BATTING RECORD ★ ★ ★

	Games	At Bat	Runs	Hits	2B	3B	HR	RBI	Avg.
1962	151	542	73	168	25	6	17	75	.310
LIFE	257	881	124	256	38	11	23	109	.291

★ ★ ★ No. 72 ★ ★ ★

Willie Kirkland

CLEVELAND INDIANS — OUTFIELDER

Ht. 6'1"; Wt. 205; Bats Left; Throws Right; Born Feb. 17, 1934; Home: Detroit, Michigan
For the fourth consecutive big league season, Willie hit more than 20 HRs. He tied the major league record for most consecutive HRs (4) in two games, July 9-13, 1961. Launching his career in 1953, he led the Mountain States League in triples (24), RBIs (164), and outfielders in assists (26). His .360 batting average put him in the lead of the Northern League. Willie played with the the Giants in 1958, 1959, and 1960 before being traded to the Indians on Dec. 14, 1960.

★ ★ ★ MAJOR LEAGUE BATTING RECORD ★ ★ ★

	Games	At Bat	Runs	Hits	2B	3B	HR	RBI	Avg.
1962	137	419	56	84	9	1	21	72	.200
LIFE	677	2340	311	584	99	25	105	356	.250

The Willies (and a Chuck).   One sometimes gets the feeling that white baseball wanted every black kid named Willie to become the next Mays—and one of them did.   In the early Sixties, it looked as if they all might.   Kirkland (out of the Giants' organization) actually had several second chances, despite his poor average.   Tasby and Hinton were better rounded but drew little interest when they didn't homer at Mays-like rates.

1 Specifically, Curt credits none other than George Crowe—whose career was now winding down in St. Louis—with teaching him to "shorten my stride and my swing", and to make other adjustments conducive to contact (*op. cit.*, 47). It is worth stressing here, as Curt does, that hitting instructors often did far less to assist their young disciples than did veteran ballplayers. Anyone who thinks that an ambitious kid, eager to hold onto his promotion, would not alter his swing one way or another in response to the slightest hint from someone in authority imagines the baseball world of that time very differently from the reality.

2 *Stranger to the Game* (*op. cit.*), 208-209.

3 See Moffi and Kronstadt's *Crossing the Line* (*op. cit.*), 199.

4 *Cincinnati Seasons* (*op. cit.*), xii-xiii.

IV

Negro League Baseball: A Study in Speed, Versatility, Resourcefulness, and Bending the Rules

I have written repeatedly about something I call the Negro League style of baseball without ever really explaining myself. It occurs to me that I should do just that along about now, since I have begun to develop the charge that the style of play in the Negro Leagues was not welcome in the predominantly white Major Leagues—was, in fact, responsible in no small measure for the unease with which young black players were greeted by white ballplayers (and, more consequentially, by white coaches and managers). I am suggesting, further, that in seeking to abandon that objectionable style and fit themselves better to the white ballplayer's mold, many black players sabotaged their game, belied their talent, and made themselves eligible to be overlooked and discarded for reasons that had nothing immediately to do with racism.

Well, then... just what *was* the Negro League style? Buck O'Neil (immortalized now by Ken Burns' PBS documentary series *Baseball*) puts it thus:

> And it wasn't like white baseball, either. While the major leagues relied on the longball that Babe Ruth brought to the game, black baseball was fast and aggressive, with lots of stealing, bunting, hit-and-run play. It was the game Jackie Robinson learned and then brought to the majors twenty-four years later—speed, intelligence, unbridled aggressiveness on the basepaths—and for a twelve-year-old boy from Saratoga, it was *thrilling*.[1]

This is as good a thumb-nail sketch of the style as I have seen. No doubt, it is exaggerated. There were most certainly black stars like Josh Gibson and Mule Suttles who could hit a baseball right out of any park ever constructed; and, on the other side of the question, Babe Ruth did not put a screeching halt to Ty Cobb's style of baseball, which was very similar to that described by Buck.

Earle Combs, Kiki Cuyler, Goose Goslin, Joe Judge, Pie Traynor, Sam Rice, Edd Roush, Paul Waner... these white ballplayers had several things in common, one of which was *not* a propensity for hitting home runs. They all played into the decade of the Thirrties, all compiled a career batting average of over .300, all amassed over 150 triples in the course of their baseball life, and almost all managed to post far more walks than strikeouts (Rice and Roush being the only two exceptions—and narrow exceptions they were). The scrappy player who put his bat on the ball, moved runners along, took pitches at times to reach base himself, and advanced two bases rather than one if the defense dozed off (most of this group were also accomplished base-stealers, by the way) did not vanish when the Babe started monopolizing headlines. That breed of ballplayer will always survive wherever baseball is "played smart"—wherever franchises play to win, that is, rather than to pack in strategy-innocent fans hungry for a home run derby.

Negro League star Dave Malarcher figuratively tipped his hat to Ty Cobb in an interview on the subject of how to play ball—but then proceeded to argue that Cobb had very few heirs in white baseball, after all:

I say that Ty Cobb was the only white ballplayer that we observed who played somewhat like we played on the American Giants. None of the teams in the major leagues in those years—and up to now—really concentrated their attack against the opposition. The batters come up and they swing away and okay, it's a double play or a triple play—or a home run. But they so often fail....

Malarcher goes on to explain his personal approach to hitting—obviously the antithesis of indiscriminate flailing away.

And so I developed this strategy against pitchers: I became a very good waiter. If I went to bat with nobody on the bases, I never hit anything but the third strike—I never hit at the first nor the second. But when I came up with men on the bases, I hit the first good thing that came in there because of Rube [Foster]'s principle. "Now is the time." Why? Because when I came to bat with men on the bases, the pitcher would figure I was going to wait anyway and he would give me that pitch right down the middle, belt high, and that's when I would hit it. So that's why I was called a great clutch hitter. It wasn't because I was a great hitter at all; it was because they pitched good balls to me at the times I really needed to hit.[2]

I remain unconvinced that white baseball beyond the person of Ty Cobb did not recognize the soundness of Dave's methods. Successful ballplayers are always aware that certain situations call for certain adjustments—that the home run should no more be the objective of every at bat than the strikeout should be the pitcher's objective in every confrontation with a hitter. But it may well have seemed to people like Malarcher—black

people who knew white baseball mostly from the radio and the sports page—
that the contrast between the Major Leagues and their own leagues was just so
stark. Such a perception, indeed, may have made them more pliant when
white coaches eventually ordered some of them to stop stealing, to stop
bunting—or may have made them more eager, though unordered, to forget the
legacy of Rube Foster and swing for the fences every time.

Foster was perhaps black baseball's greatest genius. He was a
player's player, and a thinking man's thinker. Long before managers adopted
the routine of flipping through clipboards full of statistics, Rube would
approach every game with an image of its likely progress—based upon his
vast personal experience as both player and manager—clearly etched in his
mind. Rube once confided,

> If you let a player make the pitcher pitch four and five balls to him,
> he [the pitcher] will tire around seven innings, and if you can hit
> him at the beginning you can hit him when he is weaker and less
> effective. It is at this point I always center my attack. In most cases
> it is successful. On the other hand, if you allow your players to
> make a few runs at the beginning of the game they become careless.
> Should these few runs be overtaken they are in most cases beaten.
> That is why I vary my attack in the field....[3]

Peterson summarizes Foster's success in these terms, which are more or less a
reiteration of Buck O'Neil's comments about the Negro Leagues generally:

> He was a strong advocate of the bunt and the steal, and his players
> were expected to be adept at both. A player literally had to be able
> to bunt the ball into a hat to play for Rube Foster. He developed to
> a high art the hit-and-run bunt in which the runner on first raced for
> second and went on to third as the play was made at first on the
> bunter.[4]

It is hard to dispute either that running and bunting were an essential
part of Negro League ball or that one found rather less of each in the white
Major Leagues. Simply tracking the many World Series between the Yankees
and the Dodgers during the Fifties is highly instructive: film clips are widely
available. Campanella and Robinson both bunted for a hit in the final game of
the 1953 Series, and of course Jackie would steal home two years later in the
only Series that Brooklyn ever won. (Billy Martin tried the same feat in the
1955 fall classic: he came up short.) The images of Jackie dancing down the
third base line—whenever he made it so far—to drive the pitcher crazy are
unforgettable. Find an old newsreel and see for yourself.

Negro Leaguer Bill Yancey stressed that it was even rougher where
blacks played blacks: no holds were barred then.

We had these little felt things that went from your ankle up to your knee. Because some of them guys would jump on you trying to get safe. Now you see ballplayers sliding all around—you never see anybody getting spiked, and if they do it's an accident. But them guys would deliberately jump on you. Oh, rough![5]

In the process of summing up the importance of base-running in the Negro Leagues, Peterson once again advances the tried-and-true formula that Babe Ruth had changed everything for white baseball. Whether the dichotomy he insists upon was true of the Majors in the Thirrties, it was certainly coming to be so by the Forties and Fifties, precisely when Negro League talents were making their Major League debut.

Daring baserunning was always a feature of Negro baseball. The advent of Babe Ruth as a slugger of prodigious home runs changed the face of major-league baseball, bringing a souped-up, lively ball to meet the demands of the fans for longer drives, and with the lively ball came caution on the basepaths. Why risk being thrown out trying for an extra base when the next batter might well hit one into the seats?[6]

Why? Because, as Dave Malarcher commented, the sluggers so often fail. The very best of their ilk throughout baseball history have never homered more than about once every ten or twelve at-bats: once every three games, say. That leaves two games when you restrain your speedy base-runner from getting into scoring position so that Mighty Casey can strike out or pop up (and the third game may feature a Mightier Casey on the other team). Seasoned baseball minds may be dull about taxes, investments, and neoclassical poetry, but they understand this much: close ball games are usually won by the team that plays better "small ball". A good pitcher can thwart a home run hitter most of the time. The best of pitchers cannot so confidently deny a successful drag bunt to a speedster—and once on, the speedster can degrade the superstar fire-baller to a nervous rookie without even stealing second base.

My question (I may now frame it fully after dropping many a hint) is this: why wasn't Jackie Robinson's brand of baseball embraced by the white establishment? That is, why wouldn't bunting, base-stealing, and the rest be taken over wholesale by the Majors, not because a few white players also practiced "black baseball", but because this style was simply *winning* baseball? Negro League teams regularly defeated teams of white all-stars rambling around the country in the off-season: this, I suspect, is part of what made many white players nervous—that they would lose their jobs if forced to compete in the black player's kind of context. Peterson claims that, for black teams, "a game against white semipros was a holiday after the rigors of a Negro league contest." He recounts that the Negro Leaguers "might clown a bit" in such interracial scrimmages, indulging in such antics as flipping a hard grounder to several infielders before getting it to first base for the out.[7] Such reports are so common from those old enough to have been eye-witnesses than one can scarcely doubt their veracity.

Yet baseball is and has always been a business, first and foremost. Owners have seldom shown any particular shyness about laying off players of any race as long as the reshuffling was viewed as helping them to a pennant. Why, then, was the game carried in the direction of a station-to-station slugfest during the late Forties, throughout the Fifties, and for much of the Sixties? The phenomenon was strangely self-destructive (like today's Major League trend in the same direction, it seems to me). What I have found in the work of baseball's greatest statistical guru, Bill James, is so far from applying the magnifying glass to this paradox that it shrinks the Negro League alternative, rather, into an appearance of sameness with white baseball. For James doesn't believe in the difference: he hears all the conventional chatter about Negro League bunting and stealing with impatience. "Negro League teams carried fourteen to sixteen men, which forced players to be more versatile than in the white leagues," he concedes—or underscores; for his intent is to explain how a given Negro League hitter might have qualities both of the lead-off man and the clean-up slugger.[8] But he is reserved about the characterization of these leagues as all "Punch and Judy" hitting and base-path dazzle:

> When you read the oral histories of the Negro Leagues, you could get the impression that the game was like dead ball era baseball. The spitball, banned in white baseball since 1920, remained legal in the Negro Leagues.... Such stories [about variously doctored or conditioned balls] create the image of a dead ball game, dominated by strategy and baserunning. Donn Rogosin wrote [in *Invisible Men*] that "Negro Leaguers realized that they possessed a distinctive style of baseball. The central difference stemmed from the Negro League's emphasis on speed and its rejection of the Babe Ruth-inspired long-ball game."
>
> Phil Dixon gives a different impression in *The Negro Baseball Leagues*, reporting what happened after Bill Robinson (Bojangles) offered to pay members of the Los Angeles White Sox $5 per home run. The White Sox hit so many home runs that "Robinson reduced the offer to $1 per home run. He finally stopped giving money altogether when Norman (Turkey) Stearns hit four home runs in one game. Robinson stated 'It's time for me to stop handing out money; you fellows are breaking me.'"[9]

James concludes by statistically demonstrating that several Negro Leaguers besides Josh Gibson—Oscar Charleston, Chino Smith, Turkey Stearns, Mule Suttles, Willard Brown, Buck Leonard—homered at about the same rate throughout their far-flung careers as Hack Wilson, if not Babe Ruth.

It seems to me that Mr. James has proved with the "Bojangles" incident exactly the opposite of what he imagines. Think about it: Bill

Robinson elicited home runs instantly and constantly from his players by dangling some extra cash before them. This tells us a) that many Negro Leaguers were well able to step up their home run production to white baseball's levels at will, and b) that the will to do so was not normally there, since Bojangles' bribe was needed to shift the gears. James's ensuing comment about the lifetime homering stats of figures like Stearns, Suttles, and Brown actually contradicts the lesson of the Bojangles story somewhat, since it suggests that Negro Leaguers were merrily homering away all along.

I suspect that the truth here is somewhere between "always" and "never". All good ball clubs have one or two sluggers in the middle of the order whose job is to collect the big hit, the *long* hit; and all great hitters, too, know when to peck away and when to bet everything on one roll of the dice, one mighty swing. No sensible analyst would propose that the home run was alien to black baseball—or, for that matter, that spitballs were unknown in the white Major Leagues. (I shall have more to say about doctored baseballs later—particularly the timing of mainstream baseball's crackdown on them.) The point is, rather, that the long ball used to be employed more judiciously in the Negro Leagues than in the white leagues. *The black ballplayer knew the home run's proper time and place.* His attitude, if he were a veteran who had studied at Rube Foster's school, would be well summed up by Negro Leaguer Thomas Turner's spirited reflections on power-hitting:

> I almost want to throw up sometimes watching these professional guys go up to bat and being suckered with these pitches. It's really something to be professional and be suckered like that with a pitch. They aren't watching anything! They can't bunt a ball; they can't do anything! Anytime a professional man strikes out four times in a row, there's something wrong. And continues to do so![10]

Turner isn't implying that sluggers shouldn't go for the downs: he's saying that a home run hitter cannot afford to think of home runs all the time. You give the pitcher too many advantages when you signal to him that you have only one kind of swing for any count and any situation.

This sort of approach was consciously taught in the Negro Leagues, by all accounts. There were plenty of big hulks who wanted to swing out of their shoes and were counseled to do otherwise, just as Tommy Davis was warned against bunting and Bob Boyd against base-stealing in white baseball (see Chapters One and Two of this section). Negro League slugger Tommy Simpson was taken in hand by his manager and turned into a multi-dimensional hitter:

> Yeah, I could hit. I really don't know how many home runs I hit, but I had *great* power. Remember the Senators in Washington? I hit 'em up in that center field stand. Boy, I used to wear that ball out.

Joe Lewis, my manager when I was playing at Bellville, he used to tell me, "Don't swing for the fences and start hitting that ball to right field." I started hitting it to right field.[11]

One of the greatest ironies I encountered in putting this book together was that black players too young to have worked their way through the Negro Leagues, when given the very advice by a white hitting instructor that Joe Lewis offers above, suspected racist sabotage. They thought that the rare white coach who clung to Pie Traynor/Paul Waner baseball in the Sixties was simply trying to cheat them of the home runs which had made Mays, Banks, and Aaron famous!

Of course, therein lies part of the answer to the question which has shadowed this chapter's exposé of Negro League style: why did white baseball reject that style? The partial answer is that not all of white baseball did any such thing. There were managers like Solly Hemus and Harry Walker (see the following chapter) who strongly encouraged their young black players to learn "small ball"—and, for their troubles, were reviled by the youngsters (privately, then quite publicly after retirement) for trying to keep them out of the "big time". I have no doubt that many such figures were indeed bigots in their social outlook; but I have every doubt that most of these unsavory types would have sacrificed their managerial careers to leave black talent unexploited. I think such men tried to impart what they regarded as winning baseball, and some of them must have done it rather well. The Dodgers, the Cardinals, and the White Sox (nobody ever called Al Lopez a racist) racked up a pile of championships and near misses over these years by essentially playing the kind of ball that Rube Foster would have taught.

So I conclude that the more race-motivated coaching strategy would have been precisely the exhortation to take big swings or, as a base-runner, to stand on your bag patiently while someone else took those swings. Let me try to phrase my allegation very clearly. I do not say that Branch Rickey and his scouts were racists for wanting their black prospects to pull and elevate the ball, or that Paul Richards was a racist for refusing to let Bob Boyd engage in base-theft. Again, certain men in every Major League organization probably held bigoted social views; but baseball was big business, and even the sainted Branch Rickey (as Mr. Rogosin reminds us) was bringing in black players to sell tickets as well as to ease his conscience.[12] These coaches, managers, and front-office suits *believed in* the home run's power to vanquish the foe— wrongly, in my opinion: but the home run has always had its adherents, including Bill James and Earl Weaver, whose allegiance is completely color-blind.

Why, then, would I suggest that some of "long ball's" adherents in the Fifties were less than color-blind? The best harbored no significant racial prejudice at all... *but the rest mistrusted "small ball" at least partly because it was "black ball".* As a manager, you don't necessarily want to see your players dropping bunts and swiping bases on their own initiative, particularly if you savor being in control (as Paul Richards plainly did) *or if you think certain players won't make very good decisions.* Negro League players often had to manage themselves to some extent, for their teams carried few coaches (if any at all) and a manager who himself was often a player. Many of them entered white baseball having grown accustomed to showing a degree of initiative that a Major League manager would bestow only on a veteran. That some of their new handlers thought people of African descent to be wanting in quick-wittedness, anyway, did not help matters. (Recall the general reluctance to let American-born blacks play up the middle on defense, discussed in Part 1, Chapter 3). The station-to-station, home run style of play was the antidote to this influx of black kids with their potentially chaotic notions. I believe it became the white style by default: it was a way of keeping young Jackie Robinsons from running the team out of big innings. The men who saw it as such, once again, must have fancied that they were just doing their job. If they could keep baseball more like a checkers match than a juggling act, then their winning percentage would go up.

And one can see how some managers might have felt this way without having the more rabid kinds of bigotry in their hearts. No less a prince of the Negro Leagues than Buck Leonard has described the game in terms which almost leaves us thinking that any wheel could fall off the wagon at any moment:

> We did not know about backup plays or pickoff plays or how valuable they were. We weren't told the certain positions you were supposed to get in for certain plays. We did know a few, but the few we knew we picked up ourselves. We weren't told on our beginning teams where you were supposed to be on certain plays— how you are supposed to back up plays or how an outfielder is supposed to relay the ball to an infielder, and how the infielder is supposed to stand in line with the throw to keep the hitter from advancing an additional base. We didn't know all that; how we learned was by playing. After playing so many years we found out that was the best.[13]

Some of this negligence may have been peculiar to Buck's own training—or lack of training. I could produce other accounts that contradict his examples. In general, however—granting that the details of the negligence must have varied from team to team—we cannot dispute his major point that the Negro Leagues simply didn't have the manpower to instruct as white baseball did. Some black players clearly learned marvelous tricks by trial-and-error which rendered them almost invincible. Others may well have lost their way in confusion, even though a ballplayer who was befuddled across the board—in hitting and fielding and base-running—would have been released without much ceremony. Bob Boyd, as we saw in the first chapter of this section, once shattered his arm trying to make a strong throw from left field. Such bizarre mishaps (though, frankly, I have never heard of another quite like this one) do not bespeak sound fundamentals.

The vast majority of the time, however, a Negro League "upbringing", for all its anguish of on-the-job training, must have produced an extraordinarily creative player, especially by Major League standards. Playing style can become riveted quite inflexibly at certain times in baseball history and within certain organizations age in, age out. Only consider the resourcefulness with which Satchel Paige pitched, varying his motion, his release point, and his delivery's tempo (the most dramatic example thereof being his notorious "hesitation pitch"). Ted Williams, pondering the science of pitching purely as a hitter (the game's premier hitter, one might add), couldn't understand why so many hurlers neglected such fine points. "I know it's important to make adjustments, to upset the batter's timing, to throw him off with a little different delivery, a little change in motion," he insisted. "I'm continually amazed how often pitchers don't know these things."[14] The spectacular success of Satchel Paige in white baseball long after his fastball had cooled off punctuates Ted's remarks with an exclamation point. The Majors had never seen anybody perform such "antics" (and, in fact, its outraged lawgivers would soon outlaw the "hesitation pitch"). Not everyone was as inventive as Satchel, of course, but using your noggin was a required credential for longevity on the Negro League mound. Writes Peterson:

> Like infielders, pitchers fought a constant battle for survival. Because a Negro club played nearly every day with a small staff of pitchers, they were rarely rested; and so, many of them relied on guile when their arms were too weary to whip a fastball or break off a curve. Spitballs, shine balls, and emery balls were among their weapons long after such trick pitches had been officially outlawed in the Negro leagues.[15]

The point I seek to make here, of course, is not that Negro Leaguers were seasoned cheaters: as far as pitching is concerned, cheating has always been an interracial, multi-cultural activity. My point is that guile gets hitters out—but that much of what artists like Satchel Paige did was indeed perceived as mere "antics", an unprofessional clowning around that could be forgiven only in a master showman. To this day, pitchers at all levels are usually taught to use pretty much the same motion in every situation, even to the degree that many pitch from the stretch with the bases empty.

The case could also be made, it seems to me, that the Major League's crackdown on spitballs and scuff-balls accelerated as the stock of the home run went up rather than that new rules and strict enforcement were the specific cause of increased homering (as Bill James contends). In other words, it may be that the white establishment's interest in eradicating illegal pitches grew in tandem with its interest in promoting the long ball. Might both of these worthy ambitions have shared in a desire (a hidden desire, perhaps of the sort that one hides from oneself) to minimize or neutralize Negro League tactics? Quincy Trouppe recalls that Bob Feller's white All-Stars were extremely upset over their inability to handle what the pitchers of black All-Star teams from the Negro Leagues dished out:

> Nick Stanley finished the game [an exhibition in Yankee Stadium] in good form. Nick could do everything to the ball. He threw a spitball curve, fast-ball sinker, screwball, and shine ball—that scuffed-up baseball Roosevelt Davis was so mean with. We hung a goose egg on them that game, 4-0.
>
> Feller's boys had never hit against this type of pitching before, especially the spitball.
>
> Nick really made them look bad, in front of all those fans. They were so upset over Nick's pitching that they would not play another game until we released him from the team. That made me wonder about the younger generation of hitters. There were many pitchers like Nick, twenty-five years before he threw his first ball.[16]

Quincy neglects to say that Nick's brand of pitcher was not necessarily black—or perhaps he truly believed that white big-leaguers had never even seen a spitball or scuff-ball. One could well conclude that he was *made* to believe this by all the fuss with which Negro League ball-doctoring was received (although Preacher Roe, just to drop a name, would share his formula for a spitter with anyone who wanted to know after his retirement[17]). The policing of such dastardly practices, I suspect, probably *did* become more rigorous as the knowledge spread that Negro League pitchers relied heavily upon them. All the same, to hear John Roseboro tell it, practically every member of the Dodgers pitching staff at least tried to throw a spitter during the Sixties, with Stan Williams and Phil Regan showing particular promise (though not a match, either of them, for those masters of surreptitious lubrication, Gaylord Perry and Lew Burdette). "It's cheating," Roseboro concludes his discussion philosophically, "but it's also competitive pitching."[18]

Competition, of course, can be controlled by those who make and enforce the rules to favor one style of attack over another. If you think that big-league baseball's movers and shakers were unaware of the directly proportional relationship between clean, smooth baseballs and frequent homering, look at some videos of ball games before the 1994 players' strike and note how pitches which hit the dirt behind home plate were not automatically tossed out, as they are today. The white baseball establishment surely knew of the same connection half a century ago, and almost as surely exploited it to deter the "wild style" of Jackie and his successors.

If I may finish this review of the Negro Leagues by summarizing the argument that I have squeezed in among so many colorful vignettes, I would say this: to the extent that black baseball meant "free style" (or maybe just *style*, in the sense of "individualism"), it was probably not widely welcomed into white baseball. The white approach consisted of learning the system: don't think, just do as you're told. That the teaching-intensive white organizations into which black players were very gradually admitted seem to have taught them nothing, all too often, about defense is one of the situation's many puzzling ironies. I have not really succeeded in understanding why I run across so many criticisms of black outfielders who miss their cut-off man in the literature of the times, for such lessons should require all of one good half-hour session to be taught. Since white baseball concluded so readily that blacks couldn't play the infield, where were all the coaches who might have straightened out Bob Boyd's or Leon Wagner's throwing motion with an hour-per-day's work over a week's span? I don't see them charged with bigotry anywhere for hanging around the water cooler; but, to be honest, such sluggards strike me as more deserving of the charge than some "small ball" advocate with a slur-rich vocabulary who vigorously taught his black recruits to hit to the opposite field.

Were there white coaches who just plain neglected untutored black players for racist motives? Would they really have undermined the team's chances of success just to scratch such an itch? How could anyone begin to answer a question like that more than a half a century after the fact? But from what I know of human nature, I'd guess that the coaches and managers themselves didn't know how short they were selling the youngsters entrusted to them, along with the whole organization. They weren't profound enough to be deemed racist saboteurs. "Look at that clown's wind-up... look at that one's stance! Hell, you can't do anything with these jokers—you'd have to start from the ground up." I can just about hear the words from half a century away.

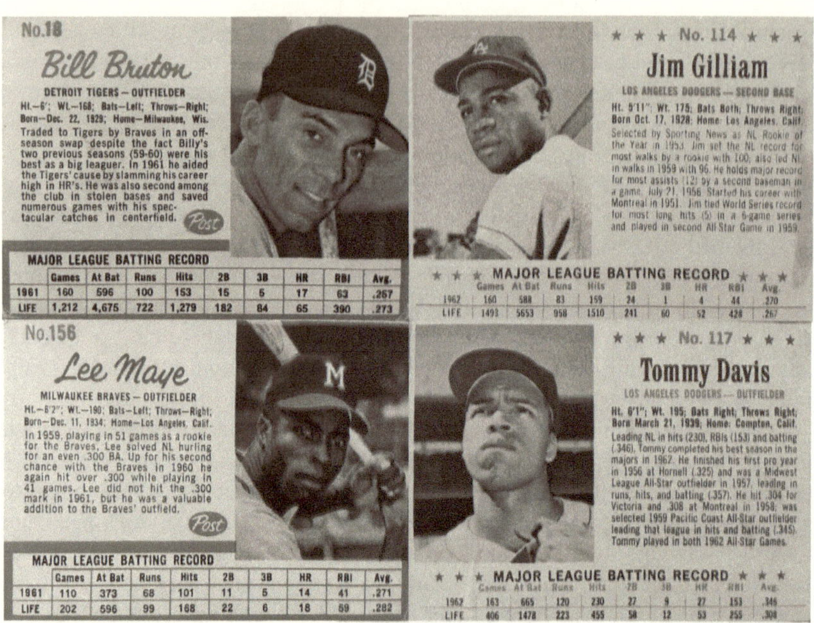

MAJOR LEAGUE BATTING RECORD

	Games	At Bat	Runs	Hits	2B	3B	HR	RBI	Avg.
1961	160	596	100	153	15	6	17	63	.267
LIFE	1,212	4,675	722	1,279	182	84	65	390	.273

★ ★ ★ MAJOR LEAGUE BATTING RECORD ★ ★ ★

	Games	At Bat	Runs	Hits	2B	3B	HR	RBI	Avg.
1962	160	588	83	159	24	1	4	44	.270
LIFE	1493	5653	958	1510	241	60	52	428	.267

MAJOR LEAGUE BATTING RECORD

	Games	At Bat	Runs	Hits	2B	3B	HR	RBI	Avg.
1961	110	373	68	101	11	5	14	41	.271
LIFE	202	596	99	168	22	6	18	59	.282

★ ★ ★ MAJOR LEAGUE BATTING RECORD ★ ★ ★

	Games	At Bat	Runs	Hits	2B	3B	HR	RBI	Avg.
1962	163	665	120	230	27	9	27	153	.346
LIFE	406	1478	223	455	58	12	53	255	.308

Bill Bruton and "Junior" Gilliam both came up through the Negro Leagues: bat control and speed were their hallmark. Maye and Davis had a very different baptism. Lee (like another left-hitting righty in the Braves' organization, Mack Jones) was encouraged to pull home runs, which he did with modest frequency. Tommy was once scratched from the line-up for successfully bunting his way on base instead of swinging for the fences.

Charles Schulz's creation Luci once told her pianist-playmate Schroeder that Beethoven couldn't be famous if he wasn't on a bubblegum card. These three fine players from 1962 would have been happy to know that: they never reached the back of a cereal box. Notice how far Jones held his bat from his body—often the sign of a hitter who is trying to keep from shifting fully to his front foot. Mack was continually urged by coaches to "stay back".

1 See Buck O'Neil (with Steve Wult and David Conrads), *I Was Right on Time: My Journey from the Negro Leagues to the Majors* (New York: Fireside, 1997), 24.

2 This and the immediately preceding citation are quoted in Robert Peterson, *Only the Ball Was White: A History of Legendary Black Players and All-Black Professional Teams* (New York and Oxford: Oxford University Press, 1970), 111-112.

3 Peterson (*ibid.*), 110-111.

4 Peterson (*ibid.*), 111.

5 Peterson (*ibid.*), 116.

6 Peterson (*ibid.*), 117.

7 This and the previous citation are from Peterson (*ibid.*), 116.

8 See James's *Baseball Almanac* (*op. cit.*), 170.

9 Bill James (*ibid.*), 171.

10 See Brent Kelley's collection of interviews, *Voices From the Negro Leagues* (*op. cit.*), 249.

11 From Brent Kelley's second collection, *The Negro Leagues Revisited* (*op. cit.*), 125.

12 Rogosin quotes Negro Leaguer Dave Malarcher on Rickey's motives: "Branch Rickey had something else in his mind than a little black boy. He had those crowds [the capacity audiences at Negro League East-West games]." From Donn Rogosin, *Invisible Men: Life in Baseball's Negro Leagues* (New York: Atheneum, 1983), 189; and see all of Rogosin's final chapter. Bill Veeck, it might be added, viewed Rickey's motives as distinctly venal.

13 See Peterson (*op. cit.*),127.

14 *The Science of Hitting* (*op. cit.*), 75.

15 *Only the Ball Was White* (*op. cit.*), 118.

16   From Quincy Trouppe, *20 Years Too Soon: Prelude to Major-League Integrated Baseball* (St. Louis: Missouri Historical Society Press, 1995. The first edition appeared in 1977; interested readers should also be warned that Quincy added the second "p" to his last name later in life.

17   In an A&E production (written and directed by Marty Bell) during the early Eighties, *The Boys of Summer*, based on Roger Kahn's book of that title, a retired Roe shows the camera exactly how to throw a spitball. The trick was to exhale moisture while tugging at the bill of your cap.

18   *Glory Days with the Dodgers* (*op. cit.*), 197.

V

Rogues' Gallery: A Catalogue of Racially Suspicious or Hostile Behaviors Beyond the Pale of Statistics

a) *Racial prejudice in coaching, managerial, and front-office appointments*
    This subject has been written and spoken about by people infinitely more qualified for the task than I am. In most cases, they are none other than retired black ballplayers who have decided to go public with their experiences rather than wait by the phone another five years while they build up a tree-trimming business or try to get on at the Post Office. Situations immersed in tragedy on a massive scale can take surprising turns: they can exceed their human viewership's normal capacity to witness pain (like the starving, toothpick-limbed children on late-night television's appeals for money), in which case the audience rushes past them for fresh air... or they can become downright ludicrous. Baseball's denial of upper-echelon positions to highly qualified black applicants had become ludicrous as the twentieth century closed. One had to laugh. Frank Robinson wrote a book titled *Extra Innings* partially in response to the Al Campanis incident in 1987. (Campanis appeared on *Nightline* in his role as Dodger general manager to celebrate—of all things—the fortieth anniversary of Jackie Robinson's step across the color barrier; he proceeded to announce that there were not more blacks in management positions because they "lacked the necessities".) Frank's first chapter says more than I would ever know how to say, and says it with authority. I think, too, that he probably intended to say it with a dark humor—at least in places. What about this?

    The Yankees later hired Dick Howser and Lou Piniella to run the big club even though they had no managing experience [the typical reason for rejecting black applicants]. They are both white, of course. But whites are not required to go to the minor leagues as managers before they are hired by major league clubs. Yogi Berra, Ted Williams, and Lou Boudreau didn't manage in the minors, and

259

neither did Jerry Coleman, Pete Rose, or George Bamberger. Joe Torre, Jim Fregosi, and Harvey Kuenn didn't manage in the minors before being judged capable of managing in the majors, and neither did Ray Miller, Roger Craig, or Bobby Valentine. The list goes on and on.[1]

Henry Aaron writes lengthily in his autobiography about his own efforts to land a job in the baseball hierarchy after retirement. Aaron's efforts were more fruitful than most black former-players'; yet despite owning the most famous record in baseball history, Hank did not readily find a spot in the Braves' organization, nor was he allowed to scale very high up the ladder.

When I completed the original manuscript of this volume in 2005, Aaron's book was approximately a decade old, Robinson's more than two. Once again, I do not consider myself to be in a position that allows me to declare authoritatively whether the situation has improved or not—but things certainly *seem* to have gotten better. Robinson was managing the new Washington Nationals as I finished my first draft, a team that spent several weeks atop the Eastern Division during its inaugural year and then faded quickly down the stretch. Dusty Baker completed a stint of calling shots from the Cubs' dugout, continued at the Reds' helm, and still later succeeded Robinson as Washington's skipper. Other black Americans have enjoyed, or are enjoying, a generous run in their managerial jobs (as such things are measured)—and most, like the particular two I have named, are well liked by the public.

But Frank and Dusty had a high profile: they had achieved renown even as players. What about less glamorous figures? Just as the typical utility player once tended overwhelmingly to be white instead of black, so the typical low-profile manager tends overwhelmingly to be white. Lloyd McClendon was briefly skipper of the Pirates, and then the Mariners; Ron Washington took the Texas Rangers to the World Series. Neither had enjoyed a national following as a player. How many of their ilk are at the helm as I write in 2018? Alex Cora and Dave Roberts have piloted the champions of their respective leagues deep into October, one would immediately stress. Does it matter that one is of Latin extraction and the other partly an African American whose mother is Japanese? We noted earlier in this book that the baseball establishment once pictured Latinos as gifted with the subtlety necessary to play second base and shortstop, and that even blacks from the Caribbean appeared mysteriously more trusted in those positions than their mainland-born brethren. Could it be that such thinking lingers in managerial hires? For the strange fact is that, as of this moment, no American of unequivocally African genetic heritage is employed as a big-league skipper. Yet such minor performers in yesteryear's line-ups as Gabe Kapler and Scott Servais are very secure in their position—deservedly so; but does Terry Pendleton not want to manage? What about Ozzie Smith or Tim Raines?

To be sure, managers probably bring rather little to any team, all things considered. I've heard ballplayers say over and over again, in effect:

"He manages best who manages least." The most critical decisions any manager makes during a game concern the relief of pitchers and the insertion of pinch-hitters—and the latter stratagem, for that matter, is such a by-the-book move that a child could accomplish it flawlessly. American League managers don't even have to worry about pinch-hitting, thanks to the designated hitter. One would think, then, that owners would be willing to "take a chance" on minority skippers more often. From the owner's point of view, managing is marketing. Comparatively few African-American citizens spend their money going to baseball (as opposed to basketball or football) games, except perhaps in New York; so... has that affected the equation?

If I may conclude this sub-section with an editorial comment: I recall wincing when Terry Francona allowed Pedro "The Yankees Are My Daddy" Martinez a chance to enter the 2004 LCS play-off's final game and taunt the Bronx audience. No doubt, Pedro's suffering ego was much bolstered—but he also very nearly blew the game. He created a situation where one swing of the bat could have turned it around completely. And then Martinez would have been the goat, I suppose... but the fault belonged entirely to the manager. Similarly, though Bill Buckner will always be remembered for booting a ground ball to lose Game Six of the 1986 World Series, the fault was all John McNamara's for letting an old warrior with two bad knees play extra innings.

Now, Pedro has since been elected to the Hall of Fame, and Terry won't be far behind him when he retires as a manager. I salute them both—and I love them both. But it's a fact that franchises like the Red Sox sometimes appear to hire managers on the understanding that they showcase superstars. (No doubt, this comment should be addressed with more emphasis to other organizations.) A black manager—especially someone who didn't quite make the Hall of Fame but knows baseball inside-out, like Tim Raines—might insist upon managing by his own lights, with no front-office interference. Who knows whether a given owner wishes to win more than to make money—or whether he wishes to make money more than to hob-knob with the superstars whose salaries he pays? Maybe certain owners feel more comfortable having a "drinking buddy" type in this facilitator's role.

b) *The beanball and the first black players*

In the midst of his legendary career, Henry Aaron was quite convinced that pitchers at all levels of predominantly white baseball had deliberately thrown at him—much more so than they did at white hitters.

> Pitchers have knocked me down a lot, and sometimes it goes
> through my head that they're throwing at me because I am a Negro.
> What makes me think so is that Eddie Mathews is just as much of a
> hitter as I am, and I've batted right behind him for nine years now
> and have never seen him knocked down. I've been knocked down
> too often. [Wes] Covington used to get knocked down often, too.
> [Bill] Bruton used to get picked on. I've seen some of the white
> players knocked down once in a while, but most of the time it's

261

been the Negroes.[2]

The mention of Covington is especially revealing, because Wes batted left—and most pitchers, being righties, will not "accidentally" knock down left-handed hitters, since the lefty can distinguish between a fastball and a breaking ball without sticking his nose in the ball's path. After retirement, Hank would reiterate in his autobiography the suspicion that a target was placed on black players. He observes at one point that his teammate Felix Mantilla seemingly "got beaned every night."[3] Felix batted right-handed, and stood rather close to the plate, into the bargain. Perhaps he was asking for trouble... but Aaron is convinced that such incidents had little to do with his stance.

On the other hand, Bill White (also in the middle of a distinguished career when Jackie Robinson elicited his comments) was unwilling to concede that the X between his eyes was any bigger than that between a Caucasian player's:

> I can say this, too—any player can take care of himself in any situation if he knows how. Take these reports about pitchers throwing at Negroes. This has never happened to me in the majors and only once in the minors. At Shreveport we had a little throwing trouble, and handled it pretty good.[4]

Now, White was a lefty: few balls from a right-handed pitcher would have ridden up above the letters on the inside corner. Bill White was also the kind of man who refused to let crippling thoughts enter his mind. A fear is only true, one might say, if you allow it to be true—if you admit the reality of the feared object. White probably ignored a lot of situations simply because they would have undermined him as a ballplayer. And the reverse could also have been true of players like Felix Mantilla: they may have created an issue out of bean-balling by forming a generality out of several specific occurrences when the better course, as far as hitting was concerned, would have been to resist generalizing.

Caucasian player Fred Hatfield grew a little touchy about the touchiness of black players.

> If you knocked down white guys, nothing was said. A black guy gets knocked down and it was racial prejudice. He's not a baseball player, he's a black guy. I thought it was a compliment to get knocked down. At least they had respect for you. Luke Easter wasn't thrown at because he was black—he was thrown at because he was a good hitter and was hurting you. When the blacks and the Latins came along, they thought you were picking on them when all you were doing was seeing if they could be intimidated and what they were made of.[5]

To be sure, Hatfield was not particularly sympathetic with integration generally. A faithful member of the Boston Red Sox, he expresses confidence right before this passage that the franchise failed to call up black ballplayers sooner than it did simply because there were so few good black players. The substance of his remarks should not be completely ignored, however, just because they are phrased with a certain hostility. Getting "low-bridged" was part of a rookie's initiation at the time—any rookie's. The new guy had to prove that he could not be intimidated: the veteran on the mound wanted to know if he *could* be intimidated. Fear is one of the pitcher's weapons, after all. Overpowering pitchers almost always have a reputation for being somewhat wild.

There was a perception current among white ballplayers, furthermore, that the new black recruits were especially susceptible to such intimidation. I discuss the stereotype (as detailed by Bill Veeck, who saw it applied up close) in the following chapter. The assumption about black hitters that you could "take away their power" just by making them sit in the dust a couple of times most certainly had racist undertones, and—in retrospect—most certainly seems to have been incorrect. However, it was part of what went through the minds of white pitchers: that is, the objective of their knocking down black hitters, to the extent that they believed those hitters easy to intimidate, was to win the game, not to kill a member of a hated race.

Still, the logic of Hatfield's comments above does not withstand narrow scrutiny. For if black players were thrown at so much because they were so respected as hitters, then the hitting which won them respect must not have been much affected by being thrown at (not to mention that the Red Sox ought to have shown some interest in suiting up one of these offensive marvels). As for the initiation theory, the evidence is preponderant that whatever big-boy hazing went on in these cases lasted quite some while and was extraordinarily thorough. Don Newcombe believed that Roy Campanella would not have survived if he had been the very first black ballplayer:

> He had the right temperament, but I don't know how much he could have taken physically. Even in the majors, he used to get hit in the head a lot. I never saw Jackie get hit in the head—the ribs, the arm, but never in the head. (The same with Willie Mays, after he joined the Giants in 1951.) Roy didn't have those kinds of reflexes. I saw him get hit in the head by Bill Werle on a curveball. They would have killed Roy. They would actually have set him up and killed him with a baseball.[6]

It should be said at this point that a "beaning" is significantly different from a "brush-back". Every ballplayer understands the distinction. If a pitcher wants to back a hitter off the plate, he hums in a fastball high and tight. The batter may get nicked on the wrist or, if he turns away instead of falling back, take the ball off his shoulder: painful, but not life-threatening. The true "head-hunter" is the pitcher who attempts to shoot a fastball *behind the batter's ear*. Since batters almost never see a pitch thrown behind them at the most expert levels of competition, they do not have a well-rehearsed response to it—and if they should back up instinctively, they will be carried right into the pitch. Beanings could indeed end careers—and potentially lives—in the days before batting helmets. The initiation pitch of which Fred Hatfield spoke just above would be a dust-off or brush-back: the pitches which Hank Aaron saw coming at Felix Mantilla, and which Don Newcombe feared for Campy's sake, were meant for keeps. Only a complete fool—or a homicidal lunatic—would aim at the batter's head as a joke.

If the beanballs whizzing around black players' ears had not been serious business, their white teammates would not have exacted reprisals on the mound. Such was the strategy adopted by Bill White's Minor League teammates in Shreveport, and such was the response of Al Smith's white teammates in Cleveland. "I learned quickly that black players were knocked down all the time," recalled Al.

> Doby, [Dave] Pope, and myself—and Luke Easter, Harry Simpson, and Dave Hoskins when they were on the Indians in 1953—were often decked. So [Early] Wynn, who always spoke his mind, told the other pitchers that "we can't score runs with those guys on the ground." He protected Doby and me by knocking down opposing batters. No one wanted to fool with him. He got our other pitchers to protect our black players, too. This helped unify the team for the successful pennant run.[7]

Wynn's patronage didn't keep Al from setting an Indian record in 1954, however, for being hit by pitches. The rookie season was past, along with whatever initiation it involved—and the dust-baths kept coming. Noted Al acidly, "It seemed that blacks were setting just about every team's record for that."[8]

I had considered putting the hit-by-pitch figures of black players and white players side by side in Part 2 above, and of correlating those figures to number of plate appearances. One certainly gets the impression from glancing over the raw numbers that black hitters on average were pitched more tightly than white hitters. But the stats tell a very murky tale, at best. Henry Aaron was struck only 32 times in over 12.000 at-bats, and his brother Tommie was never hit at all in almost 1,000 at-bats. Caucasian slugger Bob Alison barely reached 5,000 at-bats, yet was hit by pitches two more times than The Hammer. Ernie Banks got thumped 70 times in 9,421 official at-bats. That's not really exorbitant, considering how long Ernie played and how he crowded the plate in his effort to pull the ball (a technique still more vigorously—and painfully—employed by Frank Robinson). On the other hand, it seems almost incredible that the fearsome Mickey Mantle, who set up with his front foot very close to the plate, pulled nearly everything, and was the only heavy lumber in the Yankee line-up for much of his career should have been plunked *a mere 13 times*! Lithe, light-hitting Jim Gilliam was struck 33 times with 1,000 fewer official visits to the plate than Mantle.

Well... but one player ducks better than another or crowds the plate more or plays with a team staffed by more headhunters (how many of Gilliam's war wounds were paybacks for Drysdale's razor-close pitching?). How could one possibly take so many factors into account? The bottom line is that statistics take a back seat to the anecdotal evidence here. We must remember that a grazed shirt sleeve is not the same as a fractured cranium, and we must listen to what the players themselves have to say.

c) *Blue on the outside, white on the inside: prejudice in umpiring*

There is no question that young black ballplayers trapped in the Deep South's minor-league circuits on predominantly white teams often received the short end of close calls from what passed for umpires in the hinterland. Ralph Johnson tells the following hair-raising tale about his Negro League team's giving a local squad a run for its money during an exhibition game:

> There were a lot of problems, man. A lot of problems. Especially in the Southwest and in the South. Mostly in the South, like Mississippi, Louisiana, Florida, Georgia—places like that. It was tough on us.
>
> I really got scared with the [Indianapolis] Clowns. We were playing right out of Mobile there, in Pritchard, Alabama, I think it was. We got to the ballpark and there was a sheriff out there; he was the umpire. He said, "You boys ain't gonna beat our niggers here in town, now."
>
> Our manager said, "Don't pay that man no mind. Y'all go play ball."
>
> 'Bout the fifth inning, we had about ten runs. He come in our dugout. "I told y'all, you ain't gonna beat my boys"....
>
> So after a while, we started taking that thing seriously. He had two guns on his side. He started calling balls strikes. A man'd be safe on base and he'd call him out. 'Bout the eighth inning, our manager come and said to us, "I'll tell y'all something. Y'all better start losing this damn ballgame".... "Boy, if it's hit to you, either you better miss it or throw it away or something. Let these guys get some runs."
>
> About the last of the eighth inning, them guys had caught up. I think we was tied up. In the last of the ninth inning they won that game and that umpire looked at us, said, "I *told* you, didn't I?"

Whether or not umpires at the Major League level consistently perverted calls in favor of white players at any point in the Fifties (and the incident above, notice, involves local rather than racial favoritism), one can well imagine that young players who ascended to the top through this stew of intimidation would not have the utmost confidence in receiving the benefit of the doubt.[9]

Frank Robinson makes a convincing case that certain umpires rode him excessively hard in his original managing stint with the Indians. "Ron Luciano admitted that the umpires were not being fair with me or my ballclub," he observes, referring to public comments made by an especially outspoken and flamboyant umpire. Frank was indiscreet enough to protest his treatment before reporters, with the result that the condition lingered even though he himself became more reticent in the dugout. Within baseball, as within any system that has its dirty little secrets to hide from general view, uttering honest, open remarks about the skeleton in the closet is far more severely punished than simply letting the boss know that you don't like murder. The umpiring crew of Lou DiMuro, Rich Garcia, Bill Kinkle, and Dave Phillips tossed Frank, his coaches, and his players from games almost on a whim. "By July they had worked 15 of our games, and my team had suffered 12 ejections at their hands. We had only one other ejection in that time." Robinson concludes with admirable cool-headedness, "I still have no way of knowing if racism had any bearing on the way certain umpires came down on us without letup through the first half of my first two seasons at the Indians' helm."[10] And, in a way, his reserve in reaching what seems an inescapable judgment is justified. Frank was black, and he was the first black manager in the Major Leagues—but he was also a new boy in the broadest terms, and freshmen are often hazed and bullied. No doubt, his being new in several ways at once made him a more than usually tempting target for whatever evil demon in us likes to torment the tyro. No doubt, also, his reputation as an aggressive ballplayer preceded him: certain umps decided in advance that they would go out of their way to teach him who was boss, no doubt.

But there is a racial element to a rookie manager like Frank that has nothing to do with the shade of his skin. As blacks schooled by the Negro Leagues were somewhat off-beat players, hitting to all fields and bunting in any situation and stealing at the drop of a hat, so the first black manager proved to be exceptionally resourceful and intense. Umpires were more accustomed to an aging Walter Alston or Casey Stengel: a figure who did not abstain from arguing calls, to be sure, but who on a given day was vulnerable to the charge of having his mind elsewhere. People in any line of business entrusted with monitoring performance do not appreciate keen bystanders monitoring their monitoring. Frank's newness was a threat, I suspect, because it was so *complete* a newness—a willingness to try any angle and to shine a light into any corner.

Did black players suffer from the same double standard in the field: that is, was the unorthodoxy in their play a source of irritation to umpires because it required the official monitor of the game to wake up and do some close monitoring? I have never seen such an allegation made in such terms. Henry Aaron had an uncomfortable feeling, early in his career, that close calls at the plate would not go his way. "I wouldn't go so far as to say that black players had a different strike zone than white players, but I didn't want to test the umpires. When you've grown up black in the South—at least, in my times—you're conditioned not to rely on the white man's justice. If the pitch was close, I wasn't taking any chances."[11] In a way, it doesn't really matter whether the young Aaron was right in his suspicions or not: merely the belief that they would be rung up on a low-and-outside pitch with two strikes, false though it may have been, is bound to have induced plenty of black players to wave at that pitch. Jake Wood acquired a rap for striking out too often which the Tigers never gave him an opportunity to overcome. Chuck Hinton struck out about 20% of the time, as did Jim Pendleton: it was a common failing among unproved black talents of the era. This fact seemed to me a statistical aberration throughout my research, for the baseball of the Negro Leagues stressed putting the ball in play and advancing runners. I concluded that the players in question must have been extremely nervous when at last given a chance, not just to perform in the big leagues, but to show the world that their race was on a par with any other. That many of the group should have feared a hostile umpire's uncharitable rulings would not be at all unlikely, especially since the umpires in venues like the Carolina League and the Sally League had done much to validate these fears.

In one case, however, I can voucher my own eye-witness testimony of a white umpire blowing an easy call against a black ballplayer. It occurred at a crucial moment in Game 7 of the 1968 World Series. Bob Gibson and Mickey Lolich had dueled each other to a scoreless standstill when Lou Brock led off the bottom of the sixth with a single. Brock apparently had his next move already planned: knowing that Lolich's throw to first was no bullet and that Norm Cash had a mediocre arm, at best, Lou was going to take such an enormous lead that Mickey could not resist the throw over—and then sprint for second. It was an incredibly daring maneuver. Lolich must have doubted his eyes when he saw Brock edging *beyond* the point where the infield grass straightens out of its arc around first base. Sure enough, Brock was gone as soon as Mickey lifted his forward leg. He made it to second safely: his knee was already bending under the pressure of the bag on his forward heel while shortstop Mickey Stanley's glove was still two feet away. I know, not because I was there to see it—no paying customer could have seen the play one one-thousandth as clearly as I did—but because I have studied the sequence in slow motion. Replays were rare on broadcasts of the Sixties, but Brock's steal was actually replayed by the filming crew from two different angles. From the center-field camera, one sees beyond any question that he beat the tag easily.

Yet he was called out. Commentators Curt Gowdy and Harry Caray volunteered nothing about the evidence staring them—and millions of viewers—in the face (broadcasters, too, were expected to be "team players" at that time and not expose the game's weaknesses to the public). Brock exchanged a few quiet words with the second-base umpire as he rose from the dust: no arms gesticulating, no feet stomping, no neck muscles flexing.[12] What else could he have said, except, "You blew that one big-time," or, "You just cost us the series." For a run at that point could very possibly have given Gibson the adrenaline he needed to shut out the Tigers for three more innings, and it might also have opened the gate to further runs. Instead, Curt Flood would become the goat for slipping as he went to chase down Jim Northrop's liner over his head. Flood's miscue is always pegged as the pivotal moment of the game, though, in fact, it was not. That moment was Brock's being called out on a brilliant base-stealing attempt which succeeded with room to spare.

Racism? Bob Gibson, who doesn't mince words in his recent book, devotes not a single line to the umpiring gaffe; neither did the late Curt Flood in his equally candid exposé. Perhaps Brock said nothing to his teammates after returning to the dugout, a kind of "classy" reticence that would be typical of him. My own suspicion, once again, is that the umpire suffered a kind of brain cramp. He was wholly unprepared for anything so absolutely outlandish as Brock's inducing a throw over in order to beat Cash's lob to second. I'm sure that none of the umpiring crew had ever seen anything like it in year upon year of arbitrating the same old ploys and gambits. A runner who breaks for second base when the pitcher throws over to first will end up being out unless the defenders drop the ball: always has been, always will be. In that situation, the runner has made a mistake—*always*—and can only stumble about in No Man's Land prior to the inevitable conclusion. The scenario etched indelibly in this umpire's mind overrode what he saw with his own eyes. How many times, I wonder, had something similar happened since players from the Negro Leagues started turning the Majors upside-down?

In a way, perhaps it really was Lou's fault. Maybe he should have approached the second-base umpire before the game and let him know what was cooking. He had overestimated the petty functionary's ability to process genius.

d) *"I told you so": forms of managerial sabotage*

Occasionally I have seen suggestions that managers or coaches would "set up" their young black players to fail. It was as if they were trying to create a situation where they could turn to the GM or the owner (with the public invited to view the whole highly staged pantomime) and say, "You see? I told you so! We gave this kid a chance, but he just couldn't do the job." The GM or owner would then utter the formulaic lines, "Yes, Butch, I had my doubts, too. But the times are changing, and we owed it to our nation and our conscience at least to give the young man a try. Well, send him back to Pawtucket, and bring Spike back up."

Did such Oscar-worthy performances ever actually take place? Probably. Human beings are nothing if not hypocritical, and baseball front offices are not known for producing saints. At the same time, the more I look into specific charges of this kind, the less I am inclined to believe that the alleged sabotage could have been quite as deliberate as charged.

Joe Morgan asserts that his erstwhile manager on the Houston Astros, Harry "The Hat" Walker, was, "without question, the most blatant racist I have ever met in baseball," and that Walker tried deliberately to undermine some of the team's very promising black youngsters in the late Sixties. Writes Joe,

> From the moment he donned an Astros uniform in 1968, Harry
> began targeting black players. He constantly deprecated my

roommate Jimmy Wynn, who was only the best player on our club….. [Bob] Watson, known as "The Bull", was six feet two, 220 pounds; [John] Mayberry was six feet four and weighed around 240. These guys were built for power, but Harry tried to ruin their careers by transforming them into dainty singles hitters. If Watson, a right-handed hitter, drove the ball down the left-field line for a booming double, Harry would fine him for not slapping the pitch the other way.[15]

This Hall of Famer has here patently contradicted what I have claimed about the baseball establishment and home run mania! Yet I regard this curious case as the exception that proves the rule. I believe that not all of baseball's movers and shakers—especially the ones who had actually played the game for years—were infatuated with the long ball. Certainly an old hand like Walker, managing a team in a pitcher-friendly ballpark, might well have reflected during The Year of the Pitcher that the Astros' best bet was to be "dainty singles hitters". Watson and Mayberry, to be sure, were not the most likely converts to this gospel. It may just be, though, that Walker had observed too many young black talents swinging from the heels, and that he concluded that they all needed to be thus disciplined. His conclusion may well have had a bigoted pedigree: he may have said to himself, for instance, that his black understudies were too dumb to figure out the fine art of hitting, especially now that the Negro Leagues' tutoring was no longer available to them. I feel fairly confident that some such reasoning kept young black second basemen and shortstops out of those key positions earlier in the decade once they reached the Majors. A black kid couldn't think fast enough to be a shortstop… and so on, and so on.

But in the matter of malignly chaining Watson's power, Joe may be giving Harry credit for too much clairvoyance. Walker had, after all, fixed upon the right formula for winning in the Dome: he was simply applying it with the blunt inflexibility so typical of know-it-all coaches everywhere. "The Hat" had himself been a low-line-drive hitter in his day (leading the National League with 16 triples and a .371 batting average in 1947—along with one home run). He would as naturally think that his players should poke pitches through defensive holes and sprint as Ted Williams would teach his protégés how to elevate and pull pitches over the fence. Walker wouldn't have given much thought to the typical fate of black ballplayers who eschewed power-hitting. Frankly, if the baseball world had been prepared to reward a black player for hitting .371, the Walker hitting regimen might have been career-saving for a George Altman or a Vada Pinson… who knows? Rod Carew, perhaps the greatest hitter of the coming generation, lost his bid for a raise after hitting a league-high .364 in 1974 because (as he was expressly told by Twins owner Calvin Griffith) he "was merely a singles hitter and could not produce the long ball."[14] Apparently home run mania wasn't about to subside in some quarters, even as the Seventies loomed. But Harry Walker, who knew nothing except hitting and knew only one kind of hitting, wouldn't have known *that*. Any way you cut it, he doesn't make a very convincing saboteur.

(With apologies to Joe Morgan, I must also squeeze in a few statistics indicating that Walker's hat wasn't occupied by an entirely empty space. Bob Watson would place among the top ten hitters in batting average five times over a nineteen-year career. Among the top ten home run hitters, he never claimed a spot for a single season. His career high in homers was a middling 22. Of course, he played most of his career in Houston's Astrodome, scarcely a long-baller's paradise. But then, maybe that's exactly what Harry had anticipated.)

Morgan continues that Walker "would tell me to bunt in obviously inappropriate situations. At times when a stolen base could help the club, Harry often flashed the 'do not steal' sign to me or Jimmy Wynn, even though we were the team's best base thieves."[15] This looks like the same picture to me: Walker was trying to re-invent the bunt and opposite-field hitting in the most offense-hostile park known to the Major Leagues, yet he feared that his young black talents were not sufficiently cerebral to be turned loose on the base paths. Bigotry? I'll take Joe Morgan's word for it. He was there, and he produces plenty of evidence. Deliberate sabotage tailored delicately to undermine each black player's special abilities? I think it far more likely that Harry Walker, like Rogers Hornsby and so many other managers and coaches of the old school, was a genius-unto-himself whose recipe for victory was to replicate in every player what *he* would have done in *his* playing days. Walker (like Hornsby in his managing days) was universally loathed by those who fell under his sway. In a world sundered by partisan strife, it is indeed heartening to read with what unanimous detestation both black and white players viewed his mentoring. Jim Brosnan, having already blasted him in *The Long Season*, would later describe Walker as "an egomaniac who didn't know how to teach hitting."[16] Sometimes a jerk is just a jerk.

The "do not steal" incident, it seems to me, smacks more of standard bigotry than any other. It is highly reminiscent of the anchor that Paul Richards tied securely about Bob Boyd's fleet feet during the late Fifties. Probably nothing unnerved white baseball orthodoxy quite like the audacious base-running which Jackie Robinson, Jim Gilliam, Al Smith, and others imported from the Negro Leagues. Bunting was not unheard-of; in fact, several white "Punch and Judy" hitters excelled at it. No less a slugger than Mickey Mantle had refined drag-bunting to a degree scarcely equaled in baseball history. So for opposite-field and all-field hitting: such tactics did not routinely produce home runs, but they *did* produce batting titles. Musial hit drives to the whole park; so did another Polish superstar, Carl Yastrzemski. In contrast, base-stealing, while mastered by pesky hitters like Ty Cobb and Richie Ashburn, had grown comparatively rare in the Major Leagues. Hit-and-run plays were far more popular as a means of moving runners along. At a minimum, the base-stealer had to be extremely wily—not wild, but wily. These new dusky-skinned speedsters just didn't get it—they didn't know when or how to throw on the brakes. Best just to issue a standing order that they stay put unless told otherwise in a given situation.

Solly Hemus was straight out of the Hornsby-Walker mold with regard to his love of scrappy playing and his dearth of interpersonal skills (not, alas, in regard to his own successes as a ballplayer, which were few and rare). Hemus drew some of the charges from Curt Flood and Bob Gibson which Joe Morgan levels above at Walker.   (In fact, Hemus chose Walker to be his hitting coach!   The coaching fraternity was, and still is, a very tight-knit bunch.) Flood attributes Solly's position at the Cardinal helm to a sycophantic letter whose afterglow warmed Mr. Busch's heart for two and a half seasons of losing baseball.   He implies that Hemus deliberately played Bill White painfully out of place—in center field, where the stiff-jointed giant was positively humiliated.[17] Gibson recalls the same stupefying mismatch, adding that Bill had no speedsters flanking him in the outfield to minimize his awkwardness. On the matter of bunting, however, the players whom Bob shrewdly singles out for being mis-assigned the sacrifice by Hemus are not Bill White and other blacks, but white All-Star slugger Ken Boyer and the incomparable Stan Musial. The silly Solly had them "bunting and hitting behind the runner, a strategy best restricted to utility infielders like Hemus" himself.[18] Gibson rightly discerns, in my opinion, that bigotry is most often a species of vast folly: folly is rarely a specific by-product of bigotry. In other words, if you're a fool about race, you're probably just a fool.

Perhaps I should be writing these next words in a footnote, or at least parenthetically… but it's impossible for me to let pass without comment the amazing fact that I have now collected testimony from *two* Hall-of-Fame black players denouncing coaches for chaining up home run hitters! What would the late Bob Boyd have said, who was pressured in just the opposite direction but insisted on safeguarding his success as a line-drive, high-average hitter? There's absolutely no doubt whatever that Bob Watson, Ken Boyer, and their ilk should have been cut loose to have their hacks in many situations—but for every manager who sought to restrain such sluggers, these same years must have seen ten who let their young black stars go to ruin swinging for the seats. When he retired, Joe Morgan had belted more homers than any second baseman in history: naturally, he thinks like a power-hitter. Bob Gibson was among the most frequently homering pitchers ever to play the game. They were youngsters when home run mania was at an epidemic pitch, and the type of coaching oppression which they felt most keenly was that which dissuaded them and their peers from "airing it out" at every cut. Yet I persist in believing—more strongly than ever—that *this very mindset sabotaged a great many careers among young black players.* No, I don't suppose George Altman would ever have been paid like Willie Mays if he had gone on to win three batting titles, as he might well have done. But he would have had a respectable Major League career. Harry Walker probably couldn't have helped George, because Harry Walker couldn't help anyone—but watching Ken Boyer clout home runs didn't help George much, either. Just because Walker couldn't teach a rock to sit still doesn't mean that his hitting style was flawed. By the same token, just because Ted Williams and Joe Morgan are most remembered for their offensive power doesn't mean that their approach to the ball should have been widely replicated. Most of the time, if three infielders can safely play on the same side of second base when you're at the plate, you are destined for a brief tour of duty in that league.

What, then, shall we say—that managers never miscast black players or never thwarted their talents in order to humiliate them at the cost of a game or a season? Well, if you really think about that suggestion, maintaining its contrary (i.e., that managers *did* sometimes sabotage their players) would call for a racist of fanatical proportions to be at the helm. The man would have to be willing to throw away his present job as manager, and to jeopardize his chances of receiving any such job in the future, just for the satisfaction of "getting" a few kids of African descent. It's a rather extravagant notion. I was willing to entertain it when I began this study, but I'm much less so now. I don't think many managers were on a mission to say, "There, see? I told you so—these black guys just can't play up here!" When they did say it (and I would never doubt that some of them did), I think the cause was more a matter of simply not knowing how to utilize the extraordinary talents entrusted to them. I think that some skippers, perhaps a great many, were nervous around their black players during these years—afraid they might try to steal home with the game on the line, or something of the sort. Vic Power, a dark-skinned Puerto Rican who knew all too well what the black ballplayer went through, gauged the situation perfectly:

> In baseball I notice I have two managers who are real cold to me, Jimmy Dykes and Harry Craft. The others—Lou Boudreau, Eddie Joost, Bobby Bragan, and now Sam Mele with the Twins—they different, they treat me like anybody else. I don't say Jimmy Dykes and Harry Craft treat me cold because I am colored—there's something they don't like about me.[19]

"Something they don't like about me"…yes, Vic probably had them worried for reasons that neither he nor they could have explained. The problem was precisely that his skin color represented an indefinable threat, an unknown which they could only keep from corrupting their simple calculations if they rigidly channeled the rest of the player's performance into familiar quantities. Most of these authority figures, after all, were anything but risk-takers, however original they may have been as young blades with a bat in their hands. And, after all, they inhabited a gray-flannel era where one was expected to be a "company man", a loyal slave to the Boss. Consider this loving portrait which Mickey Mantle draws of the second doubtful Harry in our line-up of suspects, the one just mentioned by Vic Power:

> I can still see, in my mind's eye, rugged Harry Craft walking down the street, well set up, neatly dressed, looking like a man of the sort you do not bump into at every corner. And I know that this posture of his made a deep impression on his charges, made it easier for him to maintain control, and made us all ready to accept him as a

leader. I do not mean that he swaggered or appeared impressed with his own importance. Quite the opposite. He was always quiet and unassuming in manner, and he never looked as if he were trying to make a show of himself. But he stood up straight and looked the whole world in the eye. And his appearance was always neat, brushed, and polished.[20]

Would a man like this set one of his young charges loose on the base paths? Would he stake his professional future on letting a dark, moping, distant kid from an alien background occupy the most crucial positions on the infield? Maybe he would force that kid—and all his lighter-skinned footsoldiers, as well—to hit low drives up the middle, or maybe he would exhort them all to pull the ball hard and high. That would all depend on which part of the trenches he himself had toiled in when *he* was their age. His views would be tinged with bigotry, probably—because he was a company man, and scarcely anyone had yet heard of Martin Luther King, Jr. Whatever didn't fit securely under the boat's thwarts rocked it dangerously. But deliberate sabotage? I am skeptical.

Let me conclude by examining two somewhat opposed cases from the late Fifties. In my comments about Bob Boyd (see Chapter One of this section), I ventured an opinion that Orioles manager Paul Richards really needn't have platooned this potential batting champ at first base—that Boyd made reliable contact producing taut liners (hence his nickname, "The Rope"), and that platooning makes little sense in such cases. Yet Boyd tended to believe (though interviews show him vacillating) that Richards had done right by him and even, in some ways, looked out for him to an extraordinary degree. Henry Aaron was much less inclined to see Richards as a benevolent leader; on the contrary, Aaron found his style as general manager to be that of a ruthless autocrat.[21] Perhaps what most irritated Hank about the Richards regime was the cavalier handling of Braves legend Eddie Mathews—who, of course, was Caucasian. Was Paul Richards, then, a bigot, or just another of baseball's strong men lamentably devoid of finesse?

I would contrast Boyd's optimistic attitude with what Aaron's book reports of how black pitcher Brooks Lawrence viewed his handling by Reds manager Birdie Tebbetts. Lawrence went 19 and 10 in 1956, and apparently had plenty of time to achieve Win Number 20. Recalls Aaron, "Down the stretch, when any game might have meant the pennant, he [Lawrence] didn't pitch. Later he told me the reason was that his manager, Birdie Tebbetts, didn't want a black man winning twenty games."[22] Now, Tebbetts by all accounts more nearly resembled the "good old boy" managerial specimen than the iron-fisted Paul Richards type. Former players do not line up to testify to his bigotry as they do in the case of Harry Walker or Solly Hemus. Jim "Mudcat" Grant had no lofty opinion of Birdie's managerial genius, but on this particular issue he remarked, "The best thing I can say about Tebbetts is that he understood what problems black players would have in the majors."[23] This is not to say that Tebbetts was clean of racial prejudice; but it makes little sense to me that a man who invested rather heavily (by his profession's standards) in keeping people happy would sacrifice a pennant to put down a black player. I would more readily believe that he held Lawrence out of the starting rotation in the backward belief that a black pitcher would not be able to withstand the rising tension of a pennant race. It should be said, as well, that Brooks received far more starts under Tebbetts than he would under subsequent managers, and that Birdie also allowed black stars like George Crowe and a young Frank Robinson to scintillate in the regular line-up. Robinson went so far as to declare as he looked back over his career, "Birdie was like a father to me."[24]

So here is my parting question: could a ballplayer's performance not be somewhat undermined by the conviction, or even the suspicion, that he was playing for a racist even if he were right—perhaps *especially* if he were right? What good would it do him to take the field knowing (or thinking himself to know) that nothing he did that day would make the boss happy? Though Bob Boyd was probably serving under an imperious, cocksure captain whose silent prejudices would leak into command decisions, was not Bob's approach to the situation more healthy for his performance?

I am not defending the bigot—far from it. The purpose of this book is to work closer to the truth through a cloud of witness rather than to extol the power of positive thinking, and the truth about human beings is often upsetting. I close with these questions because I wish to suggest the subtle kind of pressure—the veritable psychological warfare—with which young black ballplayers of the time had to contend. Were they getting a raw deal from the manager, or were they just imagining things? If they had imagined these things, had they imagined others? Were they just not strong enough inside, or were their minds insufficiently focused? Was there the least little bit of truth in some of those idiotic remarks about their flaws, their weakness under pressure?

Self-doubt and success rarely mix. Some handle doubt by trying harder in order to suffocate the inner questioning... but far more grow surly and, eventually, surrender. And when I write "some" and "more", I am referring to all human beings.

e) All the wrong reasons: promoting the unprepared to ensure failure

From the specific charge of managerial undercutting, we move to the more general charge that decisions about placement or promotion, usually made in the front office, sometimes aimed at humiliating young black players. I'm not quite sure where I first ran across this accusation: I know that I have seen it once or twice, but also that it is among the less noisily voiced criticisms of Major League practice over the years of desegregation. The idea is that certain organizations may have brought young black ballplayers to the top too soon—or have intentionally promoted the less talented from the available pool—in order to turn to the public with open palms and proclaim innocently, "You see? We gave you the integration you wanted... but Joe just doesn't play as well as his white teammates. We want to be fair, but baseball is competitive. And these black kids just can't compete with our white boys."

One can see why prosecuting this charge would be a delicate matter. In the first place, how would you ever prove it? There may be enough evidence in some cases for an indictment... but for a conviction? How do you say that when one of a team's first black players fizzles under pressure, the front office had planned it all from the start in a kind of bigoted sabotage? How do you distinguish between an outfit that takes a big chance on a promising but unknown lad—which is precisely what you want out of desegregated baseball—and an outfit that knows the big team's new recruit to be too young, or too short of the necessary ability? How young is too young... was Henry Aaron not just a kid? How talented does the kid have to be... would anyone have pegged a young Yogi Berra as a future Hall of Famer?

For another thing, of course, this line of argument requires that one be brutally frank about the experiences of human beings who have already been put through quite enough. They would have to hear that no sane person would ever have promoted them to the Major Leagues without a hidden agenda. No man likes to be told that the knight's armor of his glory days was cardboard— that he was really just a pawn, all along. I remember seeing some B-movie a very long time ago about a covert operative who, quite unknowingly, was set up by his own side to be captured by the KGB: the cynics at the CIA, confident that so weak a character would cave in under questioning, had filled him with false information that they wanted passed along "realistically". In an extraordinary feat of heroism, the agent kept mum under the severest tortures—and deeply disappointed his handlers in Washington, of course. Most of the movie was about his later disillusion when, battered but proud back in the States, he discovered the truth behind his ordeal. It would be similarly shattering to be told by someone that your lackluster, short-lived Major League debut was engineered from the very beginning to be a flop. It would likely be the most unkindest cut of all.

With the resolution of doing this as kindly as I can, therefore, let me put forward some of the evidence and see if we cannot at least arrive at a few meritorious indictments.

First of all, consider the Brooklyn Dodgers, an organization that called up Jackie Robinson, Roy Campanella, Don Newcombe, and Jim Gilliam within a few short years. No one would ever contend that Jackie was the best ballplayer in the Negro Leagues at the time—but, it was argued, he had the best shot at succeeding in the white Major Leagues. He had the mental toughness and emotional durability that the assignment required. If Branch Rickey had wanted the experiment to fail, he could easily have chosen a player possessed of a more dazzling "skill set" and a hot temper, to boot. (This tableau is somewhat tongue-in-cheek: I will explain later why I do not implicitly buy Rickey's act, which he actually strutted in person for the cameras in *The Jackie Robinson Story*.) There was no set-up for failure in the works, say the mythmakers; and indeed, the black players who followed Jackie to Brooklyn, one after another, were all of the highest caliber. Though a few inevitably proved disappointing, most, like Junior Gilliam, were really even better than they are given credit for today.

The New York Giants brought up Hank Thompson, Monte Irvin, and Willie Mays among their first picks; the Chicago Cubs chose Gene Baker and Ernie Banks. These were all solid players who made solid contributions, although some of them (to wit, Baker and Thompson) probably had more to give when they were finally released than the Major Leagues were willing to accept. That's baseball, whatever your skin color: sometimes you go cold for a while and fail to win that vital benefit of the doubt. Not everyone ends up in the Hall of Fame—though the other three of this group did. All five of them made a splash, and nobody with any sense would have shaken his head when they were first penciled into the line-up.

In the American League, ponder the quality of player that the pioneering Cleveland organization brought into the game. Larry Doby, Satchel Paige, Luke Easter, Minnie Minoso, Sam Jones… Satchel, to be sure, was well past his prime by the time he put on an Indians uniform, and he was given little opportunity to be more than one of Bill Veeck's crowd-pleasing stunts. (Veeck denied that the signing was a mere gimmick; but his command decision was not, after all, the club manager's, and the fact is that Satch pitched not quite 156 innings during two seasons at Cleveland, most of it out of the bullpen.)[25] Even in this case, however, there could be no question of intent to humiliate. At worst, Veeck was robbing a younger prospect of a spot on the roster to show off one of the game's greatest players while he could still play tolerably well. The other men who reached the Indians through the Negro Leagues could readily be described as dominating, thanks largely to Bill Veeck's eye for talent and blindness to color.

Now consider some rather more dubious cases. The most infamous team in the well-hidden history of white baseball's desegregation-resistance would have to be the Boston Red Sox, the very last outfit (out of an original sixteen) to suit up a black man. The faintly unsavory honor of wearing that Boston uniform fell to… Pumpsie Green. Now, my own feeling is that Pumpsie had a great deal of potential. He was a defensively sound second baseman who could switch-hit and run the bases with speed. But no one would have laid a heavy bet on him to succeed as any keen baseball observer would have, say, on Luke Easter or Minnie Minoso. I suspect that, having made Green's hopes ride a roller-coaster for several Minor League seasons, Red Sox owner Tom Yawkey and manager Pinky Higgins (whose bigoted opinions are a matter of public record) saw that Pumpsie was primed to second-guess himself—to take any negative judgment of his abilities as gospel. Unlike Frank Robinson, Pumpsie was no dynamo of confidence. Predictably sent down after his original mediocre achievements, Green would acknowledge for reporters that he "wasn't ready to play big-league ball last spring", that "being the center of attention isn't really my style," and so forth.[26] He hadn't the character to put up a loud, blow-for-blow self-defense. The Boston organization could as easily have prophesied his acquiescence to circumstances as Mr. Rickey had foreseen Jackie's quiet but determined opposition to the same circumstances.

Pumpsie's numbers actually tell the story of a player who got better whenever he was given more time on the field—the vector of which improvements might one day have carried him to All-Star heights. Though he received just 651 at-bats in his only three significant seasons of big-league play, he scored 99 runs in that time and banged 47 extra-base hits. These are very close to the single-season figures one would expect of a slugging outfielder. In fact, I suspect that Pumpsie did rather better than Boston's brain trust had expected him to do *or wanted him to do*, and that the self-effacing side to his character proceeded to become crucial as his accomplishments were belittled and further playing time was refused. Pitcher Earl Wilson arrived in Bean Town about the same time as Green (who needed a black roommate, naturally)—and a similar attempt was made to place Wilson's talents under a bushel. For two seasons, Earl came out of the Boston bullpen for rare mopping-up operations. When he finally escaped from the Sox to the Tigers in 1966, he proceeded to compile a 65-and-44 win/loss record over the next four seasons (including a league-leading 22 wins in 1967). Boston is also the franchise where might-have-been stars Al Smith and Felix Mantilla were stuck on a high shelf. I would submit that one can't reasonably view this franchise's use of black players through the early and mid-Sixties in the belief that it expected these players to do other than fail.

And the Tigers, despite Earl Wilson's success with them, don't appear in a much better light during the early Sixties. (Walter Briggs had staunchly opposed the integration of baseball until his death in 1952, and his family continued to dabble—or muddle—in the team's affairs until 1961, no doubt leaving an after-odor down the chain of command.)[27] Bill Bruton found a happy home in Detroit; but then, Bruton had become a local hero around the Great Lakes with the Milwaukee Braves—and was, besides, fair-skinned and well-spoken, not someone who would have great difficulty "fitting in". Ozzie Virgil was the first black Tiger in 1958. He, too, could be called a gradual kind of transition for the Motor City, since he hailed from the Dominican Republic. Yet to avoid an unsettling haste, Tiger management ensured that Virgil wasn't played at Briggs Stadium (the home field) until halfway through the season. Virgil must have surprised the Tigers as Pumpsie Green surprised the Red Sox: that is, though seldom allowed as many as 200 at-bats in a season, he plainly performed better the more playing time he was given. Detroit jettisoned him to Kansas City in 1961, which effectively ended his career.

That was the same year in which rookie speedster Jake Wood led the league with 14 triples and crossed the plate 96 times. This seems to have been altogether more than the Tigers wanted to see out of him, too, for Jake never again played a full season of Major League ball. His three-digit strikeout total during his rookie campaign was offered in explanation to a gullible public; but (as I have written in the first chapter of this section) anybody possessed of Jake's speed would have been able to cut the K's in half with a little coaching. The Tigers clearly had other plans. Maybe the front office was expecting something more like the 1959 debut of pitcher Jim Proctor. Jim went two-thirds of an inning in a mean-nothing game at the season's end, was pulled in time to keep his ERA securely pumped up at 16.88, and never donned a big-league uniform again. You see? You give 'em a chance, and the game falls apart....

There is another fascinating resemblance in the way Boston and Detroit used their young black players in the early Sixties: Pumpsie Green and Jake Wood were both second basemen. As we have noted before, black players of this era very rarely got a chance to play Major League ball in the middle infield. The implicit assumption appeared to be that they lacked the necessary quick-wittedness to handle an assignment calling for such split-second adjustments. How peculiar, then, to find two of the more bigoted teams on the circuit bestowing these crucial defensive roles upon young black rookies! Maybe the Red Sox and the Tigers weren't so mean-spirited, after all.

Or maybe they believed the fairy tale about blacks and the middle infield with such naïve confidence that they fully expected Green and Wood to self-destruct when put under the second-base magnifying glass. One must wonder if the other Boston team of the early Fifties, the Braves, had called up the stunning shortstop recruited by their farm system from the Negro Leagues, Buzz Clarkson, with the same snare set to spring. Maybe not: since Buzz appeared in only 14 games for the team and received only 25 at-bats, it's hard to surmise just what was going on. Manager Tommy Holmes had expressed an eagerness to have the legendary Clarkson bat in his line-up... but the stats tell the story of a man who couldn't have started more than four or five games—or who, perhaps, was used almost exclusively as a pinch-hitter.[28] The Boston Braves had also called up Sam Jethroe and George Crowe—two more Negro League stars who, like Clarkson, would have been considered much too old to waste time on by most Major League teams. Give this Boston club credit: it advanced proven performers—and, at least in Crowe's case, it opened the door to a sadly delayed but nonetheless respectable career of big-league play. Perhaps the real lesson is that the *other* team in town could have brought along black players a lot sooner with the least trace of good faith (unless anyone today seriously believes in the Red Sox' manufactured obstacles).

Actually, the employment of seasoned Negro Leaguers for the remaining four or five productive years of their ball-playing life was a sensible and benign strategy, it seems to me: the insistence on youth, all things considered, sounds more like an excuse a) for refusing those players plainly qualified in the present and b) for humiliating less experienced black ballplayers in an environment of fierce pressure. Had the Philadelphia Phillies something like the latter in mind when they brought up Ted Savage? He scarcely made a bungling fool of himself, scoring 54 times in just over 300 at-bats and stealing 16 bases (still an impressive tally in 1962). Was his relative success the reason for his being dealt at once to Pittsburgh in the off-season? Of all the teams I have studied, the Phillies had perhaps the most ingenious solution to the problem of how to field blacks without having to sacrifice all their prejudices. They went with dark-skinned Latinos, almost entirely. Wes

Covington was allowed to haunt the bench between bouts of pinch-hitting while Pancho Herrera struck out 256 times in two seasons: Pumpsie Green finished his frustrating career batting .276 for the ghastly Mets while Ruben Amaro, the Phillies' answer to second base, posted the same average *as an on-base percentage* for the same year. Make of that what you will.

Let us now follow Savage to Pennsylvania's western frontier. Ted spent only one season with the Pittsburgh Pirates, as well, during which he received half the at-bats awarded him in Philadelphia. (His homering rate actually increased—dramatically—but it seems that much more was expected out of his five at-bats per week.) The Pirates were also taking the Latino page out of the Phillie playbook. Roberto Clemente was their dark-skinned star throughout the late Fifties. Outfield prospect Luis Marquez received 21 at-bats as a Buccaneer late in 1951. Two years later, Carlos Bernier actually played about half a season (perhaps thanks to a French surname). He led the Pirates in stolen bases and scored 48 runs—not quite as good as Ted Savage, but good enough to get him permanently shipped down to the Minors. When the Pittsburgh front office was not looking for blacks who spoke Spanish, it seems to have been seeking black players clearly on the way out who might be detained for a cup of coffee. Negro League superstar Sam Jethroe, already well past his prime when the Boston Braves brought him up, finished his big-league days with *one at-bat* in a Pittsburgh uniform. Jim Pendleton earned 59 at-bats with the Bucs in 1957, during which he sadly socked no homers and came dangerously close to hitting below .300. Suitcase Simpson may never have gotten all of his underwear in a Pittsburgh drawer as 1959—and his hapless Major League career—wound to a close. When the Cubs' star second baseman Gene Baker developed a bad knee after the '57 campaign, the Pirates greedily plundered him so that he could adorn their bench (about 100 at-bats over three years) and, later, the lowest rung of their Minor League system. No bigots here!

Of course, Baker and Ernie Banks had played the Cub middle infield throughout the mid-Fifties with gratifying success, just as Neal and Wills would do it when the Dodgers moved to LA. Had the Pirates given Curt Roberts a good-faith chance to do the same in 1954? One may very much question in this instance whether a no-namer had been put on the hot spot, as with Pumpsie Green and the Red Sox half a decade later—and in this half of the decade, top-notch middle infielders of Negro League provenance were still abundant. Curt was a superb prospect, to be sure, but he was suspiciously hastened to the big team from Class A ball. Essentially, he was given one full season to show his stuff; and, of course, he was found wanting, despite being a defensive genius. His mediocre hitting began to heat up when manager Fred Haney had him fitted for glasses... but the decision had been made, and Curt soon plummeted off the Major League radar.[29]

Moffi and Kronstadt (to whom I am indebted for most of my information about Roberts) seem to think that a place just had to be cleared for Bill Mazeroski. I have read the same words about R.C. Stevens and Dick Stuart. But, you know, Maz was not Maz for years, and Stevens could easily have put up better career numbers than Stuart if he had been offered something like the same chance. How are we to suppose that talents like Bill and Dick were instantly apparent to white managers, requiring black players of promise to yield way to greater ability? Yet it's hard to believe that the Pittsburgh Pirates—the team which would soon give us Stargel, Sanguillen, Dock Ellis, Bill Madlock, and Dave Cash—would be playing a shell game with their dark-skinned recruits, especially on the watch of Branch Rickey (general manager for much of the Fifties). Perhaps Rickey's presence accounts for the extreme subtlety of the evasions; perhaps, while the great but aging man was busily combing the horizons, his discoveries were being quietly traded away or slipped overboard behind his back. Or perhaps you might wonder—if you're a real cynic—whether the old man was up to his old tricks.

For Mr. Rickey's record, upon close examination, is not quite the brief for sainthood which some would have us make of it. Since the subject at hand is the possible setting up of young players for failure, and since we have noted that being played out of position might sometimes have been the specific means to this dastardly end, let me first circle back to Gene Baker—and then focus on Jackie Robinson himself. Was Baker put at one of the most difficult infield positions so that he would publicly fall on his face? Gene performed well for the Cubs, but it seems quite clear from Ernie Banks' autobiography, *Mr. Cub*, that he was called up from the Los Angeles Angels (then a Minor League franchise) to be Ernie's roommate and shepherd the adolescent star through a segregated world largely unknown to him.[30] The motive doesn't do justice to Baker's own talent—but he got a chance to play, and the whole strategy, after all, was meant to pave Banks' road smoothly. I see no indication of sabotage here. Ernie was the Cubs' starting shortstop for a decade, while Gene played three very full seasons at second with distinction before being traded—guess where?—to Branch Rickey's Pirates. It was here that Baker's playing time was severely cut and his career allowed to trickle away.

But what about Jackie Robinson? We've all seen *The Jackie Robinson Story*, where Jackie plays himself, beautiful Ruby Dee plays his wife, and the saintly Mr. Rickey reprises whatever role he played in "real life" with great verve. Quite a show: Jackie Robinson and Branch Rickey, the one name forever united with the other in a warm halo of higher humanity… but the facts are less than compelling. The truth is that Robinson's case disturbs me more the more I ponder it. Donn Rogosin raises the objection universally acknowledged among Negro Leaguers that Jackie was not the ballplayer of their ranks best qualified for promotion. Rogosin adds more petulantly that Jackie "did not fit in very well…[since] he never drank and he never smoked."[31] Of course, this may be precisely why Branch Rickey selected him: i.e., because Robinson had extraordinary possession of himself. (When Mr. Rogosin's book was published, it was considered insufferably "square" in educated circles to abstain from virtually anything.) I find far more serious the revelation that Jackie was slated to play second base in the big leagues without adequate preparation. Rogosin describes a happy encounter that may have kept Robinson's big-league debut from being an ongoing fiasco:

> Negro league veteran Willie Wells saw Robinson that spring and was stunned to see him at second base. Robinson was less than enthusiastic himself. "Wells," he said, "they got me playing second base, and I don't even know how to pivot." Wells immediately offered his assistance. "I'll meet with you after practice and I'll show you how to pivot," he volunteered.[32]

Branch Rickey setting up Jackie Robinson to receive egg on his face at second? Rogosin does not outrightly lodge this accusation, and I cannot see how a complete and deliberate subversion would have advanced Rickey's interests in any way. But there is this to be considered: if Jackie *had* failed, in whatever terms failure should be defined here—if Jackie had simply stirred uncontrollable amounts of trouble around the league or in the stands—Rickey would have possessed an option capable of salvaging his investment. Robinson's defensive skills were deficient: he needed to be sent back to Montreal for further seasoning. In the meantime, perhaps another black star could be tried out... and perhaps Jackie would never be heard from again. The formidable volume of black fans at the turnstiles could be placated with a somewhat technical explanation and put off until, say, the coast was clear for Roy Campanella.

This scenario really seems very probable to me. In fact, Jackie's insertion into a spot where he could scarcely have been expected to succeed hardly makes any sense *except* as an overture to Mr. Rickey's Plan B. Bill Veeck, who lacks Rickey's "alderman" image but was really much more conscientious about doing right by Larry Doby's Negro League patrons (Veeck paid $10,000 for Larry's legally flimsy contract: Rickey refused to pay a dime for Jackie's), knew that a Plan B was essential. "I only wanted to sign one Negro," confessed Bill, "because, despite those glowing credentials I had given myself, I wanted to be in a position to extricate the club fairly easily in case we ran into too many problems."[33] There is nothing particularly devious here—certainly nothing so malign as thrusting a young man, already under tremendous pressure, into a job for which he has not been trained. Yet Veeck remains the P.T. Barnum of integration, and Rickey the Billy Graham.

The further fact remains that Rickey imported Dan Bankhead from the all-black Memphis Red Sox almost overnight—i.e., both without exposure to integrated play and without tutelage in the more rigid Major League style of play—to be Jackie's roommate and pitch for the Dodgers. To be sure, the former function may have been the more urgent; but why not, then, call up a black position player who was already somewhat prepared for the psychic shock? Rickey piously insisted, "We need pitchers and we need them badly. I know this boy has the physical equipment to help this club."[34] Other pitchers were available, however, who possessed *more* than the necessary physical equipment. Why not bring up a white pitcher and a black outfielder and bump a white utility man from Brooklyn's bench? Branch Rickey was known to play both ends against the middle, and his bank account would not have suffered if the Dodgers had scooped up the cream of the Negro Leagues even as the experiment seemed dubious enough that those leagues continued to prosper. Part of Rogosin's argument, at any rate, is that Rickey fiercely craved the revenues denied to him when Brooklyn's Brown Dodgers folded, and which his abortive United States League would perhaps have resuscitated through a new Brown Dodgers team or in some other form. The whole thing is a little too Byzantine for my brain… but then, I am no businessman. All I can say as a student of baseball is this: no one in his right mind would have supposed Dan Bankhead to have a realistic shot at success under the conditions of his Major League debut. Branch Rickey was entirely sane: therefore, the smell of dead rat in this affair cannot be imaginary.

Speaking in broad terms, then, may we conclude that big-league teams sometimes set up young black ballplayers to fail, and thereby to discredit the game's desegregation? I see no evidence of a vast, united conspiracy—but plenty of evidence that cards were occasionally dealt off the bottom of the deck. How does this evidence jibe with my claims elsewhere in this chapter and section that no professional coach would deliberately undermine his team's performance and jeopardize his own job just to express his inner bigot? Well, I don't think the two conditions—sabotaging desegregation and giving the team its best chance—would seem contradictory to certain decision-makers; indeed, to such minds, doing your all for the team might well *require* doing your all to keep black players off of it. But there's a difference between trying to minimize an unwanted player's time on the field and deliberately teaching or signaling him to do foolish things while a game is in progress. I can see a racist coach sticking a black player into a fairly meaningless game and smiling when the kid goes 0-for-4. I *cannot* see a racist coach forcing that kid to swing the bat the wrong way once the kid has been announced as a regular starter.

Besides, the maneuvering discussed in this section would have to come largely from the level of ownership or general management. The front office wanted the public to perceive an effort to integrate—for a black man's dollar and a white man's dollar are just as green. At such air-conditioned heights, the problem presented itself as one of showmanship: of giving the audience what it wants while introducing minimal changes to the way things have always been done. As Bill Veeck had implied, the Old Guard was by and large convinced that its habits were tried-and-true just because they had been around for decades—not because any of them had been thoughtfully analyzed. So an ongoing pantomime of change, with much publicity about the new but little departure from the old, was surely, for some of baseball's leaders, just another patriotic service to "the good of the game".

Or maybe I should let Willie Grace, a Negro League star who never quite made it to the Majors, have the last word:

Yes. I was in the Washington Senators chain—that's why I
played here with Erie, but I know what that was for. That was a

cover-up. You see, Washington didn't want no blacks on their ballclub. Boston [Red Sox] didn't, although Boston was the first team to look at black ballplayers—Jethroe and Jackie and those guys—but they didn't want none on the team. Boston was the *last* team to take a black player and they'd taken Pumpsie Green. The press was givin' 'em the devil.

The same thing was happenin' in Washington, so they signed myself and another boy named [Maurice] Peatross—he was from Pittsburgh—and another boy, Hill I think was his name. That's what they had in their system, so when the press started getting' on 'em they'd say, "We're not that way. We got blacks in our system."[35]

Image is everything, as a professional athlete once muttered witlessly on a commercial for a great deal of money. Create something that would look good in a picture, and then call the guy with the camera.... That, too, is baseball.

f) *The invisible bottleneck: limiting the number of blacks on teams*

Willie Grace's cynicism about big-league clubs boasting, "We got blacks in our system," is echoed in fellow Negro Leaguer Neale Henderson's sobering reflections:

When Negroes first broke into professional baseball—just like St. Louis picked up a lot of us, a lot of my old teammates—and they put 'em on the farm. They put 'em out on the farm and wouldn't bring 'em up. A lot of us, if they'd have given us a chance, we could've been a Willie Mays or a Jackie Robinson or anybody, but they just swept us under the carpet and forgot about us. It's a shame that things were like that because it wasn't meant to be, but that's just the way it was.[36]

The substance of these observations cannot be overemphasized. The black ballplayers who were brought into the Majors young (and the argument against promoting seasoned Negro Leaguers, made over and over again, was that they were already too old) labored under tremendous pressure. They knew only too well that they were likely to be judged on a few at-bats per week—perhaps a rare start after seeing only batting-practice fastballs for a month. They must have suspected, indeed, that they had already been judged, and that the big boss, while eagerly offering evidence to black ticket-holders that he was broad-minded, was at the same time just looking for an excuse to send this or that dark face on the bench back down for "seasoning". And these young men, under the circumstances, must often have appeared to need more seasoning. Kids who had seldom struck out at baseball's humbler levels struck out all the time now, and kids who had seldom made foolish defensive gaffes in the Minors threw the ball into the bleachers now.

If Leo Durocher had not taken a young Willie Mays aside and assured him that his place on the Giants was secure, the "Say Hey" Kid would never have been born. As Neale opined above, there were many Willies we shall never know about—but Willie himself might easily never have existed, as well.[37]

Pumpsie Green, the reluctant hero of the Red Sox' eventual desegregation, was perhaps not ready to be so elevated—either psychologically or technically. That made him eminently eligible for the promotion, no doubt, to certain influential people: he could be brought back down as quickly as he had been lifted up. Pumpsie's reflections upon this high-profile experience show that, in fact, the mental and the physical cannot really be distinguished. Boston would never have to worry about having "too many" black players on the team as long as they could be kept in a state of mind opposite to what Durocher had inspired in Willie Mays:

> I never felt I had it made with the Red Sox. I never got that feeling I had at Minneapolis [Triple A], where I knew the job was mine and I could handle it. Almost every game I played, I felt like I was trying out. I *never* felt comfortable. It had nothing to do with the way I was sent down the first time. Maybe it was self-imposed. If I had felt more at ease, I might have done a better job. Unfortunately, I was given only one opportunity, and three or four days in a row in the lineup isn't really a fair opportunity. You put too much pressure on yourself realizing that "if I don't do well, I'm back on the bench—or back in the minors." I was also aware that major league teams rarely kept [black] players who were not starters. If you didn't play, you were outta there. That was the constant pressure I felt.[38]

If you could keep a good player second-guessing himself in this manner, he might end up not even *wanting* to stay very much. And that would lubricate the revolving door which assured that black faces would exit at the same rate as they entered.

Indeed, induced demoralization and "not quite yet" delays with/returns to Minor League clubs were the inseparable flip side of the bad-faith promotions investigated under the previous heading. When the public cried for you to prove your willingness to integrate, you called up somebody unlikely to succeed. When the new call-up's stats were disappointing or ambiguous (and they almost always were, with a little finessing: Curt Roberts led the Pirates in assists in 1954—and also in errors), you sent him back down or bundled him into a package deal, being careful to swap for another black kid (an equally untested one) if at all possible. Bench, pinch-hit, spot start... "seasoning" on the farm, trade for another "promising" prospect... the whole circuit described a kind of figure-eight itinerary; and the eight, as we know, becomes a cipher for infinity if laid on its side. It wasn't that certain influential parties in Major League baseball didn't want a man of African descent playing the game... they just didn't want him playing it too much or in one place for too long.

Jackie Robinson was well aware that white baseball's owners and executives presented themselves as confronting an issue of public health, civil order, and communal harmony. To them, this was no black-and-white moral crossroads, but the proverbial gray area under the proverbial cloud. He recalls the terms used by one exponent of the greater good:

> Then there was the veteran morning paper writer who croaked: "Rickey's nuts! He'll ruin the game! Those dinge fans of Robinson's'll tear down the ballpark if an umpire dares to put him out of the game! And there'll be a race riot the first time he steals second, spikes high, on a Southern infielder!"[39]

It is often remarkable in questions of racial or ethnic tension what sensitivity to mounting pressures the majority can betray after having denied the basic problem for, perhaps, generations. I can dimly remember snatches of conversation from my childhood. Jet fighters would rattle our dishes as they broke the sound barrier far overhead... but adults scarcely ever talked (within my hearing, anyway) about nuclear war or the Soviets: far more often, on the topic of violent disturbances, they talked about the fragmenting color barrier. There would be riots in the streets. Individuals who seemed friendly enough would join mobs whose one criterion for letting you live or tearing you apart would be your skin. And the integration of baseball, as Jackie reports with a blend of amusement and simmering indignation, was supposed to pose a hazard because an afternoon at the ballpark could readily become the touch-point for racial war.

What I cannot say is how many white people actually believed this. I cannot even say how many owners sincerely believed it, and how many simply used it to veil their own natural distaste for change of any kind. Whatever the ultimate truth of the matter, the superficial policy was plainly one of "little by little... one step forward, half a step back... haste makes waste." It is always a mistake, I find, to assume that professional baseball is about winning. *Primarily, it is about money.* We true fans of the game would like it to be about quality of play, with the best rising to the top... but those who own the plant and equipment (so to speak) want to sell tickets, first and foremost. Excellent play (i.e., winning) sells tickets to true fans, and to a ticket-buying fan, the excellent team's racial composition is a matter of utter indifference; but how many ticket-buyers are true fans of the game, and how many simply have an afternoon on their hands?

This was the question that baseball owners painfully tried to feel out through one half-measure and subterfuge after another. I wrote in Chapter 4 of Part 2 about the unwritten law—the "gentlemen's agreement"—that no more than four black players would ever be on the field at once. That stricture was quite subtle. I needed an encounter with Felix Mantilla's description of it before I understood how well it explained much of what I had read and seen, and I doubt that most white fans of the Fifties—true fans, without the least anxiety over race—would have thought to determine the "color ratio" of the faces on the field. The whole calculation was an exercise in entrepreneurship at its most oily: give this group something… but give that group something, too. Give that group a little more, because it provides more customers.

Bill Beverly of the Negro Leagues just didn't believe that most ticket-buyers of his generation were *not* true fans, and I am very much inclined to agree with him:

> What it was all about was, if you had a good black ballplayer and the gentleman's agreement was you wasn't gonna have no more than three or four blacks at the most on the club and [if] you had good white ballplayers, there wasn't any room for you [as a black ballplayer]. If you were better, there wasn't any room for you. They thought it wasn't a good business move to bring in undesirables that the public didn't wanna see. It wasn't the public that was makin' the decision. They didn't try 'em. The public wants to win. The guy can be from Canada, but if he comes to Houston, Texas, and produces a winner—participating in a winner—they don't care where he's from 'cause he's representin' their city. His morals can be ever so low and they'll be behind him.[40]

Beverly may have underestimated the white fear of riots—or have mistaken it for a fear of "lower class" ways rather than of impending violence. He may have confused snobbery with physical unease—and both were indeed motives in white discomfort. The white public worshiped Joe DiMaggio and Mickey Mantle, however, despite the former's Mafia-tinged connections and the latter's alcoholic binges. It was quite ready to embrace Willie Mays and Ernie Banks as adopted sons, whatever their parents did for a living. The baseball establishment entirely underrated the ability of life in the sun to gild—of a boyish livelihood to bestow innocence—in the eyes of the great American middle class.

I would even venture to say that the Brooklyn Dodgers were "America's team" in their day (though no one thought to use that slightly mawkish phrase) *because* of their successful integration. White Middle America loved the story of desegregation done right—of meritocracy allowed to work its magic and bring the worst to first. A white kid might admire Peewee and the Duke and Gil Hodges and Carl Furillo, who themselves represented a wide variety of ethnic and regional pasts; but he could also—he *would* also—admire Jackie and Campy and Newk. Together, they beat the odds and won it all. They lived the myth, the dream, upon which an entire society was founded.

But the Dodgers had caught lightning in a bottle. Much of the rest of baseball continued to market cheap imitations and hope for the best.

g) A lingo of their own: black ballplayers and "black language"

In my research, I often ran across the outlandish and rather comical notion than black ballplayers had a language all their own, as if they were immigrants from another country (if not beings from another planet). Perhaps the most outspoken, widely publicized, and pompously self-gratulatory of these "discoveries" of an alien tongue is to be found in Jim Brosnan's tell-all tome, *The Long Season.*

> "Hey, Mullion-man!" Lawrence said to [Benny] Daniels, and they grinned at each other.
>
> Lawrence and I turned to run back to the left field line for our last lap. "How do you spell 'Mullion', Brooks?" I asked him.
>
> "I don't know. I just say it. I don't spell it."
>
> "It's a Negro term, isn't it?["] I asked. "I first heard it this spring over at St. Louis. Every colored player in the league seems to be using it this year. Who started it?"
>
> "How do I know, Brosnan? Don't bug me on that, now. You're always buggin' people on words."
>
> "But what does it mean, Brooks?" I persisted. "Even the o-fays on this club are using it now." "*O-fay*" is a Negro word that means white man, and is one word from the fascinating Negro language that I'm familiar with.
>
> "Where'd you pick up *that* expression, Brosnan?" asked Lawrence.
>
> "O-fay? I read a lot. Don't bug me on words, man."
>
> "Well, I couldn't spell 'Mullion' but it means… like, not pretty. Not a queen. You know. Ugly, you might say," he said.
>
> "Okay. I dig. How come everybody's a Mullion-man this year?"
>
> "There aren't many good-lookin' ones goin' nowadays, I guess. How do I know? Let's go play us some bridge."[41]

As is typical of any of us in our vainglorious moments, Brosnan naively reports Lawrence's faintly indignant surprise with perfect accuracy, mistaking it for a hidden operative's weak evasiveness upon finding that his cover has been blown. Like a good sport, Brooks finally plays along… within the limits of reasonable patience. After all, he didn't have a lot of choice, as he must have recognized. To deny the existence of the secret code would only stir more suspicion: better just to humor this brilliant detective.

Baseball, of course, has all sorts of secret codes. Catchers flash signs to pitchers, coaches flash signs to hitters, catchers change their signs when a runner reaches second base, runners attempt to steal signs for the hitter as they lead from second, guys in the dugout attempt to figure out the opposing coaches' signs… why, the home team has even been known to post a spy with binoculars and walkie-talkie in the center-field bleachers, where an excellent view opens up straight into the catcher's lap. And I wouldn't be surprised to learn that dugouts and clubhouses have been bugged.

But the entire team engages in this arcane communication. It binds the group. When a subset of the group is seen as having its own shibboleths, the glue can begin to melt. That's why, I suppose, Brooks Lawrence let Brosnan in on his race's "secret". On occasions when another language really was at issue and its minority of users could not simply admit the rest of the team to conversations with a quick lesson, tempers have sometimes flared. Curt Flood reports one of the more disturbing incidents of this kind. "Among [Giants manager Alvin] Dark's master strokes was an edict forbidding the Latin-Americans to speak Spanish on the team bus. According to Orlando Cepeda, a reliable source, the Latins assumed that Dark suspected them of using their mother tongue for the sole purpose of blasting him. Possible."[42] Now, neither Flood nor Cepeda nor anyone but God Almighty could have known exactly what Dark had in his mind; but the point is, as Flood indicates, that a wall of suspicion and hostility sprang up because two dozen men living at close quarters were not mutually intelligible. I have never heard of similar incidents involving Italians speaking Italian, Poles speaking Polish, Jews speaking Yiddish, or perhaps even Irish speaking Gaelic, though there must surely have been such exchanges in the twentieth century's early years. One could speculate about how much of the hostility to Spanish-speaking (which continues in some baseball venues to this day) is motivated by bigotry, and how much attaches to the ebullience of the typical banter pouring from young Hispanic males compared to (say) the typical Polish coterie. Maybe Cepeda's laughter created a problem with Alvin Dark. Cepeda liked to laugh.

In any case, the "black language" is something else again—since, obviously, it wasn't really a language at all, but a combination of regional accents and slang imbibed from sources unfamiliar to most white players. A white player would know approximately what black players were saying among themselves in a way that he wouldn't know what Cepeda was saying to José Pagán or Felipe Alou. So there was no real collapse of communication at stake. To some extent, I think the myth of a black language may have helped white players to justify (if only subconsciously) the segregation of their teammates—first in separate parts of town when the team traveled, later in the pairing off of roommates even after hotels were accepting all comers equally. At this level, the "black language" was indissolubly linked with social problems. It smoothed them over by emphasizing that blacks really were distinct. Yet a word from the "language" in tense circumstances could also ignite the proverbial powder keg by gesturing toward that very distinction. Such seems to have been the source of combustion in the infamous Copacabana brawl, which landed several celebrated Yankees in court. Vic Power explains:

In 1957, I started calling [Minnie] Minoso "Mau Mau" and he had no idea I was referring to those black terrorists in Kenya who were in the news. In New York, I'd call Elston Howard "Mau Mau." Soon, all the blacks in the league were jokingly calling each other

"Mau Mau." Then, in fun, the white players started calling the black players "Mau Mau." The Copacabana incident? I was told Whitey Ford, Mickey Mantle, Hank Bauer, and Johnny Kucks were celebrating Billy Martin's birthday and had been drinking and Billy Martin or someone at the table jokingly called Sammy Davis, Jr., who was performing, a "Mau Mau." The people at the next table may have heard that and then called him some worse names and there was a fight that spilled into the men's room.[43]

Power's yarn is especially fascinating in that it shows the creation of a term in the "language" completely from scratch by one ingenious wag—a Puerto Rican wag, at that, who spoke only broken English of any kind at the time. Nothing in the world was originally going on here beyond a comradely joke… but because the joke was based on racial difference, it could (and, in this case, did) cut a cruel wound when rotated to prod at the difference contemptuously.

A student in one of my writing classes surprised me a few years back with the following observations about being black in circumstances where the majority is lighter-skinned:

To be black is to run up constantly against many stereotypes, which can be either positive or negative. One of the negative stereotypes is that all black people have a certain menu that they eat. The typical black menu includes chicken, collard greens, watermelon, grits, and anything else that can lead to high blood pressure. The drink on the black menu is Kool-Aid. There is even a stereotype of the flavors of Kool-Aid blacks drink: red or purple. Not cherry or grape, but red or purple. Blacks supposedly refer to Kool-Aid flavors by their color rather than their taste.... An additional stereotype relating to blacks is the form of language that they speak, called Ebonics. Ebonics is English mixed in with black "slang" and is the way that blacks are thought to talk. Not all blacks greet each other by saying, "What's up, dawg?" or, "How you livin'?" Black people may use slang to talk, but it is an unnecessary stereotype to label all black people as using it. (NO, there should not be an Ebonics dictionary.)[44]

Of course, one cannot read such silliness without a smile—and I'm sure that my student meant for his readers to be amused. But the silliness would not be amusing if it were not largely true of our every-day practice: we smile because we recognize in this caricature a perception of reality embraced by a great many among us. And when I say that I was surprised to read the account, I mean that the author's ability to show such manifest good humor about the situation impressed me—not that the situation itself came as a shock to me. I myself am a Texan who speaks with little trace of an accent (though I can modify the trace up or down to suit present company), who is indifferent to steak and detests football, who is uninterested in the internal combustion engine and would like to see all car traffic transformed to a distant memory, and who takes an immediate dislike to any man who squeezes the tar out of one's hand on first encounter and bellows with the design of excluding all other conversation. It's hard being a white male from Texas when your prior ambition is to be a thoughtful, civilized human being.

But then, no one will know that I am from Texas unless I announce the fact. My student is in a different situation; and so, of course, were those ballplayers of African descent who attempted to nestle comfortably into Major League clubs half a century ago. Some no doubt managed to see no harm in the cajolery about their special language—the jests which amounted to imposing a dialect on an entire race because of its skin color. Others bristled. Ernie and Willie took it in stride (with the result that we are all on a first-name basis with them), Frank Robinson objected, Jim Gilliam shrugged and kept quiet, Henry Aaron said little and stewed slowly, Leon Wagner teased the jokesters with their own dialects… as many responses as personalities, and as many personalities as people. But one would like to be considered an individual without having to prove oneself so through a unique response. The constant effort of self-assertion—or of postponing or renouncing that effort, depending upon the person—was one more little strain that white ballplayers of the time never endured with such intensity.

h) One step forward, two half-steps back: the steepening ascent ten years after Jackie

I didn't know quite where to put this brief reflection. Its subject is perhaps not on the order of the dastardly behavior discussed above. Yet, if my suspicions are true, young black players did indeed encounter still another curve ball if they entered the Major Leagues late in the Fifties expecting to find their rough road smoothed by Jackie's generation. Jim "Mudcat" Grant verified my hunch in his prefatory remarks to some thoughts already quoted (under "Al McBean" in Part 3, Chapter 1). Jim was observing specifically that black pitchers had to suffer the indignity of having their entire game called by white catchers and white managers, the assumption being that they themselves were too obtuse to follow two fastball strikes with a slider out of the zone. Speaking more generally, Mudcat had begun with the following spirited observation: "The feeling among many people is that after Jackie Robinson and Larry Doby integrated baseball, it was easy for the black players who followed. That's bullshit."[45]

My suspicion is that life was in fact a little harder for the second wave of Jackie's successors—or a lot. Think about it. The first black recruits to the Majors were for the most part already established stars for their African-American audience. Jackie himself was practically alone in not being a household name throughout much of black America. Dan Bankhead and Willard Brown were hot items in the Negro Leagues, even though they would not fare well in the "bigs" (the former because he was too young, the latter because he was too old). Larry Doby, Luke Easter, Monte Irvin, and Hank Thompson were also pre-existing heroes; and Satchel Paige, of course (imported by Bill Veeck with a certain amount of controversy), was a demigod. With the exception of Bankhead, whose handling by Branch Rickey was redolent of complex motives, these men received plenty of playing time before admiring black fans who now passed through the turnstiles with white fans. To be sure, some were booed, jeered at, threatened, and otherwise harassed from the bleachers even as they were being thrown at and spiked on the field. The point I am trying to make, though, is that such treatment had the real psychological advantage of being objective, concrete, and clearly aimed at all players of color. The struggle was generalized, and its participants already knew darned well that they were equal to the task before them.

Ten years after Jackie's entry into the Majors, the psychological warfare had grown much more subtle. Black rookies had no longer proved themselves in another venue to such an extent, and their names were no longer common coinage to a large portion of their franchise's fandom. The Class of '57 included obscure figures like Frank Barnes, Bennie Daniels, John Kennedy (John *I*. Kennedy), Larry Raines, and Valmy Thomas. Because these young men had no claim to fame, they could be sat down in dugout or bullpen for an unconscionable number of innings. When they finally did get a chance to play, they were naturally not very sharp, most often; and their mediocrity on the field, in turn, justified sitting them down still further—or perhaps sending them back to the Minors, from which depths they would never again emerge.

Did Jake Wood have an easier time playing in Detroit than Bill Bruton? Billy had already popularized himself in the Great Lakes region by starring on the pennant-winning Milwaukee Braves. Wood was one of 1961's most splendid rookies, leading the league in triples—and he was placed on the fast track to disappearance because a hitting instructor couldn't teach him how to swing more compactly and selectively with two strikes. A great many fans might have cried foul if Bill had been so handled in '53: nobody cried anything in '62.[46] Did Joe Gaines have smoother sailing in Baltimore in 1963 than Bob Boyd in 1956? Both were traded by other franchises, and neither was greeted by the Birds' management with open arms; but Boyd enjoyed something close to a full season of play for three straight years. The speedy Gaines (a leading base-stealer in the American Association) hit .286 for the Orioles and slugged almost .500... which earned him a spot in another trade the next spring. Did R.C. Stevens have even a fraction of the chance in 1958 to show his stuff to the Pirates which Roberto Clemente had enjoyed a mere four years earlier? It's no good saying that Stevens wasn't Clemente: the point is that *he might have been*—that he was never put in a position to demonstrate otherwise. It's true that Curt Roberts, Pittsburgh's first black player, had essentially a one-season career in 1954. He had been far from any kind of stardom in the Negro Leagues, and Pittsburgh (in the person of Branch Rickey) seemed to like it that way—*just in case* things didn't work out. Even so, Curt had about three times as long an audition on the field as the much-traveled, little played Ted Savage, who came to—and left—the Bucs in 1963.

It would take a truly extraordinary character to convince himself while stewing in the pressure cooker of three or four at-bats per week that, yes, he had the right stuff—that he was just being stalled and sandbagged, that white managers were playing "mind games" with him. Though this proposition might seem transparently true to any calm, rational onlooker, the performer of intricate athletic feats needs to *believe in his heart* that he can prevail. Few tactics are more diabolical, it seems to me, than seducing a man's spirit away from what his mind knows to be fact. Then he walks away from it all not only hating those who beguiled him, but also hating—very secretly—himself for having been beguiled.

This, I repeat, was a torture necessarily distinct to the late Fifties. Jackie and Larry had made it, Willie and Ernie were making it... don't blame your skin color if you, too, can't make it. Be a man: admit that you're just not good enough.

No wonder so few of this generation wanted to talk to me about baseball....

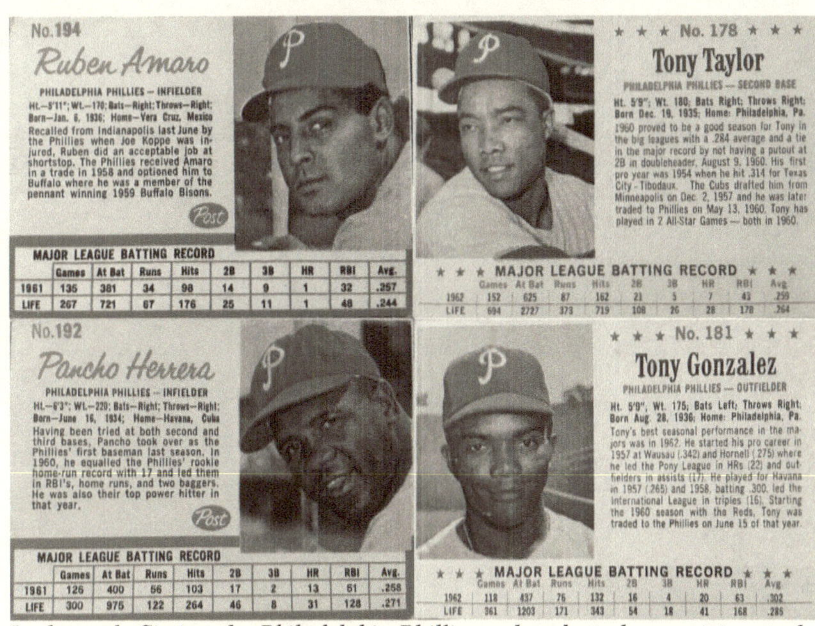

No.194

Ruben Amaro

PHILADELPHIA PHILLIES — INFIELDER

Ht.—5'11"; Wt.—170; Bats—Right; Throws—Right; Born—Jan. 6, 1936; Home—Vera Cruz, Mexico
Recalled from Indianapolis last June by the Phillies when Joe Koppe was injured, Ruben did an acceptable job at shortstop. The Phillies received Amaro in a trade in 1958 and optioned him to Buffalo where he was a member of the pennant winning 1959 Buffalo Bisons.

MAJOR LEAGUE BATTING RECORD

	Games	At Bat	Runs	Hits	2B	3B	HR	RBI	Avg.
1961	135	381	34	98	14	9	1	32	.257
LIFE	267	721	67	176	25	11	1	48	.244

★ ★ ★ No. 178 ★ ★ ★

Tony Taylor

PHILADELPHIA PHILLIES — SECOND BASE

Ht. 5'9"; Wt. 180; Bats Right; Throws Right; Born Dec. 19, 1935; Home: Philadelphia, Pa.
1960 proved to be a good season for Tony in the big leagues with a .284 average and a tie in the major record by not having a putout at 2B in doubleheader, August 9, 1960. His first pro year was 1954 when he hit .314 for Texas City - Tibodaux. The Cubs drafted him from Minneapolis on Dec. 2, 1957 and he was later traded to Phillies on May 13, 1960. Tony has played in 2 All-Star Games — both in 1960.

★ ★ ★ MAJOR LEAGUE BATTING RECORD ★ ★ ★

	Games	At Bat	Runs	Hits	2B	3B	HR	RBI	Avg.
1962	152	625	87	162	21	5	7	43	.259
LIFE	694	2727	373	719	108	26	28	178	.264

No.192

Pancho Herrera

PHILADELPHIA PHILLIES — INFIELDER

Ht.—6'3"; Wt.—220; Bats—Right; Throws—Right; Born—June 16, 1934; Home—Havana, Cuba
Having been tried at both second and third bases, Pancho took over as the Phillies' first baseman last season. In 1960, he equalled the Phillies' rookie home-run record with 17 and led them in RBI's, home runs, and two baggers. He was also their top power hitter in that year.

MAJOR LEAGUE BATTING RECORD

	Games	At Bat	Runs	Hits	2B	3B	HR	RBI	Avg.
1961	126	400	56	103	17	2	13	61	.258
LIFE	300	975	122	264	46	8	31	128	.271

★ ★ ★ No. 181 ★ ★ ★

Tony Gonzalez

PHILADELPHIA PHILLIES — OUTFIELDER

Ht. 5'9"; Wt. 175; Bats Left; Throws Right; Born Aug. 28, 1936; Home: Philadelphia, Pa.
Tony's best seasonal performance in the majors was in 1962. He started his pro career in 1957 at Wausau (.342) and Hornell (.275) where he led the Pony League in HRs (22) and outfielders in assists (17). He played for Havana in 1957 (.265) and 1958, batting .300, led the International League in triples (16). Starting the 1960 season with the Reds, Tony was traded to the Phillies on June 15 of that year.

★ ★ ★ MAJOR LEAGUE BATTING RECORD ★ ★ ★

	Games	At Bat	Runs	Hits	2B	3B	HR	RBI	Avg.
1962	118	437	76	132	16	4	20	63	.302
LIFE	361	1203	171	343	54	18	41	168	.285

In the early Sixties, the Philadelphia Phillies—already under suspicion as the National League's last franchise to integrate—often satisfied their allotment of four dark-skinned players on the field (as stipulated in an unwritten "gentlemen's agreement") with Latinos. Wes Covington was odd-man-out when he came over in a trade, and spent most of his time riding the bench.

★ ★ ★ No. 119 ★ ★ ★

Willie Davis

LOS ANGELES DODGERS — OUTFIELDER

Ht. 6'2"; Wt. 180; Bats Left; Throws Right; Born April 15, 1940; Home: Gardena, Calif.
Willie had a great sophomore season in the big leagues in 1962. In his two seasons of minor league ball he led the league in hitting — the California League in 1959 with Reno (.365) and the Pacific Coast League in 1960 with Spokane (.346). He led both leagues in runs, hits, triples and the California League in doubles. Willie received All-Star honors both years and was MVP of the California League in 1959.

★ ★ ★ MAJOR LEAGUE BATTING RECORD ★ ★ ★

	Games	At Bat	Runs	Hits	2B	3B	HR	RBI	Avg.
1962	157	600	103	171	17	10	21	85	.285
LIFE	307	1027	171	285	42	17	35	140	.278

★ ★ ★ No. 89 ★ ★ ★

Ed Charles

KANSAS CITY ATHLETICS — THIRD BASE

Ht. 5'11"; Wt. 170; Bats Right; Throws Right; Born April 29, 1933; Home: Jacksonville, Fla.
One of the outstanding rookies of the 1962 season was Ed Charles, who had a fine year with the Athletics, after hitting .314 in 9 years in Braves' farm system. Was obtained by A's from Braves on Dec. 15, 1961 after a fine season at Vancouver in 1961, when he led Pacific Coast in runs (114), hits (181), doubles (36) and BA (.305) as well as third basemen in put-outs and assists.

★ ★ ★ MAJOR LEAGUE BATTING RECORD ★ ★ ★

	Games	At Bat	Runs	Hits	2B	3B	HR	RBI	Avg.
1962	147	535	81	154	24	7	17	74	.288
LIFE	147	535	81	154	24	7	17	74	.288

Davis may have been the fastest man in the big leagues at one time—but Charles was surely one of the best offensive/defensive packages. That Willie played a decade longer than Ed highlights the difference between the enlightened Dodgers and the unhinged Athletics. Charles, furthermore, had played a very slick second base in the Minors, a feat which only seemed to stir discomfort in ML front offices when a black man did it.

1 From Frank Robinson, *Extra Innings* (New York: McGraw-Hill, 1988), 6. The first chapter, 1-22, is written in this same very specific vein, detailing incident after incident.

2 From Jackie Robinson's collection of testimonials, *Baseball Has Done It* (*op. cit.*),127.

3 From *I Had a Hammer* (*op. cit.*), 81.

4 *Baseball Has Done It* (*op. cit.*), 139.

5 From *We Played the Game* (*op. cit.*), 202.

6 *Ibid.*, 91.

7 *Ibid.* , 271.

8 *Ibid.*, 304..

9 Brent Kelley, *The Negro Leagues Revisited* (Jefferson, NC: McFarland, 2000), 161.

10 This and the succeeding citations in the paragraph appear in Robinson's *Extra Innings* (*ibid.*), 129-133.

11 *I Had a Hammer* (*op. cit.*), 145.

12 I have been unable to confirm exactly who the ump at second base was. The crew for the series included Tom Gormon, Bill Haller, Doug Harvey, Jim Honochick, Bill Kinnamon, and Stan Landes—not a cast of characters known for being racked by self-doubt. Perhaps it is fitting that the face remain nameless in this case, because any umpire of the time might have botched the call in the same way for the same reason, as I shall shortly explain.

13 *Long Balls, No Strikes* (*op. cit.*), 266. The charge of racism immediately precedes this passage.

14 See Fred McMane, *The 3,000 Hit Club* (Sports Publishing, Inc.: 2000), 147.

15 *Ibid.*, 267. Joe also notes just above this passage that Watson had once tried to strangle Walker—but that, alas, is not an unusual sort of transaction between players and managers.

16 *We Played the Game (Op. cit.)*, 426.

17 *The Way It Is (op. cit.)*, 50-51. Bill White, by the way, refused to second his teammates' objections to Hemus. In Jackie Robinson's anthology, *Baseball Has Done It (op. cit.)*,Bill remarks that Solly helped him with his batting. ""I got along fine with him—I don't see why any player should not get along with his manager if both recognize that they have different jobs (139). To be sure, this is the only testimony in Hemus's behalf that I was able to find.

18 This citation and my previous of Gibson's remarks about White may be found in *Stranger to the Game (op. cit.)*, 52.

19 From the transcript in Jackie Robinson's *Baseball Has Done It (op. cit.)*, 171. Minnie Minoso, by the way, recounts a story about Jimmy Dykes shouting every racial epithet in the books at him from the opposition's dugout, then greeting him politely later on at the hotel (*We Played the Game [op. cit.]*, 207). People like Dykes knew that the mere suspicion of being discriminated against for racial reasons could get into a black player's mind and so preoccupy him that he had trouble functioning.. It was a disgusting tactic; but the Old School held that nothing was out of bounds, and the resulting behavior was really more vulgarity than bigotry.

20 *The Education of a Ballplayer (op. cit.)*, 80.

21 See especially *I Had a Hammer (op. cit.)*, 257-258. I have taken a closer look at Richards already in my paragraphs on Bob Boyd in this section's first chapter.

22 *Ibid.*, 157.

23 From *We Played the Game (op. cit.)*, 578.

24 *Extra Innings (op. cit.)*, 37. Frank, of course, was no easy audience to please. Perhaps hitters related better to Tebbetts than pitchers.

25 "I foolishly believed that nobody could possibly accuse me of signing Paige for a gag," wrote Veeck. "Not when we were in the middle of a four-way pennant fight. But my talents for underestimating the Old Guard's resistance to reason and logic remained unimpaired. The cry went out that I was—yes—making a travesty of the game and—yes—cruelly exploiting an old man's reputation in his declining years." See *Veeck—As in Wreck* (New York: Bantam, 1962), 188.

26 See Moffi and Kronstadt, *Crossing the Line* (*op. cit.*)211-212. Green also participated in several sections of Peary's *We Played the Game* (*op. cit.*), virtually all of which are a testimony to his self-effacing nature.

27 Writes Richard Bak in *Cobb Would Have Caught It: The Golden Age of Baseball in Detroit* (Detroit: Wayne State UP, 1991), "Coming at such a pivotal time in baseball, when clubs like Brooklyn, Cleveland, and the New York Giants were improving their fortunes by loading up on black talent, Briggs's attitude was more than shameful, it was almost criminal" (137).

28 See Moffi and Kronstadt (*op. cit*), 76, for Homes's comment. Clarkson was thirty-four years old, I should add, when he was called to Boston—an extraordinary age, then and now, for any man to be honored with a Major League audition.

29 See Moffi and Kronstadt, *Crossing the Line* (*op. cit.*), 120-121, for these and other details about Roberts.

30 See especially *Mr. Cub* (*op. cit.*), 81-83.

31 See *Invisible man* (New York: Atheneum, 1983), 189.

32 *Ibid.*, 215.

33 From *Veeck—As in Wreck* (*op. cit.*), 178.

34 See Moffi and Kronstadt (*op. cit.*), 12.

35 From Brent Kelley's collection of Interviews in *More Voices From the Negro Leagues* (*op. cit.*), 138.

36 See Brent Kelley's collection of interviews, *The Negro Leagues Revisited* (*op. cit.*), 263.

37 Willie hit .236 with 4 home runs in 127 at-bats in 1952. Figures like this might very easily have earned him the same fate as Curt Roberts and Ted Savage.

38 From *We Played the Game* (*op. cit.*), 446.

39 *Baseball Has Done It* (*op. cit.*), 53.

40 From Brent Kelley's *Voices From the Negro Leagues* (*op. cit.*), 285.

41 *The Long Season* (*op. cit.*), 247-248.

42 *The Way It Is* (*op. cit.*), 63.

43 *We Played the Game* (*op. cit.*), 369-370.

44 My thanks to Mr. Chris Robinson for consenting to my use of his very apt remarks; Chris was a student at The University of Texas at Tyler at the time of this paper's composition (Spring of 2006).

45 See Danny Peary (*op. cit.*), 440.

46 In *We Played the Game* (*op. cit.*), 242, Vic Power recounts that "in the mid-'50s, the Puerto Rican fans would hold a day for me in Yankee Stadium"—this because they knew that Vic, who had come up in the Yankee organization but never played a day in pen stripes, had been stalled shamelessly. In other words, masses of minority fans were fully aware of how the integration of their local team was proceeding (or *not* proceeding) in the mid-Fifties, a circumstance which would largely have disappeared by the Sixties.

VI

The Leopard's Immutable Spots: How Black Ballplayers Were Shadowed by Judgments About Their Appearance

The content of this chapter has necessarily been touched upon already in places; indeed, some of it is implied throughout the book. I feel that the concluding pages of the narrative section are the logical place to assemble various prejudices about black ballplayers into a composite, since all of the foregoing statistics and testimonials are needed to get at the big picture; but, by the same token, the big picture has always been dimly visible behind the detail for anyone with a quick eye. I apologize, then, for certain repetitive passages in what follows, yet I think that restating some of the obvious facts may be largely justified as emphasis.

When I was a wee bairn, I dimly recall seeing reruns of the television version of *The Amos and Andy Show.* I laughed at it the way we also laughed at *The Honeymooners.* Most of the characters in both shows were buffoons: *all* comedies place buffoons at the center of the action. I don't know that the scheming Kingfish and the gullible Andy were any more racist in conception than the blowhard Ralph Kramden and the loony Ed Norton. (In fact, if Gleason and Carney had not bestowed these ethnically neutral names upon their *personae*, they might plausibly have been called race-traitors just like the cast of *Amos and Andy*—for the Eastern United States has a long, rich tradition of despising the Irish.) The single character, it seems to me, who really did trespass far beyond the bounds of taste in *Amos and Andy* was Lightning—so called for the same reason that corpulent people are sometimes nicknamed "Tiny". A janitor whose tall, thin body seemed to slouch in a perpetual "s" around his mop, Lightning did nothing in a hurry. Even his speech was drawn out into a doze-quality whine. Yet one had the feeling that Lightning could be off in a flash if powerfully motivated—say, by a sudden, extreme terror, for he was not stout of heart.

Now, if we had to recruit a ballplayer from this motley crew, our choice would fall upon Lightning by default. The Kingfish was too old, Andy too out-of-shape, the benignly omniscient Calhoun also rather advanced in years... and Lightning, of course, was the one figure who actually did hard manual labor to earn his bread. For those who don't understand the connection (which would probably have included some of the show's white viewership at the time), let me explain that hard labor *does* make your feet drag. If you have to return to the pick-up truck for a crowbar because the shovel won't budge a big rock, you shuffle. You're going to have a long, long day of digging holes that don't want to be dug, and there's not a reason in the world why you should waste your precious energy hustling when you don't have to. There's certainly no financial incentive to do so.

Henry Aaron came from a background where men did such hard manual labor, and he "walked the walk". Consequently, he spent a lot of time—his whole career, off and on—trying to overcome the perception that he was a "shuffler" rather than a "hustler":

> I was in Bradenton, Florida, trying to make the club and convince everybody that I wasn't a lazy kid just off the cotton field, which is what they all seemed to think.
>
> In those days, there was no problem with saying it, either—as if nobody would mind but the coloreds, who didn't really matter, anyway. It wasn't regarded as bigotry for a white person to make lighthearted reference to a black person's laziness or ignorance—it was just being a good ol' boy. I remember the manager, Charlie Grimm, calling me "Stepanfetchit" in the newspaper. It was in the headline of the Milwaukee *Journal*: "Aaron Has Nickname of Stepanfetchit, Because He Just Keeps Shuffling Along." I remember Joe Adcock, our first baseman from Louisiana, calling me Slow Motion Henry and saying I looked like a pretty good hitter but smart pitching would probably fool me.[1]

A few pages further on, Aaron returns to the subject, focusing somewhat more on the widely circulated view that he had a kind of animal aptitude for hitting which didn't require much in the way of brains:

> Because I was black, and because I didn't speak Ivy League English, I came into the league with an image of a backward country kid who could swing the bat and was lucky he didn't have to think too much. Along the way, there were plenty of stories that played along with the image. A lot of them came from Charlie Grimm. Charlie never meant anybody any harm; he was just an entertainer—when he wasn't telling tales, he was picking the banjo—but his stories about me contributed to an image that I'm still trying to shake.... There are... different kinds of intelligence, and I found out that if you don't express yours in the same way that the critics express theirs, then they assume that you're dumb. For years, the newspaper and magazine stories described me with words

like "uncomplicated", "slow-talking", "shuffling", "lethargic".
They said that hitting was something that just came naturally to me.
Maybe it was. But part of that natural ability was the natural ability
to think in the batter's box.[2]

The more worldly Curt Flood—who matured on the streets of
Oakland, where a kid frequently had to scamper—was no stranger to haste and
was never chided for dragging his feet. Nevertheless, Curt understood full
well that the outward show of "hustle" was a kind of salesmanship having
little to do with the real product. In this passage, he does not expressly address
race, but the "hustler" stereotype clearly does not describe many black players
of his day:

So long as a team *looks* spirited, the owners seem happy enough.
Being concerned more with form than substance, they prefer
hustling players—the kind who never walk when they can trot and
never trot when they can gallop. The dumb show of racing full tilt
from the outfield to the dugout when the teams change sides is
regarded as the sincerest possible sign of competitive integrity.
And it is publicized as such. And presumably helps at the gates....

Alas, team spirit is something quite different. The showmanly,
stereotyped hustler may or may not be a good team man. His
colleagues may despise him if, like one or two famous hustlers, he
races to and from the dugout, tears to first base after being walked,
yet sometimes shows no enthusiasm about chasing a batted ball that
has gone through his legs.[3]

How deeply had the "Lightning" image penetrated the psyche of
white America in the Fifties? Demobilized soldiers who had finally found
jobs after World War II, these upwardly mobile legions in gray-flannel suits
were "company men" whose device was, "Please the Boss." Hustle was
central to their way of life, even when it served no particular purpose. If they
had to carry a memo down the corridor, they *hustled* it, for the Boss might be
watching. If they were going to the coffee pot on break, they *hustled* there, for
the Boss might see them and not know that they were off the clock. Their
ethic was white-collar and urban—and, I suppose, probably military in many
cases, as well. (Comedian Phil Silvers was the Fifties' greatest satirist of this
ethic, in not one half-hour show, but two: he was first Sergeant Bilko and later
a shop foreman, a master in both roles of appearing to be a dynamo while
getting nothing done.) In the minds of white Middle Americans belonging to
the Eisenhower era, hustle directly and profoundly correlated with
productivity. "Anti-hustle" was therefore connected inseparably with what
they did *not* want their lives to resemble: manual drudgery, low pay, absence
of opportunity, imminence of unemployment. When they saw the guy
sweeping up after hours—and he was probably a *black* guy—they may well
have smiled to themselves and shaken their heads. They may even have

thanked their lucky stars (like the Pharisee wincing over the publican) that *they* were not in *his* shoes.

In my opinion, it would be a mistake to dismiss the "sluggish janitor" stereotype's power until about the mid-Sixties—or the damage that it did to young black ballplayers. Nowadays, a white American who thinks reflexively (as opposed to *reflectively*) about his neighbors of African descent is likely to grab the image of a rapper, or maybe of an outspoken millionaire *prima donna* wide-receiver. (Such are the associations, at any rate, that college freshmen make.) They can be disturbing images, to be sure, with their resonance of in-your-face cockiness—but they are also worlds apart from Lightning and the Fifties' stereotypes. Readers, especially younger readers, must make an effort to imagine how pejorative the suspicion of laziness—of *deficient hustle*—would have been in baseball's overall hiring practices. Consider, particularly, that the teams' owners held the purse strings and hence the right of final decision, which they may or may not have chosen to waive in favor of someone's judgment who had actually played the game. Not that these latter were always to be found on the second rung down the ladder of command: general managers, too, were often businessmen. If the rank and file of white America believed that a significant percentage of black males resembled their beloved fool Lightning, then a great many owners and GM's probably shared this same belief.

Lightning was no Zulu warrior, naturally, in terms of his inner qualities. Indeed, the paradox of his being at once so slow on the job yet so rocket-like in retreating before danger is resolved if we see him as essentially "beaten into submission"—edging his mop down empty corridors almost apologetically lest some swell suddenly open a door and run into him. Bill Veeck believed that this estimate of the black man had much to do with a very specific baseball maneuver: the knock-down pitch. "All colored players were thrown at for years," wrote the perspicuous Veeck, "a practice arising from an old coach's tale that Negroes didn't have the guts to come up off the ground and dig back in. It is usually called, with a delicacy unusual in baseball, 'taking their power away'."[4] I don't honestly know if the cliché claptrap of which Veeck writes may have been fed by the evident fact that many good black hitters liked to stand away from the plate rather more than white Major Leaguers and poke the outside pitch, their arms fully extended, down the opposite field's foul line. Roberto Clemente modeled the style, as has Julio Franco more recently. I suspect that a great many young hitters brought it with them from the Negro Leagues—whereupon a great many white coaches, in turn, tried to make them muscle up on the plate and pull everything. Perhaps the "old coach's tale" began in the period's romance with the dead-pull hitter... or perhaps it was no more than a logical outgrowth of projecting Lightning onto every black male.

Henry Aaron, of course, was able to stand the "timid lollygagger" stereotype on its ear with his accomplishments (although he never has received credit for being a first-rate base-stealer: care to guess who was runner-up in steals when Maury Wills swiped 104 bases in 1962?). Other players were hounded by a reputation for sloth throughout their all-too-brief careers. The uninquisitive Ed Walton, who seems to have gobbled up everything the sports page fed him, reveals to us that Charlie Neal was one such victim in a passage I have already cited: "Neal was characterized as temperamental, no hustler, and needing to pull the ball to hit over .250, but was rated as a good fielder."[5] Notice Walton's passive formulation: he doesn't even try to conceal that he is simply warming over old gossip rather than offering eye-witness testimony. But what an absurd sentence he has written! How could someone be a good Major League second baseman who couldn't get himself going? We have already become very familiar with the condemnation for not pulling the ball. Here, however, its vague association with lack of hustle is perhaps not a mere accident. I don't suppose Lightning would have pulled the ball, either—too much quick effort needed to whip that bat through the zone! So now jerking the ball down the line for a home run was not only the manly way to score, but also a measure of your ability to concentrate and react. Pulling a homer is nothing less than an indicator of *the moral will's development*!

No less a speedster than Tommy Davis was apparently fitted for this same collar—tailor-fitted, for the charge wasn't really attached to Tommy's fleetness afoot any more than it had been to Neal's. Allegations were made, rather, that Davis was groggy in his first trip or two to the plate. His black teammate on the Dodgers, Maury Wills, has said for the record, "Tommy didn't really wake up until after his first time or two at bat." Wills hasn't exactly endeared himself to former teammates or to anyone else with his well-lubricated tongue; but Davis is supposed to have fired back on this occasion, "They used to call me lazy, but the lazier I felt, the better I hit."[6] Any ballplayer could grasp the truth behind Tommy's good-natured repartee: tensing up is fatal to hitting. The relevant point in the present discussion, however, is that a man who twice led his league in hitting—despite having Aaron, Ashburn, Clemente, Mays, and Robinson as competitors—was branded lazy (by a lot more people than Maury Wills, who was merely an echo chamber) because he liked to see what the pitcher had in the early innings. Nothing at all to do with race?

Having seen only his stats rather than his actual play, I would never, never have suspected to find Vada Pinson accused of lollygagging. Maybe this isn't quite what Jim O'Toole had in mind when he reminisced, "He [Vada] really could get around the bases. He led the league in several categories [in 1959] and some people were already saying he was going to be a Hall of Fame player. His trouble was that he was too laidback. I think if he had more heart, he could have been the best player in baseball."[7] Is Jim perhaps trying to suggest through the word "laidback" that Pinson's *mind* was less lively than his feet—that he didn't give sufficient thought to how he was using his great gifts? That interpretation is much more plausible. It's the basis, in fact, of Earl Lawson's feud with Vada, Lawson insisting that Pinson should use his splendid speed by bunting for hits.

And I can't say that I disagree with Earl. But the "Lightning" stereotype, in other cases if not in this one, must have had major consequences in determining where a player would be positioned defensively. Speed afoot and cold molasses between the ears is a recipe for exile to the outfield. We have also seen already how many good black shortstops and second basemen were nudged over to third or into the outfield; and we have noted the relation between playing left and right field, especially, and having a brief career. Guys who embarrass their team with their glove are sent to left, where they will be tolerated as long as they hit well—meaning, in particular, as long as they hit for power. The stereotype at issue implied that blacks did *not* have an essential quality for playing middle infield—quick wits—but that they *did* have, in almost unnatural abundance, the essential quality for shagging flies: speed. "Everyone knew" that young black males could run. Jimmy the Greek infamously spoiled his broadcast career by suggesting (or acknowledging, if you prefer) that people of African descent make better sprinters.[8] The forms that this proposition assumed in dugouts and bleachers of the Fifties were apt to have a rather less complimentary ring about them. The absence of exceptional speed in Elston Howard once inspired Casey Stengel to blurt (in what was intended as a joke), "Goddamn, we finally got one and he has to be slow."[9] The amiable Mickey Mantle apparently thought this rigid categorization of an entire race under a single quality so self-justifying—and Elston's breaking of the mold so outrageous—that he tells the tale cheerily in his 1985 book as evidence of the Yankee bench's freedom from racial tensions!

Like Jim O'Toole's "laidback", the creative epithet "loosey-goosey" used below to describe Harry "Suitcase" Simpson may not mean that Simpson was suspected of feet-dragging. The source—former Negro Leaguer Bob Scott—is certainly a sympathetic witness; and Bob himself, in any case, defends Harry against the implication of not being involved in the action. It looks to me, however, as though this *was* the implication. See for yourself:

> Suitcase was, like, happy-go-lucky, like a lot of ballplayers. They take the game seriously, but they don't play it like they do. He was that type of ballplayer. He was a *good* ballplayer and he was a nice guy. And real loose, what we call in baseball "loosey-goosey". He could hit and he could run. And he was a good outfielder.
>
> They called him "Suitcase" because they kept trading him. But he had that reputation for not being serious, and when you get a reputation like that, it's hard to get over it. A lot of ballplayers get a reputation like that, but they're good ballplayers.
>
> When these guys make an error, it goes like, "Well, he didn't try. He didn't care about it," and that's what happens. They just play loose, some of these guys. Baseball is a pressure game and some guys don't show it.[10]

If "loosey-goosey" means something other than "dragging one's heels" (and I think it probably does, although there is also clearly an overlap on the point of not caring), then perhaps the same word might have been applied to Leon Wagner. Or maybe not. Leon was loose, all right, as was everyone else around him. You couldn't very well stay tight around a man who described his attitude about delicate racial matters this way to Jackie Robinson:

> Whenever a discussion comes up about myself being a Negro I try to beat the other fellow to the punch with some humorous jokes that relieve the pressure around the clubhouse. I let the fellows know that I consider myself a Negro and love to be a Negro, just like they love to be Polish or Italian or Irish. I let them know I have an open mind and speak from reality, that I don't get insulted by a few names being called me, or by so-called Negro racial jokes. This relaxes the situation. This makes these fellows know they don't have to worry about placing their words exactly, and keeps up the spirit of the team. Besides, I want them to know that with the Negro people under tension and fighting for their rights in the United States and around the world, I have the courage to lead them into humorousness for the sake of the team. When they rib me because I have high cheekbones and call me Indian, I say, "I'm not Indian. I'm colored and like my colored people." I say, "I like all people, including Indians. Right here, I'm playing baseball, and right here that's what I'm fighting for, equality everywhere, and most of all right on this ball club."[11]

If this broad-shouldered, burly ambassador of good humor kept the bench from becoming uptight, however, he could scarcely be thought of as a laid-back, lollygagging laggard. "Daddy Wags" possessed a pleasantly in-your-face assertiveness which, among the emerging forms of declaration that "black is beautiful", was rather less somber than what much broader audiences would hear from the likes of Sidney Poitier and Richard Roundtree. In fact, Wagner opted for Hollywood when he decided he had had enough of being shuffled among various Major League franchises. I have already discussed the "rap" about his being a butcher in the outfield—which a multiplicity of evidence must incline us to accept, but which nevertheless fails to explain why no defensive coach could ever take a little extra time with such an offensively valuable player. Leon seems to have made light of criticisms savaging his outfield play. Maybe that convinced some sour sports of his lack of dedication, of "seriousness". But then again, maybe the good-natured counter-ribbing with which he asserted his rightful place among the team leaders rubbed some the wrong way. Maybe a guy who desperately needed to work on his fielding wasn't supposed to be in high spirits... maybe he was supposed to "hustle" while on the diamond and brood while off. The Red Sox certainly didn't try to arrange any deals for the young Ted Williams as he stood in left field practicing his swing, oblivious to the action around the plate... but maybe a black player was supposed to show a little more gratitude just for being in left field, and a little more concern about staying there.

Speaking of poor fielding, I cannot conclude this chapter on noxious stereotypes without mentioning that unpardonable sin of so many young black outfielders, missing the cut-off man. Earl Lawson once indicted (*at least* once) his beloved Vada Pinson for the offense. Writes Earl of the unfortunate events leading up to Vada's assaulting him in 1962, "Our relations had been strained since spring training when I had criticized him in print for his repeated failure to hit the cut-off man with his throws from the outfield."[12] Of course, Lawson may well have been correct to chide Pinson, if one judges the case by its specifics. Yet I suspect that the Hall of Fame reporter had overlooked, here as when he took Pinson to task for unruly swinging at the plate, the prickly dilemma of any young black ballplayer. Routine plays are not good enough. Routine plays will make you the equivalent of an average white performer, who never misses his cut-off man but never guns down the runner trying for an extra base. When the choice is between an average white player and an average black player, the black guy starts packing his bags. To remain in the starting line-up, you, as an unestablished black player, must not only clout 20 homers a year: you must show a flare for defensive genius— especially if you are apt to have a mere 12 or 15 homers by year's end.

If I overstate this dilemma in reality, I don't think that I exaggerate it *as it appeared to the young ballplayers concerned*—and that subjective reality, after all, is the one at issue here. Pinson and others in his position probably went for the spectacular too often. George Altman incurred a separated shoulder when diving for a low drive during a spring-training game: would he have risked his career in such needless "hustle" (and the injury arguably did hasten the end of his Major League days) if he had not felt compelled to sparkle in the outfield? I don't know how often George observed the all-important ritual of hitting the cut-off man—but certainly Willie Mays sinned over and over in that fashion, nor was he beyond playing a bloop single into extra bases by attempting such an ill-advised dive as had torn George's shoulder apart. These young men felt it incumbent upon them to *do more* than expected; and sometimes, as a result, they did less. Curt Flood writes amusingly of how Harry Caray used to sear him for that gaffe which no sportswriter ever failed, apparently, either to notice or to highlight:

> I still have a tape of his [Harry's] broadcast from Chicago on the day I made a leaping catch so improbable that a photograph of it wound up on the cover of *Sports Illustrated*. I cherish the tape for that reason, but also for a typical Carayism that occurred earlier in the inning. I had retrieved a ball and thrown it back to the infield. Enemy base runners were in full flight, the crowd was screaming and so was Harry: "Oh no! Flood missed the cut-off man again!" *Again!*[13]

I can just hear Harry saying it, may he rest in peace.

The broader question is this. With so much emphasis placed on "oversights" like missing the cut-off man (there's really no requirement to hit him: if you throw out a daring runner on your own, you're a hero) and with the tendency among ambitious black outfielders to make such errors of enthusiasm, how did their image suffer? One cannot point to statistics or even cite damning commentary from white managers, for the reasoning must have been largely subconscious. Yet it would also be obvious, and perhaps inevitable: as a group, black players lacked judgment on defense. They didn't think things through. They played like crazy kids, or wild men. They didn't have the equipment to appreciate the game's finer points. Thank God, that kid was moved to left field from shortstop!

I will close this gloomy retrospective by casting a glance into the future. The kinds of stereotype I have discussed are not dead, even today. I recall hearing two ESPN announcers (whom I shall not name, not out of respect for them, but because my contempt for their views is so close to the surface) indulging in a kind of contest to devalue Fred McGriff's career. The exchange occurred during a lull in one of Fred's final games, wherein he wore a Tampa Bay uniform. The prattling pair in the booth reminded me of a couple of high rollers seeing and raising each other back and forth in a poker game, with Fred's bleak chances at the Hall of Fame piling up like so many chips. "Oh, yeah? Well, I don't think McGriff will make it to Cooperstown even if...." Nothing could have been more transparent to these two infallible analysts than that Fred's achievements didn't measure up to the standards for enshrinement.

Why not, I wonder? McGriff had about 300 more at-bats than Mickey Mantle in his career: a negligible difference. He struck out about 100 more times than the Mick, and hit about 40 home runs fewer. His .284 average was not far behind Mickey's .298 (and was almost dead even with Robin Yount's lifetime mark), while Mickey was actually 75 hits behind him—enough that those extra 300 at-bats might well not have been enough to make up the gap. (Mickey's more frequent walks account for the difference in average.) McGriff had seven 100-RBI seasons: Mantle had four. (Mays, by the way, had 10, and Aaron 11.) McGriff batted in 1550 total runs to Mantle's 1509, and hammered 465 total extra-base hits other than homers versus the Yankee superstar's 416. Mantle would have been hard-pressed to make up either of these disparities with that additional half-season, even in his prime. Mickey was the cornerstone of a Yankee dynasty—and Fred, having powered the Blue Jays to several winning seasons, ignited the Atlanta Braves over a critical period in their almost incredible sequence of divisional titles.[14]

Mantle is a first-ballot, no-brainer Hall of Fame inductee. To many talking heads in the press box, Fred McGriff is a non-starter. Why the distinction—because Mantle also played great defense? But, thanks to injuries, he didn't really do so for very long. Fred wasn't a Gold Glover at first base, but neither was he a liability. He is commonly adjudged so, however, by detractors who consider, not his stats, but *his stiff, lumbering style*. Fred McGriff doesn't suit their Charlie Hustle image of a ballplayer.

A shrewd observer will point out that McGriff and Mantle played in very different eras and physical surroundings. You bet they did! Mickey was still in his prime when the pitching of both leagues was stretched thin by a multi-team expansion, and whenever he batted left at Yankee Stadium, he faced one of the most hitter-friendly porches in baseball. Fred McGriff didn't exactly play in notorious pitcher's parks... but he *did* share a spotlight in the Nineties with several other sluggers who would flirt with (and surpass) 500 homers, *all* of whom (but for Ken Griffey, Jr.) have since been tarnished by steroids, corked bats, steroids, bats of non-regulation hardness, steroids, human growth hormone, and steroids. Lanky Fred was practically the only one from this dubious generation of whom nobody would ever dream of asserting, "He used performance-enhancing drugs." If the Hall of Fame is not to become a Hall of Infamy, eventually waving in Bonds and McGwire and Sosa and Palmeiro and Gonzalez in an "everybody does it" shrug of flower-child thought-nullification, then McGriff should be admitted purely on the strength of character he manifested before a temptation which seduced virtually every heavy hitter among his contemporaries. But lanky Fred, in the mind's eye of certain bloviating desk-jockeys, will forever evoke an awkward stiffness that just doesn't fit the paradigm.

Maybe if Fred had just collected more of those many strikeouts by tying himself into a pretzel, like Mickey! But Fred would always give the outside corner to the pitcher; and if a pitcher could thread that needle for the third strike, Fred would walk politely back to the dugout, never so much as muttering a word to the umpire. Fred didn't show his emotion on such occasions—or on any occasion—and the public (as well as certain gentlemen of the Fourth Estate, apparently) demands to see that a player "cares", that he is not "laid back". Jeff Kent also gave up the outside corner: so did Ted Williams. Both of them could also get rather heated in their displays. Neither of them, most definitely, has ever been branded a slouch. But Fred... Fred, you know, just didn't have that fire, that spirit. You might even say he *shuffled.*

1 *I Had a Hammer* (*op. cit.*), 117-118.

2 *Ibid.*, 132-133.

3 *The Way It Is* (*op. cit.*), 65-66.

4 From *Veeck—As in Wreck* (*op. cit.*), 183.

5 *The Rookies* (*op. cit.*), 132.

6 Both citations are drawn from Moffi and Kronstadt, *Crossing the Line* (*op. cit.*), 205.

7 *We Played the Game* (*op. cit.*), 436.

8 Canadian journalist and high school sprinter Malcolm Gladwell, himself of African descent, wrote a very enlightening article titled "The Sports Taboo" for *The New Yorker* (May 29, 1997) on this subject which has been reproduced in several anthologies. Gladwell observes that since there is more diversity in African genetic material than among all the rest of the human race put together, exceptional speed or dexterity or jumping ability or any other genetically influenced quality is likely to be highly represented at the extremes by Africans.

9 *The Mick* (*op. cit.*), 130.

10 From an interview in Brent Kelley's *The Negro Leagues Revisited* (*op. cit.*), 230.

11 From Leon's interview in *Baseball Has Done It* (*op. cit.*), 189-190.

12 *Cincinnati Seasons* (*op. cit.*), 123-124.

13 *The Way It Is* (*op. cit.*), 74.

14 The metaphor of "igniting" the team was used endlessly and mercilessly after Fred played his first game in a Braves' uniform, because a section of seats in Fulton County Stadium had literally caught on fire shortly before the opening pitch. McGriff contributed a home run to an Atlanta victory, and the team's fortunes abruptly turned around in the ensuing weeks.

Part Four

Tentative Conclusions Drawn
from Sketchy Evidence

I

Inner Circles and the Eccentric: A War That Never Ends

As well as I can recall, I began this book early in 2005—quite early enough, I thought, to have it ready for the sixtieth anniversary of Jackie Robinson's entry into the Major Leagues. Obviously, I undershot the mark in predicting my work load. The problem was that I hadn't foreseen all the speculative gray spaces into which I would be carried. My choosing a sample of players to study seemed straightforward, and some of the statistical anomalies I observed right off appeared to tell me that I was building a great case for the abiding reality of underground radical discrimination in the Fifties. Then, in my third section, things started to get complicated. In fact, as I better appreciated the role of injury, substance abuse, career alternatives, and other factors in the lives of big-league ballplayers circa 1960, I even began to find my statistical arguments a little less compelling. Not that I ever doubted the objective presence of unequal treatment in many of these cases... but when is inequality an outrage, and when is it just a sad fact of the human condition? For a lot of white ballplayers never got the kind of shot that they deserved, either... not as big a lot, proportionally, as the young black men I was studying, and usually not to as great an extent; but where is that clear boundary which permits one to say with confidence, "This was over the line"?

And another question: what good does it do any of us, half a century later, to cry foul? I happen to believe that the truth should be told whether it "makes life better" (whatever that means) or not; but what is the real truth of such issues and events? That racial discrimination lingered in big-league ball long after formal integration? If such observations "do good" to people of color by sounding vaguely like an apology and "do good" to white folks by making them feel morally superior to their ancestors, what is their rock-bottom truth value? I would like to purge all grandstanding, posturing, preaching, and quasi-hysterical repenting from this exercise as much as possible. I would like to understand as accurately as possible just what we're looking at when we confront the experiences of these young athletes of past generations.

One theme that emerged over and over as I developed Section Three was the role played by "system" at these racially lopsided tables. The phrase "company man" had a long currency in the Fifties: the loyal drudge who would put in twenty-five years of clock-punching for faceless owners in a large corporation, then be packed off with a gold watch and a meager retirement. The GI's had lately returned from a world war that required a massive team effort to win, preceded by a global depression that had required massively centralized government programs (or so most of that generation believed) to overcome. There weren't a lot of jobs lying about as the economy scaled down from churning out fighter planes and destroyers. Men like my father were happy just to have a place where they could carry their lunch pail. These Americans had not come to maturity in a time of rugged individualism; on the contrary, everything in their formative years had warned them that safety lay in staying close to the herd.

For good measure, the war's end had enveloped them in the shadow of a mushroom cloud. In the back of all their minds sat the sobering awareness that they, along with every human being everywhere, might not live to see much of the century's second half. They felt smaller than ever as the Cold War proceeded: they felt like ants scurrying about under the heel of an inscrutable giant.

I have the impression in studying baseball of this era that the game reflected a broader—a society-wide—discomfort with the individual, the eccentric, the creative, the experimental. The elevation of the home run over "small ball" is surely the game's clearest example of this resistance to the diffuse and the exotic. Even though they appear to emphasize lone heroes, homers demand relatively little technical ingenuity or impromptu adjustment. They reduce strategy to a minimum and concentrate offensive training upon a single focal point. I intend no disrespect here or elsewhere, by the way, to students of the game like Earl Weaver and Buck Showalter who have constructed their offenses largely around power-hitting; but in baseball as in life, Aristotle's golden mean applies. Even a good thing can be cultivated in excess—and the Fifties celebrated power at the plate with a monomania that left high-salaried, heavy-slugging teams constantly exposed to the small minority of pesky roadrunners like the Chicago White Sox and the St. Louis Cardinals.

The home run emphasis of the Fifties, furthermore, was largely management-driven. The homer craze of the steroid-plagued Nineties may have had much to do with television; for the round-tripper is very screen-friendly, unfolding at just the pace that a panning camera can follow. (Televised highlights have, indeed, become little more than home run documentaries.) Many households still didn't own a TV in the Fifties, however—and even those that did could view no more than Saturday's Game of the Week. So relatively resistant was the baseball public to home run fever in those days that the Mantle-and-Maris chase after Ruth's single-season record in 1961 drew only moderate crowds. "At the end," notes Bill Veeck, "there were only 23,154 in Yankee Stadium on a warm Sunday afternoon to see Babe Ruth's record broken."[1] (Most photos of Maris's Number 61 reveal a lot of empty seats.) Veeck evenly divides the credit for this stunning feat of entrepreneurial underachievement between an asterisk-brandishing Ford Frick and a somnambulant Yankee publicity department; but it suggests, as well, that people were not obsessed with home runs in the early Sixties.

During the other years of my study, too, I find no convincing evidence that the public was the driving force behind home run mania. The rate of home run hitting had risen more or less steadily throughout the Fifties, and not just because of the influx of black sluggers. Mantle, Mathews, Mize, Musial... the letter "M" could already account for about 2,000 home runs in this era without Mays's even being added to the tally. Kluszewski reached or surpassed 40 home runs in each of the three seasons from 1953 to 1955. Roy Sievers hit a total of 81 during 1957 and 1958. Rocky Colavito walloped an even 200 homers in the five years from 1958 to 1962... and so it goes. Not since the 1930's had so many sluggers racked up so many "taters".

This, I'm convinced, is part of why young black players struggled as they did: the ethos of the day wanted a narrowly circumscribed kind of play, and they represented alternatives that were untested or had passed out of style. By no means do I insinuate that racial discrimination was not part of their ordeal. What I suggest, rather, is that their visible difference from mainstream (i.e., Caucasian) players was associated with the suspect skill set. Black players—nudge, nudge—were apt to run wild on the bases, to drop bunts instead of swing for useful doubles, to overthrow the cut-off man, to showboat on the mound instead of pitch to the defense... and so on, and so on. White coaches and front offices had reservations about them based not strictly on their skin tone, but on the "other way" that their color implied.

This state of affairs, it seems to me, offers useful lessons. If it makes the baseball establishment appear less like the KKK, and if that strikes some readers as self-serving, I can only insist that I am not trying to be anyone's apologist—but that I find conceiving of a large portion of humanity as irredeemable moral imbeciles (for what else is a hooded thug with a torch and a noose?) to be neither very helpful nor very realistic. If baseball's inner circle exhibited racist behavior, *why* did it do so? There has to be a reason. Existing at a subhuman level is no reason, even though a few humans do appear to degenerate beyond recognition. When aimed at a vast group of people, such an "explanation" would be a paranoid nightmare. I think we have to do better than that.

So let me hypothesize that people sometimes get excessively caught up in the requirements of "belonging". Sociability means conformity in some measure (I'll leave it to Aristotle to figure out the amount). Whenever you have membership in any group, you must meet certain minimal standards with regard to that group's rules. In cultures, the standards involve such behaviors as speaking the common language, wearing "decent" clothes, and eating kosher food. Sub-groups, of course, have more finely tuned standards. A group of car mechanics would expect you to understand the basics of building an engine. A group of chefs would expect you to understand how to marinate a chicken.

Physical features are generally considered in group-formation only secondarily. For instance, it is a gross misstatement to speak of any race as a culture. By definition, cultures have *cultivated* their unique habits: their ways are taught to each new generation, not embedded in genetic material. Certain races, however, have often been identical with certain cultures for most of human history because human beings have done very little traveling until the past few centuries. A culture whose habits are adapted to a severe climate may well belong mostly to people of certain racial characteristics, since few other tribes have likely ever shown any interest in occupying the same space.

In situations of shared crisis, we often see how readily superficial differences are ignored in the interest of common objectives. A Scots farmer whose barn is burning down doesn't care if a Chinaman joins the bucket brigade; the occupants of a building being besieged by terrorists don't care if the guy reloading their guns is white or black.

Why, then, do such distinctions seem to matter before the crisis? Perhaps because the rigors of the previous system—the "normal" system—are still operative. Even though skin color has nothing directly to do with religious beliefs, a typical American Methodist who walked into a church full of people of East Indian features might conclude that he could not be in a Methodist sanctuary. A college student who had signed up for an advanced engineering class might conclude that he had mistaken the room number if he found himself surrounded by young women. Such associations as these are careless and shallow… but, as human beings, our flesh is heir to them. We assume that what we see seventy or eighty or ninety percent of the time must reflect a deep and necessary connection. I believe it was Hume who first pointed out to us that induction is not as logically compelling as we suppose it to be.

As the purpose of a system becomes better defined and its success at that purpose more urgent, inductive exclusions seem to become more tolerated. One would hope that our Methodist might receive an Arabic-looking visitor cheerfully into his church; yet a government unit trying to locate a Near Eastern terrorist's bomb before midnight might refuse the help of an Arabic computer technician if a blond-haired, blue-eyed version were also available. The discrimination would be crude and repugnant… but those concerned would wait until tomorrow to sort it out.

Winning a pennant ranks somewhere between welcoming a visitor to church and assembling an anti-terrorist team for a ball club's management and ownership (with a steep inclination toward the latter). A coterie of blunt, red-necked people with some crude, tobacco-stained ideas (how do you like those stereotypes?) might be aware that their techniques of profiling would not look good if released to the press… but they would nonetheless probably apply their techniques in a kind of tacit conspiracy. For we must remember that these men (who have likely never heard of Hume, or maybe even Aristotle) really believe in their assumptions. Too many of a certain type on the team will ruin everything: the manager will insist that he has seen it happen before, and his coaches can supply their own illustrations to embellish his… because we must also remember that systems emerge through like attracting like. Everyone within this tight-knit group will have signed off, at least informally, on certain bedrock assumptions, either because he truly thinks the same way or because he needs the job.

Quite beyond its unfairness to the try-outs who were passed over, this kind of thinking is also self-destructive, sooner or later. Systems tend eventually to sabotage the healthy effects of imposing clear structure. They grow rigid to the point that observing organizational order is more important than accomplishing what that order was fashioned to do. The first time external circumstances change from a predictable range of forms and patterns, the system fails to respond sensibly, so bound and gagged is it in procedural rigor. The Cold War succeeded in keeping us from a "hot war"—but its great risk was always that those who had designed its parameters so well would one day be squeezed by the box they had engineered into pushing red buttons.

By the early Sixties, the Boston Red Sox had resisted integration and clung to habit for so long, calling up the bare minimum of black players and using them as seldom as possible, that even the expansion Los Angeles Angels were out-performing them. The Kansas City Athletics hadn't been much more innovative (quasi-superstar Vic Power was soon unloaded), and continued to hover near the bottom along the way to moving their lackluster franchise. Systems cannot afford to stifle creativity, even though the admission of too much creativity undermines the system. The contradiction must somehow be resolved: the healthy organization must find ways to keep changing as it remains the same.

This enigma has racial undercurrents even in relatively recent baseball. Almost any "suspicious" hitting technique that the all-American coach can name for you has been modeled with devastating effectiveness by black players, and probably since 1970. Joe DiMaggio wasn't the only guy to spread his feet wide in the box: Willie Mays did so, too, as did Manny Sanguillen. Eddie Murray had an uppercut swing. Wes Covington's extreme-rear dangling of the bat anticipated—with much exaggeration—the styles of Carew and Tony Fernandez. If Leon Wagner and Bill Madlock were the last really top-notch players to hold their hands wide apart, hitters like Andre Dawson might also open up about half an inch of wood in crucial situations.

Interestingly, you can also readily cite black players who go to the opposite extreme. If Mays's feet were spread out, then Lee May's were close together. If Clemente was almost out of the batter's box when he set up, then Frank Robinson was almost standing on the plate. Black hitters historically have brought the whole spectrum of techniques with them into Major League parks. I don't exactly know why this is. Perhaps because their fathers were away all day in mills and factories, they simply taught themselves to hit in sandlots and meadows: maybe a relative paucity of instructors nourished their creativity. Or perhaps the mood in the Negro Leagues was simply more tolerant of outlandish styles. There, a player was more likely to be judged purely on whether or not he could produce good results. (Negro League pitchers, for instance, were frequently explosive hitters; yet to this day, mainstream baseball doesn't bother to have pitchers take serious batting practice.) In the all-white Major Leagues of these same years, proven players were benched because they didn't do things exactly as the manager thought proper. (After retiring to manage the Washington Senators, Ted Williams benched John Roseboro for refusing to force a young pitcher to throw exclusively curve balls.)[2] Such a sociological explanation of the diverse styles among black players doesn't call upon us to assume that people of African descent tend to have livelier wrists or more creative impulses… which I regard as a plus, because the previous two paragraphs could also have been written of the Deadball Era's Caucasian stars.

Today the basic mechanism that drives human systems, it seems to me, is far less obscured in superficial veils: so it is in baseball, at least. Players are not being benched or passed over because of their color—but they *are* being punished (as I can testify of the game's lower echelons) if they don't squeeze themselves into the coach's cookie cutter. I don't mean to slander a noble calling: my grandfather was a professional coach, and I have volunteered as a Little League coach myself for several years. Nevertheless, it is *because* I have seen close-up how young boys get treated in such situations that I bear witness to the presence of favoritism and instructional force-feeding. Most volunteer coaches allow themselves to be drafted into the duty because, like me, they have a son playing ball… and some of these rookie coaches, alas (like so many of our politicians), become seduced by the thrill of power. After an initial uncertainty, they start telling every kid just how to hold the bat and stand in the box before they have even seen the child take his preferred cut. They place their own boy at the top of the order and in some key defensive position: other such "plums" they assign to the children of assistant coaches and to the physically most imposing children of the group. If a child happens to be small and "unconnected" socially, he can be sure of halving his time between the bench and right field, and of batting at the bottom of the order.

I would hope that those who are specially chosen and modestly paid to develop talent would do a better job of identifying it. Still, there are fixed ways of doing things even at the very top—perhaps more fixed at the top than anywhere else. Frank Robinson writes of several very sensible ideas he sought to implement as manager of the Giants, such as having runners tag at first base on long fly balls that would obviously be caught and having the third baseman sprint into shallow left field as the relay man on a drive down the line. Both maneuvers, though their advantages were transparent, violated baseball's hallowed wisdom. The former worked very well for Frank's Giants, all the same: the latter had to be discarded because "the players were so steeped in the old way of reacting".[4] To this day, you can easily go an entire season watching Major League games without seeing either of these heretical strategies used.

Curt Flood's ostensible autobiography, *The Way It Is*, might more correctly be called one long, eloquent indictment of systematic abuses. Since the book was published originally in early 1971, and since it looks back over a career that began in the mid-Fifties, the charges leveled against the coaching establishment are aimed directly at the era which I have addressed in the present book. All of Flood's Chapter Four, "Geniuses Need Not Apply", is dedicated to the managers and front-office types employed by baseball ownership. On the specific subject of professional coaching's quality, I might excerpt the following from Curt's steady flow of ringing denunciations (which really ought to be read in its entirety):

> Despite the tedious fiction about the perspicacity of grizzled old managers and coaches, few examples have been recorded of instruction bringing success to players who might otherwise have failed. Johnny Sain, a pitching coach constantly at war with his employers because of his player-oriented outlook, has helped every pitcher with whom he has ever worked. Neither front offices nor field managers care for his insistence on husbanding a pitcher's strength (and prolonging a pitcher's career, I might add). Accordingly, the best pitching coach in baseball was without a job in baseball when this was written.[4]

Consider the vagaries of base-stealing. The reemergence of station-to-station baseball during the Nineties in anticipation of home runs resurrected the old orthodoxy of the Fifties. Such is the standard game plan once again in professional baseball, as it was during the Fifties. Of course, base-stealing was perhaps the single most distinctive and flamboyant import from the Negro Leagues into modern baseball, despite its being largely stifled by white managers in the American League. After sluggers of the Sixties had begun tying themselves into futile knots with their mighty cuts, the base paths became pretty lively in the Seventies, and part of the Eighties. Now the "good old days" of long ball are back. In 1997, Brian Hunter of the Detroit Tigers led the Majors in steals with 74. No ballplayer since then has broken into the top 100 leaders for single-season steals: Hunter is tied with several others for a position on the very bottom rung. Indeed, without Rickey Henderson, the Nineties could scarcely boast of anyone in the top 100. I learned recently, in viewing a videotaped game from two decades ago, that the National League's three top base-stealers in 1984 were Tim Raines, Juan Samuel, and Alan Wiggins: 75, 72, and 70. Four of the five players I have named in this paragraph are African-American, and the other (Samuel) is a Latino. One has to assume that the Caucasian kids brought up on expensive clinics and state-of-the-art instructional gear aren't learning how to galavant with joyful abandon around a playground.

What I'm trying to do here is suggest how "the system"—any system—may be viewed as cheating recruits, applicants, or rookies with enormous potential of a fair chance to succeed, yet do so without any real malice. The age or race or religion of the cheated parties is likely not the central factor in their being shortchanged: this factor, rather, is probably their mere association with the new or different. The superficial markers are "add-ons" that flash a warning for dull functionaries mired deep within the system—people readily programmed to believe that all quadrupeds are horses because a horse is a quadruped. When the outward sign is skin color rather than height or speech habits or gender, then we see behavior that looks racist.

Part of the lesson to be learned here, sadly, is that such over-generality in thought is an abiding human characteristic. As individuals, we can guard against it: as larger groups or entire societies, we cannot. This is a war in which small victories may be won but not final and permanent triumph. Revolutionaries who overthrow systems simply set up new ones. Even if they are anarchists, their successors will create an "orthodoxy of anarchy". The cycle never ends. The labyrinth has no exit.

Yet thoughtful people should find some comfort in knowing that they form a kind of mystical fraternity. Racial minorities are but one species of "standout".   Anyone endowed with exceptional creativity, or exceptional insight, or (for that matter) exceptional honesty, must fall under suspicion over and over again as he or she is passed in review from one group, clique, tribe, order, company, or sodality to another. And I don't know that very many people have the "good fortune" to be such complete sheep that they are never exceptional in any way. I think there must be far fewer of these "sheeple" than a typical day would leave one thinking.

By way of stressing these conclusions, I would like to share my own experiences of the baseball establishment (and various broader social establishments) as the father of an up-and-coming player. Though race has almost nothing directly to do with this story, it is yet the same story as I have been telling over and over in previous chapters.

1 See *Veeck—As in Wreck* (*op. cit.*), 250.

2 The incident is related in Roseboro's *Glory Days with the Dodgers* (*op. cit.*), 243-244. The exchange actually went like this: "I said, 'Okay, Skip, we'll start working in some curves.' He [Williams] said, 'I don't want you to work in curves. I want him to throw only curves.'" When Roseboro refused to set up his pitcher to "get killed", his career essentially ended: he never started another game. The immortal Williams's handling of the situation was arrogant to the point of stupidity—but it was also par for the course in that era.

3 *Extra Innings* (*op. cit.*), 180-181. Also recommended by Frank is having a runner on second sprint for third rather than playing it safe on a grounder which the third baseman has to charge.

4 *The Way It Is*, with Richard Carter (New York: Pocket Books, 1972), 45. Flood, of course, issued the ultimate challenge to baseball's ossified system when he refused to be traded to Philadelphia by the Cardinals after the 1969 season, making the "extravagant" claim that he should have the right to peddle his services where he wished if St. Louis no longer wanted them.

II

Money, Egotism, and Ineptitude: A Father's Tale About Youth Baseball

a) Most of my advice was wrong, and all of it was mainstream

About the time that I was clipping baseball cards off of cereal boxes—or just a little later—I began teaching myself how to hit the way thousands of kids have learned for over a century: throwing a ball up in the air and swinging at it whenever it decides to come down. Since nobody my age lived on our block, this autodidactic endeavor could not be avoided; and when we moved to a larger house in a yet undeveloped subdivision, my drill became lonelier than ever. It also grew more refined. In the old house, I had essentially mastered hitting left-handed. I wanted to switch-hit like Mickey Mantle, and since I really didn't know how to hit at all, the extra time I devoted to the left side quickly concentrated my skills there. It was mostly at our new residence that I realized how I could replicate fastballs or off-speed pitches by varying the heights to which I tossed my ball (the really fast ones hardly getting a toss at all). There I also soon acquired an inside-out stroke; for the couple that eventually moved next door had an annoying little dog that yapped at my heels if I pulled the ball over the new arrivals' chain-link fence and had to retrieve it, whereas the lots beyond "left field" were still uncleared and pristine.

The long and the short of it is that I was an exceptionally good hitter in a few very odd ways once we began to play organized ball at school. Thanks to the big hitch my methods had taught me, however, I didn't adjust well when pitching started to accelerate with my group's age; and thanks, furthermore, to the reigning football obsession in Texas, my coaches could dish out such useful advice as "attack the ball" but couldn't offer any specific hints about how a successful attack might be launched.

To this day, I think I might have been good ballplayer, since I could drive a ball substantially farther than anyone else my age if I could only lay a bat on it. Who knows... I might even have had the rudiments of an effective if off-beat pitcher, for I had so well mimicked Willie Mays's style of flipping the ball underhanded back to the infield that I was something of a playground wonder. From the mound, this is called "submarining", and it's something I could do with ease. I think I had some basic ability. What I didn't have was

320

instruction. Whatever "lessons" I received from football coaches during their off-season were worse than no lessons at all.

When my son was born several decades later, therefore, I had to "go to school".

What I mean is that I felt obliged actually to hit the books as well as resume hitting baseballs. I read Ted Williams' classic which somewhat pompously claims to teach the science of hitting—as well as Charlie Lau's, which prefers to treat hitting as an art; and I recall other books by Walt Hreniak, Mike Schmidt, Johnny Mize, Willie Mays, Dusty Baker, Ty Cobb, and Cal Ripken, Jr. I also did photographic and video research. I bought up dog-eared books from libraries that no longer had shelf space for yesteryear's forgotten warriors on the chance that I might see how Pie Traynor gripped a bat or how Eddie Collins finished his swing. I purchased old-model bats from e-Bay and constructed experiments based upon hypotheses. (I always used pitching machines that fired plastic whiffle balls in these undertakings: with my timing eroded by the years, I didn't want to risk splintering a museum piece!)

I swung right- as well as left-handed. I spread my hands sometimes, and sometimes I interlaced the top hand's pinky and the bottom hand's index. Upon my forward leg I used a lift, a kick, a glide, and no motion at all. I covered styles from Honus Wagner to the Babe to Joe D to Andre Dawson to Arod. I even crossed my wrists, as a young Henry Aaron had done in the sandlots (and as Hall-of-Famer Dan Bancroft apparently did: I'm convinced to this day that the mysterious Baltimore Chop of nineteenth-century renown was executed with wrists crossed.)

I searched for the science of hitting as only an amateur artist can. I wanted to give my son the expert tutelage that I never received. Of course, I also realized pretty soon that my baseball infection had lain dormant for about twenty-five years without ever really vanishing. Once bitten is bitten for life.

I taught my boy (for convenience's sake, I'll dub him with the pseudonym "Kevin") to the best of my ability. I gave him the benefit of the most sensible and best-documented pedagogy that I could amass. To a much-reduced extent, I did the same for pitching—for I had never been a pitcher and couldn't imagine that Kevin would ever be anything but a hitter. We Celts are broad-framed but usually a bit on the short side: a build far better suited to swinging a claymore than hurling a quoit.

As my son prepares to enter college, I can now confidently pass two judgments upon my efforts to teach both hitting and pitching: 1) my lessons were deeply flawed, and 2) everything I taught the boy was and is a part of mainstream coaching doctrine.

I would ask that you remember that twofold revelation, for it is not unconnected to the experience of black ballplayers in the Fifties, strange as that may seem.

b) The plot sickens: moneyball

Now I must move on to the dramatic portion of my story. Every good yarn has a villain, and the man whom I shall call Coach Rasp was about as grating a personality as I have known in this life (though not the wickedest soul). Our stars were obviously crossed from the dawn of time: the events that led me over and over smack into his oncoming load of ego were as improbable as they were numerous. In fact, I seem to have been introduced to him in a very unfavorable light before I even knew that he existed. I had, in slightly foolish enthusiasm, typed up some of my research about hitters of yesteryear and put it into a book manuscript about different hitting styles down through the ages. A kid who was taking Freshman Composition with me at the time somehow got to talking with me about baseball, and my manuscript came up. He insisted that he wanted very much to read it. Authors are always flattered by such requests, so I copied the text onto a disc for the young man. Little did I know that he had been the star ballplayer at the local private school where I would one day send my son. The disc was apparently shared with Coach Rasp by my student—and I doubt that he read much of it, for reading has never been his preferred means of passing time; but he must have seen enough to cast me in his mind as an educated idiot, for there were veiled references to my opus when Kevin signed up for the coach's summer baseball camp a few months later—the first time either of us had actually met the irascible Mr. Rasp.

I hasten to add that I eventually shoved that manuscript to a distant back burner after realizing how many errors littered it. Hitting is hard, and figuring it out clinically is almost impossible. Yet Rasp's subtle sneers at my work seemed to aim only at my viewing the great hitters of yesteryear with deep respect. He had no logical reason, for instance, to suppose that holding the bat at or a little below rather than above the shoulder would not produce a more level swing with a higher probability of intersecting the ball: he just knew that the technique was old-fashioned, and therefore—in his mind— wrong. The lessons he gave Kevin over the ensuing years in opposition to this and similarly dated techniques produced far worse results than my own mistakes (one of which, by the way, was *not* the lower hand-hold, in my view); so the objective evidence cannot justify my being written off immediately as a meddling fool. Rasp's justification for that treatment, rather, was that I belonged neither to the professional coaching fraternity nor to the elite group of his financial benefactors.

For money has as much to do with ruining young baseball talent as egotism and incompetence. I cannot neglect its role in this story, at any rate, even though I must stray farther into scattered, superficially unconnected circumstances. In twenty-first century America, all baseball in the suburbs is moneyball. Long before anyone in my family ever ran into Coach Rasp, we were finding out that you don't just sign your kid up for Little League any more and sit back to enjoy the fun. In the white suburbs of my Texas town, here's how it works.

Men who have ambition and common sense—but not enough money to be comfortably wealthy—realize that working all the way through medical school or penetrating the inner circle of a law firm will involve vast expense. If they have sons, then a generous athletic scholarship is a good way to accomplish at least the first leg of the journey. The shortest path to scholarship money is probably baseball. Football and basketball... not the likeliest bet. The importance of a certain inherited physique is critical in both of those sports, and the successful car salesmen and burger-franchise owners of Blandsboro seldom carry the DNA of gigantic freaks in their veins. Virtually any boy can be molded into a baseball player, however, if he has the right training at the right moments. Baseball is a game of many fine skills intricately connected. A boy can't really teach himself to hit by tossing a ball in the air the way I once tried to do; but if I had been a foot taller, I might have spent those same hours shooting hoops and become a superior basketball player, largely by myself. Baseball demands a much more involved plan of attack.

Hence the relatively modest cost of baseball instruction actually represents a welcome exclusionary factor in the race for the free college ride. Lessons and high-tech training equipment are affordable on an upper-middle income, but not really below that level... so move over, freakish athletes from single-parent families! Our suburban movers and shakers may pay as much as a hundred bucks an hour for their child to receive lessons from a one-time Triple A star who blew his arm out... and sometimes the star truly teaches his pupil a thing or two. In any case, that's not the end of the production orchestrated by impresario-dads. As skill levels rise with the boy's age, many elite camps and ever more high-tech training equipment figure in the budget (enough, usually, to have paid a big chunk of that college tuition which baseball is supposed to be funding eventually). Dad has grown accustomed at his "day job" to delegating specific technical tasks to technicians, so he feels that the process must be moving along smoothly every time he writes a check to "Fan 'em Frank" Fannin—little suspecting that his child, too, is rather often being nudged out of serious contention by charlatans in a multi-billion dollar industry. But that, of course, is another story.

As a white-collar type who doesn't have (but, in his view, doesn't need) in-the-trenches experience, Dad attempts to help his sprouting superstar by messing about in the system's administrative cogs and wheels. For starters, he manages the boy's Little League team. He ensures that his Tigers or Twins win the championship—and have a chance to go to a regional tournament, if not the Little League World Series—by packing the team with top players on draft night. The rest of us dumb grunts simply submit our boy's form to the league office: we assume, in our naïveté, that other fathers do the same. Meanwhile, these elite operators have invested dozens of hours in scouting the upcoming talent so that they know just which three or four studs to snap up when the draft is conducted. (A surer method is to butter up each "target boy's" father, beg him to assist with the coaching, and then "reserve" the kid. Two or three reserved players are always sequestered from the draft list by every coach: specifically, the sons of his coaching subordinates. Slick.) At young adolescent levels, wining teams revolve around a mere handful of players, the rest being randomly chosen "cannon fodder" or perhaps visibly imposing specimens noted during tryouts; for another hard fact of youth baseball is that size counts. Tall boys with no skill to speak of can nevertheless hit a ball very far if they only connect, for their superior reach causes the bat head to accelerate well above average speeds.

The father-managers in question are utterly convinced that their ten- or twelve-year-olds will be noticed by some college or big-league scout and entered into an exclusive database if the team can just make it to a regional tournament. There's little evidence that this is true. Even showcases hosted by dozens of college scouts are often boondoggles: they make money for the organizers without drawing any professional attention in what turns out to be a weekend vacation for jaded assistant coaches. Yet the dad-managers I have in mind didn't get where they are in the business world by keeping their fingers out of the works and letting nature run her course. Their philosophy of life demands that one throw elbows, lay out cash, secure the post position, and do everything else possible to become an "insider". The also-rans—the losers— are those suckers who kept their place in line and trusted in the system.

Kevin was on several of these teams, some less benign than others. The worst coach he had was an adipose redneck who made the game of baseball disgusting even to me. This man boasted of his trophies as if he were a past Olympian and insisted that he had discovered the alchemy of victory. His step-son and a couple of his reserved players threw hard and threw strikes: that alone, for the age group, put the team immediately in contention. His offensive strategy was to have hitters take pitch after pitch, perhaps waving their bat in the zone as if intending to bunt. He was especially delighted that Kevin batted left-handed, for he moved every lefty up on top of the plate in the fairly accurate conviction that the boy would either be hit by a pitch or walked. He never actually learned Kevin's name, for his elite three were constantly playing tournament ball as well as Little League (against the rules), and the cannon fodder was not viewed as requiring practice. What's to practice when you stand in the field watching strikeouts, then stand at the plate watching balls sail at your head and feet?

By the end of this "championship" season (we strategically planned a vacation in order to avoid the playoffs), Kevin, all black and blue, was ready to quit baseball. Because of his diminutive size and his dad's relative obscurity in the local community, he had been "filler" for about three years in a row—but never before at such risk to his personal safety. I had made him tough out the season in the insecure belief that I might be assisting the formation of strong character in him. Whether or not umpires are haunted by missed calls, I know for a fact that dads are. That's one of the three I would most like to have back.

This is not a chronicle of my son's early baseball life. I will say only briefly, then, that Kevin passed the next two springs playing YMCA ball— which in this town, for some reason, is black kids' baseball. He was actually given a chance to pitch and discovered a real talent for the mound. The fire was reignited. Our second season on "that side" of town was as dismal as the first one was delightful. Kevin's buddies from the previous year mysteriously disappeared from the team when it became evident (to everyone but me, I suppose—for I had foolishly volunteered to manage the group) that we had been made the dumping ground for every trouble-maker in the league. There was no draft that I ever witnessed: I simply started receiving big, bulky kids as "gifts". They couldn't play ball, but they could sure start fights.

The other painful memory of that season was the concession stand— or, I should clarify, the obsession of three of the league's organizers with that enterprise. Our kids were often kept out very late on school nights, and always beginning at the dinner hour, for no reason other than to "raise money" for the league's operation through the sell of Cokes and hot dogs... all for cash and coin: no checks or credit cards. The boys also sold hundreds of raffle tickets in the cause, ostensibly, of building some batting cages. Those tickets went for greenbacks, too: foldable cash that fits in your pocket. I never heard who won the raffle, or even that it took place; and the league shut down operations the next year, so that junk-food money couldn't have bought a lot of floodlights. I kept thinking of all those bills floating around, and of three men in luxury vehicles who never got worked up about baseball or school but quickly started shouting at me if I threatened the business of the concession stand.

We logged one victory that season: a "fake" victory that actually went down as a forfeit because we had to recruit a ninth player on the spot. (Several of our team had gone home when it was discovered that the game had been scheduled two hours too early—an occasional stratagem used by the "organizers" to ensure an abundant, starving clientele near their precious concession stand.) I didn't have the heart to tell my remaining boys that they'd been disqualified before the first pitch, and the opposing coaches were good sports and kept mum.

You could call the pocket-lining around the cash register before the last light went dark a kind of moneyball, too. It resolves into quite an interesting little snapshot of black culture versus white culture in one Middle American town: *Raisin in the Sun* versus *All My Sons*, the pilfering of petty cash versus a long-term investment in rigging the recruitment game. It's a damned depressing portrait.

c) Money, egotism, and ineptitude converge

The only good news to come out of that season was that Kevin started throwing submarine. He had seen me fooling around with it in the back yard, and he took to it without any encouragement, spending long hours in the perfection of his technique with a rubber ball thrown at the side of the house. When I finally prevailed upon him to give the motion a try in a real game, he completely shut down for three innings a team that had been regional champion the previous year.

Kevin's modest successes were about to converge with Coach Rasp's know-it-all vanity and our Little League culture of micro-managing dads. The weekend John McGraw in our midst who had the deepest pockets and the most determination to advance his son was a man I shall call Bob. Robert, Jr., was always bound for high achievement in the sports world, if you listened to his doting sire: not just for a scholarship ride through a D-I college, but all the way up to the pros. The boy didn't strangle anacondas while in the crib like Baby Hercules (or not that I was ever told); but Bob assured me at one time that his heir, when eight or nine, had beaten the sox off a bunch of teenagers in a golf tournament. Why Robert didn't continue in that preferred pastime of the affluent, I have no idea. Our lives would have been much simpler and happier if the gods had not whispered to Bob that this youngest wonder of the world was destined for the baseball diamond.

And Robert, to be fair, was a good ballplayer. He should have been: he had height on his side from an early age (hence his proficiency at golf, no doubt), and Bob had also secured him all of the best instruction that money could buy. Somehow or other, the head coach at our local university--an extraordinarily capable man who had led the school repeatedly to the national finals of the Division III heap (and who had given off-season instruction to Mark Texeira)—happened to be Robert's godfather. Had that anything to do with Bob's underwriting big chunks of the university baseball program year after year? (But then, you don't really have to be bribed to become someone's godparent, do you? If asked, wouldn't you just say "yes" without being a *cul de cheval* about it?)

Bob's Little League reputation had preceded him all around the town. Kevin had never played in his division: we were East, where residences were more humble, and he was West, where domiciles tended to spread out and lift up. Yet we knew that some of the intra-league wars over there had grown very intense; we heard that they were even worse than ours. Bob was in the thick of these rumors. It was said that he shouted and raged at his kids and demanded victory at all costs. Most of that was probably said, however, by those whose teams lost to his. I would not be the man's best choice as a character witness, but I would have called him more of a charmer than a bruiser. I never heard him shout at anyone.

It was just our luck, when we finally shifted Kevin to private school (with his grandmother's financial assistance), that Bob and his arch-rival from the Western division were sending their boys to the same school. I'll call the rival Casey, since he had an estimable baseball name (though not that one). In fact, the name was the most "baseball" thing about Casey. His son was really a very poor athlete, and he himself seemed more likely to read a long biography or calculate the interest on an investment than to re-stitch a catcher's mitt. I never truly understood his enthusiasm for baseball. Was it simply one of several ways to compete with Bob on the local social scene?

If so, the chosen battleground was not at all to his advantage. I'm sure Bob's team must have trounced his team—and Bob's son must have played circles around his son—for years before I strayed all unwitting into a heavily mined No Man's Land. Casey latched onto me first. We had begun to think about a summer league for Kevin as he entered middle school, and Casey was forming a traveling team that would play in Dallas over the weekends. He was paying Coach Rasp to be the team's manager—paying him pretty handsomely, I'm sure. And Coach Rasp, who now lived his life among kids whose least plaything could have bought his whole toy chest when he was their age, had decided that money was something he'd like more of.

If I could erase all of the shadows that I now know lurked around the events of those two summers, when Kevin had finished seventh and then eighth grade, they would be among the happiest in my life. Kevin's pitching accounted for most of the team's successes (we just about broke even), and his hitting also began to shine. I have already written that my lessons in that fine art were severely flawed. I had selected Charlie Lau as my guru, and I had Kevin pulling the bat through with an almost straight front arm. This is no way to hit for power... but it actually does produce lots of contact. A smaller-than-average kid, Kevin seemed very happy with his clusters of singles. He would end up his final middle-school season hitting exactly .750!

Throughout this time, we heard little about Bob and Super-Robert. The latter, we were told, also played around Dallas in weekend tournaments, but not in any capacity where we would ever run into him. His team was an elite bunch. They were the best and played only the best.

I came to regard Casey as my friend. My son had prospered from the occasions to play ball that he provided, he was a quiet man who didn't boast or force his views on anyone, and he had drawn the high school coach's interest to my son (and to his own: it was really to Rasp's advantage to manage the team, in fact, because he was not only well paid but also able to work with rising talent on a campus that had all too few players to choose from). If Coach Rasp and I got off to a rocky start, these months also saw a relaxation of tensions. While I remained an idiot intellectual and the two of us weren't exactly on friendly terms, neither were we adversaries to the death. I even convinced him to look at Kevin throwing left-handed—something the kid had also picked up from our backyard foolery. The coach was completely skeptical, as he had every right to be; but when he and Kevin came back up from the field that afternoon, he was grinning ear to ear. He joked about becoming Kevin's agent. It was the first and last truly jovial conversation we ever had.

The specific detonating event of this deceptively tranquil time-bomb was Robert's failure to dominate his select team in the manner that Bob expected. This all happened as Robert and Kevin were just finishing the freshman year of high school: hence both would have been playing summer ball with a lot of older kids around them. No matter. Age-schmage. Robert should still have been the starting pitcher in every important game, according to Bob ("important" being defined as "college scout possibly in attendance": Bob could no doubt have bought a small college—but his son had to enter the big-league rumor mill properly). Plan B developed. Bob would create his own select team and appoint Rasp to be its coach. Since Bob could buy the coach's allegiance with his pocket change, his son would be assured of occupying every ray of limelight the team managed to blunder into.

The snag was that the Coach's summer tutelage had already been bought and paid for by Casey. Bob decided that there was no conflict—that the two teams were registered in different leagues whose charters allowed coaches to double-dip. And players, too; for out of the blue, Bob approached me with a proposition that Kevin play for his elite Angels summer traveling team. I thanked him—I was genuinely flattered on Kevin's behalf—but said that we had already made a verbal commitment to Casey's team. Bob replied that Kevin could play on both teams without violating any rule. We were satisfied, so Kevin got measured for an Angels' uniform.

I can't fully remember the order of all that happened next. Casey insisted that Bob had drawn us into an illegality, and seems to have thrown a wrench into some of Bob's paperwork. Somebody told us at some point—it must have been Bob, because it certainly wasn't the Coach—that Rasp had refused to manage the Angels unless Robert and Kevin both signed on. The idea of working with two of his promising sophomores at once was supposedly a significant factor in his agreeing to manage the team. I know that Kevin did eventually practice with the Angels for a while, so the initial problems (if they had ever existed at all) must have been ironed out.

Then came the day when I observed Bob filming all the players in the batting cage. I asked the purpose of his camera work: he told me that he and the Coach were going to review each player's swing later—or maybe he just said that Coach Rasp would, but I recollect having heard a dual number. In any case, I emailed Bob that evening asking that I be apprised of any changes they had in mind for Kevin's stroke. I wanted to be kept in the loop.

There are a lot of incidents behind my christening this man "Rasp", but none more influential than what happened next. Bob showed my email to the Coach... or said that he had. I'll never know for certain just what he printed out that punched all of this strange fellow's buttons: what I wrote was no more provocative than what I've set down here. Like a thunderbolt on a clear day, there fell before my eyes through return email the rudest communication that any primate as ever aimed at me who didn't have bars in front of him. I didn't read it all. It went on and on, informing me of what a highly trained professional the author was, what a meddlesome incompetent I was, and what a vast number of students the author had gotten into college baseball programs. The last of these claims was demonstrably false, but apparently true in Coach Rasp's steamy brain. Or maybe not... maybe he remembered this absurd boast years later, and maybe he felt "shown up" when Kevin's baseball scholarship had nothing whatever to do with him.

The Angels adventure blew apart after that—not just for us, but for the entire team. Perhaps Casey was right and Bob had not properly filed his paperwork. But Casey's team blew up, too. It lacked sufficient players, and Coach Rasp was also refusing to have anything further to do with it. We found Kevin a place on a summer team that got him a handful of at-bats and dragged us all over the country—the best I could do on short notice. I never suspected what a hornets' nest of bruised egos we had left behind.

Somehow Bob had pulled Coach Rasp permanently out of Casey's pocket, though Bob's own team had foundered in the process. It was said that wives even exchanged Words Which Can Never Be Taken Back. Had Bob ever really wanted Kevin to be an Angel, or was it planned from the beginning that his recruitment would be a mere ploy to destroy Casey's team? Were the Angels ever meant to stay together? All that remained clear after the dust eventually settled was that Coach Rasp, in complete control now of Kevin's high school future, would devote his full resources to keeping Robert center-stage, even if it meant thrusting kids like Kevin off into the wings.

And as time went on, Kevin would be nudged especially far into the wings… yet the dust took its time settling. I believe the boy played every inning of every game as a sophomore. That was when Casey, having determined that Rasp was permanently Bob's "boy" now, declared all-out war on the coach, as well. He undertook a community-wide campaign of slamming Rasp as a danger to children and (of all things) to wildlife. Newspapers, radio… whatever medium had an audience broadcast Casey's indignant outcry. I found the strategy disgusting, but I never had occasion to say so directly to my "friend". The last time Casey ever spoke to me was when he sought my support in a school-wide initiative to have Rasp fired. I responded that I didn't much like the man but that my son worshiped him—and that the coach/player relationship was what counted. So much for our friendship.

I cannot speak to the kind of treatment that Casey's son received from Rasp. At the time, I wouldn't have believed that the coach could stoop low so low as to avenge himself on another adult through a boy. Now I know otherwise. I still view with extreme distaste the cowardice of Casey's strategy: undermining a man's reputation with wild allegations in the public press. But when your own kid is a target, I guess you might do some pretty desperate things.

My kid, as I say, was not a target in his sophomore year. It may have been because Rasp didn't need any extra enemies if he were to keep his job. Maybe he was even "sucking up" to me by playing Kevin as much as he did.

If so, that all ended once Casey terminally disgraced himself by overplaying his hand. It took about a year, a very slow year… but eventually Casey conceded victory to Bob and transferred his kids to another school. Only then, when he had "picked off" one adversary, did Coach Rasp appear to me to focus his energies on sabotaging Kevin. I think he actually liked my son, and was perhaps even particularly fond of him. It was me he hated: for, in his mind, I would forever be Casey's ally as well as the idiot intellectual. Getting at me through my son must therefore have been really tough on the guy. Can you imagine… having to foul up the success of someone you sincerely like because no better way presents itself of having revenge on someone you sincerely detest?

Coach Rasp, I might add, is an ordained minister in whatever hard-line denomination he claims to follow. One would have hoped that the example of Christ might have suggested to him a way out of his emotional predicament.

d) More tell-tale facts and stats

Statistics were my starting point with the young black ballplayers of the late Fifties and early Sixties. In my son's case, they are the crescendo of a tortuous (and I hope not insufferably tedious) chain of events. With yesteryear's big-leaguers, I possessed only mathematical fact at first and had to work backward from there to reconstruct motive. In this most personal of cases, my head was so aswirl in motives that I often asked myself if I were being unfair. Then I would ponder the mathematical facts for a short while and realize that I could hardly be imagining foul play.

1) Batting

Kevin made All Conference Honorable Mention as a freshman, during which season he was almost exclusively used as a designated hitter for a senior who couldn't swing his way out of a wet paper bag. With an average of about .320 and an on-base percentage of around .450, Kevin was clearly a very handy guy to have in the line-up. He also led his high school team in sacrifices by a substantial margin.

As his sophomore year began, however, Kevin unwittingly faced a coach who was stewing over the "Angels incident", if temporarily minding his manners while Casey attempted to have him fired. Rasp's efforts at sabotage were subtle this year, if they existed at all. I noticed that he insisted on Kevin's batting only left-handed from now on, which really puzzled me (for he had hit .300 from the right side during the previous year). Thanks to this "adjustment", Kevin's average and OBP proceeded to decline thirty or forty points, though they remained within the respectable range.

So further subversion, apparently, had to be undertaken. In his junior year, Kevin was advised by a new hitting coach (a kid about eight years his elder) that his swing needed complete reconstruction. The idea was to give him more power... but the result was that he hit scores of fly balls medium-deep to waiting outfielders. Some of these pop-ups were quite majestic, but the umpires don't give you any style points in baseball. Kevin finished the season at .236.

During his senior year, Kevin began very hot because of some adjustments he had made during summer ball. The hitting coach soon "corrected" that. I don't know where Kevin's average ended up—somewhere below the Mendoza line. He was so unproductive that Coach Rasp benched him for the final half-dozen games of the season. Yet he had returned to his summer form in practice (with the hitting coach's resigned, "I wash my hands of this" blessing) and was scorching the ball on low trajectories, while his replacements—all underclassmen—were not even hitting long flies, but striking out weakly. (You can have a "quality at-bat" on a strikeout... and then again, you can make a miserable showing.) Rasp seemed to have found whatever excuse he needed to bury Kevin, and he kept him six feet under.

I should add a couple of footnotes. The hitting instructor was unquestionably a very competent hitter himself, and I also fully believe that the changes he had in mind for Kevin were good ones. They would have corrected the flaws that my own teaching had introduced into Kevin's swing: specifically, they would have had him driving into the ball with his back side rather than pulling down on the ball with his front side. But the young man (who was probably more devastated by Kevin's failure than I was) didn't know how to get all the movable parts working together. Hitting is hard.

And here's the second point. Rasp, who had at last tacitly admitted that he knew nothing about hitting by hiring this coach, nevertheless knew full well that Kevin was capable of leading the team in most batting stats. I say this because the Rasp/Bob axis had invaded the Dallas Patriots organization—with which Kevin and I had hooked up to play summer ball before Kevin's junior and senior years. The two men had essentially taken over the summer traveling team of which we just happened to be a part, now a showcase for Robert's pitching prowess. Rasp had seen up close with his own eyes, then, that Kevin had discovered a leg kick that made his straight and overemphasized front arm work effectively and with power. This was just before his junior year—the summer season after which the new hitting coach insisted that Kevin abandon everything he had been doing. Then, in the summer before his senior year, when Rasp was yet again coaching the Patriots (a.k.a. the Roberts), Kevin actually did log the highest BA on the team, at .389. He had lowered his hands to his back armpit, which was making him drive off the rear side more powerfully and stay inside the ball better.

No, I'm not trying to write a hitting manual... but my point is that even a coach who knows nothing about how to hit knows hitting success when he sees it. Rasp had it entirely within his power to pull the struggling young hitting coach and the struggling young hitter aside together and say, "Hey, I watched this kid hit the hide off the ball all last summer. Let's go back to what he was doing then." This man who had never been reticent before about anything connected to baseball savvy suddenly wouldn't let on that he had stood in the third-base coaching box all summer—for two summers—and had seen a wholly different hitter in Kevin. He simply let his first-time instructor (a boy not even finished with college) completely dismantle Kevin's stroke and try to reassemble the pieces.

Or did he "simply" do so? Did he say to the instructor, instead, "Take this boy's swing and tear it apart completely"? No other starter on the high school team, I noticed, had his approach at the plate completely altered. Few others changed anything at all.

2) Fielding

Kevin has always had good hands and good coordination. As I wrote earlier, he can throw tolerably well left-handed (and did so in one relief appearance on a "fall ball" team). That doesn't sound like the typical attribute of a klutz, does it?

331

Nothing Rasp did to Kevin reminded me so forcefully of the experiences of early black big-leaguers as his "developing" the boy to be an infielder. I didn't really expect Kevin to play infield as a freshman: he was a little too small and his arm a bit too weak. In subsequent years, however, he was never once drilled in pre-season training to play the position where Rasp put him once the games went on the record. He played some third base in his sophomore year with a few mistakes here and there, but overall showing steady, substantial improvement; this was the year of "laying the ambush", as I now think of it bitterly, when the coach had to hold his fire and isolate Casey. The following year, Kevin was inexplicably shifted to second base with little to no preparation. He hardly made a mess of it, starting every conference game at that position without making an error. Must have been really frustrating. So Rasp again had him messing around on the infield's left side for his senior year, where he wasn't given an instant's peace.

The spring-training time at shortstop was especially suspect, since Kevin never saw a single pitch from that position during his senior season. The thought occurred to me later that such "practice" was intended to de-familiarize him with third base and ensure that he would foul up his assignments there. Inevitably, he made the occasional error: grounders come to third in a hurry sometimes, and sometimes very slowly or with a lot of spin. None of these little miscues was overlooked. When Kevin was benched in that final year, his various replacements at third performed so miserably that teammates began to complain about the arrangement in the dugout. And to think that Coach Rasp often rebuked his squad for having no spirit! It's hard to cry, "Charge!" when you know that the general intends to have your buddy shot as soon as the platoon leaves the trench.

I'm not a coach; in fact, I'm a very partisan observer in this instance. I could say that I saw Kevin make plays at second and third that no one else on the team made all season, and I would be telling the truth. Yet I know that coaching assessments can be complex: sometimes what the player fails to do has a stronger negative effect than the positive influence of what he succeeds in doing. I understand that. I will even attest to the fact that Kevin did not always face-plant himself in the dirt to attempt the knock-down of an errant throw (though I never saw him fail to do this in any instance where the "plant" would actually have stopped the throw—but some coaches can be very impressed by futile gestures). Who knows... if another kid were to be stuck at third, maybe he would get himself dirtier. You don't know till you try... yes, I understand all that.

What I shall never understand is how any coach at any level, professional or amateur, could possibly expect a kid to learn a difficult position knowing that he is likely to be benched or exiled to the outfield if he makes one gaffe. You can't flag down a skipping grounder with the thought throbbing in the back of your head, "Don't boot it! Don't make an error!" Players tense up when they're in such a state. They may actually avoid the ball to avoid being charged with an error. Some of Coach Rasp's products have often seemed to me more concerned about getting a 9.6 from the Russian judge for their belly-flop into the dirt than about snagging the ball. Kevin, I'm proud to say, was never one of these.

Yet I know that his confidence as an infielder was often completely sapped by the treatment he received. That makes my blood boil. The subversion of his hitting was mostly passive aggression—but this was a fully aggressive act of sabotage.

Still, fielding is a nebulous area. It has few reliable statistics associated with it; and even if Rasp was guilty of being a horrible teacher who tyrannized his subjects, perhaps he treated all the boys the same way.

But he didn't. I wouldn't know how to rate the "degree of hounding" to which every boy on the team was submitted... but there was certainly a sliding scale. Moat notable—downright unmistakable—was the kid-glove treatment he accorded to Robert. Even as a freshman, Robert was dubbed our starting third baseman when he was not pitching. His errors were legion and routine. He lost us a district championship on a simple boot; and I'll never forget how he pouted over the fumble rather than picking the ball up and touching third, where there was a force. He was elevated to starting shortstop for the remainder of his high school career, yet he never lost this propensity to brood and sulk after letting one scoot between his legs. Coaches ordinarily recognize such attitudinal problems as terminally crippling. You can teach a kid to have softer hands by having him take grounders without a glove on— but you can't get rid of that pout, which focuses his attention uselessly inward rather than on the game.

Robert racked up errors galore in Patriots summer ball, as well, yet he always started (when not pitching) at the most pivotal, highly skilled defensive position in fair territory: shortstop. Why? Because someone might be watching, and because Rasp was in Bob"s pocket. Robert was always being thrust front and center in the casement window just on the chance that a scout might happen by. Coach Rasp's job was to market Robert.

3) Pitching

Kevin had refined his pitching skills considerably since his YMCA days, but he remained undersized—especially for a hurler—as he entered high school. I thought that Rasp worked him into his eventual role very adroitly... up to a point. The boy wasn't at first used in conference games or at critical junctures. His confidence grew with his small successes. Only as a sophomore did he begin to appear in short relief with runners on base, and only as a junior did he become the regular closer. The coach was clearly capable of professional behavior on occasion.

Unlike many baseball dads, I don't actually have reams of my son's stats at my fingertips. I know that the sidearm motion employed by Kevin got him a lot of ground balls and swings-and-misses. In wooden bat tournaments over the summers, he usually managed to break a few sticks; in other words, the opposition tended to make weak contact. This pitching style also had liabilities. Umpires too often call pitches where they're caught rather than where they cross the plate, which can be a real nuisance to a sidearmer.

Ground balls also have a way of sneaking through for hits if you have mediocre infielders behind you. Kevin was victimized on both counts. In compensation, he developed superior pick-off moves to first and second. He must have led every league he ever played in over those years in runners caught leaning. It couldn't even have been close.

I do recall that his strikeout-to-walk ratio hovered around three- or four-to-one in both high school and summer seasons when he was a freshman and sophomore. That's a very good proportion, and also a better measurement of success than something like Earned Run Average, which doesn't account for fielders with weak arms or inferior range. Nevertheless, his ERA couldn't have been that bad, either; for on a stray sheet of stats relating to his sophomore year, I find it recorded at 2.45. In his senior year, the local newspaper listed him as having the fourteenth best ERA in all of East Texas, no distinction drawn between public and private schools or various levels of play. He was within six hundredths of a percentage point of cracking the top ten.

In his junior year, an article in the same newspaper had recorded his strikeouts-to-walks ratio as 35 to 7: exactly five to one. After his senior year, this ratio topped seven to one.

As his offense was systematically undermined, then, and as his defense was ridiculed to his face and before his teammates every time he made a rare error, Kevin was incontestably becoming a better pitcher, by any measure. His progress accelerated in his senior year, even though he had gained little height throughout high school and still never reached 80 mph on the JUGS gun. The reason was that he was again throwing submarine rather than sidearm.

It had been Coach Rasp's decision to elevate Kevin's arm angle from submarine to sidearm in the freshman year. I didn't question the rationale: Kevin had more velocity from the side. Forgive me, though, if I now wonder retrospectively whether the man were trying to screw Kevin up on the mound as he was doing to him in the batter's box. Maybe Kevin's ability to get hitters out from the new angle came as an unpleasant surprise to Coach Rasp.

For during summer ball before Kevin's junior year, I finally asked Rasp why Kevin didn't throw from both angles. His answer made no sense to me then, and makes less to me now: he said that, if Kevin dropped down extra-low to throw submarine, the hitter would instantly know that a fastball was coming, since Kevin had no other pitch from that angle. Absolutely absurd! Where to begin? In the first place, a hitter seeing Kevin for a stint of short relief would have no idea what to expect from the lower angle. In the second place, a submarine fastball moves so much that one can know it's coming and still not be able to track it. In the third place, Kevin also had a change-up—and if he hadn't, it could have been taught to him in five minutes. (I should know: Kevin taught me how to throw a submarine change in the back yard: my first attempt went wide, but you could have framed the next two and hung them in the Louvre.) In the fourth place, the two arm angles can be reached out of the same wind-up, so that nothing is given away until the last instant.

And in the fifth place, a submarine fastball thrown to rise above the letters is an entirely different pitch from one thrown to drop below the knees.

I shouldn't have needed to say any of this to a professional coach who pitched at a Division I college... and I didn't bother to say it, because the objection was patently made up. I realized that something was amiss after that brief discussion (very brief: the testy Rasp was benching Kevin that day for throwing his glove after blowing a save the previous evening—a punishment I never knew the coach to dish out to anyone else). Now I began to wonder, once again, if Kevin was being held back deliberately from achieving his potential.

I began to insist that Kevin throw submarine to me in the back yard. It was like pulling teeth: Rasp had convinced him that the motion was a waste of time. Yet it was working so well for him by his senior year that the coach, upon seeing him fool with it during practice, exclaimed, "Why haven't you been doing that the whole time?" He made a tug here and a tweak there, and satisfied himself, apparently, that the creation was all his own. Kevin half-believes the same thing to this day. Dad, the idiot intellectual, never played ball at a high level... so, obviously, Rasp must have taught him to throw submarine!

Kevin can hardly dispute, though, that Dad forced him almost physically to make a video of his submarine pitching. It was on the basis of that video, posted by the National Collegiate Scouts Association, that he was offered a college scholarship.

About which, more anon. I will say here only that I believe the scholarship to be yet another axe that Rasp was grinding. When he found out about it, the senior-year benchings started almost at once. And although Kevin had posted one of the very best ERA's in East Texas, as I have said, he threw not one pitch in the final game that knocked his team out of the play-offs. Four pitchers made appearances: an ineffective Robert, and then three sophomores trying vainly to stop the hemorrhaging. Kevin never even warmed up.

This is a critical detail. I have often asked in the foregoing chapters how we are to suppose that professionals, full of competitive spirit and paid to win (or often fired if they didn't), would put an inferior team on the field just to indulge their bigoted inclinations. My own experience has taught me that such inscrutable things do happen. Coach Rasp craved victory as much as any ballplayer who ever suited up. (Once, on a midnight bus ride back from a loss, he screamed at a poor freshman for daring to nibble a sandwich rather than fast and brood over their humiliation.) Yet various vendettas and ambitions were always colliding within him. There are losses... and then, there are losses. Having Kevin come in and claim a victory that might have belonged to Robert would have slapped Rasp's psychic face up one side and down the other. Robert had to shine: he had been paid to make Robert shine, and—perhaps more importantly—he had staked his professional reputation on Robert's shining. Yet Robert's star was growing dim by the senior year. Between his father's and his coach's grandiose ambitions, he had been overworked until his arm had gone dead. After the season, it was found that his labrum had almost separated.

For Robert had also started every game in the summer that might have been observed by a scout, and he had been kept in those games, too, until he could hardly stay on his feet. The little sidearmer/submariner was never brought in to relieve him in those circumstances, for it just wouldn't do for the scout who came for the tall flame-thrower to walk away thinking about the small sidewinder. This was all borne home to me painfully during one summer tournament when I had all but secured a certain college coach's promise that either he or his assistant would be in the bleachers. I told Rasp straight out of Kevin's interest in the school and the coach's interest in Kevin. Rasp seemed already apprised of what college staff members would attend which games. The result? Kevin didn't throw a single pitch for the weekend's first three games. On the fourth—an early-morning Sunday game that no scout would have attended at gunpoint—he threw three shut-out innings. Now, our college coach's assistant was indeed very interested in Robert after the first game... but Robert's dad wasn't remotely excited by a Division III school's sniffing around. Kevin didn't even start that game at second base: Rasp practically sent him to patrol the parking lot.

The following spring we had the same song's second verse. It was the end of the boys' junior year in high school, and their team carried a 1-0 lead into the final inning of a game that might have landed them in the state championship round. Robert's junior season was brilliant: he had been all but unhittable, and he would end up being the district MVP. In this instance, however, he was visibly exhausted and flustered. The afternoon was exceptionally hot, and his younger teammates couldn't seem to lay off first pitches during their plate appearances, which resulted in his having little time to sit on the bench and grab a drink during our at-bats. (And why could Coach Rasp not prevail upon these kids to take a few pitches?) The first two hitters of that fateful last inning reached on errors by Kevin's klutzy teammates at the corners. Robert began to pout: I could see it from the bleachers. He managed to record another strikeout. Then a misplayed fly to left field rolled to the fence... and the tying and winning runs crossed the plate.

Why was Kevin, who struck out five times as many as he walked that season and practically never gave up fly balls, not brought in to relieve? Because a scout from Baylor was rumored to be in the press box. That worthy had to be shown nothing but the merchandise on which Rasp was receiving a fat commission.

It should be said explicitly that kids like Robert suffer a far more tragic fate in these situations than kids like Kevin. That's an entirely different topic... but the fact deserves acknowledging. Robert was collateral damage in Kevin's sabotaging, and the surroundings perhaps suffered more wreckage than the target.

e) More money and ego

The first and third basemen who made critical errors in that crucial game both received All Conference Honorable Mention recognition, though Kevin played a brilliant second base and pitched as I have described. Yet these two error-prone, no-hit kids (Kevin's troubles at the plate were negligible compared to theirs) had certain "advantages". The first baseman, a hulk of a boy whose true love was football, received the same honor every year despite costing the team runs every other game. His parents were major donors to the school. The second boy has rapidly improved; but as a freshman, his was certainly no standout. I recall Kevin's receiving Honorable Mention when he was a freshman, and when Rasp was fighting for his professional life against Casey. Coach Rasp, over the years, has appeared to me to take on only one family at a time. Now that ours is out of range, maybe this boy's will be next. I noticed that his father, a very outspoken man who's also quite knowledgeable about baseball, has already removed himself from the bleachers to beyond the center field fence during games. I smell a doghouse.

Our high school's Athletic Director once explained to me, quite unsolicited and laughing all the way, that All Conference selections are voted on by district coaches collectively, but that the individual coach chooses the Honorable Mentions from his own school—"which, of course," chuckled Milord, "are the ones he has to choose in order to keep his job." Naturally, Coach Rasp included the AD's gangly son in that secondary honor once the boy came of age.

I should think a job of this nature might be one you'd want to quit, especially if you were a rugged individualist, a highly trained professional, a fearless warrior, and a practicing Christian—or even a single one of the above. For any of several reasons, I should think you might decide that the life of a lying, fawning toady isn't worth living. But apparently my opinion is not generally held in the coaching world. Put it down to my being an idiot intellectual.

One very real and specific moral problem that the idiot at this keyboard sees in such practice is that college applications invariably have slots wherein prospective athletes are to type their high school honors. This means that, by certifying our block-footed first baseman to be a rising star, Coach Rasp and his ilk are misleading institutions that wish to build a string baseball program. It also diminishes the chances that talented ballplayers like Kevin from poorer families will find scholarship money. It deceives recruiters, this fraud over which the AD jovially smirked, and it cheats hard workers. That's not even to mention the effect on the delicate ego of an adolescent who looks on, trying to smile and clap, as a teammate not worth half his salt receives a plaque.

Do the ring-leaders of, and collaborators in, these "old boy" networks ever give a second thought to what a vile service they perform as they belt out their hymns at the head of the congregation on Sunday?

Mere weeks after this meeting with the Athletic Director, I took Kevin with me to confer with Coach Rasp in his snug little office. I had never penetrated that inner sanctum before. It was September of Kevin's junior year, and we were to discuss how my son might be getting his ducks in order to play college baseball. I really had no ideas at the time: NCSA was still over a half-year from my horizon. Naturally, I expected to get some pointers from Rasp... but I also hoped that the gesture might lay to rest any lingering doubts he had about my respect for his professionalism. Kevin was only halfway brought high school. The incident involving the email that Bob showed around (and perhaps embellished) wasn't that far behind us yet, and I thought I was discerning signs of a grudge.

Rasp was polite enough, and probably even flattered that his opinion was being sought. Yet he really had nothing to say, although he delivered it with his usual air of authority and expertise. Kevin, he advised, would do well to stay cool, not expect a commitment from any college until after he had graduated, and then—in the very summer before he was to become a college boy—poke around among local junior- and community-level institutions. Someone somewhere would likely pick him up. The coach also warned Kevin not to let jealousy eat him up (was this the preacher talking?) if Division I schools started to nose around Robert this very year. He as much as declared, "Robert should be signed by a D-I school within a year from now, but you should look for JUCO opportunities and, even then, not expect a firm answer before you actually graduate."

Now, I have always been realistic about my son's talents. I thought Rasp undersold him a bit in that interview—but I also had heard that college scouts pay lots of attention to physique, and Kevin was no John Sena. I certainly didn't go seeking other options on the Internet in the spirit of trying to show up the coach. I wanted what was best for my son—and I still presumed, over all, that Rasp did, too.

Yet when Kevin was not only offered a spot on an NAIA roster midway through his senior year, but thousands in scholarship money to come play, I think Coach Rasp took it very personally. Coupled with Robert's failure to find a spot on any roster anywhere (not that Bob and Rasp would let him consider a school below D-I), Kevin's success became in that feverish brain a mortal insult. That's my conviction. The abusive email sent to me four years earlier that boasted so grandly of Rasp's ability to pull college strings... the rather pompous prophesying about how Robert would be hounded by elite scouts... the "stacked deck" with which we played out both high school and summer seasons in order to make that prophecy come true... the coach must have seen in Kevin's simple, honest triumph something like the ultimate sneer from the idiot intellectual. And so he berated Kevin's defense that spring, sabotaged his hitting, limited his pitching, finally sat him on the bench, and—in short—did just about everything he possibly could to say to me, "Well, your kid's not gone just yet, and in my opinion he's a nobody, a nothing. Got it? He's not even good enough to start on my team. Got it?"

III

Why Systems Rigidify: The Sad Human Tendency to Build an Identity Out of Memberships

a) Vanity: the lifeblood of bad coaching, with or without racism

Money and egotism: these are the two influences I have observed to be in constant competition with talent and hard work during the nearly two decades now that I have been involved in baseball as a coach and a father. (Ineptitude doesn't compete as an influence: it simply saturates every deck of cards with jokers.) Money, of course, always seems to insinuate itself into every human enterprise. I truly believe that kids of my generation must have loved baseball more, even if we had fewer good teachers, because it was not at that time—not quite—a fast track to big bucks. Dads didn't pressure their kids to play because success ensured a college education, and perhaps even (best-case scenario) a multi-million dollar annual income. Everything now is an "investment": the lessons, the special instructional technology, the latest gear, the traveling teams, the showcases, the "Webinars"... parents are always balancing the not-so-slow drain of dollars by the hundreds against the possible jackpot. Signing a kid up for Little League today is buying a lottery ticket.

That hard fact brings out the worst in some people: for if you can somehow invalidate X number of tickets, then the chances improve that all that money's still in the pot for the next drawing, even if you don't have the winner this time. What I'm saying, and what I have just illustrated through my personal experiences, is that certain "predator dads" will try to have your son pushed out of the limelight just to bring their son relatively closer to it. Winning a war means disabling your adversary as well as equipping your own forces to the hilt. Success in junior-level baseball has become a war, apparently... and you know what they say about fairness in love and war.

I'm not sure that this "slow down the other sprinters to speed up my son" approach has any analogue in the black experience of playing ball after Jackie. A parallel might exist in the way that some organizations brought up less-than-the-best players in order to slow the experiment down (if not sabotage it) while maintaining to the public that they were committed to it. Jackie himself may have been an example. He was certainly not the most polished black ballplayer of the late Forties. The myth has it that Branch Rickey wanted Jackie for his college-boy savvy, his ability to assess the situation fully. This condescending explanation served Rickey well once the experiment worked; but the sly fox would have been equally well served if tensions had eaten into ticket sales, the experiment had had to be called off, and Jackie's not-quite-ready level of performance could be cited as an excuse. It's really the same phenomenon as using one's wealth to promote a certain player by burying others around him... except in reverse. This way, you bury the superior players by elevating one to represent them who is not of their caliber.

In contemporary times, we see organizations devote unlimited tender-loving-care to costly high-draft picks in order to recoup a whopping signing bonus while quickly pulling the plug on kids who signed for a box of Crackerjack. Matt McCarthy discusses this with good humor in his recent book.[1] Of course, that all has nothing to do with desegregation.

Allow me, then, to highlight a few solid connections between my son's experience and that of the young black men in my sampling. In defense of the analogy (which I know many must view with suspicion), I would stress that the seven techniques of sabotage listed below are merely points of resemblance that caught my eye right away. Several more probably exist.

a) bait-and-switch: a "set-up" wherein the player is trained at one position, then brought up to the big team to play another. The Dodgers' AAA franchise was starting Jackie Robinson at shortstop just before he was brought up to play second—possibly to provide Mr. Rickey with justification for sending him back down again if things didn't run smoothly. Coach Rasp never gave my son a single pre-season of training at the position where he started once the season began (this in distinct contrast to the "steady home" that players like Robert found). It's an extremely effective strategy of disorientation.

b) quick hook: a phrase often used of pitchers pulled early from a game, but intended here to signify a fielder's losing his job after one or two miscues. This is a particularly subtle technique of suppression in that the objective evidence of a player's having made a mistake can't be argued with. Everyone makes errors. Most coaches themselves probably can't tell you how many formal errors and unofficial mental lapses Player X has made in comparison to Player Y. They'll just say that X doesn't "look as sharp" to their highly trained professional eye. One thing's for sure: if a fielder senses that he will lose his job the first time he makes an error, he won't become a good fielder. This is true even if his perception is incorrect. I was able to see up close how destructively Coach Rasp worked his way into my son's subconscious mind. I can't say how many young black players had the same experience, because most of them were no doubt successfully ruined as fielders before they ever made it to the top. I wonder if Jake Wood's fielding at second might have been cited when he was permanently bumped from the starting line-up? Curt Roberts' certainly was, although he also set a record for put-outs.

c)	"you've had your chance": a version of the quick hook applied to entire seasons, or even careers, rather than to a game or two. Curt Roberts had had his chance with the Pirates in 1954—a chance of which he made the most defensively, but marred it with weak offense. Despite his having corrected the problem (materially—with glasses) by the '56 season's start, the ship had sailed. The bad-faith analogy that coaches and management seem to operate on in these cases is that of a carnival game: you pay your money and you get three balls to hit the bull's eye. If you realize after the third miss that you were throwing at the wrong target (maybe you didn't have your glasses on)... well, that's just too bad. Step aside for the next contestant! This is a perfectly idiotic way to develop ballplayers. The only motive that can explain such practice, beyond sheer stupidity, is a covert desire to be rid of a certain player. I watched Coach Rasp bench my son and substitute for him one player after another whose official errors numbered many times Kevin's and whose mental errors were lethal... yet the coach was "shopping for something new", which seemed to him an approach superior to developing an already solid talent with repetitions.

d)	hit for power: a good ploy for irreparably damaging a pretty swing— tell the kid he's a failure unless he starts driving the ball over the fence. Well-intentioned, competent coaches will actually urge their players *not* to swing for homers: Mike Schmidt and many other legendary sluggers have stressed that the objective of the power-hitter is simply to make solid contact. Yet I saw my son's development as a hitter undermined year after year by threats that he might lose his starting spot if he didn't "put more backspin" on the ball (trendy code for taking a steep swing from above your back shoulder). In the Fifties and Sixties, these same sages of the swat were telling young black players to "stay back and elevate the ball" with an uppercut swing. Willie Kirkland modeled this stroke, whether naturally or after "coaching" I do not know... and it probably garnered him a few extra years of big-league play. Was the advice, then, deliberate sabotage? Again, who can say? It certainly interrupted George Altman's meteoric ascent, did little for Mack Jones, and very likely fouled up Vada Pinson and Floyd Robinson. Even a hopeful white lad from Georgia, Coot Veal, saw his dreams dashed when he was forced to adopt "the swing" and could never recover his hitting effectiveness.

e)	switch off the switching: another strategy useful for undermining hitters, this one very specific. If you have a switch-hitter and you want to hack forty or fifty points off his average, tell him he can't switch any longer but must choose one side or the other. Coach Rasp pulled this one on my son with dramatic effect. Conscientious, well-meaning coaches typically try to talk a talented player *into* switch-hitting (as the Dodgers did with Maury Wills, and as Minor League coaches would later do with Eddie Murray). A player who has already put a couple of years into switching and has shown some slight aptitude for it should be encouraged by the well-wisher. Having suddenly to hit lefties from the left side, for instance, is a much more arduous and scary task than simply refining one's skills from both sides. If Rasp felt that Kevin had too little pop from the right side... well, show him how to get more bat speed. Isn't a coach supposed to be a teacher? (Of course, this was also a deployment of the "more power" canard: most switch-hitters are get-on-base guys like Wills and Gilliam, not sluggers like Eddie Murray.) And if Pumpsie Green's switching just didn't justify keeping him in the big leagues... well, give him more at-bats, not fewer. A switch-hitter needs more repetitions than others hitters; and if you're not willing to give him the reps he needs in that special capacity, why bring him up, to begin with? Unless you wanted him to fail from the start...

f) playing the right way: a more general category that could include "hitting for power", but may be extended to fielding, base-running, and even such silly minutiae as dress and "hustle". Players are usually not offered any rationale for the "right way": they're essentially told that the coach just doesn't like what they're doing. It seems to me that this is a formula for elevating conformity over adequacy. Willie Mays's famous basket catches certainly weren't "the right way"—but Willie got away with them, probably because any emphasis of his uniqueness was seen as good marketing (like the tease before a freak show). Coach Rasp forbade my son's submarining until, years later, he finally figured out how effective it was. I know that Kevin was very confused, too, over the propriety of being "passionate about winning" that allowed Rasp to throw gear all over the dugout but didn't allow Kevin himself to hurl his glove after a bad outing. I'm reminded of certain traffic cops in our little Southern towns who will ticket you either for stopping in front of the stop sign or stopping behind it: the proverbial no-win situation. Frank Robinson was probably traded by the Reds because Bill DeWitt didn't like his off-field deportment: it just wasn't "the Cincinnati way".

g) specialization: the technique of relegating the player to minor or obscure roles (pinch-hitter, reliever) where his talents will be little noticed and lightly valued. Of course, in contemporary professional baseball, specialization has opened several doors. There's no faster ticket to the top than being a specialty reliever—a submariner, for instance! But in the Fifties and Sixties, these functions were still emerging and had attracted little respect. Al McBean's exile to the bullpen after a brilliant rookie season as a starter was definitely a demotion, and Valmy Thomas's "career" as a third-string catcher cum pinch-hitter left him ready to be cut or traded from one day to the next. Kevin's being restricted to short relief appearances did not upset me, particularly since he threw ground balls and, with our porous infield (anchored by Robert), he might have worn his arm out trying to record seven outs an inning for several innings. Yet it bothered me that he was seldom, if ever, used in games where "somebody" might be watching from behind the press box's dark window. On those occasions, the kid might as well have been hog-tied in a closet.

My son isn't black, yet his experience with several members of the coaching community mirrors that of many of my subjects in stunning ways. If he had been black, that might have knocked around in the back of Coach Rasp's mind, as well. (The coach doesn't like the "work ethic" of black kids; and the specific cause of Kevin's and my joint conference with the Athletic Director, by the way, was to hear an ultimatum about my son's publishing his "tasteless" rap music on the Internet!) What may really be at the bottom of discriminatory treatment, here and elsewhere, is pure—or toxically impure—egotism. People want to be first, to be smartest, to be in command; and when they see their superiority challenged, they discredit the challenger. If he has an advanced degree, then he's an idiot intellectual. If he succeeds despite doing "everything wrong", then he's a nine-day wonder or a freak of nature. And if his epidermis is an unusual shade... well, you know, people from that culture just can't seem to learn our ways.

My objective in this and the previous chapter has not been to suggest that being a victim of racial prejudice in the Fifties was no different from having a coach out to get you for any reason in any era. I understand the differences. Kevin could always walk through the front door of a restaurant with his teammates and sit at the same table as they. If the team went on a road trip, he didn't have to find special lodgings on the shabby side of town while the others stayed at the Hilton. Whatever troubles he had on the field, he wasn't obliged to dodge bottles and batteries and worry about some lunatic leveling a pistol at him. On that basis, there is utterly no comparison between the two experiences.

But that's not the basis of my comparison. I have been writing specifically about how the black player might have been slighted by his coaches, not about how he was historically and criminally harassed in many instances by the general populace. I have posed myself the question many times (and continue to do so), "How can a professional who is paid to win games and wants to keep his job go about deliberately sabotaging one of his players? Wouldn't this be a classic case of cutting off your nose to spite your face?"

b) The egotist's profile: fear, arrogance, incompetence, vengefulness

The answer I expressed in this section's first chapter was excessive devotion to system; but the analogy I have just unfolded points yet more directly to human vanity—to egotism. Indeed, at the deepest level of bigotry's abyss, I don't even think we find much money washing around. To the extent that money had anything to do with the black ballplayer's struggles, it actually must have worked in his behalf. Negro League teams were minimally compensated for the players raided by white baseball, these players often gave a lively transfusion to gate receipts by drawing black spectators, and their salaries were seldom on a par with those of their white counterparts. What's not to love about this arrangement, from the owner's financial point of view?

Note, furthermore, that if baseball is all about money for some big-league owners, the money itself is sacrificed in hecatombs to the egotistical dreams of certain dads. Fathers like Robert's can virtually destroy their sons in a quest to force greatness upon them, and the tragedy of such stories is heart-wrenching. Coaches, likewise, love money—as much as the rest of us— yet could surely make it in some more stable way than marketing themselves as prophets and oracles if they didn't feel a personally defining attachment to baseball. They lose their jobs if they're not in the know: but the job they have all freely chosen is to be professional fountains of knowledge. Their vanity as well as their financial status is engaged in being right, and was so half a century ago.

Hence the form of such egotism that must first leap out at us is a blend of arrogance and fear. The coach fears the loss of his livelihood, and he therefore powerfully projects to others (maybe or maybe not convincing himself along the way) that he is a leading guru, a Zen master, when it comes to all aspects of the game. Everyone who makes him look bad is a klutz or an idiot. His instruction (or lack thereof) is never the problem: if a problem exists, it's that he hasn't been given players with the wit and talent to execute his brilliant counsel.

This is a formula for incompetence, another facet of egotism. The person who can't admit that he has limitations is bound to overreach. Incompetence, naturally, breeds further fear in a kind of vicious cycle. A man like Rasp who backs himself into insisting that he understands hitting while knowing full well that he does not must suffer terrible anxiety when his team can't hit. Did this particular coach hire a hitting instructor to improve offense, I wonder, or to give himself a fall guy if offense didn't improve? Probably both. If things worked, then he would take all the credit for hiring the young man; and if things didn't work, then he would fire the kid in a lather of indignation over his "incompetence". (The latter, by the way, is precisely what happened.)

Then we have vengefulness, which is also related to fear. People don't like being afraid: it may be the most uncomfortable emotion of them all. Someone who has plunged them into fear is thus likely to find a bullet in his back if he later walks into their crosshairs. The lust for revenge is also and primarily related to egotism, however, and is hence the true child of that parent and only the step-child of fear. Our friends frighten us all the time, whether in jest or because we worry about their getting hurt—and we don't plot revenge upon them. Yet if a very vain person were publicly made to lose his cool by being tricked into supposing his car stolen, and the whole thing were later publicly unveiled as a joke pulled by his friends, he might well plan to "get back" at the pranksters in some unfunny, harmful way. To be sure, people like that don't keep friends for long.

If a coach associates you with the forces that almost made him lose his job or his professional honor, and if he later acquires power over you, then you'd better watch your back. Not all coaches are vain—I don't mean to make that flaw a firm requirement for the position; but if a vain coach goes on record as saying that a player isn't capable of doing this or that and the player later proves him a fool, then the player had better not found his career on said coach's support. The matter of competence also surfaces here. A coach who cannot adequately assess his players' abilities is incompetent at his job, and he's bound to see that an "unplanned success" makes him look exactly that way to anyone who has been listening to him.

I don't have nearly enough information to cite specific cases of such vanity in the coaching of young back players decades ago. Nobody on earth could have the necessary information, in most instances: the coaches themselves, when they were alive (and most are long gone), probably practiced a lot of self-deception to keep up their spirits. Yet because of what I've learned about human beings, I'm absolutely certain that what I have just written is not irrelevant to the treatment of black ballplayers in the Fifties. Some managers and front-office types (Walter Briggs and Tom Yawkey spring to mind) sincerely believed that recruits from the Negro Leagues couldn't compete at a higher level.[2] Was their persistence in this opinion pure racism... or was it somewhat or mostly egotism? Was their scorn for black people greater than their fear and loathing of being proved wrong?

Negro League baseball differed from Major League baseball in numerous ways. The contrast was not unlike that between Japanese and American baseball today—"sortie-and-ambush" ball versus "by the book" play (guerilla warfare versus pitched battle, if you like). White managers and coaches during the decade in question genuinely believed that their way was better: it was all they had ever known, and it was what they taught their understudies. Joe Morgan reminds us that the skipper also exerted substantially more control over his players in those days than we see his counterparts doing now. "Unless you were a superstar, he controlled your playing time and, by extension, your compensation. You had to remain in a manager's good graces back then. If you didn't he could sit you down, demote you to the minors, or ship you to another team."[3] We can hardly suppose that many of these rough-and-ready men would have admitted to themselves (let alone to others) the possibility of being wrong and of having to learn a new gospel. Even a Little League coach like me can tell you how hard it is to command attention and respect by prefacing drills with, "Now, this is one of several theories. Let's try it this way, and if it doesn't work, we'll go back to the drawing board." Managers were fully expected, rather, to project expertise and demand discipline.

A few players were skillful enough to give their manager abject obedience in practice while doing what worked for them in a game. Hank Aaron reproduces a reminiscence of Ralph Garr's about his all-time favorite "Aaron advice"—which is indeed golden, if you're good enough to follow it:

> The coaches will tell you how they want you to hit, and when you're in the batting cage, do what they say to do. But when you get up to that plate and it's just you and the pitcher, do what got you here. Take advice from everybody, but do what you have to do.[4]

Yet let's face it: most of us would play the way we practice. Telling a kid not to let a coach ruin him amounts to warning that kid never to fail; for apostasy will be countenanced only if and as long as it produces positive results. It's true enough that following instructions and still failing will not earn the struggling youth any "obedience points": Kevin learned that the hard way from Coach Rasp. All successes are shared by the coach; all failures belong to the individual player. (Remember the saying, "Success has many fathers, but failure is an orphan"?) If an Aaron did the "wrong" thing at the plate but lit up the scoreboard, then his unique and even bizarre African wrists were the cause (drawled shrugging coaches). If a Mack Jones did just what he was told with mediocre results, then his poor preparation in an inferior black sub-culture was the cause (said the same coaches). Race could dress up the conclusion in either direction. As long as the search for causes was steered away from the coach's teaching, one might have added Alabama water or Polk salad to the list of influences.

So if a white manager belittled and somewhat bullied a black player for doing things the "wrong way", was that a stronger indication of racism or of good old-fashioned arrogance and vanity? Even if he later made racial remarks about the kid's ignorance of proper method or slowness to learn, was bigotry the most likely source of those remarks... or was bigotry merely summoned to support opinions favoring the coach's extreme competence and wide experience?

c) A major paradox: selfishness is the glue of impersonal systems

Think of how you respond when someone cuts you off on the freeway and almost spins you into a major accident. Your instinctive reaction is one of brief terror, followed by fury when you realize that you're safe. Then you start to let loose on the moron in front of you... and you embellish your curses with impromptu descriptors. If he looks very young, you vituperate teenagers; if he looks very old, you revile the nation's senior citizens; if he is a she, you might uncork a few choice clichés about woman-drivers. Are these remarks "agist" or "sexist"; and if race unhappily finds its way into them, are they racist? Maybe so... but only secondarily. You had not already determined that the person's demography was a traffic hazard before he made his risky move. The uncharitable classifications occur *after* the specific event of unpleasantness.

346

This is not an alternative theory to the one about systematic rigidity with which my final section opened. Rather, egotism is integrally related to system. The cocksure confidence that certain people project has probably been bestowed upon them by a deep, thorough programming. It is precisely when you cut such people off from their broader network of roots that fear, vengefulness, and other emotions mentioned above flare up. Anxiety invades them when they have to stray from well-known boundaries; and this anxiety, though it doesn't seem to belong in a rugged individualist, is in fact egotistical, too. We often define our individuality (far too often, I would say) by our membership in groups; and if the group's virtues and powers suddenly vanish like a mirage, then our sense of self vanishes, too.

In these ways, then, egotism is more fundamental than reverence for system: the former is indeed necessary fully to explain the latter. I know what a paradox that presents: for worship of the group can turn people into cattle if unchecked, whereas we think of egotists as consumed by their selfish importance. I have a feeling, though, that life's profoundest truths are always paradoxes. For it is also true that the courage to break with the crowd comes from selflessness—from a commitment to higher principles whose abstraction does nothing to promote a flamboyant, stylish identity. In a nutshell, without selfishness, there would be no secret societies.

I'm sure that to some I now appear too speculative about a problem—racism—which they prefer to view as utterly unlike any other in our society, and hence not to be philosophically blended into airy comments about human nature. A friend of mine insists that neither I nor any other white man can understand the condition of being black in America. Well, none of us can understand any of his fellow beings completely: we don't even understand ourselves! But I would respond to my friend more specifically, if I thought it wouldn't hurt his feelings, that having racial discrimination to blame for setbacks is almost a luxury sometimes. A black kid who had fifty big-league at-bats in 1958 and then got bundled home might tell himself that racism short-circuited his career, and he might well be substantially correct. What's the white kid's excuse in the same situation? How does he explain the coach's apparent indifference to him? Was it something about his family name, or where he was from? He batted .320, even though he collected only two extra-base hits, and his fielding was almost perfect. Wasn't that good enough... or has he been kidding himself? What is it about him that marks him for failure? It's certainly not his skin color! Does he just not know how to admit to himself that he's mediocre, an "also ran"?

For there's no denying that people get shortchanged in life for all kinds of reasons: they certainly did in baseball of the Fifties. Running the Major Leagues of the mid-century represented a challenge to the abilities of coaches, managers, and owners. This group of authorities often did only a modest job of handling rare talent or extraordinary circumstances even when race, with its attendant social and political fallout, wasn't a factor. Somebody, it seems to me, made a hash of Albie Pearson's brilliant but brief career, probably because he wasn't quite five-and-a-half feet tall. Somebody failed to exploit Don Demeter's many abilities to the maximum.

Surely the most egregious example, however, of a white player's being cheated of the chances he deserved was Roger Maris. Clavin and Peary's new book reveals secrets that the New York Yankees in particular, and the MLB establishment in general, must have wanted sealed in an enchanted vault of the pyramids. Team doctors actually allowed Roger to play ball with a broken hand for much of the 1965 season without telling him of his condition. In fact, manager Ralph Houk and the front office sat by passively as fans and media excoriated Roger for "dogging it" and "whining" about a minor bruise.[5] The resulting further damage done to Maris's hand was permanent, although he continued to play ball for three more years—two of them very productively, on pennant-winning Cardinal teams.

It's well nigh impossible to say why grown men do such things to other men who have done them no wrong, and indeed are considered to be comrades in arms. I suppose the malefactors are probably doing the best they can with limited ability and in difficult circumstances: I suppose they just get in over their heads. They want to keep their jobs, an—if they are to do those jobs at all—they have to believe implicitly that they do their jobs well. So when a lad falls into their hands who needs special training or about whom upper management is sending mixed signals, they start working on Plan A and Plan B at the same time. Plan A calls for preparing the kid properly, Plan B for crucifying him. Certainly Roger Maris arrived bearing his own cross, in that the press took an instant dislike to his terse interviews and thinly veiled contempt for their fine art. That he was an uncouth Northwesterner was a touch readily added to an unflattering portrait. "Wahoo" Sam Crawford was even more northwestern than Roger, though—and I never heard Sam referred to as boorishly uncouth.

Details such as hailing from the hinterlands or being from the Deep South or having the red hair of the Irish can be added like toppings on a pizza in order to confirm the judgment behind which one's ego shelters. Race, of course, is one of these seasonings. If a black kid like Jake Wood has equivocal success—great speed and power but lots of strikeouts--and a white kid named McAuliffe is waiting in the wings, then maybe the fact of Jake's complexion is not irrelevant. There's a question, you know, about whether these black kids are quick enough upstairs to handle the middle infield! But if there's no McAuliffe, or if the kid fills a gaping hole in center field, maybe his race never comes up. Race, in other words, may be a secondary factor that legitimizes and "objectifies" the verdict most flattering to one's personal competence. Rather than admit that he doesn't know how to reduce Jake's strikeouts and hence isn't very good at his job, a coach would prefer to call Jake unteachable on the basis of genetic hard-wiring.

d) Murky optimism: the cruel blessing of the obstacle
Maybe, then, the coaches and team officials who shortchanged some of the players in my study were not "primary racists", but only functionaries of

limited competence who were trying to hold their world together (with their own position at or near its center intact). That, at least, must be my final verdict—which is as much as saying that the jury is hung. Most human beings, in all their fallibility, are capable of determined persistence neither in doing good nor in doing bad. Far more often, a cloudy situation develops like that described poignantly by Willie Mays during the very years that we have studied. Willie tells a story (surely a true one—so many details could scarcely be made up) in which a high school coach gives a freshman named Lewis a few at-bats with rather disappointing results. The coach follows Lewis's progress in summer ball, where the boy is playing against kids his own age rather than hitting against eighteen-year-old pitchers... but the boy still doesn't do well. Little does the coach know that Lewis's summer coach has overhauled his stance; or if he does know, then he thinks, "Well, why not? Lewis wasn't hitting, anyway." Willie continues:

> And this is what happened to Lewis. On account of two men who were both good baseball men, and who meant nothing but the best for Lewis himself, he was coached out of what should have been a good and easy confidence-building Pony League season as a 14-year-old. He knew now that his high school coach had real doubts as to how he might perform as a sophomore. And what might have been a baseball career for a boy just went down the drain.
>
> This, as I say, was a classic: a product of overcoaching.... I think youngsters who have a future in baseball can survive undercoaching—things they're not taught because their Little League manager just doesn't know them to begin with—far better than they can weather overcoaching![6]

Could my son's high school coach have been one of these men, well meaning but in over his head? To this day, Kevin regards the man almost as a big brother; and indeed, the figure I have called Coach Rasp has often shown a genuine affection for Kevin when the two of them weren't in uniform. A guilty conscience? Who can say? But it strikes me that the opposite reactions of my son and me to those years of being snubbed, shortchanged, misadvised, and bullied are again mirror images of how black ballplayers handled their treatment half a century ago. Some would rather not dwell upon shadow and what it might conceal, while some will always heat to a low boil when they look back. Without doubt, it does one's heart and soul no good to linger over the injustices of the past; but is the higher objective of life to live in tranquility, or to drag the whole truth—snarling like Cerberus, the three-headed dog of Hell—out into the light of day? Some of us, I suppose, just can't be tranquil while the truth stays in hiding.

I'd like to give this reflection a happy ending, not to condescend to my audience (you can decide for yourselves if optimism is justified), but because I really do believe that a certain rugged optimism emerges from all my ambivalent stats and clouds of witness. I'm sorry that Al Smith was embittered about how baseball had treated him: he certainly had good reason to feel so. But Roger Maris probably had even more reason, and his abuse had nothing to do with race. Baseball has treated a lot of men (and boys, like Lewis) very badly. Maybe the chance offered to you when a door slams in your face is better than the easy admittance given to those who need only knock to enter; maybe what you gain is not the knowledge that you're as good as (or better than) the next guy, but the "dare" of making a further discovery—of finding whether you have it in you to be Superman. The unfairness resides in your indeed being the other guy's equal yet not getting his easy pass; the exhilaration lies in your having a run at Superman, even though you probably discover in the end that you're a mere mortal. The other guy, with his ready opening, has no incentive to jump out a window and try to fly. You, as the one unfairly nudged aside, have nothing to lose if you jump. You may carry a limp through the rest of your life because of that jump—but you can bear it like a trophy, with true pride rather than arrogant vanity. You will have learned something that most people would never have the nerve or creativity even to dream about.

Without Al Smith and George Altman and Vada Pinson and Leon Wagner, there would have been no Hank or Ernie or Willie or Robby.

And without some bad coaching, I would never have pressed my son to try something very different; and without his submarine pitching, he would probably not be playing ball in college—at a Division II school, thank you! Now he has a chance to see if he can fly, while kids with more raw talent than he are choosing to party in the dorms and be fitted for their gray flannel suit thereafter.

As a Welsh proverb has it, *Cyfyngder dyn yw cyfleustra Duw*: "A man's tight squeeze is God's opportunity."

Notes

1 *Odd Man Out* (Penguin: New York, 2009).

2 John Skipper (*Charlie Gehringer, op. cit.*, 146), attributes a measure of Gehringer's failure in the General Manager position to "Walter Briggs' refusal to sign black ballplayers." The Red Sox' mishandling of an opportunity to nab the young Willie Mays has grown legendary; cf. John Klima's account in *Willie's Boys* (Hoboken, NJ: Wiley, 2009). Klima appears, like most commentators, to hold owner Tom Yawkey responsible for the heel-dragging rather than General Manager Joe Cronin.

3 *Long Balls, No Strikes* (*op. cit.*), 76.

4 *I Had a Hammer* (*op. cit.*), 302.

5 See especially ch. 22, "Betrayal" (287-292), Tom Clavin and Danny Peary, *Roger Maris: Baseball's Reluctant Hero* (New York: Touchstone, 2010).

6 Willie Mays, as told to Charles Einstein, *My Life In and Out of Baseball* (New York: E.P. Dutton, 1966).